16th Conference of the European Chapter of the Association for Computational Linguistics (EACL 2021)

Student Research Workshop

AA001568

Held online due to COVID-19

Kiev, Ukraine
21 – 23 April 2021

ISBN: 978-1-7138-2915-7

Printed from e-media with permission by:

Curran Associates, Inc.
57 Morehouse Lane
Red Hook, NY 12571

proceedings.com

Some format issues inherent in the e-media version may also appear in this print version.

Copyright© (2021) by the Association for Computational Linguistics
All rights reserved.

Printed with permission by Curran Associates, Inc. (2021)

For permission requests, please contact the Association for Computational Linguistics
at the address below.

Association for Computational Linguistics
209 N. Eighth Street
Stroudsburg, Pennsylvania 18360

Phone: 1-570-476-8006
Fax: 1-570-476-0860

acl@aclweb.org

Additional copies of this publication are available from:

Curran Associates, Inc.
57 Morehouse Lane
Red Hook, NY 12571 USA
Phone: 845-758-0400
Fax: 845-758-2633
Email: curran@proceedings.com
Web: www.proceedings.com

EACL 2021

The 16th Conference of the European Chapter of the Association for Computational Linguistics

Proceedings of the Student Research Workshop

April 19 - 23, 2021

©2021 The Association for Computational Linguistics

Introduction

Welcome to the EACL 2021 Student Research Workshop!

The EACL 2021 Student Research Workshop (SRW) is a platform for students in the field of Computational Linguistics and Natural Language Processing to come together to discuss and advance their research with help from more experienced researchers from both academia and industry.

The workshop is uniquely placed to provide valuable feedback to students about their research both before and after paper submissions. It provides them with ample opportunities to improve writing and research dissemination skills in the process. Following the tradition of the previous student research workshops, we have two tracks: research papers and thesis proposals. The research paper track is a venue for Ph.D. students, Master's students, and advanced undergraduate students to describe completed work or work-in-progress along with preliminary results. The thesis proposal track is offered for advanced Masters and Ph.D. students who have decided on a thesis topic and are interested in receiving feedback for their proposal with suggestions for both making the ideas achievable, as well as discussions related to future directions for their work.

The student research workshop has received considerable attention from many different parts of the world, and papers have addressed research questions in several different languages, which reflects the growth of the workshop. After excluding the withdrawn submissions, we received 59 submissions in total: 6 thesis proposals and 53 research papers. We accepted 4 thesis proposals and 22 research papers, resulting in an overall acceptance rate of 44%. We have also added a best paper award in the process. All the accepted papers will be presented virtually, as a part of the EACL conference, spread across three days (April 21st–23rd, 2021).

Mentoring is a core part of the SRW. In keeping with previous years, we organized pre-submission mentoring to improve the writing style and presentation of submissions. A total of 11 papers participated in this program. It offered students the opportunity to receive guidance from an experienced researcher before their submission was peer-reviewed for acceptance.

We thank our program committee members for providing careful and comprehensive reviews for the papers, and all of our mentors for donating their time to provide feedback to our student authors. Thanks to our faculty advisor, Eneko Agirre, for the essential advice and suggestions, and to the EACL 2021 organizing committee for their support in the entire process. Finally, we would like to thank all the authors whose participation has made the workshop a success!

Organizers:

Ionut-Teodor Sorodoc, Pompeu Fabra University

Madhumita Sushil, University of Antwerp

Ece Takmaz, University of Amsterdam

Faculty advisor:

Eneko Agirre, University of the Basque Country

Pre-submission Mentors:

Raquel Fernandez, University of Amsterdam

German Kruszewski, Naver Labs Europe

Xiaoyu Shen, Amazon

Valerio Basile, University of Turin

Bhuwan Dhingra, Google

Jeska Buhmann, University of Antwerp

Eva Vanmassenhove, Tilburg University

Alan Akbib, Humboldt-Universität zu Berlin

Hamed Zamani, University of Massachusetts Amherst

Sudipta Kar, Amazon Alexa AI

Lifu Huang, Virginia Tech

Fernando Alva Machego, University of Sheffield

Chris Brew, LivePerson

Program Committee:

Giovanni Cassani, Tilburg University

Sabine Schulte im Walde, University of Stuttgart

Thomas Brochhagen, Universitat Pompeu Fabra

Odette Scharenborg, Delft University of Technology

Sebastian Schuster, Stanford University

Sepideh Sadeghi, Google

Sebastian Pado, University of Stuttgart

Iacer Calixto, New York University

Vera Demberg, Saarland University

Ehsan Kamalloo, University of Alberta

Chris Brew, LivePerson

Lina M. Rojas-Barahona, Orange-Labs

Thomas Kleinbauer, Saarland University

Chaitanya Shivade, Amazon

Anusha Balakrishnan, Microsoft Semantic Machines

Thomas Kober, Rasa

Bonnie Webber, University of Edinburgh

Vered Shwartz, AI2 & University of Washington

Emily Bender, University of Washington

Andrea Horbach, University Duisburg-Essen

De Clercq Orphée, Ghent University

Sowmya Vajjala, National Research Council, Canada

Bruno Martins, University of Lisbon

Roberto Basili, University of Roma

Robert Logan, University of California, Irvine

Jacob Eisenstein, Google

Sewon Min, University of Washington

Nitish Gupta, University of Pennsylvania

Oshin Agarwal, University of Pennsylvania

David Adelani, Saarland University

Jack Hessel, AI2

Marius Mosbach, Saarland University

Enrique Manjavacas, University of Antwerp

Folgert Karsdorp, KNAW Meertens Instituut

Florian Kunneman, Vrije Universiteit Amsterdam

Mona Jalal, Boston University

Lucy Lin, University of Washington

Paul Rayson, Lancaster University

Shruti Rijhwani, Carnegie Mellon University

Arnab Bhattacharya, IIT Kanpur

Nivedita Yadav, Janssen Pharmacuetica

Timothy Baldwin, The University of Melbourne

Esther van den Berg, Heidelberg University

Lucas Weber, University Pompeu Fabra

Tim Kreutz, University of Antwerp

Carolina Scarton, University of Sheffield

Fernando Alva-Manchego, University of Sheffield

Sian Gooding, University of Sheffield

Sebastian Gehrmann, Google Research

Albert Gatt, University of Malta

Ben Zhou, University of Pennsylvania

Kevin Lin, Microsoft

Denis Newman-Griffis, University of Pittsburgh

Omid Memarrast, University of Illinois of Chicago

Marta Ruiz, Universitat Politècnica de Catalunya

Alina Karakanta, Fondazione Bruno Kessler / University of Trento

A.B. Siddique, University of California, Riverside

Marco Damonte, Amazon

Alberto Testoni, University of Trento

Divyansh Kaushik, Carnegie Mellon University

Massimo Nicosia, Google

Bernhard Kratzwald, ETH Zurich

Florian Mai, Idiap Research Institute

Pieter Fivez, University of Antwerp

Chris Develder, Ghent University

Michael Hedderich, Saarland University

Louise Deleger, Université Paris-Saclay, INRAE

Filip Ilievski, USC Information Sciences Institute

Lifu Huang, Virginia Tech

Laura Ana Maria, University of Stuttgart

Alan Akbik, Humboldt-Universität zu Berlin

Najoung Kim, Johns Hopkins University

Vlad Niculae, University of Amsterdam

Diego Marcheggiani, Amazon

Michael Heddrich, Saarland University

Dirk Hovy, Bocconi University

Chris Alberti, Google

Roberto Dessi, Universitat Pompeu Fabra / Facebook AI Research

Louise McNally, Universitat Pompeu Fabra

Ru Meng, University of Pittsburgh

Phong Le, Amazon

Anna Currey, Amazon AWS AI

Arda Tezcan, Ghent University

Mattia Antonino Di gangi, AppTek

Katharina Kann , CU Boulder

Marcos Garcia, Universidade da Corunha

Murathan Kurfalı, Stockholm University

Manex Agirrezabal, University of Copenhagen

Burcu Can, The University of Wolverhampton

Taraka Rama, University of North Texas

Ahmet Üstün, University of Groningen

Laura Aina, Pompeu Fabra University

Gosse Minnema, University of Groningen

Aina Gari, Université Paris-Saclay, CNRS, LIMSI

Ludovica Pannitto, University of Trento

Mario Giulianelli, University of Amsterdam

Qianchu Liu, University of Cambridge

Meishan Zhang, Tianjin University, China

Enrica Troiano, Institut für Maschinelle Sprachverarbeitung (IMS), Stuttgart

Shabnam Tafreshi, George Washington University

Zeerak Waseem, University of Sheffield

David Jurgens, University of Michigan

Els Lefever, Ghent University

Saadia Gabriel, University of Washington

Miguel A. Alonso, Universidade da Coruña

Hardy Hardy, The University of Sheffield

Bernd Bohnet, Google

Ruket Cakici, NTENT, METU

Table of Contents

Computationally Efficient Wasserstein Loss for Structured Labels

Ayato Toyokuni [1,3] **Sho Yokoi** [2,3] **Hisashi Kashima** [1,3] **Makoto Yamada** [1,3]
[1] Kyoto University [2] Tohoku University [3] RIKEN AIP
{toyokuni.ayato@ml.ist.i, kashima@i, myamada@i}.kyoto-u.ac.jp,
yokoi@ecei.tohoku.ac.jp

Abstract

The problem of estimating the probability distribution of labels has been widely studied as a label distribution learning (LDL) problem, whose applications include age estimation, emotion analysis, and semantic segmentation. We propose a tree-Wasserstein distance regularized LDL algorithm, focusing on hierarchical text classification tasks. We propose predicting the entire label hierarchy using neural networks, where the similarity between predicted and true labels is measured using the tree-Wasserstein distance. Through experiments using synthetic and real-world datasets, we demonstrate that the proposed method successfully considers the structure of labels during training, and it compares favorably with the Sinkhorn algorithm in terms of computation time and memory usage.

1 Introduction

Label distribution learning (LDL), which is a generalized framework for performing single/multi-label classification and estimating the probability distribution over labels, is an important machine-learning problem (Geng, 2016). Its applications include age estimation (Geng et al., 2013), emotion estimation (Zhou et al., 2016), head-pose estimation (Geng and Xia, 2014), and semantic segmentation (Gao et al., 2017). In particular, multi-label classification is an important problem in many NLP areas, and has several applications including multi-label text classification (Banerjee et al., 2019; Chalkidis et al., 2019).

Typically, Kullback-Leibler (KL) divergence is used to measure the similarity between two distributions. However, the KL divergence can tend to infinity if the supports of the two distributions do not overlap, resulting in model failure.

To solve this support problem, Wasserstein distance is used instead of KL divergence (Arjovsky et al., 2017). Wasserstein distance is defined as the cost of optimally transporting one probability distribution to match another (Villani, 2009; Peyré and Cuturi, 2018). Because it can compare two probability measures while considering the ground metric, it is more powerful than measurements that do not consider geometrical information.

An LDL framework with Wasserstein distance has been recently proposed (Frogner et al., 2015; Zhao and Zhou, 2018). This framework employs the Sinkhorn algorithm (Cuturi, 2013) to calculate the Wasserstein distance, which requires quadratic computational-time. Thus, when we consider extremely large label-sets, for example, 10^5, the computation cost can be significant. However, the Wasserstein distance on a tree (hereinafter called *tree-Wasserstein distance*) can be written in a closed-form and calculated in linear computation time (Evans and Matsen, 2012; Le et al., 2019).

In this paper, we propose a tree-regularized LDL algorithm with a tree-Wasserstein distance. The key advantage of the tree-Wasserstein distance is that it considers the hierarchical label information explicitly, whereas the Sinkhorn-based algorithm needs a cost matrix using tree-structured data. Moreover, the tree-Wasserstein distance has an analytic form that can be computed in linear time using significantly less memory. We experimentally demonstrate that the proposed algorithm compares favorably with the Sinkhorn-based LDL algorithm (Frogner et al., 2015; Zhao and Zhou, 2018) with considerably lower memory consumption and computational costs. We demonstrate that the calculation is more efficient than that of the existing Wasserstein loss.

Contribution: Our contributions are summarized as follows. (1) We propose training a model by minimizing the tree-Wasserstein distance for hierarchical labels, and (2) we experimentally show

Proceedings of the 16th Conference of the European Chapter of the Associationfor Computational Linguistics: Student Research Workshop, pages 1–7
April 19 - 23, 2021. ©2021 Association for Computational Linguistics

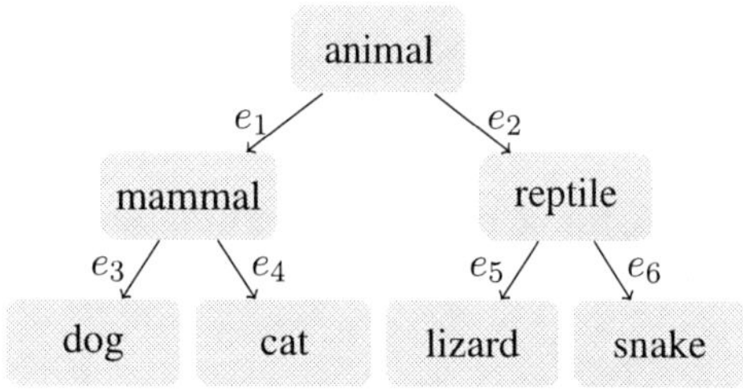

Figure 1: Illustration of a tree-structured label with the root "animal". $\Gamma(\text{"mammal"}) = \{\text{"mammal"}, \text{"dog"}, \text{"cat"}\}$, $v_{e_2} = \text{"reptile"}$.

that the proposed method is computationally more efficient than the existing methods with Sinkhorn-based methods.

2 Problem Setting

We observe n input and output samples $\{(\boldsymbol{x}_1, \boldsymbol{y}_1), \cdots, (\boldsymbol{x}_n, \boldsymbol{y}_n)\}$ from $(\mathcal{X}, \mathcal{Y})$, where $\mathcal{X} \subset \mathbb{R}^d$. We consider the problem of learning a map from a feature space $\mathcal{X}$ into $\mathcal{P}$, which is a set of distributions over a finite set $\mathcal{Y}$.

For example, multi-class classification is included in this problem, $\boldsymbol{y}$, which represents the ℓ-th class, and it is expressed as the following one-hot vector:

$$\boldsymbol{y} = (0, \ldots, 0, \underbrace{1}_{\ell}, 0, \ldots 0)^\top \in \mathbb{R}^L,$$

where L denotes the total number of classes, and $\boldsymbol{y}^\top \mathbf{1}_L = 1$. Additionally, $\mathbf{1}_L \in \mathbb{R}^L$ denotes a vector whose elements are all 1.

When multi-label classification is considered, $\mathcal{P}$ denotes binary vectors that indicate existing labels. For example, if the sample $\boldsymbol{x}$ belongs to classes ℓ and ℓ', $\boldsymbol{y}$ is given as

$$\boldsymbol{y} = (0, \ldots, 0, \underbrace{1}_{\ell}, 0, \ldots 0, \underbrace{1}_{\ell'}, 0, \ldots, 0)^\top \in \mathbb{R}^L,$$

where $\boldsymbol{y}^\top \mathbf{1}_L = 2$. Accordingly, we can transform $\boldsymbol{y}$ into a probability vector as $\boldsymbol{p}_{\boldsymbol{y}} = \boldsymbol{y}/\boldsymbol{y}^\top \mathbf{1}_L$. Notably, we assume that $\mathcal{Y}$ is discrete and has a tree structure similar to hierarchical labels.

We aim to estimate the conditional probability vector $\boldsymbol{p}_{\boldsymbol{y}}$ for $\boldsymbol{x}$ by considering the structure information of $\mathcal{Y}$ from $\{(\boldsymbol{x}_1, \boldsymbol{p}_{\boldsymbol{y}_1}), \cdots, (\boldsymbol{x}_n, \boldsymbol{p}_{\boldsymbol{y}_n})\}$.

3 Proposed Method

In this study, we assume $\mathcal{Y}$ has a tree-structure. Accordingly, we propose LDL with tree-Wasserstein distance.

3.1 Wasserstein distance on tree metrics

Let $\mathcal{T}$ be a tree with non-negative weighted edges and $\mathcal{N}_\mathcal{T}$ be the set of nodes of $\mathcal{T}$. A shortest path metric $d_\mathcal{T} : \mathcal{N}_\mathcal{T} \times \mathcal{N}_\mathcal{T} \to \mathbb{R}$ associated with $\mathcal{T}$ is called the *tree metric*. Let v and v' be the nodes in $\mathcal{T}$. Accordingly, $d_\mathcal{T}(v, v')$ is equal to the sum of the edge weights along the shortest path between v and v'. Next, we know that $\mathcal{M}_\mathcal{T} = (\mathcal{N}_\mathcal{T}, d_\mathcal{T})$ is a metric space and can be naturally derived from $\mathcal{T}$.

It is assumed that $\mathcal{T}$ is rooted at r. For each node v, the set of nodes in the sub-tree of $\mathcal{T}$ rooted at v is defined as $\Gamma(v) = \{u \in \mathcal{N}_\mathcal{T} \mid v \in \mathcal{R}(u)\}$ where $\mathcal{R}(v)$ denotes the set of nodes in a unique path from a node v to the root r in $\mathcal{T}$. For each edge e, v_e denotes a deeper level node. Figure 1 illustrates a tree-structured label.

Given two probability measures μ, ν supported on $\mathcal{M}_\mathcal{T}$, the 1-Wasserstein distance between μ and ν is expressed as follows (Evans and Matsen, 2012; Le et al., 2019):

$$\mathcal{W}^1_{d_\mathcal{T}}(\mu, \nu) = \sum_{e \in \mathcal{T}} w_e |\mu(\Gamma(v_e)) - \nu(\Gamma(v_e))|, \quad (1)$$

where w_e denotes the weight of edge e. The key advantage of the tree-Wasserstein distance is that it can be computed with the linear time complexity, whereas the time complexity for the Sinkhorn algorithm is quadratic (Cuturi, 2013).

3.2 LDL with tree-Wasserstein distance

We define the tree-Wasserstein regularizer as follows.

Definition 1 (tree-Wasserstein regularizer). *Let $\boldsymbol{h}_{\boldsymbol{\theta}} : \mathcal{X} \to \mathcal{P}$ be a model with learnable parameters θ. Let $T_\mathcal{Y} = (V, E, W_E)$ be a tree associated with $\mathcal{Y}$, where V denotes the set of nodes, E is the set of edges, and $W_E(e)$ is the length of edge $e \in E$. Given input $\boldsymbol{x} \in \mathcal{X}$ and the ground-truth distribution of $\boldsymbol{y}$ $\boldsymbol{p}_{\boldsymbol{y}} \in \mathcal{P}$, then the tree-Wasserstein regularization term $\mathcal{TW}(\boldsymbol{x}, \boldsymbol{p}_{\boldsymbol{y}})$ is defined as follows:*

$$\begin{aligned}&\mathcal{TW}(\boldsymbol{x}, \boldsymbol{p}_{\boldsymbol{y}}) \\ &= \sum_{e \in \mathcal{T}} W_E(e) |(\boldsymbol{h}_{\boldsymbol{\theta}}(\boldsymbol{x}))(\Gamma(v_e)) - \boldsymbol{p}_{\boldsymbol{y}}(\Gamma(v_e))|,\end{aligned}$$

where $\boldsymbol{h}_{\boldsymbol{\theta}}$ denotes the prediction model.

Using the tree-Wasserstein regularizer, we pro-

Table 1: The results for the Synthetic dataset. The label distributions are given on a random tree with 1000 nodes.

Loss	Wasserstein ↓	KL ↓	Cheby↓	Clark ↓	Canbe ↓	Cos ↑	IntSec ↑
$\mathcal{KL}$	$9.701 \pm (.050)$	$\mathbf{0.431} \pm (\mathbf{.001})$	$0.209 \pm (.001)$	$1.777 \pm (.011)$	$14.512 \pm (.060)$	$\mathbf{0.877} \pm (\mathbf{.000})$	$\mathbf{0.754} \pm (\mathbf{.001})$
$\mathcal{KL} + \frac{1}{2}\mathcal{W}^1$	$10.831 \pm (.044)$	$0.452 \pm (.001)$	$0.230 \pm (.001)$	$1.666 \pm (.009)$	$13.834 \pm (.064)$	$0.868 \pm (.000)$	$0.739 \pm (.001)$
$\mathcal{KL} + \mathcal{W}^1$	$11.631 \pm (.048)$	$0.475 \pm (.001)$	$0.244 \pm (.001)$	$\mathbf{1.618} \pm (\mathbf{.008})$	$\mathbf{13.474} \pm (\mathbf{.063})$	$0.859 \pm (.000)$	$0.727 \pm (.001)$
$\mathcal{KL} + \frac{1}{2}\mathcal{TW}$	$7.257 \pm (.110)$	$0.595 \pm (.007)$	$\mathbf{0.193} \pm (\mathbf{.001})$	$2.098 \pm (.040)$	$19.636 \pm (.171)$	$0.833 \pm (.002)$	$0.729 \pm (.003)$
$\mathcal{KL} + \mathcal{TW}$	$\mathbf{7.158} \pm (\mathbf{.117})$	$0.631 \pm (.007)$	$0.195 \pm (.001)$	$2.143 \pm (.030)$	$19.923 \pm (.441)$	$0.825 \pm (.003)$	$0.721 \pm (.004)$

Table 2: The results for BlurbGenreCollectionEN.

Loss	Pseudo-Recall	Top5	AUC
$\mathcal{KL}$	$0.679 \pm (.008)$	$1.013 \pm (.015)$	$0.971 \pm (.001)$
$\mathcal{KL} + \frac{1}{2}\mathcal{W}^1$	$0.675 \pm (.008)$	$1.009 \pm (.013)$	$0.970 \pm (.002)$
$\mathcal{KL} + \mathcal{W}^1$	$0.678 \pm (.004)$	$1.008 \pm (.018)$	$0.970 \pm (.001)$
$\mathcal{KL} + \frac{1}{2}\mathcal{TW}$	$0.678 \pm (.010)$	$0.993 \pm (.013)$	$0.971 \pm (.002)$
$\mathcal{KL} + \mathcal{TW}$	$0.678 \pm (.009)$	$0.991 \pm (.017)$	$0.970 \pm (.001)$

pose the following LDL:

$$\widehat{\boldsymbol{\theta}} = \underset{\boldsymbol{\theta}}{\operatorname{argmin}} \sum_{i=1}^{n} \lambda \mathcal{TW}(\boldsymbol{h}_{\boldsymbol{\theta}}(\boldsymbol{x}_i), \boldsymbol{p}_{\boldsymbol{y}_i}) + \mathcal{KL}(\boldsymbol{h}_{\boldsymbol{\theta}}(\boldsymbol{x}_i), \boldsymbol{p}_{\boldsymbol{y}_i}), \quad (2)$$

where

$$\mathcal{KL}(\boldsymbol{h}_{\boldsymbol{\theta}}(\boldsymbol{x}_i), \boldsymbol{p}_{\boldsymbol{y}_i}) = \sum_{\ell=1}^{L} \boldsymbol{p}_{\boldsymbol{y}_i}^{(\ell)} \log \frac{\boldsymbol{p}_{\boldsymbol{y}_i}^{(\ell)}}{\boldsymbol{h}_{\boldsymbol{\theta}}(\boldsymbol{x}_i)^{(\ell)}}, \quad (3)$$

is the multi-class Kullback-Leibler loss function, and $\lambda \geq 0$ is its regularization parameter.

Notably, $\mathcal{TW}(\boldsymbol{h}_{\boldsymbol{\theta}}(\boldsymbol{x}_i), \boldsymbol{p}_{\boldsymbol{y}_i})$ is calculated in $O(L)$ time, where L denotes the number of labels. Unlike the Sinkhorn-Knopp algorithm, we need not compute and hold a distance matrix. For tree-structured labels, including hierarchical labels, the tree structure can be used directly as a tree metric. If we have prior knowledge about labels (e.g., similarity), we can set edge-weights using the prior knowledge.

4 Related Work

4.1 Label distribution learning

LDL (Geng, 2016) is the task of estimating the distribution of labels from each input. While age estimation (Geng et al., 2013), head-pose estimation (Geng and Xia, 2014), and semantic segmentation (Gao et al., 2017) are well known LDL tasks, in this study, we consider the task of estimating a distribution on a hierarchical structure. The key difference between LDL and a generative model is that the "true" distribution on labels is given in LDL.

4.2 Wasserstein distance

Given two probability vectors $\boldsymbol{a}, \boldsymbol{b} \in \mathbb{R}^n_{\geq 0}$ and a distance matrix $\boldsymbol{D} \in \mathbb{R}^{n \times n}_{\geq 0}$, the 1-Wasserstein distance $\mathcal{W}^1(\boldsymbol{a}, \boldsymbol{b})$ between $\boldsymbol{a}$ and $\boldsymbol{b}$ is defined as:

$$\mathcal{W}^1(\boldsymbol{a}, \boldsymbol{b}) = \min_{\boldsymbol{P} \in \Pi} \langle \boldsymbol{D}, \boldsymbol{P} \rangle, \quad (4)$$

where $\boldsymbol{\Pi}$ denotes the set of transport plans such that $\boldsymbol{\Pi} = \{\boldsymbol{P} \in \mathbb{R}^{n \times n}_{\geq 0} \mid \boldsymbol{P}\boldsymbol{1}_n = \boldsymbol{a}, \boldsymbol{P}^\top \boldsymbol{1}_n = \boldsymbol{b}\}$.

Because Wasserstein distance can incorporates the ground metric in the comparison of the probability distributions, it has been widely used in applications, including domain adaptation (Courty et al., 2017), generative models (Arjovsky et al., 2017), and natural language processing (Kusner et al., 2015). A loss function that uses the Wasserstein distance can improve predictions based on a structure of labels (Frogner et al., 2015; Zhao and Zhou, 2018). Additionally, an entropic optimal transport loss can provide a robustness against noise labels by finding the coupling of the data samples and propagating their labels according to the coupling weight (Damodaran et al., 2020).

Frogner et al. (2015) proposed learning using a Wasserstein loss to consider the geometric information in predicting a probability distribution. Because computing a sub-gradient of the exact Wasserstein loss is expensive, they estimated the sub-gradient by introducing an entropic-regularization term and using the Sinkhorn-Knopp algorithm. Although they also suggested extending the Wasserstein loss to unnormalized measures, we do not consider this case. Zhao and Zhou (2018) showed that Wasserstein loss influenced LDL in terms of simultaneously learning label correlations and distribution. We proposed learning using an exact Wasserstein distance with efficient computations when the ground metric is represented by a tree.

Le et al. (2019) suggested the tree-sliced Wasserstein distance, where the Wasserstein distance is approximated on a continuous space by averaging the Wasserstein distances on tree metrics constructed by dividing that space. An unbalanced variant of the tree-Wasserstein distance has been recently proposed (Sato et al., 2020).

5 Experiments

We applied our proposed method to LDL on trees based on a synthetic dataset and to multi-label text classification of a hierarchical structure based on a real dataset. We implemented all the methods using Pytorch (Paszke et al., 2019). Our models were optimized using a gradient method with the *Adam* (Kingma and Ba, 2015) optimizer.

Baselines: We compared our proposed method to the Wasserstein-loss-based LDL framework (Frogner et al., 2015; Zhao and Zhou, 2018) and a multi-class KL loss mentioned in (3). Notably, in the original paper (Zhao and Zhou, 2018), they did not include KL loss and used only Wasserstein loss, but (Frogner et al., 2015) used a linear combination of KL divergence and Wasserstein distance as the loss. To ensure fair comparison, we also report the combination of Wasserstein loss and multi-class KL loss as a strong baseline. Therefore, we set the combination parameter $\lambda = \{0, \frac{1}{2}, 1\}$ defined in Eq 2 and the weight of all edges to 1. The Wasserstein loss was computed using the Sinkhorn-Knopp algorithm in the log domain(Schmitzer, 2019; Peyré and Cuturi, 2018) on GPUs. For the proposed method, we computed the tree-Wasserstein loss on the CPU and then passed it to the GPU to compute the gradient. Then, we set the number of iterations of the Sinkhorn-Knopp algorithm to 10 and the regularization parameter to 50, respectively.

5.1 Synthetic data

We generated a synthetic dataset that comprises pairs of a real vector and a target probability distribution on the nodes of a randomly generated tree. This dataset was created as follows: First, we defined a parametric distribution on a graph. Given a graph, $G = (V, E)$, the shortest path metric, d_G, and the probability distribution, $F_{vu\sigma}$, over V parameterized by $v, u \in V, \sigma > 0$ is defined as:

$$F_{vu\sigma}(s) = \frac{1}{C}(\exp\frac{d_G(v,s)}{\sigma^2} + \exp\frac{d_G(u,s)}{\sigma^2})$$
$$C = \sum_{s\in V}(\exp\frac{d_G(v,s)}{\sigma^2} + \exp\frac{d_G(u,s)}{\sigma^2}).$$

Algorithm 1 shows the algorithm used to generate the dataset used in the experiments. In this experiment, we prepared datasets with the distribution on a random tree with 1000 nodes using NetworkX (Hagberg et al., 2008). The size of each of the training and testing datasets is 1000. We set the number of epochs to 500 and the batch size to 10, and we fixed the learning rate at .001. We reported the average scores of the experiments using 10 different random seeds.

Predictive model: We adopted the following model for class ℓ:

$$\boldsymbol{h}_{\boldsymbol{\theta}}(\boldsymbol{x})^{(\ell)} = \frac{\exp(\boldsymbol{w}_\ell^\top \boldsymbol{x} + b_\ell)}{\sum_j \exp(\boldsymbol{w}_j^\top \boldsymbol{x} + b_j)},$$

where $\mathbf{w}_i, b_i$ are learnable parameters.

Evaluation Metric: To evaluate predictions from various perspectives, we used the metric listed in Table 3. Notably we adopted the **exact** Wasserstein distance, called *Wasserstein*, between the prediction and ground-truth label distributions to assess the extent to which the ground metric was considered in the prediction. In these experiments, we used the Python Optimal Transport (POT) library (Flamary and Courty, 2017) to calculate the exact Wasserstein distance, and the weights of all the edges were set to 1. The other evaluation metrics are the same as those used in (Geng, 2016).

The scores of the experiment with synthetic data are presented in Table 1. The proposed linear combinations of $\mathcal{KL}$ and $\mathcal{TW}$ outperformed the others in terms of *Wasserstein* and *Chebyshev* metric, but they performed poorly in terms of the other metrics.

5.2 BlurbGenreCollectionEN

In this study, we used the BlurbGenreCollectionEN[1](Cortes and Vapnik, 1995; Lewis et al., 2004) dataset for performing experiments with real data. It comprises advertising descriptions of books from the Penguin Random House webpage. Each instance has one or multiple labels that are hierarchically structured. Because the hierarchical structure of these data is a *forest* and not a *tree*, we added a root node to the hierarchical tree. Of the total $91,892$ data samples 64%, 16% and 20% were used in the train, validation, and test sets, respectively. We set the number of epochs to 100 and the batch size to 100, and we fixed the learning rate to .001. We reported the average scores and standard deviations of the experiments using 10 different random seeds.

[1] `https://www.inf.uni-hamburg.de/en/inst/ab/lt/resources/data/blurb-genre-collection.html`

Canberra	$\sum_{\ell=1}^{L} \frac{\|\boldsymbol{h}_{\boldsymbol{\theta}}(\boldsymbol{x})^{(\ell)} - \boldsymbol{p}_{\boldsymbol{y}}^{(\ell)}\|}{\boldsymbol{h}_{\boldsymbol{\theta}}(\boldsymbol{x})^{(\ell)} + \boldsymbol{p}_{\boldsymbol{y}}^{(\ell)}}$
Chebyshev	$\max_i \|\boldsymbol{h}_{\boldsymbol{\theta}}(\boldsymbol{x})^{(\ell)} - \boldsymbol{p}_{\boldsymbol{y}}^{(\ell)}\|$
Clark	$\sqrt{\sum_{\ell=1}^{L} \frac{(\boldsymbol{h}_{\boldsymbol{\theta}}(\boldsymbol{x})^{(\ell)} - \boldsymbol{p}_{\boldsymbol{y}}^{(\ell)})^2}{(\boldsymbol{h}_{\boldsymbol{\theta}}(\boldsymbol{x})^{(\ell)} + \boldsymbol{p}_{\boldsymbol{y}}^{(\ell)})^2}}$
Cosine	$\frac{\sum_{\ell=1}^{L} \boldsymbol{h}_{\boldsymbol{\theta}}(\boldsymbol{x})^{(\ell)} \boldsymbol{p}_{\boldsymbol{y}}^{(\ell)}}{\sqrt{\sum_{\ell=1}^{L} (\boldsymbol{h}_{\boldsymbol{\theta}}(\boldsymbol{x})^{(\ell)})^2} \sqrt{\sum_{\ell=1}^{L} (\boldsymbol{p}_{\boldsymbol{y}}^{(\ell)})^2}}$
Intersection	$\sum_{\ell=1}^{L} \min(\boldsymbol{h}_{\boldsymbol{\theta}}(\boldsymbol{x})^{(\ell)}, \boldsymbol{p}_{\boldsymbol{y}}^{(\ell)})$
Kullback-Leibler	$\sum_{\ell=1}^{L} \boldsymbol{p}_{\boldsymbol{y}}^{(\ell)} \ln \frac{\boldsymbol{p}_{\boldsymbol{y}}^{(\ell)}}{\boldsymbol{h}_{\boldsymbol{\theta}}(\boldsymbol{x})^{(\ell)}}$

Table 3: Evaluation metrics for LDL. $\boldsymbol{h}_{\boldsymbol{\theta}}(\boldsymbol{x})$ is the predicted distribution of $\boldsymbol{x}$, and $\boldsymbol{p}_{\boldsymbol{y}}$ is the ground truth distribution of a label $\boldsymbol{y}$.

Predictive model: We adopted a *long-short-term-memory* (LSTM) (Hochreiter and Schmidhuber, 1997) model with a hidden state size of 200. Because LSTM can efficiently learn long-term dependencies of time-series data, it has often been used in the natural-language processing domain (Yin et al., 2017; Kuncoro et al., 2018). Additionally, we used *fastText* (Bojanowski et al., 2017; Joulin et al., 2017) for word embeddings. A fully connected layer exists before the output layer, and the output function is a softmax function.

Evaluation metric: We evaluated prediction accuracy using three metrics, namely pseudo-recall, top-k cost, and receiver operating characteristic area under the curve (ROC-AUC). Pseudo-recall is defined as $\frac{|\mathcal{P} \cup \mathcal{L}|}{|\mathcal{L}|}$, where $\mathcal{L}$ denotes the set of ground-truth labels, and $\mathcal{P}$ is a set that comprises $L = |\mathcal{L}|$ labels in descending order of the probability score.

Top-k cost is defined as:

$$\frac{1}{K} \sum_{k=1}^{K} \min_{\ell \in \mathcal{L}} d(\ell_{p_k}, \ell),$$

where ℓ_{p_k} denotes the label with the k-th highest probability score. This metric measures how close the predicted top-k labels are to the ground-truth labels. We calculate ROC-AUC using the output distribution of each model as a score vector, which is assigned 1 on the ground truth labels or 0 on the other labels. Table 2 presents the comparison results. Both regularization terms ($\mathcal{W}^1$ and $\mathcal{TW}$) did not have a significant impact on the results.

5.3 Computational-efficiency comparison

In the computational efficiency experiment, distributions with 10^2, 10^3, 10^4, and 10^5 supports were prepared. Subsequently, the computation time and memory required to calculate the loss of pairs of

Algorithm 1: Generating a synthetic dataset

Generate a random tree : $G = (V, E)$,
  where $V = \{s_1, ..., s_l\}$
$W_1 \leftarrow (n \times m)$-dim random matrix
$W_2 \leftarrow (m \times (l+1))$-dim random matrix
for $i = 1$ *to* N **do**
  $x_i \leftarrow n$-dimensional random vector
  $x_i \leftarrow \frac{1}{1+\exp(-W_1 x_i)}$
  $x_i \leftarrow \frac{1}{1+\exp(-W_2 x_i)}$
  $\sigma \leftarrow 10\mathbf{x_i}^{(l+1)}$
  $j \leftarrow \mathrm{argmax}_{1 \le j \le l} x_i^{(j)}$; $v \leftarrow s_j$
  $k \leftarrow \mathrm{argmin}_{1 \le k \le l} x_i^{(k)}$; $u \leftarrow s_k$
  $p_G(s) \leftarrow F_{vu\sigma}(s), \forall s \in V$
return $\{(x_i, p_G(V))\}_{i=1}^{N}$

Table 4: Comparison of computational efficiency.

L	Loss	Time(s)	Memory
10^2	$\mathcal{TW}$	**0.0024**	**1.58 MB**
	$\mathcal{W}^1$ with GPU	0.0062	3.32 MB
	$\mathcal{W}^1$ with CPU	0.0528	2.98 MB
10^3	$\mathcal{TW}$	0.0126	**2.44 MB**
	$\mathcal{W}^1$ with GPU	0.0071	16.94 MB
	$\mathcal{W}^1$ with CPU	0.1279	7.08 MB
10^4	$\mathcal{TW}$	**0.1204**	**9.82 MB**
	$\mathcal{W}^1$ with GPU	0.5277	766.88 MB
	$\mathcal{W}^1$ with CPU	25.7985	1148.22 MB
10^5	$\mathcal{TW}$	**1.6454**	**66.00 MB**
	$\mathcal{W}^1$ with GPU	-	(37.25 GB)
	$\mathcal{W}^1$ with CPU	-	(40.00 GB)

random probability distributions on the supports were measured. To avoid calculating a shortest-path distance matrix, we used the matrix $(\mathbf{1}\mathbf{1}^\top - \mathbb{I})$, where $\mathbb{I}$ denotes an identity matrix, as the distance matrix while computing the Wasserstein loss. Additionally, we used a random tree, with edge weights of 1, as a tree metric while computing the tree-Wasserstein loss. We report the average scores of three measurements.

Table 4 presents the time and memory required to calculate the losses for various numbers of nodes. $\mathcal{TW}$ outperforms the other Wasserstein losses in terms of computation time and is significantly superior in terms of memory consumption. Although $\mathcal{W}^1$ that uses a GPU is faster than the others with 10^3 supports, it cannot calculate the loss with 10^5 supports because the required memory cannot be allocated.

6 Conclusions

This study proposed the use of a tree-Wasserstein reguralizer for learning. The experimental results indicate that our proposed method can successfully predict the distributions of structured labels and that it outperforms existing Wasserstein loss calculation methods in terms of both computational speed and memory consumption.

Acknowledgments

This work was supported by the JSPS KAKENHI Grant Number 20H04243 and 20H04244. This work was also supported by JST, ACT-X Grant Number JPMJAX200S, Japan.

References

Martin Arjovsky, Soumith Chintala, and Léon Bottou. 2017. Wasserstein generative adversarial networks. In *Proceedings of the 34th International Conference on Machine Learning*, volume 70, pages 214–223.

Siddhartha Banerjee, Cem Akkaya, Francisco Perez-Sorrosal, and Kostas Tsioutsiouliklis. 2019. Hierarchical transfer learning for multi-label text classification. In *Proceedings of the 57th Conference of the Association for Computational Linguistics*, volume 1, pages 6295–6300.

Piotr Bojanowski, Edouard Grave, Armand Joulin, and Tomas Mikolov. 2017. Enriching word vectors with subword information. *Transactions of the Association for Computational Linguistics*, 5:135–146.

Ilias Chalkidis, Manos Fergadiotis, Prodromos Malakasiotis, and Ion Androutsopoulos. 2019. Large-scale multi-label text classification on EU legislation. In *Proceedings of the 57th Conference of the Association for Computational Linguistics*, volume 1, pages 6314–6322. Association for Computational Linguistics.

Corinna Cortes and Vladimir Vapnik. 1995. Support-vector networks. *Machine learning*, 20(3):273–297.

Nicolas Courty, Rémi Flamary, Devis Tuia, and Alain Rakotomamonjy. 2017. Optimal transport for domain adaptation. *IEEE Transactions on Pattern Analysis and Machine Intelligence*, 39(9):1853–1865.

Marco Cuturi. 2013. Sinkhorn distances: Lightspeed computation of optimal transport. In *Advances in Neural Information Processing Systems*, pages 2292–2300.

Bharath Bhushan Damodaran, Rémi Flamary, Vivien Seguy, and Nicolas Courty. 2020. An entropic optimal transport loss for learning deep neural networks under label noise in remote sensing images. *Computer Vision and Image Understanding*, 191:102863.

Steven N Evans and Frederick A Matsen. 2012. The phylogenetic kantorovich–rubinstein metric for environmental sequence samples. *Journal of the Royal Statistical Society: Series B (Statistical Methodology)*, 74(3):569–592.

R'emi Flamary and Nicolas Courty. 2017. POT python optimal transport library. Web: https://pythonot.github.io/.

Charlie Frogner, Chiyuan Zhang, Hossein Mobahi, Mauricio Araya, and Tomaso A Poggio. 2015. Learning with a wasserstein loss. In *Advances in Neural Information Processing Systems*, pages 2053–2061.

Bin-Bin Gao, Chao Xing, Chen-Wei Xie, Jianxin Wu, and Xin Geng. 2017. Deep label distribution learning with label ambiguity. *IEEE Transactions on Image Processing*, 26(6):2825–2838.

Xin Geng. 2016. Label distribution learning. *IEEE Transactions on Knowledge and Data Engineering*, 28(7):1734–1748.

Xin Geng and Yu Xia. 2014. Head pose estimation based on multivariate label distribution. In *Proceedings of the IEEE Conference on Computer Vision and Pattern Recognition*, pages 1837–1842.

Xin Geng, Chao Yin, and Zhi-Hua Zhou. 2013. Facial age estimation by learning from label distributions. *IEEE Transactions on Pattern Analysis and Machine Intelligence*, 35(10):2401–2412.

Aric A. Hagberg, Daniel A. Schult, and Pieter J. Swart. 2008. Exploring network structure, dynamics, and function using networkx. In *Proceedings of the 7th Python in Science Conference*, pages 11–15.

Sepp Hochreiter and Jürgen Schmidhuber. 1997. Long short-term memory. *Neural Computation*, 9(8):1735–1780.

Armand Joulin, Edouard Grave, Piotr Bojanowski, and Tomas Mikolov. 2017. Bag of tricks for efficient text classification. In *Proceedings of the 15th Conference of the European Chapter of the Association for Computational Linguistics*, volume 2, pages 427–431.

Diederik P. Kingma and Jimmy Ba. 2015. Adam: A method for stochastic optimization. In *3rd International Conference on Learning Representations*.

Adhiguna Kuncoro, Chris Dyer, John Hale, Dani Yogatama, Stephen Clark, and Phil Blunsom. 2018. LSTMs can learn syntax-sensitive dependencies well, but modeling structure makes them better. In *Proceedings of the 56th Annual Meeting of the Association for Computational Linguistics*, volume 1, pages 1426–1436.

Matt Kusner, Yu Sun, Nicholas Kolkin, and Kilian Weinberger. 2015. From word embeddings to document distances. In *Proceedings of the 32nd International Conference on Machine Learning*, volume 37, pages 957–966.

Tam Le, Makoto Yamada, Kenji Fukumizu, and Marco Cuturi. 2019. Tree-sliced variants of wasserstein distances. In *Advances in Neural Information Processing Systems*, pages 12283–12294.

David D Lewis, Yiming Yang, Tony G Rose, and Fan Li. 2004. Rcv1: A new benchmark collection for text categorization research. *Journal of Machine Learning Research*, 5(Apr):361–397.

Adam Paszke, Sam Gross, Francisco Massa, Adam Lerer, James Bradbury, Gregory Chanan, Trevor Killeen, Zeming Lin, Natalia Gimelshein, Luca Antiga, Alban Desmaison, Andreas Kopf, Edward Yang, Zachary DeVito, Martin Raison, Alykhan Tejani, Sasank Chilamkurthy, Benoit Steiner, Lu Fang, Junjie Bai, and Soumith Chintala. 2019. Pytorch: An imperative style, high-performance deep learning library. In H. Wallach, H. Larochelle, A. Beygelzimer, F. dAlché Buc, E. Fox, and R. Garnett, editors, *Advances in Neural Information Processing Systems*, pages 8024–8035. Curran Associates, Inc.

Gabriel Peyré and Marco Cuturi. 2018. Computational optimal transport. *arXiv preprint arXiv:1803.00567*.

Ryoma Sato, Makoto Yamada, and Hisashi Kashima. 2020. Fast unbalanced optimal transport on tree. In *Advances in Neural Information Processing Systems*.

Bernhard Schmitzer. 2019. Stabilized sparse scaling algorithms for entropy regularized transport problems. *SIAM Journal on Scientific Computing*, 41(3):A1443–A1481.

Cédric Villani. 2009. *Optimal transport: old and new*. Grundlehren der mathematischen Wissenschaften. Splinger.

Wenpeng Yin, Katharina Kann, Mo Yu, and Hinrich Schütze. 2017. Comparative study of cnn and rnn for natural language processing. *arXiv preprint arXiv:1702.01923*.

Peng Zhao and Zhi-Hua Zhou. 2018. Label distribution learning by optimal transport. In *Proceedings of the Thirty-Second AAAI Conference on Artificial Intelligence*, pages 4506–4513.

Deyu Zhou, Xuan Zhang, Yin Zhou, Quan Zhao, and Xin Geng. 2016. Emotion distribution learning from texts. In *Proceedings of the 2016 Conference on Empirical Methods in Natural Language Processing*, pages 638–647.

Have Attention Heads in BERT Learned Constituency Grammar?

Ziyang Luo
Uppsala University
Ziyang.Luo.9588@student.uu.se

Abstract

With the success of pre-trained language models in recent years, more and more researchers focus on opening the "black box" of these models. Following this interest, we carry out a qualitative and quantitative analysis of constituency grammar in attention heads of BERT and RoBERTa. We employ the syntactic distance method to extract implicit constituency grammar from the attention weights of each head. Our results show that there exist heads that can induce some grammar types much better than baselines, suggesting that some heads act as a proxy for constituency grammar. We also analyze how attention heads' constituency grammar inducing (CGI) ability changes after fine-tuning with two kinds of tasks, including sentence meaning similarity (SMS) tasks and natural language inference (NLI) tasks. Our results suggest that SMS tasks decrease the average CGI ability of upper layers, while NLI tasks increase it. Lastly, we investigate the connections between CGI ability and natural language understanding ability on QQP and MNLI tasks.

1 Introduction

Recently, pre-trained language models have achieved great success in many natural language processing tasks (Devlin et al., 2019; Yang et al., 2019), including sentiment analysis (Liu et al., 2019), question answering (Lan et al., 2020) and constituency parsing (Zhang et al., 2020), to name a few. Though these models have become more and more popular in many NLP tasks, they are still "black boxes". What they have learned, and why and when they perform well remain unknown. To open these "black boxes", researchers have used many methods to analyze the linguistic knowledge that these models encode (Goldberg, 2019; Clark et al., 2019; Hewitt and Manning, 2019; Kim et al., 2020).

Pre-trained language models use self-attention mechanism in each layer to compute the internal representations of each token. In this work, we investigate the hypothesis that some attention heads in pre-trained language models have learned constituency grammar. We use an unsupervised constituency parsing method to extract constituency trees from each attention heads of BERT (Devlin et al., 2019) and RoBERTa (Liu et al., 2019) before and after fine-tuning. This method computes the syntactic distance between every two adjacent words and generates a constituency parsing tree recursively. We analyze the extracted constituency parsing trees to investigate whether specific attention heads induce constituency grammar better than baselines, and which types of constituency grammars they learn best.

In prior work, Kim et al. (2020) show that some layers of pre-trained language models exhibit syntactic structure akin to constituency grammar to some degree. However, they do not analyze how fine-tuning affects models. We first follow their methods to extract constituency grammar from BERT and RoBERTa. Then, we use the same approach to analyze BERT and RoBERTa after fine-tuning. To the best of our knowledge, we are the first to investigate how fine-tuning affects the constituency grammar inducing (CGI) ability of attention heads. We fine-tune them on two types of GLUE natural language understanding (NLU) tasks (Williams et al., 2018; Wang et al., 2018). The first type is the sentence meaning similarity (SMS) task. We fine-tune our models on two datasets, QQP [1] and STS-B (Cer et al., 2017). The second type is the natural language inference (NLI) task. We fine-tune our models on two datasets, MNLI (Williams et al., 2018) and QNLI (Rajpurkar et al., 2016; Wang et al., 2018). Lastly, we investigate the rela-

[1] https://www.quora.com/q/quoradata/First-Quora-Dataset-Release-Question-Pairs

Proceedings of the 16th Conference of the European Chapter of the Associationfor Computational Linguistics: Student Research Workshop, pages 8–15
April 19 - 23, 2021. ©2021 Association for Computational Linguistics

tions between CGI ability of attention heads and natural language understanding ability on QQP and MNLI tasks.

The findings of our study are as follows:

1. Attention heads in the higher layers of BERT and the middle layers of RoBERTa have better constituency grammar inducing (CGI) ability. Some heads act as a proxy for some constituency grammar types, but all heads do not appear to fully learn constituency grammar.

2. The sentence meaning similarity task decreases the average CGI ability in the higher layers. The natural language inference task increases it in the higher layers.

3. For QQP and MNLI tasks, attention heads with better CGI ability are more important for BERT. However, this relation is different in RoBERTa.

2 Related Work

Many works have proposed methods to induce constituency grammar and extract constituency trees from the attention heads of the transformer-based model. Mareček and Rosa (2018) aggregate all the attention distributions through the layers and get an attention weight matrix. They extract binary constituency tree and undirected dependency tree from this matrix. Kim et al. (2020) use the attention distribution and internal vector representation to compute Syntactic Distance (Shen et al., 2018) between every two adjacent words to draw constituency trees from raw sentences without any training.

Additionally, researchers have investigated how fine-tuning affects syntactic knowledge that BERT learns. Kovaleva et al. (2019) use the subset of GLUE tasks (Wang et al., 2018) to fine-tune BERT-base model. They find that fine-tuning does not change the self-attention patterns. They also find that after fine-tuning, the last two layers' attention heads undergo the largest changes. Htut et al. (2019) investigates whether fine-tuning affects the dependency syntax in BERT attentions. They find that fine-tuning does not have great effects on attention heads' dependency syntax inducing ability. Zhao and Bethard (2020) investigate the negation scope linguistic knowledge in BERT and RoBERTa's attention heads before and after fine-tuning. They find that after fine-tuning, the average attention heads are more sensitive to negation.

While there are some prior works analyzing attention heads in BERT, we believe we are the first to analyze the constituency grammar learned by fine-tuned BERT and RoBERTa models.

3 Methods

3.1 Transformer and BERT

Transformer (Vaswani et al., 2017) is a neural network model based on self-attention mechanism. It contains multiple layers and each layer contains multiple attention heads. Each attention head takes a sequence of input vectors $h = [h_1, ..., h_n]$ corresponding to the n tokens. An attention head will transform each vector h_i into query q_i, key k_i, and value v_i vectors. Then it computes the output o_i by a weighted sum of the value vectors.

$$a_{ij} = \frac{\exp(q_i^T k_j)}{\sum_{t=1}^{n} \exp(q_i^T k_t)} \tag{1}$$

$$o_i = \sum_{j=1}^{n} a_{ij} v_j \tag{2}$$

Attention weights distribution of each token can be viewed as the "importance" from other tokens in the sentence to the current token.

BERT is a Transformer-based pre-trained language model. It is pre-trained on BooksCorpus (Zhu et al., 2015) and English Wikipedia with masked language model (MLM) objective and next sentence prediction (NSP) objective. RoBERTa is a modified version of BERT. It removes the NSP pre-training objective and training with much larger mini-batches and learning rates. We use the uncased base size of BERT and base size of RoBERTa which have 12 layers and each layer contains 12 attention heads. Our models are downloaded from Hugging Face's Transformers Library [2] (Wolf et al., 2020).

3.2 Analysis Methods

We aim to analyze constituency grammar in attention heads. We use a method to extract constituency parsing trees from attention distributions. This method operates on the attention weight matrix $W \in (0, 1)^{T \times T}$ for every head at a given layer, where T is the number of tokens in the sentence.

[2] https://huggingface.co/models

Method: Syntactic Distance to Constituency Tree To extract complete valid constituency parsing trees from the attention weights for a given layer and head, we follow the method of Kim et al. (2020) and treat every row of the attention weight matrix as attention distribution of each token in the sentence. As in Kim et al. (2020), we compute the syntactic distance vector $\mathbf{d}= [d_1, d_2, ..., d_{n-1}]$ for a given sentence $w_1, ..., w_n$, where d_i is the syntactic distance between w_i and w_{i+1}. Each d_i is defined as follows:

$$d_i = f(g(w_i), g(w_{i+1})), \quad (3)$$

where $f(\cdot, \cdot)$ and $g(\cdot)$ are a distance measure function and feature extractor function. We use Jensen-Shannon function to measure the distance between each attention distribution. Appendix A gives a brief introduction of this function. $g(w_i)$ is equal to the ith row of the attention matrix W.

To introduce the right-skewness bias for English constituency trees, we follow Kim et al. (2020) by adding a linear bias term to every d_i:

$$\hat{d_i} = d_i + \lambda \cdot Mean(\mathbf{d}) \times \left(1 - \frac{i-1}{m-1}\right), \quad (4)$$

where $m = n - 1$ and λ is set to 1.5.

After computing the syntactic distance, we use the algorithm introduced by Shen et al. (2018) to get the target constituency tree. Appendix B describes this algorithm.

Constituency parsing is a word-level task, but BERT uses byte-pair tokenization (Sennrich et al., 2016). This means that some words are tokenized into subword units. Therefore, we need to convert token-to-token attention matrix to word-to-word attention matrix. We merge the non-matching subword units and compute the means of the attention distributions for the corresponding rows and columns. We use two baselines in our experiments. They are left-branching and right-branching trees.

3.3 Experiments Setup

In our experiments, we use an unsupervised constituency parsing method to induce constituency grammar on WSJ Penn Treebank (PTB, Marcus et al. (1993)) without any training. We use the standard split of the dataset-23 for testing. We use sentence-level F1 (S-F1) score to evaluate our models. In addition, we also report label recall scores for six main phrase categories: SBAR, NP, VP, PP, ADJP, and ADVP.

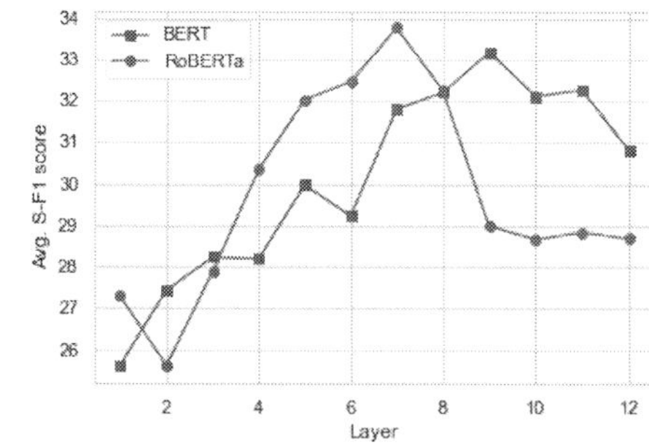

Figure 1: Average constituency parsing S-F1 score of each layer in BERT and RoBERTa.

4 Results and Analysis

4.1 Constituency Grammar in Attention Heads before Fine-tuning

In this part, our goal is to understand how constituency grammar is captured by different attention heads in BERT and RoBERTa before fine-tuning. First, we investigate the common patterns of attention heads' constituency grammar inducing (CGI) ability in BERT and RoBERTa. From Figure 1, we can find that the CGI ability of the higher layers of BERT is better than the lower layers. However, the middle layers of RoBERTa are better than the other layers. In appendix C, two heatmaps of every heads' S-F1 score in BERT and RoBERTa also show such patterns.

Table 1 describes the S-F1 scores of the best attention heads of BERT and RoBERTa. We also choose the best recall for each phrase type. We observe that the S-F1 scores of BERT and RoBERTa are only slightly better than the right-branching baseline. This implies that the attention heads in BERT and RoBERTa do not appear to fully learn constituency grammar. However, they outperform the baselines by a large margin for noun phrase (NP), preposition phrase (PP), adjective phrase (ADJP), and adverb phrase (ADVP). This implies that the attention heads in BERT and RoBERTa only learn a part of constituency grammar.

4.2 Constituency Grammar in Attention Heads after Fine-tuning

In this part, we fine-tune BERT and RoBERTa with four downstream tasks, QQP, STS-B, QNLI, and MNLI. These four tasks can be divided into two types. The first type is the sentence meaning similarity task (SMS), including QQP and STS-B. This

Models	S-F1	SBAR	NP	VP	PP	ADJP	ADVP
Baselines							
Left-branching Trees	8.73	5.46%	11.33%	0.82%	5.02%	2.46%	8.04%
Right-branching Trees	39.46	68.76%	24.89%	71.76%	42.43%	27.65%	38.11%
Pre-trained LMs							
BERT	39.47	67.32%	46.48%	68.82%	57.26%	46.39%	65.03%
BERT-QQP	39.97	67.32%	45.39%	68.79%	50.71%	45.01%	61.54%
BERT-STS-B	39.48	67.32%	44.16%	68.82%	56.68%	48.39%	57.69%
BERT-QNLI	39.74	67.32%	50.96%	68.81%	65.38%	46.08%	63.29%
BERT-MNLI	39.66	67.32%	44.89%	68.75%	62.81%	49.16%	64.69%
RoBERTa	39.60	67.43%	47.92%	69.35%	56.53%	49.00%	66.43%
RoBERTa-QQP	39.41	66.70%	43.02%	69.45%	51.06%	43.16%	60.84%
RoBERTa-STS-B	40.36	66.76%	46.82%	69.50%	54.91%	46.54%	64.34%
RoBERTa-QNLI	43.95	66.76%	52.51%	69.48%	58.30%	48.39%	69.23%
RoBERTa-MNLI	40.41	66.76%	47.97%	69.42%	57.50%	47.77%	68.88%

Table 1: Highest constituency parsing scores of all models. Blue score means that this score is lower after fine-tuning. Red score means that this score is higher after fine-tuning.

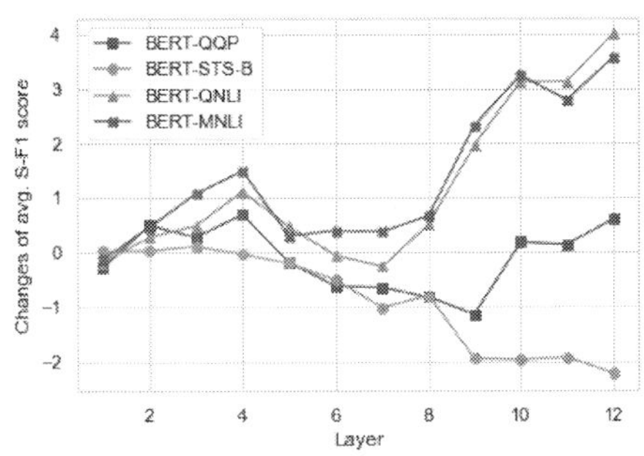

Figure 2: Changes of average S-F1 score of each layer in BERT after fine-tuning.

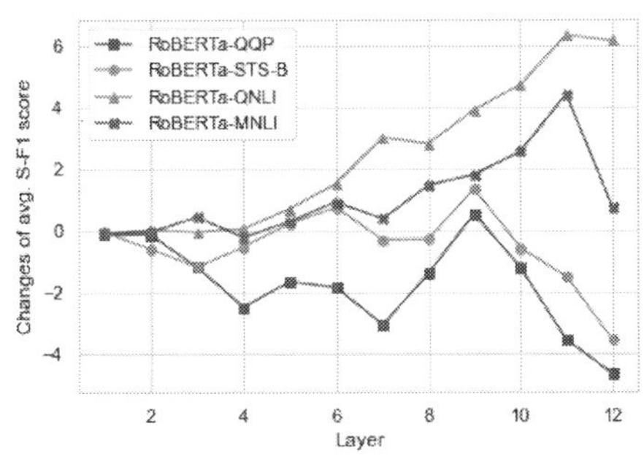

Figure 3: Changes of average S-F1 score of each layer in RoBERTa after fine-tuning.

task requires models to determine whether two sentences have the same meaning. The second type is the natural language inference task (NLI), including QNLI and MNLI. This task requires models to determine whether the first sentence can infer the second sentence. We want to analyze how these two kinds of downstream tasks affect constituency grammar inducing (CGI) ability of attention heads in BERT and RoBERTa.

Figure 2 and Figure 3 show that these four tasks do not have much influence on BERT and RoBERTa for the lower layers. For the higher layers, fine-tuning with NLI tasks can increase the average CGI ability of attention heads in BERT and RoBERTa. However, fine-tuning with SMS tasks harms it.

Table 1 shows that fine-tuning can increase the highest constituency parsing scores of all models except RoBERTa-QQP. However, fine-tuning with SMS tasks decreases the ability of attention heads to induce NP, PP, ADJP, and ADVP. For BERT, NLI tasks can increase the ability of attention heads to induce NP, PP. For RoBERTa, NLI tasks can increase the ability of attention heads to induce NP, VP, PP, and ADVP.

4.3 Constituency Grammar Inducing Ability and Natural Language Understanding Ability

In this part, we analyze the relations between constituency grammar inducing (CGI) ability and natural language understanding (NLU) ability on QQP

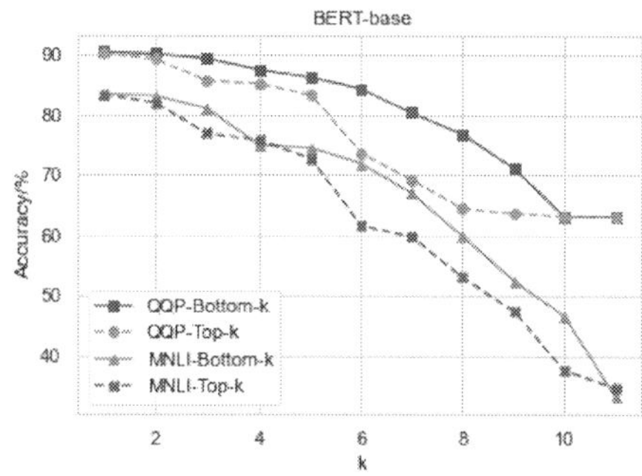

Figure 4: QQP dev and MNLI dev-matched accuracy after masking the top-k/bottom-k attention heads in each layer of BERT-QQP and BERT-MNLI.

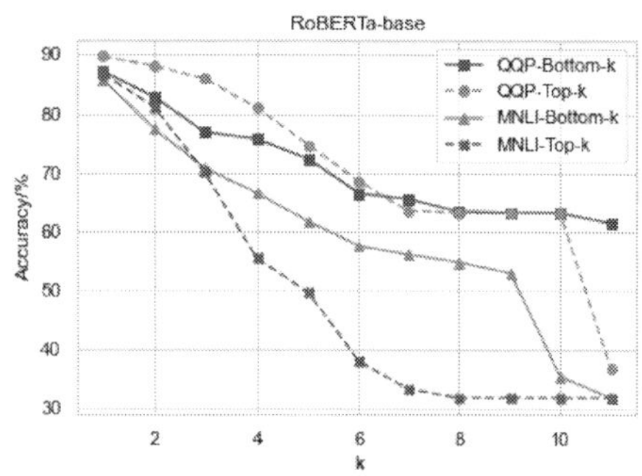

Figure 5: QQP dev and MNLI dev-matched accuracy after masking the top-k/bottom-k attention heads in each layer of RoBERTa-QQP and RoBERTa-MNLI.

and MNLI tasks. We use the performance of BERT and RoBERTa to evaluate their NLU ability. We report the scores on the validation, rather than test data, so the results are different from the original BERT paper.

First, we sort all attention heads in each layer based on their S-F1 scores before fine-tuning. Then we use the method in Michel et al. (2019) to mask the top-k/bottom-k ($k = 1, ..., 11$) attention heads in each layer and compute the accuracy on two downstream tasks, QQP and MNLI.

Figure 4 shows that downstream tasks accuracy scores decrease quicker when we have masked the top-k attention heads in BERT. Especially for the QQP task, after masking the bottom-7 attention heads in all layers, accuracy is still higher than 80%, which is more than 10% higher than masking the top-7 attention heads.

Figure 5 shows that masking RoBERTa has different results from BERT. For the QQP task, when k is smaller or equal to 6, masking the bottom-k attention heads in all layers decreases faster. For the MNLI task, when k is 1 or 2, masking the bottom-k heads decreases also faster. When k is larger than 6 in the QQP task and 2 in the MNLI task, masking the top-k heads decreases faster.

For BERT, the results show that attention heads with better CGI ability are more important for a model to gain NLU ability on these two tasks. For RoBERTa, the connections between CGI ability and NLU ability are not as strong as BERT. For the MNLI task, we still can find that better CGI ability is more important for NLU ability. However, better heads are not so important for QQP task.

5 Discussion

The experiments detailed in the previous sections point out that the attention heads in BERT and RoBERTa does not fully learn much constituency grammar knowledge. Even after fine-tuning with downstream tasks, the best constituency parsing score does not change much. Our results are similar to Htut et al. (2019). They also point out that the attention heads do not fully learn much dependency syntax. Fine-tuning does not affect these results. This raises an interesting question: do attention heads not contain syntax (constituency or dependency) information? If this is true, where does BERT encode this information? Also, is syntax information not important for BERT to understand language? Our simple experiment in §4.3 shows that the attention heads with better constituency grammar inducing ability are not important for RoBERTa on QQP task. Glavaš and Vulic (2020) also point out that leveraging explicit formalized syntactic structures provides zero to negligible impact on NLU tasks. The relations between syntax and BERT's NLU ability still need to be further analyzed.

6 Conclusion

In this work, we investigate whether the attention heads in BERT and RoBERTa have learned constituency grammar before and after fine-tuning. We use a method to extract constituency parsing trees without any training, and observe that the upper layers of BERT and the middle layers of RoBERTa show better constituency grammar ability. Certain attention heads better induce specific phrase types, but none of the heads show strong constituency grammar inducing (CGI) ability. Furthermore, we observe that fine-tuning with SMS tasks decreases the average CGI ability of upper layers, but NLI tasks can increase it. Lastly, we mask some heads based on their parsing S-F1 scores. We show that attention heads with better CGI ability are more important for BERT on QQP and MNLI tasks. For RoBERTa, better heads are not so important on QQP task.

One of the directions for future research would be to further study the relations between downstream tasks and the CGI ability in attention heads and to explain why different tasks have different effects.

Acknowledgments

This project grew out of a master course project for the Fall 2020 Uppsala University 5LN714, *Language Technology: Research and Development*. We would like to thank Sara Stymne and Ali Basirat for some great suggestions and the anonymous reviewers for their excellent feedback.

References

Daniel Cer, Mona Diab, Eneko Agirre, Iñigo Lopez-Gazpio, and Lucia Specia. 2017. SemEval-2017 task 1: Semantic textual similarity multilingual and crosslingual focused evaluation. In *Proceedings of the 11th International Workshop on Semantic Evaluation (SemEval-2017)*, pages 1–14, Vancouver, Canada. Association for Computational Linguistics.

Kevin Clark, Urvashi Khandelwal, Omer Levy, and Christopher D. Manning. 2019. What does BERT look at? an analysis of BERT's attention. In *Proceedings of the 2019 ACL Workshop BlackboxNLP: Analyzing and Interpreting Neural Networks for NLP*, pages 276–286, Florence, Italy. Association for Computational Linguistics.

Jacob Devlin, Ming-Wei Chang, Kenton Lee, and Kristina Toutanova. 2019. BERT: Pre-training of deep bidirectional transformers for language understanding. In *Proceedings of the 2019 Conference of the North American Chapter of the Association for Computational Linguistics: Human Language Technologies, Volume 1 (Long and Short Papers)*, pages 4171–4186, Minneapolis, Minnesota. Association for Computational Linguistics.

Goran Glavaš and Ivan Vulic. 2020. Is supervised syntactic parsing beneficial for language understanding? an empirical investigation.

Yoav Goldberg. 2019. Assessing bert's syntactic abilities.

John Hewitt and Christopher D. Manning. 2019. A structural probe for finding syntax in word representations. In *Proceedings of the 2019 Conference of the North American Chapter of the Association for Computational Linguistics: Human Language Technologies, Volume 1 (Long and Short Papers)*, pages 4129–4138, Minneapolis, Minnesota. Association for Computational Linguistics.

Phu Mon Htut, Jason Phang, Shikha Bordia, and Samuel R. Bowman. 2019. Do attention heads in bert track syntactic dependencies?

Taeuk Kim, Jihun Choi, Daniel Edmiston, and Sang goo Lee. 2020. Are pre-trained language models aware of phrases? simple but strong baselines for grammar induction.

Olga Kovaleva, Alexey Romanov, Anna Rogers, and Anna Rumshisky. 2019. Revealing the dark secrets of BERT. In *Proceedings of the 2019 Conference on Empirical Methods in Natural Language Processing and the 9th International Joint Conference on Natural Language Processing (EMNLP-IJCNLP)*, pages 4365–4374, Hong Kong, China. Association for Computational Linguistics.

Zhenzhong Lan, Mingda Chen, Sebastian Goodman, Kevin Gimpel, Piyush Sharma, and Radu Soricut. 2020. Albert: A lite bert for self-supervised learning of language representations. In *International Conference on Learning Representations*.

Yinhan Liu, Myle Ott, Naman Goyal, Jingfei Du, Mandar Joshi, Danqi Chen, Omer Levy, Mike Lewis, Luke Zettlemoyer, and Veselin Stoyanov. 2019. Roberta: A robustly optimized bert pretraining approach.

Mitchell P. Marcus, Beatrice Santorini, and Mary Ann Marcinkiewicz. 1993. Building a large annotated corpus of English: The Penn Treebank. *Computational Linguistics*, 19(2):313–330.

David Mareček and Rudolf Rosa. 2018. Extracting syntactic trees from transformer encoder self-attentions. In *Proceedings of the 2018 EMNLP Workshop BlackboxNLP: Analyzing and Interpreting Neural Networks for NLP*, pages 347–349, Brussels, Belgium. Association for Computational Linguistics.

Paul Michel, Omer Levy, and Graham Neubig. 2019. Are sixteen heads really better than one? In H. Wallach, H. Larochelle, A. Beygelzimer, F. d'Alché-Buc, E. Fox, and R. Garnett, editors, *Advances in Neural Information Processing Systems 32*, pages 14014–14024. Curran Associates, Inc.

Pranav Rajpurkar, Jian Zhang, Konstantin Lopyrev, and Percy Liang. 2016. SQuAD: 100,000+ questions for machine comprehension of text. In *Proceedings of the 2016 Conference on Empirical Methods in Natural Language Processing*, pages 2383–2392, Austin, Texas. Association for Computational Linguistics.

Rico Sennrich, Barry Haddow, and Alexandra Birch. 2016. Neural machine translation of rare words with subword units. In *Proceedings of the 54th Annual Meeting of the Association for Computational*

Linguistics (Volume 1: Long Papers), pages 1715–1725, Berlin, Germany. Association for Computational Linguistics.

Yikang Shen, Zhouhan Lin, Athul Paul Jacob, Alessandro Sordoni, Aaron Courville, and Yoshua Bengio. 2018. Straight to the tree: Constituency parsing with neural syntactic distance. In *Proceedings of the 56th Annual Meeting of the Association for Computational Linguistics (Volume 1: Long Papers)*, pages 1171–1180, Melbourne, Australia. Association for Computational Linguistics.

Ashish Vaswani, Noam Shazeer, Niki Parmar, Jakob Uszkoreit, Llion Jones, Aidan N Gomez, Ł ukasz Kaiser, and Illia Polosukhin. 2017. Attention is all you need. In I. Guyon, U. V. Luxburg, S. Bengio, H. Wallach, R. Fergus, S. Vishwanathan, and R. Garnett, editors, *Advances in Neural Information Processing Systems 30*, pages 5998–6008. Curran Associates, Inc.

Alex Wang, Amanpreet Singh, Julian Michael, Felix Hill, Omer Levy, and Samuel Bowman. 2018. GLUE: A multi-task benchmark and analysis platform for natural language understanding. In *Proceedings of the 2018 EMNLP Workshop BlackboxNLP: Analyzing and Interpreting Neural Networks for NLP*, pages 353–355, Brussels, Belgium. Association for Computational Linguistics.

Adina Williams, Nikita Nangia, and Samuel Bowman. 2018. A broad-coverage challenge corpus for sentence understanding through inference. In *Proceedings of the 2018 Conference of the North American Chapter of the Association for Computational Linguistics: Human Language Technologies, Volume 1 (Long Papers)*, pages 1112–1122. Association for Computational Linguistics.

Thomas Wolf, Lysandre Debut, Victor Sanh, Julien Chaumond, Clement Delangue, Anthony Moi, Pierric Cistac, Tim Rault, Rémi Louf, Morgan Funtowicz, Joe Davison, Sam Shleifer, Patrick von Platen, Clara Ma, Yacine Jernite, Julien Plu, Canwen Xu, Teven Le Scao, Sylvain Gugger, Mariama Drame, Quentin Lhoest, and Alexander M. Rush. 2020. Huggingface's transformers: State-of-the-art natural language processing.

Zhilin Yang, Zihang Dai, Yiming Yang, Jaime Carbonell, Russ R Salakhutdinov, and Quoc V Le. 2019. Xlnet: Generalized autoregressive pretraining for language understanding. In H. Wallach, H. Larochelle, A. Beygelzimer, F. d'Alché-Buc, E. Fox, and R. Garnett, editors, *Advances in Neural Information Processing Systems 32*, pages 5753–5763. Curran Associates, Inc.

Yu Zhang, Houquan Zhou, and Zhenghua Li. 2020. Fast and accurate neural crf constituency parsing. In *Proceedings of the Twenty-Ninth International Joint Conference on Artificial Intelligence, IJCAI-20*, pages 4046–4053. International Joint Conferences on Artificial Intelligence Organization. Main track.

Yiyun Zhao and Steven Bethard. 2020. How does BERT's attention change when you fine-tune? an analysis methodology and a case study in negation scope. In *Proceedings of the 58th Annual Meeting of the Association for Computational Linguistics*, pages 4729–4747, Online. Association for Computational Linguistics.

Yukun Zhu, Ryan Kiros, Richard Zemel, Ruslan Salakhutdinov, Raquel Urtasun, Antonio Torralba, and Sanja Fidler. 2015. Aligning books and movies: Towards story-like visual explanations by watching movies and reading books.

A Jensen-Shannon Distance Measure Function

Jensen-Shannon function measures the distance between two distributions. Suppose that we have two distributions P and Q, the Jensen-Shannon Distance is defined as

$$JSD(P||Q) = \left(\frac{D_{KL}(P||M) + D_{KL}(Q||M)}{2}\right)^{\frac{1}{2}}, \tag{5}$$

where $M = (P+Q)/2$ and $D_{KL}(A||B) = \sum_w A(w)\log(A(w)/B(w))$.

B Syntactic Distances to Constituency Trees Algorithm

Algorithm 1 Syntactic Distances to Constituency Trees Algorithm (Shen et al., 2018)

$S = [w_1, w_2, ..., w_n]$: a sentence with n words.
$\mathbf{d} = [d_1, d_2, ..., d_{n-1}]$: a sequence of distances between every two adjacent words.
function TREE(S, **d**)
  if d is empty **then**
    node $\leftarrow$ Leaf($S[0]$)
  else
    $i \leftarrow \arg\max_i(\mathbf{d})$
    lchild $\leftarrow$ TREE($S_{\leq i}, \mathbf{d}_{<i}$)
    rchild $\leftarrow$ TREE($S_{>i}, \mathbf{d}_{>i}$)
    node $\leftarrow$ Node(lchild, rchild)
  end ifreturn *node*
end function

C BERT and RoBERTa Heatmaps

In this section, we present two heatmaps of S-F1 score of each heads in BERT and RoBERTa. Row represents layer and column represents head.

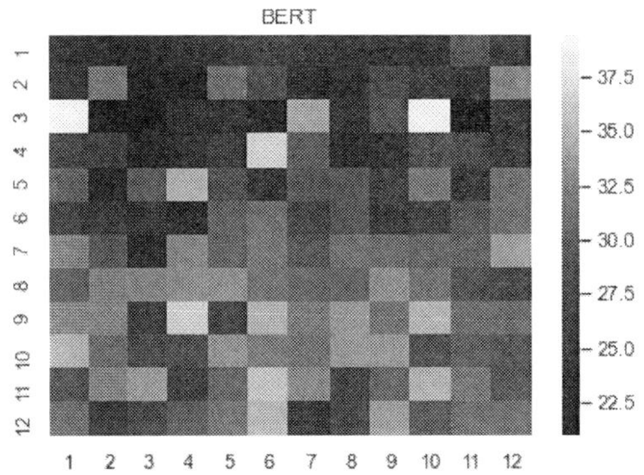

Figure 6: S-F1 score of each heads in BERT.

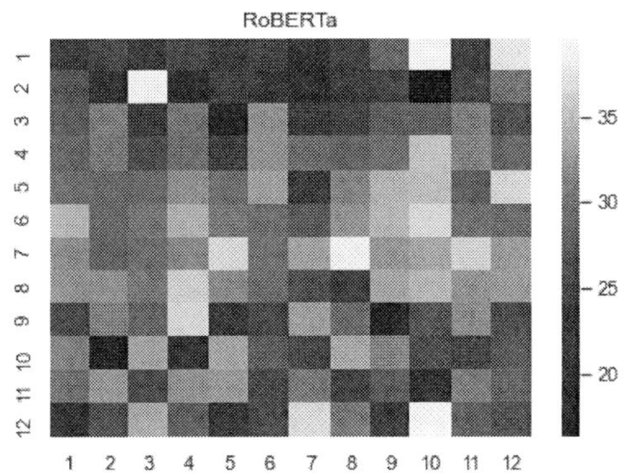

Figure 7: S-F1 score of each heads in RoBERTa.

Do we read what we hear?
Modeling orthographic influences on spoken word recognition

Nicole Macher **Badr M. Abdullah** **Harm Brouwer** **Dietrich Klakow**
Department of Language Science and Technology (LST), Saarland University, Germany
Corresponding author: macher.nicole@gmail.com

Abstract

Theories and models of spoken word recognition aim to explain the process of accessing lexical knowledge given an acoustic realization of a word form. There is consensus that phonological and semantic information is crucial for this process. However, there is accumulating evidence that orthographic information could also have an impact on auditory word recognition. This paper presents two models of spoken word recognition that instantiate different hypotheses regarding the influence of orthography on this process. We show that these models reproduce human-like behavior in different ways and provide testable hypotheses for future research on the source of orthographic effects in spoken word recognition.

1 Introduction

The abstract theory of spoken word recognition (SWR) assumes that the process of speech recognition comprises two phases: a prelexical and a lexical level (Scharenborg and Boves, 2010). The prelexical level contains prelexical representations, like phonological units, which are the result of having processed the raw acoustic signal. These units are assumed to be activated before accessing meaning representations of words in the lexical level. By instantiating the process of SWR in a computational model the underlying theory can then be validated or further refined based on insights into the model's architecture and its behavior.

Influential models of SWR are for example the Cohort model (Marslen-Wilson and Welsh, 1978; Marslen-Wilson and Tyler, 1980; Marslen-Wilson, 1987), the TRACE model (McClelland and Elman, 1986) or the Shortlist model (Norris, 1994). These models typically have a connectionist architecture with localist or feature-based representations as their inputs and outputs (Weber and Scharenborg, 2012), usually mapping phonological onto semantic representations. There is evidence, however, that orthographic information could be co-activated during phonological processing. For example, words with frequent and consistent sound-spelling relations have been proven to be beneficial for auditory word recognition (*orthographic consistency effect*, initially discovered by Ziegler and Ferrand, 1998). *Consistent* words, i.e., words with phonological rhymes that can be spelled in only one way (e.g. /ʌk/ – *uck*, as in *duck*) produce shorter reaction times in a lexical decision task, thus are easier to process, compared to *inconsistent* words whose rhymes can be spelled in multiple ways (e.g. /aɪp/ can be spelled *ipe* like in *pipe* or *ype* like in *type*). This effect is replicated in a variety of studies, using different experimental paradigms and languages (see Petrova et al., 2011, Table 1, for an overview, but also Beyermann and Penke, 2014; Qu and Damian, 2016; Chen et al., 2016, for recent studies). Furthermore, Ziegler et al. (2003) demonstrate that not only the phonological but also the orthographic neighborhood size of a word has an impact on SWR. They report two opposing effects, the *inhibitory phonological effect*, and the *facilitatory orthographic effect*. Depending on a large phonological or orthographic neighborhood of a word, the SWR process is either impeded or facilitated.

There is still a debate on how orthography exactly influences the process of SWR. However, there are two prominent hypotheses about the source of orthographic effects in SWR (Pattamadilok et al., 2014). According to the *online hypothesis*, orthographic representations are co-activated *during* phonological processing, whereas the *offline hypothesis* claims that phonological representations change through the acquisition of reading and writing such that they also incorporate orthographic information.

Proceedings of the 16th Conference of the European Chapter of the Associationfor Computational Linguistics: Student Research Workshop, pages 16–22
April 19 - 23, 2021. ©2021 Association for Computational Linguistics

In what follows, we present two models of SWR using a long short-term memory (LSTM) architecture (Hochreiter and Schmidhuber, 1997) and distributed representations, while focusing on German as a language. Our major outcomes are: (1) We design two models of SWR that instantiate the *offline* and the *online hypothesis* on the source of orthographic effects, respectively. (2) We replicate the *inhibitory phonological* and *facilitatory orthographic effect*, showing that these models are able to reproduce human-like behavior. (3) We provide testable hypotheses for future research based on the models' behavior, which allows us to further validate the *online* or *offline hypothesis*.

2 Methodology

2.1 Model architectures

We propose a recurrent model of SWR that consists of an LSTM that takes a sequence of phonemes as input and produces a meaning representation as output. The procedure of processing, e.g., the German word *Maus* (*mouse*) is illustrated in Figure 1. First, the model takes the respective phonemic sequence of [/m/, /aʊ/, /s/] as input. Then, it should build a vector representation that corresponds to a phoneme sequence, thus the phonological form of the entire word, to then produce a word meaning representation as output. This meaning representation should be as close as possible to the actual ground truth, which is the word embedding of *Maus* (*mouse*).

Phoneme embeddings learn the phonemic distribution well and implicitly capture articulatory distinctive features of phonemes (Silfverberg et al., 2018; Kolachina and Magyar, 2019). Therefore, phoneme vector representations are trained using word2vec (Mikolov et al., 2013) on the phonetic

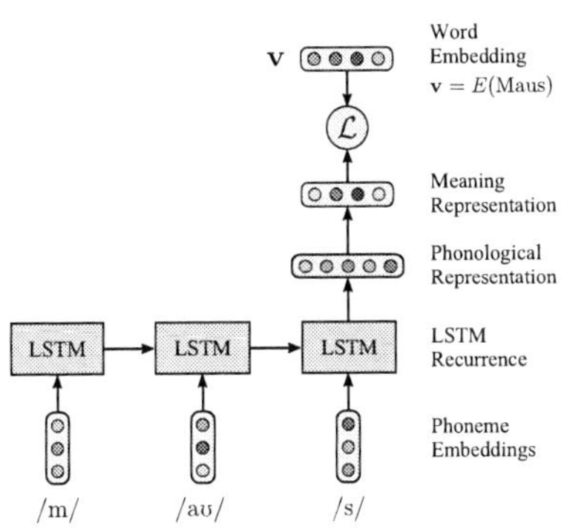

Figure 1: Sketch of a recurrent neural model of SWR.

transcription of the NEGRA corpus (Skut et al., 1997). The transcription is generated with the grapheme-to-phoneme converter tool provided by the Bavarian Archive for Speech Signals (BAS) (Reichel, 2012, 2014). The cbow model and negative sampling is used with window size 1 to obtain 30-dimensional phoneme embeddings.

Word meanings are approximated by word embeddings. We use pre-trained German fastText embeddings (Grave et al., 2018) as the output meaning representations of our models (see also Baayen et al., 2019; Chuang et al., 2020; Hendrix and Sun, 2020, for the similar use of word embeddings as semantic representations in models of word recognition).

The offline model The first architecture implements the theoretical assumption that a prelexical phonemic representation is mapped onto a lexical meaning representation, without incorporating explicit orthographic representations at the prelexical level. The offline model, which instantiates the *offline hypothesis*, processes one phoneme per time step. After the last phoneme of a phonological sequence is processed, a linear transformation is performed on the output of the LSTM layer which consists of 400 units. The resulting fully connected layer has 400 neurons and is then connected to the output layer. A tangent activation function is used on the output layer (300 units).

The online model The second proposed model architecture includes explicit orthographic information at the prelexical level, instantiating the *online hypothesis*. The online model processes two kinds of inputs – a sequence of 30-dimensional phoneme representations and a localist orthographic representation of a word that is based on character bigrams (818 units). The first input layer (30 units) is connected to an LSTM cell (400 units) which is fully connected to an intermediate layer (400 units). This intermediate layer is connected to an intermediate phonological layer (400 units). A tangent non-linearity is then used on it. On the other side of the model, a linear transformation together with a tangent non-linearity is applied on the second input layer to obtain a 100-dimensional layer. The intermediate phonological and orthographic representation are concatenated to a 500-dimensional vector which is then fully connected to a hidden layer of size 300. This hidden layer serves as an intermediate processing stage that processes both types of information, auditory and visual ones, to then give the 300-dimensional meaning representation as output.

2.2 Training

A good model should be able to learn the meaning of spoken words seen during training and generalize to similar but unseen words. We expect the model to learn that very similar sounding words have a very similar meaning (e.g., *duck* and *ducks* share nearly the same semantic concept of a water bird with short legs). By training the model on inflected forms and lemmas, e.g. *Maus (mouse)*, *Mäuse (mice)* and *Häuser (houses)*, one can afterward test whether the model can get to the correct meaning representation of an unseen lemma like *Haus (house)*, even if it never encountered the phonological sequence and word meaning representation during the training phase.

For the training and test data, the most frequent singular and plural nouns in nominative case are extracted from the German Morphology Lexicon (Lezius, 2000), leading to 3118 inflected forms and their lemmas, as well as 583 single inflected forms in the training set, and their corresponding 583 testing lemmas in the test set. In this data set, a lemma is always one of the ten nearest neighbors (measured by cosine similarity) of its inflected form such that the meaning representations of an inflected form and the respective lemma are similar to each other in the embedding space.

The offline model is trained for 100 and the online model for 150 epochs, using the Adam optimizer with its default parameters in PyTorch, as well as the CosineEmbeddingLoss to minimize the cosine distance between the output of a model and the correct word embedding.

2.3 Evaluation

To evaluate the models, the cosine similarity between a model's output and every possible ground truth vector representation is computed. The set of competing word vectors, therefore, consists of 3701 word embeddings during training, and of 4284 (3701 training + 583 testing) vectors during testing. Given these competing word embeddings, Recall@k (R@k) is computed as the proportion of times that the set of top *k* word embeddings which are closest to the model's output also includes the ground truth vector representation. If the ground truth is most similar to the output vector of a model, then this contributes to R@1. Furthermore, a word contributes to R@5 (R@10), if the corresponding ground truth word embedding is within the top 5 (top 10) most similar words to the output vector.

2.4 Simulation data

The model is considered to be successful if it can reproduce human behavioral data that is measured by Ziegler et al. (2003) in an auditory lexical decision task. The stimuli either have a large (+) or a small (-) number of phonological (PN) and orthographic neighbors (ON), which leads to the four categories ON-PN-, ON+PN-, ON-PN+, and ON+PN+. A word is considered to be an orthographic (phonological) neighbor of a target item if it is possible to create it by substituting one letter (one phoneme) in the target word (Coltheart's N, Coltheart et al., 1977). For example, *tape* is an orthographic neighbor of *type*, whereas /paɪp/ (*pipe*) is a phonological neighbor of /taɪp/ (*type*). The authors report two different effects on SWR.

The inhibitory phonological effect A large phonological neighborhood size impedes accessing the correct meaning representation of a word; whenever a stimulus has a large phonological neighborhood size (PN+), the reaction time in a downstream task like lexical decision is larger compared to a word that has a small phonological neighborhood size (PN-). A model should thus also have more difficulties to get to the correct word meaning representation for PN+ vs. PN- words.

The facilitatory orthographic effect Words with a large orthographic neighborhood size (ON+) produce shorter reaction times than words with a small orthographic neighborhood size (ON-). A large orthographic neighborhood size, therefore, facilitates SWR. Therefore, it should be easier for a model to produce the correct meaning representation for an ON+ compared to an ON- word.

2.5 Linking hypothesis

In a lexical decision task, shorter reaction times are associated with fast and effortless processing which is a result of strong word activations (Scharenborg and Boves, 2010). As word activation is assumed to be dependent on the degree of match between processed and stored information in the SWR process (Weber and Scharenborg, 2012), we infer the response time by comparing the model's output (processed information) with the ground truth representation of a word (stored information). A large difference would, therefore, indicate a relatively weak word activation, which suggests a larger response time. On the other hand, a smaller error signals a stronger word activation, which corresponds to a smaller reaction time.

A larger error score for PN+ vs. PN- words, thus, corresponds to the *inhibitory phonological effect* , as a large phonological neighborhood size (PN+) impedes accessing the correct meaning representation of a word. By contrast, a large orthographic neighborhood size (ON+) facilitates the word recognition process. Hence, a lower error score for ON+ vs. ON- words is assumed to be an analog for the *facilitatory orthographic effect*.

3 Experiments

3.1 Word meaning retrieval task

After training, the models are evaluated on the training and the test set to compute the training and testing recall (Table 1). Training recall is nearly perfect for both models, showing that they are able to memorize the data well. However, the online model achieves a higher R@1 of 100% than the offline model in the training data. Overall, both models perform well in the word meaning retrieval task, which concerns activating the correct meaning representation based on a phonological word form.

3.2 Generalization task

On the test set, the offline model reaches an R@10 of 62.95%, an R@5 of 56.78%, and an R@1 of 21.61%, whereas the online model again performs comparatively better with a testing recall of 70.67% for R@10, 59.35% for R@5, and 22.98% for R@1. This is very good, given that the models have never encountered the exact phonological sequence, nor the word embedding of a testing item during training. The generalization performance of the models is an indicator that they globally learn how word forms and their semantics relate to each other. As for future work, one can compare these results with the performance of the models on unseen words which are semantically unrelated to those in the training set. Considering both training and testing recall values, the online model performs comparatively better in learning the meaning of spoken words. However, it still needs to be verified to what extent each of the models is able to reproduce human-like behavior.

Model	Split	R@10	R@5	R@1
Offline	Train	100	100	99.32
	Test	62.95	56.78	21.61
Online	Train	100	100	100
	Test	70.67	59.35	22.98

Table 1: Training and testing recall in percent.

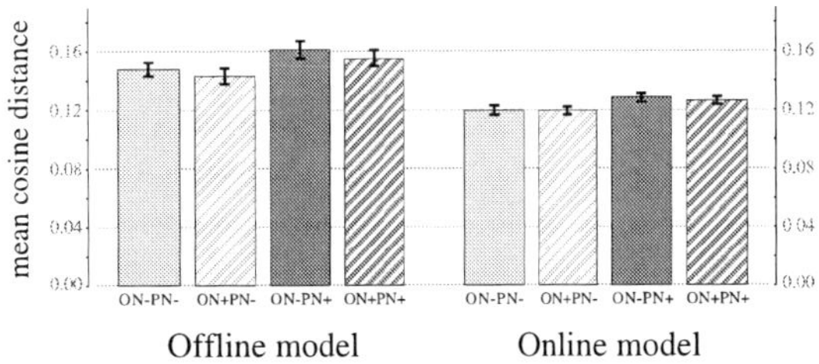

Figure 2: Mean cosine distance between the outputs and ground truths of the items of the four neighborhood categories. Error bars show standard errors.

3.3 Simulation task

To simulate the study by Ziegler et al. (2003), their experimental design is mimicked by dividing the German training data into the four neighborhood categories ON-PN-, ON+PN-, ON-PN+, and ON+PN+. Analogous to their categorisation, a word is considered to be part of the ON- category, when it has zero or one orthographic neighbor, otherwise it belongs to ON+. If a word has less than 3 phonological neighbors, it belongs to the PN- category, otherwise, it is considered to be part of the PN+ condition. For each of these four groups, we sample 70 items with similar mean word length, frequency, and density of the embedding space. The frequency of a word is estimated using the module *wordfreq* (Speer et al., 2018), whereas the density of the semantic space is approximated by subtracting the cosine distance between the ground truth word embedding and the mean vector of its ten nearest neighbors from 1.

Figure 2 shows a bar plot for each model that presents the mean cosine distance between the model's output of each word and the corresponding ground truth per condition after the models have been trained. For both models, the mean cosine distance is higher in the conditions with a large phonological neighborhood size (ON-PN+ and ON+PN+, pink bars in Figure 2) compared to the conditions with a low phonological neighborhood size (ON-PN- and ON+PN-, turquoise bars in Figure 2). This corresponds to a relatively lower word activation for PN+ items, indicating higher reaction times.

Thus, both models can reproduce the *inhibitory phonological effect.* A large orthographic neighborhood size (ON+PN- and ON+PN+, striped bars in Figure 2) has a beneficial impact on the models' performance. The mean cosine distance within the ON+PN- condition is lower compared to the ON-PN- group and it is also lower for the ON+PN+ compared to the ON-PN+ condition. This corresponds to the *facilitatory orthographic effect* and can also be observed for both model architectures. It is larger in the offline model which is surprising, because as opposed to the online model, it has no access to orthographic information. As the offline model instantiates the *offline hypothesis* which claims the phonological representation themselves contain implicit orthographic information, it is investigated whether also the phonological sequences of the training items reveal information about orthography which could have a beneficial effect on a model's performance.

Analysis of orthographic information A *friend* of a target word is a word that has the same rhyme and the same rhyme spelling, whereas *enemies* are words that have the same rhyme, but a different rhyme spelling (Ziegler et al., 2004). Therefore, words that have friends but zero enemies naturally fall into the category of consistent words (see Section 1), whereas words that have at least one enemy can be considered as being inconsistent. Based on the phonological sequence of a consistent word, one can infer its orthographic form, as its rhyme is always spelled in only one way. Therefore, consistent words provide implicit orthographic information in their phonological forms. An analysis of the friends and enemies in the training data reveals that the majority of items in the two groups with a large orthographic neighborhood, ON+PN- and ON+PN+, are consistent words. Furthermore, the mean error score for all consistent (253) and inconsistent words (62) in the training data (see Figure 3), shows that it is easier for the offline model to produce a good lexical meaning representation whenever a word is consistent, compared to inconsistent words that do not reveal reliable orthographic information. By contrast, the online model is not influenced by consistency. Therefore, the underlying reason for the *facilitatory orthographic effect* in the offline model is likely to be the phonology-orthography-consistency, rather than the size of the orthographic neighborhood.

To assess whether consistency is an explanatory

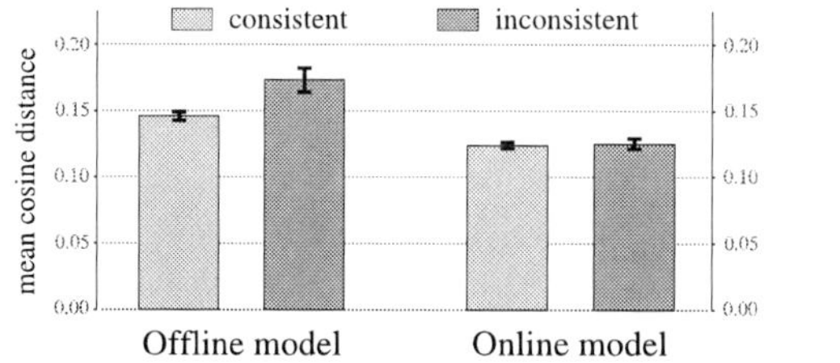

Figure 3: Mean cosine distance between the outputs and ground truths of consistent and inconsistent words. Error bars show standard errors.

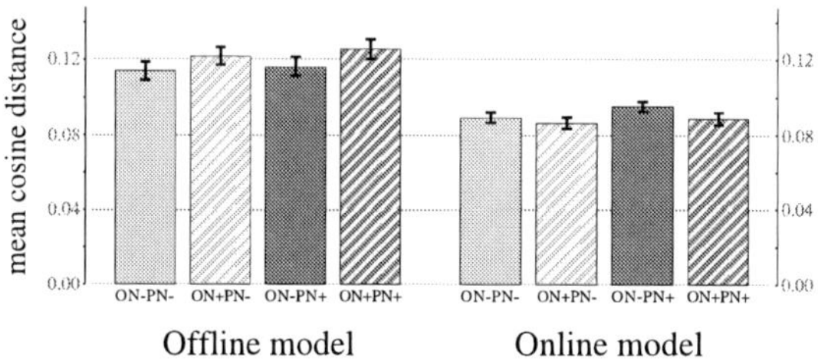

Figure 4: Mean cosine distance between the outputs and ground truths of Finnish items. Error bars show standard errors.

factor for the *facilitatory orthographic effect*, we eliminate the difference between consistent and inconsistent words by training the models on Finnish data. Finnish has a grapheme to phoneme mapping that is nearly one to one which leads to little to no inconsistent words (Joshi and Aaron, 2016).

Excluding the factor of consistency For the Finnish training data, the 2378 most frequent words are extracted from the vocabulary of the Finnish fastText embeddings (Grave et al., 2018). For the input of the models, Finnish phoneme embeddings are trained on the transcription of Finnish news texts (Newscrawl 2017, Goldhahn et al., 2012). Finnish fastText embeddings are used as meaning representations, as well as 540-dimensional localist orthographic representations within the online model. Four balanced samples of size 70 that correspond to the four neighborhood groups are drawn from the training data to then monitor the mean error score of each model per condition (see Figure 4).

The results after training the offline model on Finnish data show an inverse pattern compared to the German results. The offline model would, therefore, predict that no *facilitatory orthographic effect* can be observed in a lexical decision task with Finnish participants as every phonological sequence is nearly equally informative w.r.t. orthographic information. If this prediction proves true, this would further validate the *offline hypothesis* on the source of orthographic effects. For the online model, the general order of error scores is similar across languages. As it is not affected by consistency, the online model can also reproduce the *facilitatory orthographic effect* in Finnish. If this effect can be observed in a lexical decision task with Finnish participants, this would further validate the online model as a plausible model SWR, as well as the *online hypothesis*.

4 Conclusion

In this work, we propose two models of SWR that instantiate either the *online* or the *offline hypothesis* on the source of orthographic effects. We show that both models perform well in word meaning retrieval and in simulating the *inhibitory phonological* and *facilitatory orthographic effect*. The online model achieves the best training and testing performance, and shows the same pattern of results independent of the language of the data. It is not influenced by consistency, which indicates that the size of the orthographic neighborhood is at the origin of the *facilitatory orthographic effect* under the *online hypothesis*. This contrasts with the offline model that produces an orthographic consistency effect. When words don't differ in their consistency, the *facilitatory orthographic effect* is not present, which suggests that consistency is the underlying mechanism for this effect under the *offline hypothesis*. The models predict mutually exclusive outcomes in a lexical decision task in a language like Finnish that has a high phonology-orthography consistency. By testing these predictions, further evidence for either the *offline* or the *online hypothesis* can be provided.

Acknowledgments

This research is funded by the Deutsche Forschungsgemeinschaft (DFG, German Research Foundation), Project ID 232722074, SFB 1102. We would like to thank the anonymous reviewers for their comments and suggestions. We would also like to thank the EACL SRW for the presubmission mentorship program.

References

Rolf Harald Baayen, Yu-Ying Chuang, Elnaz Shafaei-Bajestan, and James P. Blevins. 2019. The discriminative lexicon: A unified computational model for the lexicon and lexical processing in comprehension and production grounded not in (de) composition but in linear discriminative learning. *Complexity*, 2019.

Sandra Beyermann and Martina Penke. 2014. The Impact of Orthographic Consistency on German Spoken Word Identification. *International Journal of Disability, Development and Education*, 61(3):212–224.

Wei-Fan Chen, Pei-Chun Chao, Ya-Ning Chang, Chun-Hsien Hsu, and Chia-Ying Lee. 2016. Effects of orthographic consistency and homophone density on Chinese spoken word recognition. *Brain and Language*, 157-158:51–62.

Yu-Ying Chuang, Marie Lenka Vollmer, Elnaz Shafaei-Bajestan, Susanne Gahl, Peter Hendrix, and Rolf Harald Baayen. 2020. The processing of pseudoword form and meaning in production and comprehension: A computational modeling approach using linear discriminative learning. *Behavior research methods*, pages 1–32.

Max Coltheart, Eileen Davelaar, Jon Torfi Jonasson, and Derek Besner. 1977. Access to the internal lexicon. In *Attention and performance IV*, pages 535–555. Hillsdale, NJ: Erlbaum.

Dirk Goldhahn, Thomas Eckart, and Uwe Quasthoff. 2012. Building large monolingual dictionaries at the leipzig corpora collection: From 100 to 200 languages. In *Proceedings of the Eighth International Conference on Language Resources and Evaluation (LREC-2012)*, pages 759–765, Istanbul, Turkey. European Languages Resources Association (ELRA).

Edouard Grave, Piotr Bojanowski, Prakhar Gupta, Armand Joulin, and Tomas Mikolov. 2018. Learning word vectors for 157 languages. In *Proceedings of the Eleventh International Conference on Language Resources and Evaluation (LREC-2018)*, Miyazaki, Japan. European Languages Resources Association (ELRA).

Peter Hendrix and Ching Chu Sun. 2020. A word or two about nonwords: Frequency, semantic neighborhood density, and orthography-to-semantics consistency effects for nonwords in the lexical decision task. *Journal of Experimental Psychology: Learning, Memory, and Cognition*.

Sepp Hochreiter and Jürgen Schmidhuber. 1997. Long short-term memory. *Neural Comput.*, 9(8):1735–1780.

R. Malatesha Joshi and P. G. Aaron. 2016. *Handbook of Orthography and Literacy*. Routledge.

Sudheer Kolachina and Lilla Magyar. 2019. What do phone embeddings learn about Phonology? In *Proceedings of the 16th Workshop on Computational Research in Phonetics, Phonology, and Morphology*, pages 160–169, Florence, Italy. Association for Computational Linguistics.

Wolfgang Lezius. 2000. Morphy-german morphology, part-of-speech tagging and applications. In *Proceedings of the 9th EURALEX International Congress*, pages 619–623. University of Stuttgart.

William Marslen-Wilson. 1987. Functional parallelism in spoken word-recognition. *Cognition*, 25:71–102.

William Marslen-Wilson and Lorraine Komisarjevsky Tyler. 1980. The temporal structure of spoken language understanding. *Cognition*, 8(1):1 – 71.

William Marslen-Wilson and Alan Welsh. 1978. Processing interactions and lexical access during word recognition in continuous speech. *Cognitive Psychology*, 10:29–63.

James L McClelland and Jeffrey L Elman. 1986. The TRACE model of speech perception. *Cognitive Psychology*, 18(1):1 – 86.

Tomas Mikolov, Kai Chen, G. S. Corrado, and J. Dean. 2013. Efficient estimation of word representations in vector space. In *ICLR 2013*.

Dennis Norris. 1994. Shortlist: a connectionist model of continuous speech recognition. *Cognition*, 52(3):189 – 234.

Chotiga Pattamadilok, José Morais, Cécile Colin, and Regine Kolinsky. 2014. Unattentive speech processing is influenced by orthographic knowledge: Evidence from mismatch negativity. *Brain and Language*, 137:103–111.

Ana Petrova, Gareth Gaskell, and Ludovic Ferrand. 2011. Orthographic Consistency and Word-Frequency Effects in Auditory Word Recognition: New Evidence from Lexical Decision and Rime Detection. *Frontiers in psychology*, 2:263.

Qingqing Qu and Markus Damian. 2016. Orthographic effects in spoken word recognition: Evidence from Chinese. *Psychonomic Bulletin & Review*, 24.

Uwe D. Reichel. 2012. PermA and Balloon: Tools for string alignment and text processing. In *Proc. Interspeech*, page 4 pages, Portland, Oregon.

Uwe D. Reichel. 2014. Language-independent grapheme-phoneme conversion and word stress assignment as a web service. In R. Hoffmann, editor, *Elektronische Sprachverarbeitung 2014*, volume 71, pages 42–49. TUDpress, Dresden, Germany.

Odette Scharenborg and Lou Boves. 2010. Computational modelling of spoken-word recognition processes: Design choices and evaluation. *Pragmatics and Cognition*, 18:136–164.

Miikka P. Silfverberg, Lingshuang Mao, and Mans Hulden. 2018. Sound Analogies with Phoneme Embeddings. In *Proceedings of the Society for Computation in Linguistics (SCiL) 2018*, pages 136–144.

Wojciech Skut, Brigitte Krenn, Thorsten Brants, and Hans Uszkoreit. 1997. An Annotation Scheme for Free Word Order Languages. In *Fifth Conference on Applied Natural Language Processing*, pages 88–95, Washington, DC, USA. Association for Computational Linguistics.

Robyn Speer, Joshua Chin, Andrew Lin, Sara Jewett, and Lance Nathan. 2018. Luminosoinsight/wordfreq: v2.2.

Andrea Weber and Odette Scharenborg. 2012. Models of spoken-word recognition. *Wiley Interdisciplinary Reviews: Cognitive Science*, 3.

Johannes Ziegler and Ludovic Ferrand. 1998. Orthography shapes the perception of speech: The consistency effect in auditory word recognition. *Psychonomic Bulletin & Review*, 5:683–689.

Johannes Ziegler, Ludovic Ferrand, and Marie Montant. 2004. Visual phonology: The effects of orthographic consistency on different auditory word recognition tasks. *Memory & cognition*, 32:732–41.

Johannes Ziegler, Muneaux Mathilde, and Jonathan Grainger. 2003. Neighborhood effects in auditory word recognition: Phonological competition and orthographic facilitation. *Journal of Memory and Language*, 48:779–793.

PENELOPIE: Enabling Open Information Extraction for the Greek Language through Machine Translation

Dimitris Papadopoulos[♣♦], **Nikolaos Papadakis**[♦] and **Nikolaos Matsatsinis**[♣]
[♣]Technical University of Crete, Greece
[♦]Hellenic Army Academy, Greece
{dpapadopoulos6, nmatsatsinis}@isc.tuc.gr
npapadakis@sse.gr

Abstract

In this work, we present a methodology that aims at bridging the gap between high and low-resource languages in the context of Open Information Extraction, showcasing it on the Greek language. The goals of this paper are twofold: First, we build Neural Machine Translation (NMT) models for English-to-Greek and Greek-to-English based on the Transformer architecture. Second, we leverage these NMT models to produce English translations of Greek text as input for our NLP pipeline, to which we apply a series of pre-processing and triple extraction tasks. Finally, we back-translate the extracted triples to Greek. We conduct an evaluation of both our NMT and OIE methods on benchmark datasets and demonstrate that our approach outperforms the current state-of-the-art for the Greek natural language.

1 Introduction

Open Information Extraction (OIE) techniques generally shine in high-resource languages (e.g. English, German) for which either linguistic principles leading to triple extraction have been identified or large annotated corpora and pre-trained language models can be used. For low-resource languages like Modern Greek however, there is a relative sparsity of raw textual resources and annotated corpora that could lead to the development of similar systems. On the bright side, the need for multilingual resources (e.g. movie subtitles, applications, web content) has fueled several projects of compiling parallel corpora (i.e. collections of texts translated into one or more other languages than the original) over the last years. In this work, we propose a methodology that aims at enabling OIE for low-resource languages, focusing on the Greek OIE use case. To achieve this, we rely on Neural Machine Translation (NMT) as an intermediate step to translate the texts to English, in order to exploit the plethora of methods that exist for transforming English text to its structured representation.

We present PENELOPIE (Parallel EN-EL Open Information Extraction), a pipeline for information extraction from Greek corpora. An overview of our methodology is given in Figure 1. The code and related resources can be found in https://github.com/lighteternal/PENELOPIE.

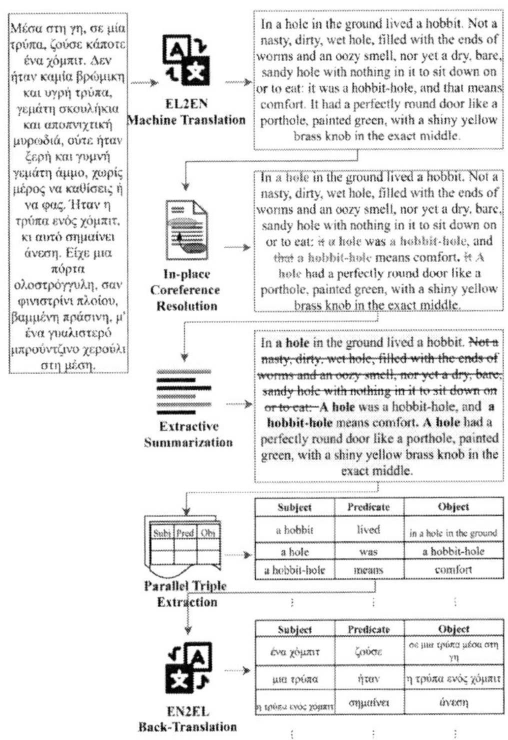

Figure 1: Steps of the PENELOPIE pipeline

Our study has the following objectives:

Proceedings of the 16th Conference of the European Chapter of the Associationfor Computational Linguistics: Student Research Workshop, pages 23–29
April 19 - 23, 2021. ©2021 Association for Computational Linguistics

1. to release a series of Transformer-based NMT models for English-to-Greek (EN2EL) and Greek-to-English (EL2EN) translation, trained on a consolidated parallel corpus and compare the translation results to the current-state-of-the-art,
2. to leverage the aforementioned NMT models for the translation of Greek texts to their English counterpart and feed them to our English-based NLP pipeline. This pipeline incorporates a series of pre-processing tasks including in-place coreference resolution and extractive summarization, as well as an OIE system comprising of three extractors based on different approaches for more robust results. The extracted triples are finally back-translated to Greek and their quality is evaluated to facilitate comparison with other methods.

2 Background

In this section, we provide background information on neural machine translation and open information extraction approaches.

2.1 Neural Machine Translation

NMT aims at modelling a direct mapping between source and target languages with deep neural networks. It has become the dominant paradigm of machine translation, achieving promising results in recent years which are usually surpassing those of traditional Statistical Machine Translation (SMT) approaches, given enough training data (Stahlberg, 2020). The invention of novel encoder-decoder architectures, from recurrent (Sutskever et al., 2014; Bahdanau et al., 2015) and convolutional neural networks (Kalchbrenner et al., 2014; Gehring et al., 2017) to self-attention (Transformer) mechanisms (Vaswani et al., 2017; So et al., 2019) has significantly pushed ahead the state-of-the-art, in terms of quality and efficiency, especially for morphologically rich languages.

Another parallel line of research towards improving translation quality is to devise effective token encoding methods that can handle out-of-vocabulary (OOV) words, targeting the lack of 1-to-1 correspondence between source and target languages, due to differences in their morphological structure. Sennrich et al. (2016) utilized variants of byte-pair encoding (BPE) methods for word segmentation to enable the representation of rare and unseen words as a sequence of subword units, showing that NMT methods are capable of open-vocabulary translation. The latest advances in the field also include pretraining cross language models on multilingual data (Conneau and Lample, 2019) or exploiting monolingual corpora for semi-supervised learning through back-translation (Sennrich et al., 2016a). It appears that not much effort has been targeted towards the Greek language with the notable exception of the Helsinki NLP group which has released EN2EL and EL2EN translation models evaluated on the Tatoeba dataset (Tiedemann and Thottingal, 2020).

2.2 Information Extraction

Open information extraction (OIE) systems aim at distilling structured representations of information from natural language text, usually in the form of {subject, predicate, object} triples or n-ary propositions. Since OIE follows a relation-independent extraction paradigm, it can play a key role in many NLP applications including natural understanding and knowledge base construction, by extracting phrases that indicate semantic relationships between entities. In order to extract triples, most approaches try to identify linguistic extraction patterns, either hand-crafted or automatically learned from the data. An abundance of such systems exists, relying on concepts ranging from rule-based paradigms that focus on the grammatical and syntactic properties of the language (Fader et al., 2011; Del Corro and Gemulla, 2013), to supervised learning-based ones that leverage annotated data sources to train classifiers, with more recent implementations making use of language models (Kolluru et al., 2020; Ro et al., 2020). Despite the existence of so many approaches however, the majority of them just focuses on evaluating the efficiency of different triple extraction tools on raw data, without incorporating any preprocessing strategies to limit the number of potentially uninformative triples (Niklaus et al., 2018). Some more recent methods go beyond the triple extraction task by encompassing more thorough preprocessing and postprocessing strategies, including discourse analysis, coreference resolution or summarization to improve the quality of the extracted triples (Kertkeidkachorn and Ichise, 2017; Papadopoulos et al., 2020). There is currently no OIE system for the Greek language, although latest approaches that leverage pretrained language models allow for multilingual extractions through zero-shot learning (Ro et al., 2020).

3 Methodology

The NMT architecture used in this paper for English-to-Greek (EN2EL) translation and Greek-to-English (EL2EN) back-translation is a variant of the Transformer model (Vaswani et al., 2017), driven by the fact that self-attentional networks tend to perform distinctly better than other architectures on translation tasks (Tang et al., 2020). Both the encoder and the decoder are composed of stacked, multi-head, self-attention and fully-connected layers. One key difference between the two implementations is that ours includes a fully connected feed-forward network with an inner-layer dimensionality of $d_{ff} = 1024$, as opposed to the original one that uses a hidden layer with $d_{ff} = 2048$, in an effort to reduce computational cost, as our training testbed had limited memory capabilities. With regard to vocabulary construction, we relied on subword units extracted with BPE, experimenting with two different configurations of merge operations

Our approach for efficient open information extraction on translated texts combines a series of distinct modules for in-place coreference resolution, extractive summarization and parallel triple extraction with the following specifications:

Coreference Resolution: We rely on a variant of the pretrained end-to-end coreference resolution model from Lee et al. (2017) using Span-BERT embeddings (Joshi et al., 2020), trained on the OntoNotes 5.0 dataset. Each translated sequence is pre-processed by the in-place coreference resolution component, where all noun phrases (mentions) referring to the same entity are substituted with that entity.

Summarization: Extractive text summarization is used on the coreference-resolved text to reduce the original documents' length by omitting peripheral information while highlighting key features that are appropriate for triple extraction. We use the transformer-based implementation from Miller (2019) where all sentences are embedded into the multi-dimensional space using BERT embeddings. K-means clustering is then used on the sentence representations to identify those closest to the cluster's centroids for summary selection.

Parallel Triple Extraction: Here we combine three popular OIE systems, relying both on rule-based (handcrafted extraction heuristics and clauses) and learning-based (semantic role labelling and sequence BIO tagging) systems, relying on the complementarity between the different approaches to ensure maximum recall.

We provide additional information regarding the technical implementation of the described information extraction pipeline in the following section.

4 Experimental Setup

4.1 NMT Setup

Dataset: We exploited most of the EN-EL resources available in the OPUS repository (Tiedemann, 2012), with main ones being the ParaCrawl, OpenSubtitles, EUBookshop, DGT and Europarl datasets. We combined these with the available parallel corpora of CCMatrix (Schwenk et al., 2019) mined in the textual content of Wikipedia, to create a dataset comprising 50451352 sentences (~6.3GB).

Preprocessing: We applied a cleaning script on the corpus that discarded any segment with a word exceeding 1000 characters, leading to a corpus of 36251157 sentences. We tokenized these using the Moses[1] tokenizer and split the dataset so that 1 every 23 sentences were assigned to the validation set and the rest to the training set. For the construction of the model dictionaries, we worked towards the creation of two different preprocessing setups leading in two training configurations:

a. For the first setup, we lower-cased all tokens in the train and test set, in an effort to reduce the dictionary size without losing translation quality. We then applied BPE segmentation[2] with an encoding size of 10000 to speed up training and inference. This resulted in dictionaries of 12892 and 9932 tokens for Greek and English accordingly.
b. For the second setup, we applied BPE segmentation directly to the mixed-case text with an encoding size of 20000,

[1] https://github.com/moses-smt/mosesdecoder

[2] https://github.com/rsennrich/subword-nmt

resulting in dictionaries of size 23220 and 15284 for Greek and English respectively.

NMT Model Settings and Training: We utilized Fairseq (Ott et al., 2019), a popular sequence-to-sequence toolkit maintained by Facebook AI Research to train our models with data from both setups and ran our experiments on a machine with a single NVIDIA GeForce RTX-2080 SUPER (8GB of VRAM). We implemented a shallower variant of the Transformer architecture with 4 attention heads, 6 encoder and 6 decoder layers, both with an embedding size of 512 and a feed-forward hidden layer dimension of 1024. During training, regularization was done with a dropout of 0.3 and label smoothing of 0.1. We used the Adam optimizer (Kingma and Ba, 2015) with 4000 warm-up steps and a maximum learning rate of 0.0005. The model was trained for 5 epochs and the best checkpoint was selected based on the perplexity of the validation set. We used mixed precision during training (Narang et al., 2018), using FP16 precision to address our hardware limitations by reducing the memory consumption and time spent in memory. The produced models (4 in total) are as follows: i. a lower-case EL2EN and a lower-case EN2EL model from the first setup based on shorter dictionaries, ii. a mixed-case EL2EN and EN2EL model from the second setup on larger dictionaries.

4.2 Information Extraction Setup

Coreference Resolution Framework: Each EL2EN translated sequence was processed by the pretrained neural model from AllenNLP which relies on Lee et al. (2017) but has the original GloVe embeddings substituted with Span-BERT embeddings. This approach considers all possible spans in a document as potential mentions and learns distributions over possible antecedents for each span. Its ability to solve challenging pronoun disambiguation problems facilitated the creation of more informative triples.

Summarization Framework: In order to reduce the size of the ingested text, we relied on the pretrained extractive summarizer from Miller (2019) made available by HuggingFace, that utilizes the BERT model for text embeddings and k-means clustering to identify sentences close to the centroid for summary selection.

Triple Extraction Engines: We integrated 3 OIE engines based on different extraction strategies: a. Open IE 5.1 from UW and IIT Delhi which is based on the combination of four different rule-based and learning-based OIE tools, b. ClausIE from MPI that follows a clause-based approach, and c. AllenNLP OIE that formulates the triple extraction problem as a sequence BIO tagging problem and applies a bi-LSTM transducer to produce OIE tuples. We further employed a deduplication process to keep only the unique triples and eliminate all redundant extractions. Since the goal of our work was to provide triples in the Greek language and the produced triples were in English, we used our EN2EL NMT model to translate them back to Greek.

5 Results and Discussion

We provide results both for the EL-EN NMT tasks and for the OIE task on Greek corpora, since the former can be evaluated independently.

5.1 NMT performance

Table 1 shows the evaluation of our models (lower-case and mixed-case) on the Tatoeba[3] and XNLI[4] test sets.

Evaluation on Tatoeba test set (EN-EL)		
Model	**BLEU**	**chrF**
Helsinki-2019-12-04-*EN2EL*	52.7	0.721
Helsinki-2019-12-18-*EN2EL*	56.4	**0.745**
OURS-lower-case-*EN2EL*	**77.3**	0.739
OURS-mixed-case-*EN2EL*	76.9	0.733
Helsinki-2019-12-04-*EL2EN*	69.4	0.801
OURS-lower-case-*EL2EN*	**79.9**	**0.802**
OURS-mixed-case-*EL2EN*	79.3	0.795
Evaluation on XNLI test set (EN-EL)		
Model	**BLEU**	**chrF**
OURS-lower-case-*EN2EL*	66.1	0.606
OURS-mixed-case-*EN2EL*	65.4	0.624
OURS-lower-case-*EL2EN*	67.4	0.633
OURS-mixed-case-*EL2EN*	66.2	0.623

Table 1: EN2EL and EL2EN NMT evaluation results & comparison with other models.

For both EN-EL and EL-EN directions we compare with the current state-of-the-art models produced by the Helsinki NLP group, evaluated on

[3] https://tatoeba.org/

[4] https://github.com/facebookresearch/XNLI

the Tatoeba dataset (Tiedemann and Thottingal, 2020). Another relevant implementation from the Facebook AI team provides results of their XLM-R model on the XNLI dataset (Ruder et al., 2019); however -given the different scope of that paper- results are presented in terms of cross-lingual classification accuracy and not in terms of NMT translation quality (e.g. BLEU), hindering direct comparisons. Nevertheless, we also provide BLEU and chrF scores on the parallel EN-EL corpus of the XNLI dataset hoping that it will facilitate comparisons with future models.

The results on the Tatoeba test set showcase a significant performance gain of our models in terms of BLEU (+10.9 BLEU for EN2EL and +10.5 BLEU for EL2EN translations) over the Helsinki ones, while all models have very close chrF scores. The apparent difference in performance gains between the two different metrics can ascribed to the idiosyncratic morphological and syntactic properties of the Greek language (accent, inflation, declension etc.) that may result in the produced translations being slightly different from the original sequences. Since chrF incorporates character matches while BLEU does not, it is possible to produce translations that achieve low BLEU but acceptable chrF scores. Therefore, given that BLEU is an n-gram-based metric and chrF is a character-based one, we consider the good results on both metrics as a positive characteristic towards producing quality estimates that are as close as possible to human judgements. The results also seem promising on the more challenging XNLI test set, although a direct comparison with other models would have been more useful. While the lower-case models seem to perform slightly better on every test, the richer vocabulary and correct casing of the mixed-case ones compensates for the slightly worse metrics scores. It should be noted that in order to ensure a fair comparison, the mixed-cased models were evaluated on the original reference translations, while the lower-case models were evaluated on a lower-case version of the same translations. Another aspect that adds to the reason why lower-case NMT models were able to showcase slightly better scores is that the former reduce the expansion of the vocabulary by neglecting some morphology information, while mixed-case models will increase the vocabulary to keep the original morphological form and as a result may lose connections with the lowercase forms of some words. Finally, while our models were trained using the Fairseq framework, we also ported them to HuggingFace Transformers format and made them publicly available[5].

5.2 OIE performance

We evaluate the performance of PENELOPIE using the CaRB benchmark which is widely used for the comparison of OIE systems (Bhardwaj et al., 2020). Given the lack of a gold standard of Greek annotated triples, we created a translated version of the original CaRB test set for our experiments, consisting of 2715 sentences and their extracted semantic triples. The test set was automatically translated using our EN2EL mixed case model. We compare our extraction results with Multi2OIE from Ro et al. (2020), an OIE engine with state-of-the-art performance on English corpora. Multi2OIE relies on the pretrained multilingual BERT model and can perform multilingual extractions through zero-shot learning (it is trained on English data); thus it can be leveraged to produce results on the Greek CaRB test set. For PENELOPIE, results are only provided using the mixed-case NMT model (similar results to the lower-case one). It should be noted that the summarization module was not utilized during the benchmark, as the gold dataset consisted of single sentences. This is a general shortcoming in the assessment of OIE systems that leverage preprocessing features (such as summarization or coreference resolution); the gold triples and the metrics involved in the evaluation process favour exact matches of the processed sentences, rather than focusing on the usability of the extracted results. As a result, some of the gold triples in benchmark datasets -although valid- may have low contextual value. The scores are presented in terms of precision, recall and F1-score in Table 2:

Model	Prec.	Rec.	F1
Multi2OIE	0.200	0.084	0.118
PENELOPIE	**0.231**	**0.284**	**0.255**

Table 2: PENELOPIE evaluation results on the translated CaRB testset & comparison with Multi2OIE.

[5] https://huggingface.co/lighteternal

Our pipeline outperforms the state-of-the-art Multi2OIE on the Greek OIE task, on all metrics. The most remarkable difference in performance is shown in terms of recall, which can be partially attributed to the fact that PENELOPIE leverages a number of different extraction tools leading to a recall-oriented approach. In addition, given that all triples are individually back-translated to Greek, it is not guaranteed that the translation output of each element will match the span of the derived sentence, especially in languages with rich morphology (e.g. conjugation, declension). This justifies the relatively low scores of PENELOPIE compared to English OIE systems, whose F1-scores may exceed 0.50 for state-of-the-art approaches (although a direct comparison between different languages is not straightforward). To this end, a source-target word alignment approach inspired by the work of Garg et al. (2020) was explored, but current implementations seem to have difficulties in aligning tokens with accents[6] (e.g. Greek ones).

6 Conclusions and Future Work

We have presented the use of NMT models integrated in an OIE pipeline to achieve triple extraction for low-resource languages, showcasing our approach on the Greek language. To this end, we trained 4 models (2 EN2EL and 2 EL2EN) that outperform the state-of-the-art by a significant margin (>10 BLEU) and made them publicly available. We leveraged these along with a set of preprocessing and triple extraction tools to construct the PENELOPIE pipeline aiming at information extraction from Greek texts. We demonstrated the efficiency of our methodology via a benchmark framework and obtained significantly better results (+116% in F1-score) compared to the best multilingual OIE system currently available.

For future work, we will focus more on word-level alignment to improve the quality of our extractions. We would also like to explore transfer learning approaches to create an end-to-end OIE system for Greek without relying on annotated datasets.

Acknowledgments

The research work of D.P. was supported by the Hellenic Foundation for Research and Innovation (HFRI) under the HFRI PhD Fellowship grant (Fellowship Number: 50, 2nd call).

[6] https://github.com/lilt/alignment-scripts

References

Dzmitry Bahdanau, Kyung Hyun Cho, and Yoshua Bengio. 2015. Neural machine translation by jointly learning to align and translate. In *3rd International Conference on Learning Representations, ICLR 2015 - Conference Track Proceedings*.

Sangnie Bhardwaj, Samarth Aggarwal, and Mausam. 2020. CARB: A crowdsourced benchmark for open IE. In *EMNLP-IJCNLP 2019 - 2019 Conference on Empirical Methods in Natural Language Processing and 9th International Joint Conference on Natural Language Processing, Proceedings of the Conference*.

Alexis Conneau and Guillaume Lample. 2019. Cross-lingual language model pretraining. In *Advances in Neural Information Processing Systems*.

Luciano Del Corro and Rainer Gemulla. 2013. ClausIE: Clause-based open information extraction. In *WWW 2013 - Proceedings of the 22nd International Conference on World Wide Web*.

Anthony Fader, Stephen Soderland, and Oren Etzioni. 2011. Identifying relations for Open Information Extraction. In *EMNLP 2011 - Conference on Empirical Methods in Natural Language Processing, Proceedings of the Conference*.

Sarthak Garg, Stephan Peitz, Udhyakumar Nallasamy, and Matthias Paulik. 2020. Jointly learning to align and translate with transformer models. In *EMNLP-IJCNLP 2019 - 2019 Conference on Empirical Methods in Natural Language Processing and 9th International Joint Conference on Natural Language Processing, Proceedings of the Conference*.

Jonas Gehring, Michael Auli, David Grangier, Denis Yarats, and Yann N. Dauphin. 2017. Convolutional sequence to sequence learning. In *34th International Conference on Machine Learning, ICML 2017*.

Mandar Joshi, Danqi Chen, Yinhan Liu, Daniel S Weld, Luke Zettlemoyer, and Omer Levy. 2020. SpanBERT: Improving Pre-training by Representing and Predicting Spans. *Transactions of the Association for Computational Linguistics*, 8:64–77, March.

Nal Kalchbrenner, Edward Grefenstette, and Phil Blunsom. 2014. A convolutional neural network for modelling sentences. In *52nd Annual Meeting of the Association for Computational Linguistics, ACL 2014 - Proceedings of the Conference*.

Natthawut Kertkeidkachorn and Ryutaro Ichise. 2017. T2KG: An End-to-End System for Creating Knowledge Graph from Unstructured Text. In *AAAI Workshops*.

Diederik P. Kingma and Jimmy Lei Ba. 2015. Adam: A method for stochastic optimization. In *3rd International Conference on Learning Representations, ICLR 2015 - Conference Track Proceedings*.

Keshav Kolluru, Samarth Aggarwal, Vipul Rathore, Mausam, and Soumen Chakrabarti. 2020. IMoJIE: Iterative Memory-Based Joint Open Information Extraction. In *58th Annual Meeting of the Association for Computational Linguistics, ACL 2020 - Proceedings of the Conference*

Kenton Lee, Luheng He, Mike Lewis, and Luke Zettlemoyer. 2017. End-to-end neural coreference resolution. In *EMNLP 2017 - Conference on Empirical Methods in Natural Language Processing, Proceedings*.

Derek Miller. 2019. Leveraging BERT for Extractive Text Summarization on Lectures.

Sharan Narang, Gregory Diamos, Erich Elsen, Paulius Micikevicius, Jonah Alben, David Garcia, Boris Ginsburg, Michael Houston, Oleksii Kuchaiev, Ganesh Venkatesh, and Hao Wu. 2018. Mixed precision training. In *6th International Conference on Learning Representations, ICLR 2018 - Conference Track Proceedings*.

Christina Niklaus, Matthias Cetto, André Freitas, and Siegfried Handschuh. 2018. A Survey on Open Information Extraction. In *Proceedings of the 27th International Conference on Computational Linguistics*, pages 3866–3878, Santa Fe, New Mexico, USA, August. Association for Computational Linguistics.

Myle Ott, Sergey Edunov, Alexei Baevski, Angela Fan, Sam Gross, Nathan Ng, David Grangier, and Michael Auli. 2019. Fairseq: A fast, extensible toolkit for sequence modeling. In *NAACL HLT 2019 - 2019 Conference of the North American Chapter of the Association for Computational Linguistics: Human Language Technologies - Proceedings of the Demonstrations Session*.

Dimitris Papadopoulos, Nikolaos Papadakis, and Antonis Litke. 2020. A methodology for open information extraction and representation from large scientific corpora: The CORD-19 data exploration use case. *Applied Sciences (Switzerland)*.

Youngbin Ro, Yukyung Lee, and Pilsung Kang. 2020. Multi2OIE: Multilingual Open Information Extraction based on Multi-Head Attention with BERT. In *Proceedings of the 2020 Conference on Empirical Methods in Natural Language Processing: Findings*, pages 1107–1117, Online. Association for Computational Linguistics.

Sebastian Ruder, Anders Søgaard, and Ivan Vulic. 2019. Unsupervised cross-lingual representation learning. In *ACL 2019 - 57th Annual Meeting of the Association for Computational Linguistics, Tutorial Abstracts*.

Holger Schwenk, Guillaume Wenzek, Sergey Edunov, Edouard Grave, and Armand Joulin. 2019. CCMatrix: Mining billions of high-quality parallel sentences on the WEB.

Rico Sennrich, Barry Haddow, and Alexandra Birch. 2016a. Improving neural machine translation models with monolingual data. In *54th Annual Meeting of the Association for Computational Linguistics, ACL 2016 - Long Papers*.

Rico Sennrich, Barry Haddow, and Alexandra Birch. 2016b. Neural machine translation of rare words with subword units. In *54th Annual Meeting of the Association for Computational Linguistics, ACL 2016 - Long Papers*.

David R. So, Chen Liang, and Quoc V. Le. 2019. The evolved transformer. In *36th International Conference on Machine Learning, ICML 2019*.

Felix Stahlberg. 2020. Neural Machine Translation: A Review. *Journal of Artificial Intelligence Research*.

Ilya Sutskever, Oriol Vinyals, and Quoc V. Le. 2014. Sequence to sequence learning with neural networks. In *Advances in Neural Information Processing Systems*.

Gongbo Tang, Mathias Müller, Annette Rios, and Rico Sennrich. 2020. Why self-attention? A targeted evaluation of neural machine translation architectures. In *Proceedings of the 2018 Conference on Empirical Methods in Natural Language Processing, EMNLP 2018*.

Jörg Tiedemann. 2012. Parallel data, tools and interfaces in OPUS. In *Proceedings of the 8th International Conference on Language Resources and Evaluation, LREC 2012*.

Jörg Tiedemann and Santhosh Thottingal. 2020. OPUS-MT — Building open translation services for the World. In *Proceedings of the 22nd Annual Conferenec of the European Association for Machine Translation (EAMT)*, Lisbon, Portugal.

Ashish Vaswani, Noam Shazeer, Niki Parmar, Jakob Uszkoreit, Llion Jones, Aidan N. Gomez, Łukasz Kaiser, and Illia Polosukhin. 2017. Attention is all you need. In *Advances in Neural Information Processing Systems*.

A Computational Analysis of Vagueness in Revisions of Instructional Texts

Alok Debnath
Kohli Center for Intelligent Systems
International Institute of Information Technology, Hyderabad
alok.debnath@research.iiit.ac.in

Michael Roth
Institute for Natural Language Processing
University of Stuttgart
michael.roth@ims.uni-stuttgart.de

Abstract

WikiHow is an open-domain repository of instructional articles for a variety of tasks, which can be revised by users. In this paper, we extract pairwise versions of an instruction before and after a revision was made. Starting from a noisy dataset of revision histories, we specifically extract and analyze edits that involve cases of vagueness in instructions. We further investigate the ability of a neural model to distinguish between two versions of an instruction in our data by adopting a pairwise ranking task from previous work and showing improvements over existing baselines.

1 Introduction

Instructional texts aim to describe the actions necessary to accomplish a task or goal, in as clear and concise a manner as possible. *WikiHow*[1] is an extensive compendium of instructional guides for various topics and domains. Any user may edit the articles, and *WikiHow* collates these revision histories. The edit history of such informal instructional articles is a source of user-generated data that can help identify possible reasons and necessities for editing. *wikiHowToImprove* (Anthonio et al., 2020) is a dataset that compiles revision histories for the analysis of linguistic phenomena that occur in edits of instructional texts, ranging from the correction of typos and grammatical errors to the clarification of ambiguity and vagueness.

In this paper, we focus on cases of lexical vagueness, defined as "lexeme[s] with a single but non-specific meaning" (Tuggy, 1993), which can potentially cause misunderstandings in instructional texts. Specifically, we study vagueness based on the change in the main verb in the original and revised version of an instruction. We say that an instruction was vague if, upon revision, the revised main verb is contextually more specific than the original version. Some examples of vague and clarified instructions are provided in Table 1. As indicated by the examples, the revised verb is usually more specific in that it provides additional information on how or why an action needs to be taken.

Original Sentence	Revised Sentence
Then, **make** the floor and walls of your house.	Then, **design** the floor and walls of your house.
When you **go** to the Hogwarts park...	When you **visit** the Hogwarts park...
Get a flexible single cord.	**Purchase** a flexible single cord.

Table 1: Examples of vague instructions and their more clarified versions from the *wikiHowToImprove* Dataset

The classification of vague and clarified instructions is a first step towards automatic text editing for clarification based on linguistic criteria such as ambiguity and vagueness at a sentence level. Existing tools for text editing focus on text simplification and fact editing (Malmi et al., 2019), while others are designed for grammatical error correction (Xie et al., 2018). Our work acts as the first step towards automated editing based on linguistic criteria by identifying vague instructions and differentiating them from "clarified" ones. Our use of the *wikiHowToImprove* corpus also utilizes a resource of edit pairs, therefore introducing a new dataset for the linguistic study of vagueness as well as exploring the general versatility of such corpora.

Our contributions are to create a dataset of vague and clarified instructions, provide an analysis based on semantic frames, and demonstrate the first results of a neural model's ability to distinguish the two versions. We create and analyze the dataset by extracting relevant instances from *wikiHowToIm-*

[1] https://www.wikihow.com/

Proceedings of the 16th Conference of the European Chapter of the Associationfor Computational Linguistics: Student Research Workshop, pages 30–35
April 19 - 23, 2021. ©2021 Association for Computational Linguistics

prove, using POS tags, dependency features, and edit distance as constraints, as well as FrameNet frames as features (Section 3). We then devise a pairwise ranking task, where we train and evaluate different neural models and analyze their performance based on frame relations and differences in distributional word representations (Section 4).

2 Related Work

Our paper focuses on revisions in wikiHow for a specific linguistic phenomenon, namely vagueness. The motivation to use revision histories as corpora for NLP tasks was introduced by Ferschke et al. (2013). The task of defining and categorizing edit intentions has been explored well for the Wikipedia edits corpus (Yang et al., 2016, 2017). More recently, Anthonio et al. (2020) performed a similar categorization on the revisions in *WikiHow*.

Traditional computational analyses of vague statements have been based on logical representations (DeVault and Stone, 2004; Tang, 2008). In contrast, our focus is on vagueness in terms of lexical changes in revisions, which is more similar to previous analyses that considered the context-dependent resolution of vague expressions such as colour references (Meo et al., 2014). Other computational approaches to vagueness include, the detection of vague sense definitions in ontological resources (Alexopoulos and Pavlopoulos, 2014) and website privacy policies (Lebanoff and Liu, 2018) as well as the verification of historical documents (Vertan, 2019).

Our approach to identifying and classifying vagueness is analyzed using FrameNet frames which provide specialized relations among conceptual categories, in a manner similar to recent advances in neural models that use sentence-level information to perform hyponymy–hypernymy classification. Roller et al. (2018) analyzes lexico-syntactic pattern-based instances of word-specific hypernymy-hyponymy constructions. Snow et al. (2004) explores the extraction of predefined patterns for hypernyms and hyponyms in the same sentence, while Shwartz et al. (2016) incorporates distributional methods for their classification using sentence-level features.

3 Data Creation, Preprocessing, and Analysis

WikiHow articles mostly contain instructions, but also include descriptions, explanations, and other non-instructional sentences that provide additional context. The *wikiHowToImprove* corpus (Anthonio et al., 2020) is an unfiltered corpus of revision histories. Therefore, we first need to extract those revisions where the original and revised versions are both instructional sentences, which can be done based on syntactic properties (§3.1). We then use a FrameNet parser to determine the frames (and their relationships) evoked by the root verb in the original and revised version of an instruction (§3.2).

The final extracted data consists of only those revisions where the root verb has been modified to be more specific to the sentence. This extracted corpus consists of 41,615 sentences.

3.1 Data Extraction and Cleaning

wikiHowToImprove is a noisy source of data with misspellings, non-standard abbreviations, grammatical errors, emoticons, etc. In order to use the data for our task, we first perform some cleaning and preprocessing.

We filter the typos and misspellings in the dataset by comparing all the vocabulary words to words in the English dictionary using the *Enchant* python API[2]. After filtering the typos, we POS tag and dependency parse the data using the *Stanza* library[3] (Qi et al., 2020). We discard all sentence pairs where the sentences are shorter than four or longer than 50 words.

We then create a sub-corpus of instructional sentneces by extracting those edit pairs in which both the original and revised version of a sentence fulfill at least one of the following criteria:

- imperative form—the root verb has no nominal subject (e.g. "Please finish the task");
- instructional indicative form—the nominal subject of the root verb is 'you,' 'it' or 'one' (e.g. "You should finish the task");
- passive form with 'let'—the sentence is in passive voice, and the root verb is 'let' (e.g. "Let the paper be put on the table.").

Finally, we retain only those sentence pairs whose character edit distance is smaller than 10. This filter was added after empirical tests to accommodate changes in the verb form and syntactic frame while ensuring that there are little to no additional edits (often just vandalism or spam).

[2]https://pyenchant.github.io/

[3]https://stanfordnlp.github.io/stanza/

3.2 Verb Frame Analysis

We perform an analysis of verb frame relations from this extracted corpus using the FrameNet hierarchy (Baker et al., 1998). In order to identify evoked frames from the data, we use the INCEpTION Project's neural *FrameNet Tools* parser[4] (Klie et al., 2018; Markard and Klie, 2020). FrameNet Tools identifies the frame-evoking elements, the evoked frames, and the context elements' roles in these frame for a given sentence. In this work, we ignore role assignments and only consider predictions of evoked frames, which we found to be generally reliable in our data.[5]

We extract the frame of the root verb in the original and revised sentences. For each pair, we identify the frame relation, if any, using the NLTK FrameNet API[6](Schneider and Wooters, 2017). We found that most edits could be categorized into one of the following frame relations between the frames evoked by the original and revised verb frames:

1. **Subframe-of**: The original frame refers to a complex scenario that consists of several individual states, one of which is the revised frame. (e.g. TRAVERSING→ARRIVING: "*Go* to the thumbs up log." is revised to "*Visit* the thumbs up log.")

2. **Inherits-from**: The frame of the revised verb elaborates on the frame evoked by the original verb (e.g., DECIDING→CHOOSING: "*Determine* the card you want to buy" is revised to "*Choose* which card you want to buy.")

3. **Uses**: The frame of the revised verb uses or weakly inherits properties of the original verb frame (e.g., PERCEPTION_ACTIVE→SCRUTINY: "*Look* for the best fit for your taste" is revised to "*Search* for the best fit for your taste.").

We also find cases of contextually relevant clarifications for phrasal verbs, such as "*Make* your bed" vs. "*Fix* your bed..." which are not covered in FrameNet. Further, there are cases in which the FrameNet Tools parser did not identify the main verb or could not assign a frame. For instance, the verb *compel* as in "you may feel *compelled* ..." is not in FrameNet. We categorize these instances, which are fewer in number than the other categories, under a single **Other** category and leave further inspection to future work. A distribution of instances over categories is shown in Table 2. Apart from instances from the 'Other' category, we indeed found the main verbs in the revised versions of a sentence to be more specific than in the original versions.

Relation	Total	Train	Test	Val
Usage	15,243	11,084	2,194	1,965
Inheritance	13,166	9,179	2,008	1,793
Subframe	9,481	6,835	1,720	926
Other	3,925	2,833	649	443
Total	41,615	30,044	6,237	5,334

Table 2: Number of sentences in the extracted dataset and distribution of FrameNet relations between original and revised verbs. We also show the distribution of train, test and validation for each frame relation.

4 Pairwise Ranking Experiments

In this section, we investigate if a neural model can distinguish between the original and revised version of the same instruction. We describe a neural architecture that uses a joint representation designed for comparing two versions of a sentence before predicting an output. We compare our results to a standard BiLSTM-Attention model used in previous work (Anthonio et al., 2020).

4.1 System and Training Details

The initial components of our system are two BiLSTM modules, LSTM_{1A} and LSTM_{1B}, that each takes one version of a sentence as input. The individual BiLSTMs are followed by a joint layer LSTM_{AB} and an additional layer of BiLSTM modules, LSTM_{2A} and LSTM_{2B}, that re-encode the sentence based on the joint representations. The final layer is trained to predict for each sentence, whether it is the original or revised version, labeling them 0 or 1, respectively.

In practice, we first encode versions A and B of an instruction using FastText embeddings or BERT. The embedded sentences S_A and S_B are then passed through LSTM_{1A} and LSTM_{1B} one (sub-word) token at a time. The hidden layers $\mathbf{h}_{1A}$

[4]https://github.com/inception-project/framenet-tools

[5]Although automatic frame identification is noisy, the tools used here are implementations of the unimodal model presented in Botschen et al. (2018), which achieves a high accuracy of over 88%.

[6]http://www.nltk.org/howto/framenet.html

and $\mathbf{h}_{1B}$ are then concatenated and passed through LSTM_{AB}, whose output $\mathbf{h}_{AB}$ is then concatenated again with the original hidden states to re-encode each sentence version in LSTM_{2A} and LSTM_{2B}. Lastly a classification layer, trained using a cross-entropy objective, transforms the final representations $\mathbf{h}_{2A}$ and $\mathbf{h}_{2B}$ into a real-valued output score using self-attention, which is normalized by softmax and rounded to $\{0, 1\}$. The equations below give a simplified summary of our implementation.[7]

$$\mathbf{h}_{1A} = \text{LSTM}_{1A}(S_A) \quad (1)$$
$$\mathbf{h}_{1B} = \text{LSTM}_{1B}(S_B) \quad (2)$$
$$\mathbf{h}_{AB} = \text{LSTM}_{AB}(\mathbf{h}_{1A} \cdot \mathbf{h}_{1B}) \quad (3)$$
$$\mathbf{h}_{2A} = \text{LSTM}_{2A}(\mathbf{h}_{AB} \cdot \mathbf{h}_{1A}) \quad (4)$$
$$\mathbf{h}_{2B} = \text{LSTM}_{2B}(\mathbf{h}_{AB} \cdot \mathbf{h}_{1B}) \quad (5)$$
$$l_A = \left[\frac{\exp(\mathbf{w}^\top \mathbf{h}_{2A})}{\exp(\mathbf{w}^\top \mathbf{h}_{2A}) + \exp(\mathbf{w}^\top \mathbf{h}_{2B})} \right] \quad (6)$$
$$l_B = \left[\frac{\exp(\mathbf{w}^\top \mathbf{h}_{2B})}{\exp(\mathbf{w}^\top \mathbf{h}_{2A}) + \exp(\mathbf{w}^\top \mathbf{h}_{2B})} \right] \quad (7)$$

Training Details We experiment with both FastText (Grave et al., 2018) and BERT (Devlin et al., 2019), using representations with a dimensionality of 300 components. The BiLSTMs modules $\text{LSTM}_{1A}, \text{LSTM}_{1B}, \text{LSTM}_{2A}$ and LSTM_{2B} each comprise one hidden layer with 256 components, whereas the joint LSTM_{AB} comprises one layer with 512 components. We train for 5 epochs with a batch size of 32 and a learning rate of 10^{-5}. The model is trained with a dropout of 0.2 for regularization. No dropout is applied to any BiLSTM layers or the self-attention layer.

For training, development, and testing, we split our data according to the existing partition given in *wikiHowToImprove*.[8] The resulting split consists of 30,044 sentence revision pairs in the training set, 6,237 pairs in the test set, and 5,334 pairs in the validation set.

4.2 Results and Discussion

Table 3 shows the results of the pairwise ranking task. We find that our proposed model with BERT embeddings is the most accurate model for this task by a margin of about 7%. We compare our results against the baseline provided by Anthonio et al. (2020), which also makes use of ranking and a BiLSTM architecture. In contrast to our model, their baseline is a simple BiLSTM-Attention classification model using FastText embeddings. It does not use an intermediate joint representation to compare representations of two versions of an instruction. The baseline model has the advantage of being trained on individual sentences, but the increase in model accuracy for training sentence pairs by sharing context highlights the efficacy of the training regime.

Their model provides an accuracy of about 64.08% when trained and evaluated on the filtered corpus. Our model with FastText embeddings achieves an accuracy of 71.16% (+7.08%), which shows the relative importance of the joint representation.

Discussion We find that version pairs that involve a subframe relation are the easiest to distinguish across our model using both FastText and BERT, while pairs involving the usage relation are most often confused. The model using BERT embeddings performs better than the FastText-based

Model Description	Dataset	Accuracy
Anthonio et al. (2020)	Entire	74.50%
Anthonio et al. (2020)	Filtered	64.08%
Our Model + FastText	Filtered	71.16%
Our Model + BERT	Filtered	**78.40%**

Table 3: Results of the pairwise ranking task, on the full wikiHowToImprove dataset (Entire) and our subset of instructional sentences (Filtered).

Frame Relation (#errors / total)	Sentence Pair
Usage (503 / 1,965)	**Make** a comic in Flash **Create** a comic in Flash
Inheritance (352 / 1,793)	**Check** the "made in" label **Inspect** the "made in" label
Subframe (137 / 926)	**Let** your hair dry **Allow** your hair to dry
Other (160 / 443)	Next, **try** to sneak out... Next, **attempt** to sneak out...

Table 4: Some examples of sentences which our BERT-based classifier could not distinguish between the original (top) and revised (bottom) versions. We find that confusable verbs (marked in bold) are mostly synonymous. The error and total counts from the validation set are provided in parenthesis for each relation type.

[7]We will make the code available upon publication.

[8]https://github.com/irshadbhat/wikiHowToImprove

model on revisions that do not involve any frame-to-frame relations according to FrameNet (referred to as 'other' in Table 2).

In Table 4, we provide examples where the model failed using both FastText and BERT. We observe that the models fail to correctly distinguish between sentences when the main verbs are synonymous. The embeddings of the most commonly confused verb pairs, which include ⟨allow, permit⟩, ⟨choose, decide⟩ and ⟨create, make⟩, have a cosine similarity of 0.8 or higher, while the average cosine similarity between the representation of verb pairs is 0.47. This insight shows that embeddings by themselves might be insufficient for this classification task. In future work, we will explore additional features such as indicator features derived from the discourse context (e.g., the position of a sentence) and from the FrameNet resource (e.g., properties of the frames evoked in a sentence).

5 Conclusion

In this paper, we extracted a corpus of clarifications of instructions from the *wikiHowToImprove* corpus. We described a methodology for extracting version pairs of a sentence that are both instructional. We then identified cases in which a revision has clarified a vague instruction by analyzing the relationship between the frames evoked by the 'original' verb and the 'revised' verb.

In our experiments, we adopted a simple pairwise ranking task, in the same vein as performed by Anthonio et al. (2020) on the entire *wikiHowToImprove* dataset. We extended a simple BiLSTM architecture with a joint component and explored different embeddings methods, observing that both modifications lead to improvements over baselines presented in previous work.

We hope that our methodology of extracting linguistically interesting cases of revisions from a noisy dataset can be extended to more phenomena and other corpora in future work. This direction has the potential of paving the way for developing automated revision and editing methods beyond typo, style, and grammar correction.

Acknowledgements

The research presented in this paper was funded by the DFG Emmy Noether program (RO 4848/2-1).

References

Panos Alexopoulos and John Pavlopoulos. 2014. A vague sense classifier for detecting vague definitions in ontologies. In *Proceedings of the 14th Conference of the European Chapter of the Association for Computational Linguistics, volume 2: Short Papers*, pages 33–37.

Talita Anthonio, Irshad Bhat, and Michael Roth. 2020. wikiHowToImprove: A resource and analyses on edits in instructional texts. In *Proceedings of The 12th Language Resources and Evaluation Conference*, pages 5721–5729.

Collin F Baker, Charles J Fillmore, and John B Lowe. 1998. The Berkeley FrameNet project. In *36th Annual Meeting of the Association for Computational Linguistics and 17th International Conference on Computational Linguistics, Volume 1*, pages 86–90.

Teresa Botschen, Iryna Gurevych, Jan-Christoph Klie, Hatem Mousselly-Sergieh, and Stefan Roth. 2018. Multimodal frame identification with multilingual evaluation. In *Proceedings of the 2018 Conference of the North American Chapter of the Association for Computational Linguistics: Human Language Technologies, Volume 1 (Long Papers)*, pages 1481–1491, New Orleans, Louisiana. Association for Computational Linguistics.

David DeVault and Matthew Stone. 2004. Interpreting vague utterances in context. In *COLING 2004: Proceedings of the 20th International Conference on Computational Linguistics*, pages 1247–1253.

Jacob Devlin, Ming-Wei Chang, Kenton Lee, and Kristina Toutanova. 2019. Bert: Pre-training of deep bidirectional transformers for language understanding. In *Proceedings of the 2019 Conference of the North American Chapter of the Association for Computational Linguistics: Human Language Technologies, Volume 1 (Long and Short Papers)*, pages 4171–4186.

Oliver Ferschke, Johannes Daxenberger, and Iryna Gurevych. 2013. A survey of NLP methods and resources for analyzing the collaborative writing process in Wikipedia. In *The People's Web Meets NLP*, pages 121–160. Springer.

Edouard Grave, Piotr Bojanowski, Prakhar Gupta, Armand Joulin, and Tomas Mikolov. 2018. Learning word vectors for 157 languages. In *Proceedings of the International Conference on Language Resources and Evaluation (LREC 2018)*.

Jan-Christoph Klie, Michael Bugert, Beto Boullosa, Richard Eckart de Castilho, and Iryna Gurevych. 2018. The INCEpTION platform: Machine-assisted and knowledge-oriented interactive annotation. In *Proceedings of the 27th International Conference on Computational Linguistics: System Demonstrations*, pages 5–9. Association for Computational Linguistics.

Logan Lebanoff and Fei Liu. 2018. Automatic detection of vague words and sentences in privacy policies. In *Proceedings of the 2018 Conference on Empirical Methods in Natural Language Processing*, pages 3508–3517.

Eric Malmi, Sebastian Krause, Sascha Rothe, Daniil Mirylenka, and Aliaksei Severyn. 2019. Encode, tag, realize: High-precision text editing. In *Proceedings of the 2019 Conference on Empirical Methods in Natural Language Processing and the 9th International Joint Conference on Natural Language Processing (EMNLP-IJCNLP)*, pages 5057–5068.

André Markard and Jan-Christoph Klie. 2020. FrameNet Tools: A python library to work with FrameNet.

Timothy Meo, Brian McMahan, and Matthew Stone. 2014. Generating and resolving vague color references. In *Proceedings of the 18th Workshop on the Semantics and Pragmatics of Dialogue (SemDial)*, pages 107–115.

Peng Qi, Yuhao Zhang, Yuhui Zhang, Jason Bolton, and Christopher D. Manning. 2020. Stanza: A Python natural language processing toolkit for many human languages. In *Proceedings of the 58th Annual Meeting of the Association for Computational Linguistics: System Demonstrations*.

Stephen Roller, Douwe Kiela, and Maximilian Nickel. 2018. Hearst patterns revisited: Automatic hypernym detection from large text corpora. In *Proceedings of the 56th Annual Meeting of the Association for Computational Linguistics (Volume 2: Short Papers)*, pages 358–363.

Nathan Schneider and Chuck Wooters. 2017. The NLTK FrameNet API: Designing for discoverability with a rich linguistic resource. In *Proceedings of the 2017 Conference on Empirical Methods in Natural Language Processing: System Demonstrations*, pages 1–6.

Vered Shwartz, Yoav Goldberg, and Ido Dagan. 2016. Improving hypernymy detection with an integrated path-based and distributional method. In *Proceedings of the 54th Annual Meeting of the Association for Computational Linguistics (Volume 1: Long Papers)*, pages 2389–2398.

Rion Snow, Daniel Jurafsky, and Andrew Ng. 2004. Learning syntactic patterns for automatic hypernym discovery. *Advances in neural information processing systems*, 17:1297–1304.

Yongchuan Tang. 2008. A collective decision model involving vague concepts and linguistic expressions. *IEEE Transactions on Systems, Man, and Cybernetics, Part B (Cybernetics)*, 38(2):421–428.

David Tuggy. 1993. Ambiguity, polysemy, and vagueness. *Cognitive linguistics*, 4(3):273–290.

Cristina Vertan. 2019. Modelling linguistic vagueness and uncertainty in historical texts. In *Proceedings of the Workshop on Language Technology for Digital Historical Archives*, pages 34–38.

Ziang Xie, Guillaume Genthial, Stanley Xie, Andrew Y Ng, and Dan Jurafsky. 2018. Noising and denoising natural language: Diverse backtranslation for grammar correction. In *Proceedings of the 2018 Conference of the North American Chapter of the Association for Computational Linguistics: Human Language Technologies, Volume 1 (Long Papers)*, pages 619–628.

Diyi Yang, Aaron Halfaker, Robert Kraut, and Eduard Hovy. 2016. Edit categories and editor role identification in Wikipedia. In *Proceedings of the Tenth International Conference on Language Resources and Evaluation (LREC'16)*, pages 1295–1299.

Diyi Yang, Aaron Halfaker, Robert Kraut, and Eduard Hovy. 2017. Identifying semantic edit intentions from revisions in Wikipedia. In *Proceedings of the 2017 Conference on Empirical Methods in Natural Language Processing*, pages 2000–2010.

A reproduction of Apple's bi-directional LSTM models for language identification in short strings

Mads Toftrup[*€], **Søren Asger Sørensen**[*€], **Manuel R. Ciosici**[$], and **Ira Assent**[€]
[€] Computer Science Department, Aarhus University
[$] Information Sciences Institute, manuelc@isi.edu

Abstract

Language Identification is the task of identifying a document's language. For applications like automatic spell checker selection, language identification must use very short strings such as text message fragments. In this work, we reproduce a language identification architecture that Apple briefly sketched in a blog post. We confirm the bi-LSTM model's performance and find that it outperforms current open-source language identifiers. We further find that its language identification mistakes are due to confusion between related languages.

1 Introduction

Automatic Language Identification is the task of identifying a document's language, an essential task for document classification and machine translation (Ling et al., 2013). General-purpose, open-source Language Identification tools like *langid.py* (Lui and Baldwin, 2012) and FastText (Grave, 2017) are the *de facto* standards for Language Identification in large documents.

During the last two decades, text messaging and social media have generated large amounts of short plain-text documents. Language identification on partial and complete short texts presents unique challenges (Jauhiainen et al., 2019). Successful Language Identification can support marketing, political, and socioeconomic analyses on large corpora of short texts such as tweets. Such analyses can, for example, study hate speech towards immigrants and women (Basile et al., 2019) or seek to understand support groups for smoking cessation (Prochaska et al., 2012).

On a smartphone, Language Identification on short texts can support several features. Language identification of incoming text messages can help virtual assistants read incoming text messages, which can be an essential tool for minorities such as visually impaired multilingual speakers.

Language identification can also help when typing short texts. Identifying language from the first few characters typed (a very short string) can allow a smartphone to select the correct spelling and grammar checker automatically. Such features motivated a team at Apple to study character-level Language Identification using bi-directional LSTMs (Apple, 2019).

This paper reproduces the architecture presented in an industry blog post (Apple, 2019) on Language Identification on extremely short strings (10 characters or less). The blog post briefly sketches the language identification system used by Apple's smartphones and computers. However, due to the use of internal, proprietary corpora, the architecture's performance cannot be compared with the current *de facto* standards for Language Identification: the open-source tools *langid.py* (Lui and Baldwin, 2012) and *FastText* (Joulin et al., 2017, 2016; Grave, 2017).

Our reproduction confirms the performance described in the original blog post (Apple, 2019). We go beyond mere reproduction and (1) compare the bi-LSTM model with the current *de facto* standards for Language Identification and (2) analyze performance on related languages. We find that the bi-LSTM is more accurate than out-of-the-box FastText and langid.py, even outperforming the re-trained FastText. Our results suggest that the bi-LSTM architecture could be an alternative to FastText and langid.py for Language Identification on short strings.[1]

[*] Equal contribution

[1] Our source code and models are available at `https://github.com/AU-DIS/LSTM_langid`. End-users can download our code as a library from the Python Package Index (PyPI) via `https://pypi.org/project/LanguageIdentifier/`.

Proceedings of the 16th Conference of the European Chapter of the Associationfor Computational Linguistics: Student Research Workshop, pages 36–42
April 19 - 23, 2021. ©2021 Association for Computational Linguistics

2 Related work

The simplest Language Identification methods discriminate using elementary distinguishing traits like unique character combinations, frequent or unique words, diacritics, or common n-grams (Dunning, 1994; Souter et al., 1994; Truică et al., 2015). Increasing model complexity, some Language Identification methods model sequences of words, characters, or bytes. Some methods focus on modeling the frequency of n-grams, e.g., frequency of character n-grams (Ahmed et al., 2004; Souter et al., 1994). Such methods outperform techniques based on unique words. Markov model-based approaches estimate the probability of a string based on n-grams of characters or bytes (Dunning, 1994), as is the case of langid.py (Lui and Baldwin, 2012, 2011). Due to its availability as an open-source library, langid.py is one of the most popular language identifiers.

Recent language identifiers increasingly use word representations. For example, in a blog post, Grave (2017) shows how to identify languages using FastText vectors (Bojanowski et al., 2016; Joulin et al., 2017, 2016), which model character n-grams. Language identification with FastText vectors is as performant as langid.py (Grave, 2017). Similar to langid.py, FastText language identification models are open-source and, therefore, popular.

LanideNN (Kocmi and Bojar, 2017) identifies languages in multilingual documents using a recurrent neural network with a single layer of gated recurrent units (GRU). Unlike Markov-based methods, recurrent neural network architectures do not model character sequences with a fixed window of context. The language identifier that Apple briefly sketched in a blog post (Apple, 2019) uses a recurrent neural network with a two-layer bi-directional LSTM to model character sequences. Apple's method differs from LanideNN in architecture complexity (two layers, LSTM cells instead of the simpler GRU cells) and in its focus. LanideNN works with long multilingual documents, whereas Apple classify extremely short monolingual strings.

In a survey, Jauhiainen et al. (2019) present more than the techniques above, discuss challenges, and identify remaining research questions. Among the remaining research questions are very short texts (the problem motivating Apple) and discrimination of related languages. In this paper, we go beyond reproducing Apple's work by analyzing the effect of related languages.

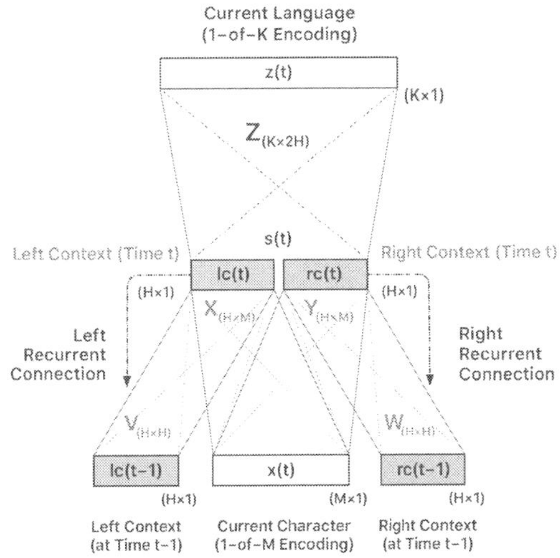

Figure 1: The bi-LSTM architecture. Figure reproduced from Apple (2019).

3 Model architecture

Figure 1 gives an overview of the two-layer bi-directional LSTM architecture powering Apple's products, as briefly sketched in a blog post (Apple, 2019).

The model takes as input strings of characters. In the following, we describe the left-to-right direction of the bi-directional LSTM. The right-to-left direction is identical but mirrored. In the first step, vector embeddings replace all characters in the input string. The network uses a single embedding for all languages since the language is unknown at this point. At each time step, the LSTM ingests a character's embedding and the hidden layer representation from the previous step. The per-character output from the left-to-right LSTM layer is concatenated with that of the right-to-left layer. The concatenated vectors pass to a second LSTM layer that is identical to the first but does not share parameters. After the second layer, the concatenated vectors go through a single linear layer, producing a distribution over all supported languages. The linear layer provides character-level language identification. In other words, for each input character, the network generates a probability distribution over the possible languages.

With the outputs from the linear layer, Apple (2019) state that *A max pooling style majority voting decides the dominant language of the string.* However, max pooling and majority voting are different techniques. A combination of the two is impossible as one cannot perform majority voting over outputs that have been max pooled, and vice versa. Instead, we sum over the linear layer's output values at each time step and *softmax* the summed output to obtain a prediction. We expect this approach to be what the original authors intended. The similarity between our reproduction's performance and what Apple report in the original blog post confirms our approach.

4 Data sets

Apple (2019) only mention the kind of data used in their experiments. Therefore, we use two large and openly available data sets of the same kind as Apple: a subset of OpenSubtitles (Lison and Tiedemann, 2016) to study performance on dialog; and Universal Dependencies (UD, Zeman et al., 2019) for prose. Following Apple, we trim strings to 50 characters per sample, with all samples starting at the beginning of a word, and remove special characters.

Apple test on 20 languages that use the Latin alphabet, but only show results on 9 of the 20 and do not specify the remaining 11 languages. Besides the 9 languages in the original blog post, we select 11 languages, some of which are closely related. Thus, our experimental setup[2] is similar to Apple's. Including closely related languages increases our data sets' difficulty but supports more interesting and more representative experiments. Specifically, it supports performance analysis on related languages, an open research question (Jauhiainen et al., 2019).

5 Experiments and results

We use five-fold cross-validation in all experiments. Following Apple (2019), we evaluate on strings of 10 characters. We test all models on the same strings.

We use the AdamW optimizer with default parameters in PyTorch; we set the character embedding dimension to 150 and the bi-LSTM's hidden dimension to 150; we train for 25 epochs using batches of 64 examples and use weighted cross-entropy for the loss function.

[2]The languages we use are: Catalan (ca), Czech (cs), Danish (da), French (fr), German (de), English (en), Spanish (es), Estonian (et), Finnish (fi), Croatian (hr), Hungarian (hu), Italian (it), Lithuanian (lt), Dutch (nl), Norwegian (no), Portuguese (pt), Polish (pt), Romanian (ro), Swedish (sv), and Turkish (tr).

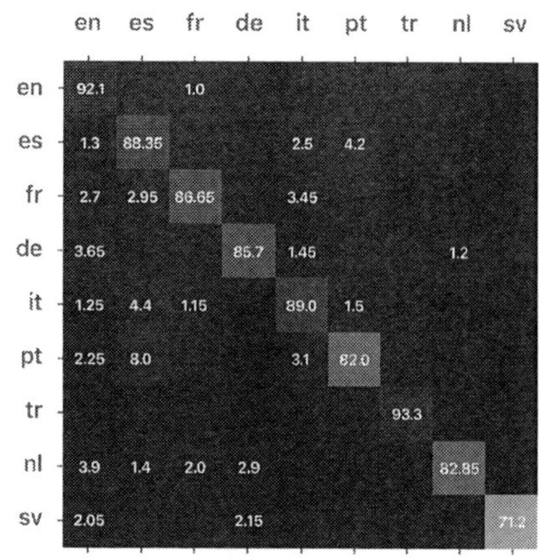

Figure 2: Apple (2019)'s original results.

Out-of-the-box, FastText and langid.py can identify more than our set of 20 languages. For fair evaluation, we limit the set of languages that the models output. For langid.py, we use a built-in method that limits the number of languages under consideration. For FastText, we take the probability distribution over all language predictions, extracting only the relevant 20. We use the large pre-trained FastText model[3]. When re-training FastText, we use 15 epochs, with a minimum n-gram length of one character and a maximum of six characters. We leave all other parameters at their default.

5.1 Comparison with original work

Figure 3 contains the results of our reproduction of the experiment in Figure (b) from Apple (2019), a confusion matrix of the bi-LSTM model trained and evaluated on the UD data set. Since Apple do not include averaged results, we use the confusion matrices for comparison. Figure 2 includes a copy of Figure (b) from Apple (2019) for easier comparison. We find that performance per language is similar between the two implementations. While in one case, accuracy is almost identical (Turkish, tr), for most languages, our implementation is either a few points of accuracy below (e.g., French, fr, −2.85 points, and Italian, it, −2.62) or above the original model (e.g., Dutch, nl, +1.87). For some languages, our implementation considerably underperforms the original (e.g., English, en, −7.4 points, and Spanish, es, −16.7). Our implementation considerably outperforms the original on German (de +6.91) and Swedish (sv +7.54).

[3]Available at `https://fasttext.cc/docs/en/language-identification.html`

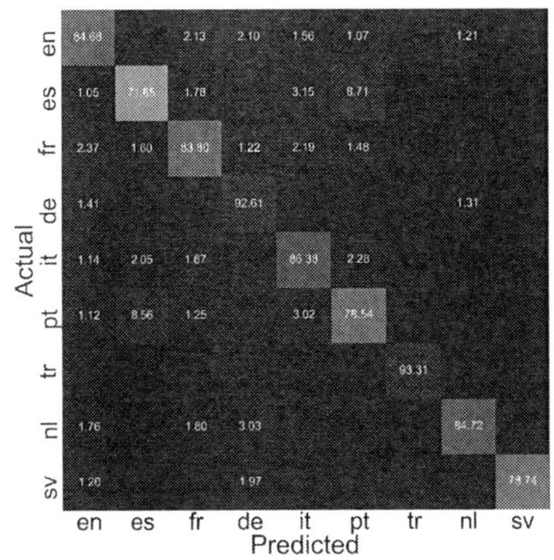

Figure 3: Confusion matrix for bi-LSTM on UD.

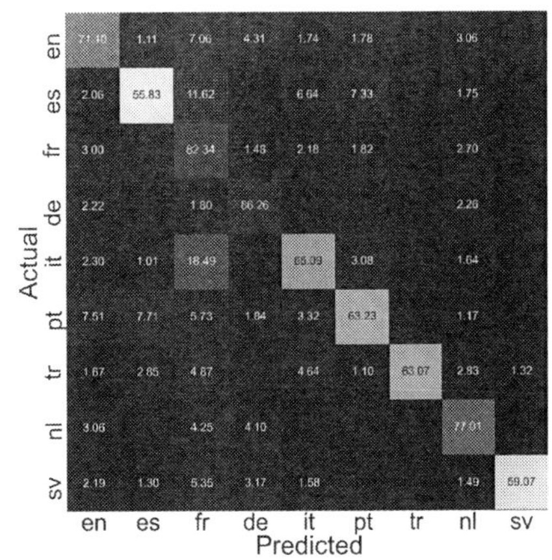

Figure 4: Confusion matrix for re-trained FastText on UD.

We attribute the difference in performance to randomness during training and differences in training data. The original blog post does not state the size nor language composition of the data set.

In Figure 3, we follow Apple and threshold values in the confusion matrix at 1.0. Thus, we can effortlessly compare error patterns. Interestingly, the patterns are almost identical. Both matrices show issues distinguishing between Italian (it) and Portuguese (pt), German (de) and Dutch (nl), French (fr) and English (en), and Italian (it) or Portuguese (pt) vs. Spanish (es) or French (fr). Unsurprisingly, most confusions appear for languages from the same families, Romance (es, fr, it, pt) and Germanic (de, nl).

5.2 Comparative analysis

In Tables 1 and 2, we include the comparative analysis results with the current *de facto* standards for Language Identification: FastText and langid.py. We use two weighing strategies for F1 to provide different insights. Macro-F1 averages the per-language results and considers languages equally important. Weighted-F1 takes into account the popularity of the different languages in the data sets. Weighted-F1 measures the performance on the data set, while macro-F1 illustrates language coverage as it is not affected by label frequency. In multi-class classification, micro-F1 equals accuracy. We, therefore, include only accuracy, denoted *acc@1*.

On both data sets, the bi-LSTM exceeds the weighted- and macro-F1 of langid.py, pre-trained FastText, and re-trained FastText. The performance difference between the bi-LSTM and the next best model (the re-trained FastText) also appears in the confusion matrix. Figure 4 shows that even the re-trained FastText exhibits confusion across all pairs. It also shows a strong bias towards some languages like English (en), French (fr), or Dutch (nl) regardless of the input language. All columns in Figure 4 that correspond to these languages exhibit confusion errors.

The OpenSubtitles data is more challenging than UD for out-of-the-box langid.py and FastText, but easier for bi-LSTM and re-trained FastText. Also, there is a considerable improvement from the pre-trained FastText to the re-trained FastText on both data sets. These observations suggest that (1) domain adaptation has a considerable impact on Fast-

	LSTM	**pFT**	**rFT**	**langid.py**
wF1	**87.41**	72.45	78.67	64.89
maF1	**79.22**	61.20	67.90	51.66
acc @1	**86.93**	70.45	77.92	61.73
acc @3	**96.07**	85.84	90.59	82.83
acc @5	**97.78**	90.92	94.45	88.99

Table 1: Results on UD. pFT = pre-trained FastText; rFT = re-trained FastText

	LSTM	**pFT**	**rFT**	**langid.py**
wF1	**91.38**	67.45	84.14	54.31
maF1	**91.38**	67.45	84.14	54.31
acc @1	**91.37**	67.73	84.13	53.47
acc @3	**98.14**	84.15	95.08	76.30
acc @5	**98.93**	89.31	97.38	84.22

Table 2: Results on OpenSubtitles. pFT = pre-trained FastText; rFT = re-trained FastText

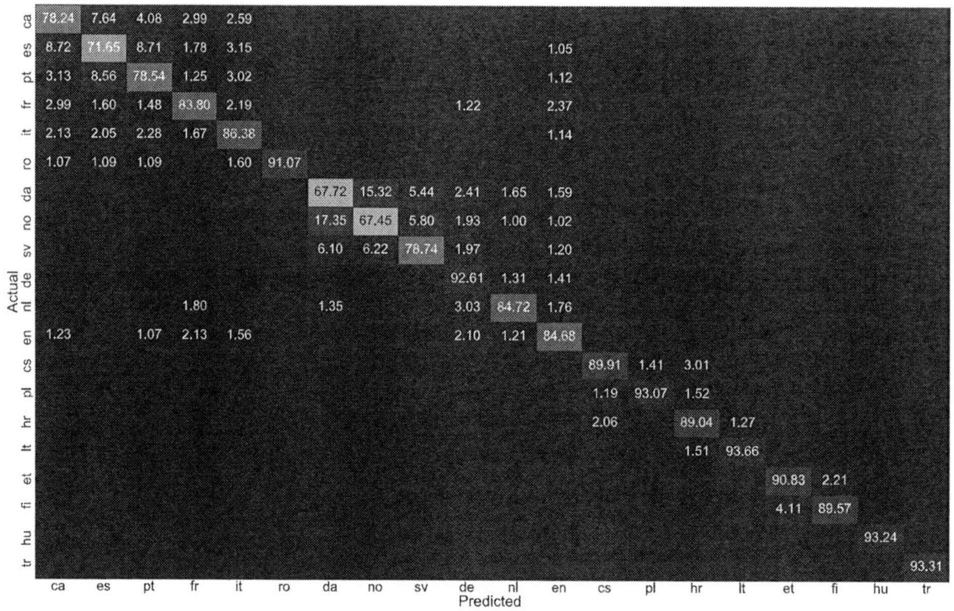

Figure 5: Confusion matrix for bi-LSTM on UD.

Text, and (2) that dialog is more difficult for the out-of-the-box models. OpenSubtitles contains subtitles of movies predominantly produced in English. Consequently, character names are also English-centered, e.g., Jane. Character names can appear in dialog, which might confuse the pre-trained models to assign such dialog lines to English, despite their translation.

5.3 Error analysis

Tables 1 and 2 show a jump from accuracy at the top of the list of prioritized predicted languages (*acc@1*) to accuracy at the top three (*acc@3*). For most models, a smaller jump follows to accuracy at the top five (*acc@5*). The sizeable jump indicates that, even when the models are wrong, the correct answer is usually among the top three. For example, from *acc@1* to *acc@3*, the bi-LSTM jumps 9.14 points on UD and 6.77 on OpenSubtitles, but only 1.71 and 0.79 from *acc@3* to *acc@5*. The gap from *acc@1* to *acc@3* is much larger for langid.py and FastText, illustrating a higher confusion. Recent work in language identification suggests that the accuracy gap might be a symptom of confusion of related languages (Haas and Derczynski, 2020).

To understand the bi-LSTM's jump in accuracy, we turn to the complete confusion matrix. In Figure 5, we show the confusion matrix of the bi-LSTM on all 20 languages in our experiments. There is intense confusion between highly similar languages. We observe three large clusters of confused languages: Romance (ca, es, fr, it, pt, ro), West Germanic (de, en, nl), and languages of Northern Europe (da, no, sv). More closely related languages are more confusing, for example, Catalan (ca) vs. Spanish (es) and Danish vs. Norwegian (no). The clusters of confusion between related languages indicate that, despite the bi-LSTM's improved performance, highly similar languages still pose a challenge.

5.4 Storage requirements

Apple (2019) also consider storage requirements. Our bi-LSTM uses 4 MB of storage, confirming the claims in the original blog post. The re-trained FastText model requires 1.5 GB of storage, but that could reduce to approximately 150 MB, following Joulin et al. (2016). langid.py's model is only 2.5 MB. Given its language identification performance and model size, the bi-LSTM is a great value proposition, especially on storage-constrained mobile devices, confirming Apple's use case scenario.

6 Conclusions

We have reproduced the bi-LSTM language identification architecture described in a blog post by Apple (2019). Our reproduction experiments confirm the performance claims in the original blog post. We evaluated the bi-LSTM against the *de facto* open-source language identifiers in experiments on two openly available data sets. Our evaluation considered dialog and prose, and targeted twenty languages, including some highly similar languages such as Danish (da) and Norwegian (no) or Catalan (ca) and Spanish (es). Our experiments illustrate the difficulty of identifying the language in very short strings. The reproduced bi-LSTM outperformed FastText and langid.py on all measures, even when training FastText on the same data. However, we went beyond a straightforward reproduction and considered related languages. Our analysis shows that the bi-LSTM can easily confuse languages from the same family (e.g., Romance, West Germanic, or Scandinavian) and highly similar languages such as Catalan (ca) and Spanish (es). We publish our implementation's source code and make a trained model available as a library. In the future, we would like to consider avenues for improving the bi-LSTM architecture. For example, we would like to replace the majority voting mechanism in the bi-LSTM with a more robust alternative.

References

Bashir Elhaj Ahmed, Sung-Hyuk Cha, and Charles C. Tappert. 2004. Language identification from text using n-gram based cumulative frequency addition. In *Proceedings of Student/Faculty Research Day, CSIS, Pace University*.

Apple. 2019. Language identification from very short strings. Online: https://machinelearning.apple.com/research/language-identification-from-very-short-strings. Accessed: 2021-02-10.

Valerio Basile, Cristina Bosco, Elisabetta Fersini, Debora Nozza, Viviana Patti, Francisco Manuel Rangel Pardo, Paolo Rosso, and Manuela Sanguinetti. 2019. SemEval-2019 task 5: Multilingual detection of hate speech against immigrants and women in Twitter. In *Proceedings of the 13th International Workshop on Semantic Evaluation*, pages 54–63, Minneapolis, Minnesota, USA. Association for Computational Linguistics.

Piotr Bojanowski, Edouard Grave, Armand Joulin, and Tomas Mikolov. 2016. Enriching Word Vectors with Subword Information. *arXiv preprint arXiv:1607.04606*.

Ted Dunning. 1994. *Statistical identification of language*. Computing Research Laboratory, New Mexico State University Las Cruces, NM, USA.

Edouard Grave. 2017. Language identification. Online: https://fasttext.cc/blog/2017/10/02/blog-post.html. Accessed: 2020-09-24.

René Haas and Leon Derczynski. 2020. Discriminating Between Similar Nordic Languages. *arXiv preprint arXiv:2012.06431*.

Tommi Jauhiainen, Marco Lui, Marcos Zampieri, Timothy Baldwin, and Krister Lindén. 2019. Automatic language identification in texts: A survey. *Journal of Artificial Intelligence Research*, 65:675–782.

Armand Joulin, Edouard Grave, Piotr Bojanowski, Matthijs Douze, Hérve Jégou, and Tomas Mikolov. 2016. Fasttext.zip: Compressing text classification models. *arXiv preprint arXiv:1612.03651*.

Armand Joulin, Edouard Grave, Piotr Bojanowski, and Tomas Mikolov. 2017. Bag of tricks for efficient text classification. In *Proceedings of the 15th Conference of the European Chapter of the Association for Computational Linguistics: Volume 2, Short Papers*, pages 427–431, Valencia, Spain. Association for Computational Linguistics.

Tom Kocmi and Ondřej Bojar. 2017. LanideNN: Multilingual language identification on character window. In *Proceedings of the 15th Conference of the European Chapter of the Association for Computational Linguistics: Volume 1, Long Papers*, pages 927–936, Valencia, Spain. Association for Computational Linguistics.

Wang Ling, Guang Xiang, Chris Dyer, Alan Black, and Isabel Trancoso. 2013. Microblogs as parallel corpora. In *Proceedings of the 51st Annual Meeting of the Association for Computational Linguistics (Volume 1: Long Papers)*, pages 176–186, Sofia, Bulgaria. Association for Computational Linguistics.

Pierre Lison and Jörg Tiedemann. 2016. OpenSubtitles2016: Extracting large parallel corpora from movie and TV subtitles. In *Proceedings of the Tenth International Conference on Language Resources and Evaluation (LREC'16)*, pages 923–929, Portorož, Slovenia. European Language Resources Association (ELRA).

Marco Lui and Timothy Baldwin. 2011. Cross-domain Feature Selection for Language Identification. In *Proceedings of 5th International Joint Conference on Natural Language Processing*, pages 553–561, Chiang Mai, Thailand. Asian Federation of Natural Language Processing.

Marco Lui and Timothy Baldwin. 2012. langid.py: An off-the-shelf language identification tool. In *Proceedings of the ACL 2012 System Demonstrations*, pages 25–30, Jeju Island, Korea. Association for Computational Linguistics.

Judith J Prochaska, Cornelia Pechmann, Romina Kim, and James M Leonhardt. 2012. Twitter=quitter? an analysis of twitter quit smoking social networks. *Tobacco Control*, 21(4):447–449.

Clive Souter, Gavin Churcher, Judith Hayes, John Hughes, and Stephen Johnson. 1994. Natural language identification using corpus-based models. *HERMES-Journal of Language and Communication in Business*, 13:183–203.

Ciprian-Octavian Truică, Julien Velcin, and Alexandru Boicea. 2015. Automatic Language Identification for Romance Languages using Stop Words and Diacritics. In *17th International Symposium on Symbolic and Numeric Algorithms for Scientific Computing (SYNASC)*, pages 243–246.

Daniel Zeman, Joakim Nivre, Mitchell Abrams, and et al. 2019. Universal dependencies 2.5. LINDAT/CLARIAH-CZ digital library at the Institute of Formal and Applied Linguistics (ÚFAL), Faculty of Mathematics and Physics, Charles University.

Automatically Cataloging Scholarly Articles using Library of Congress Subject Headings

Nazmul Kazi[1], Nathaniel Lane[1], Indika Kahanda[2]
[1] Montana State University, MT, USA
[2] University of North Florida, FL, USA
kazinazmul.hasan@montana.edu
nathaniel.lane@student.montana.edu
indika.kahanda@unf.edu

Abstract

Institutes are required to catalog their articles with proper subject headings so that the users can easily retrieve relevant articles from the institutional repositories. However, due to the rate of proliferation of the number of articles in these repositories, it is becoming a challenge to manually catalog the newly added articles at the same pace. To address this challenge, we explore the feasibility of automatically annotating articles with Library of Congress Subject Headings (LCSH). We first use web scraping to extract keywords for a collection of articles from the Repository Analytics and Metrics Portal (RAMP). Then, we map these keywords to LCSH names for developing a gold-standard dataset. As a case study, using the subset of Biology-related LCSH concepts, we develop predictive models by formulating this task as a multi-label classification problem. Our experimental results demonstrate the viability of this approach for predicting LCSH for scholarly articles.

1 Introduction

An Institutional Repository (IR) is the collection of scholarly work hosted and maintained by institutions such as universities. For example, "ScholarWorks[1] is an open access repository for the capture of the intellectual work of Montana State University (MSU) in support of its teaching and research goals". Repository Analytics and Metrics Portal (RAMP) is a web service that accurately counts item downloads for each article in the institutional repository (Obrien et al., 2016; OBrien et al., 2017). Besides counting the number of downloads, RAMP stores metadata of the articles such as title, abstract, and keywords. Currently, nearly 40 institutions have registered their repositories with RAMP.

To facilitate the easy finding of articles, the IR managers need to catalog them using different subject headings manually. One of the most popular vocabularies for cataloging is the Library of Congress Subject Headings (LCSH) (Walsh, 2011). LCSH is a subject indexing language that is actively maintained since 1898 to catalog materials in the Library of Congress and most widely adopted by large and small libraries around the world (Work, 2016). A subject heading is the most specific word or a group of words that capture the essence of a subject category. Due to the rapid growth of items in IRs, manual cataloging using LCSH or other vocabularies is becoming highly resource-consuming (Engelson, 2013).

Due to the above challenge, there have been a few previous attempts on the automatic assignment of LCSH through keyword extraction (Wartena et al., 2010; Aga et al., 2016), by collecting LCSH concepts that are assigned to similar texts (Paynter, 2005), using semantic similarity (Yi, 2010), and co-occurrence-based mapping (Vizine-Goetz et al., 2004). These techniques primarily depend on the presence of the keywords or similar words/ phrases within the actual text and do not utilize machine learning. Furthermore, one of the studies claims that the prediction of LCSH using machine learning may be infeasible due to the large size of the vocabulary leading to inadequate training data (Wartena et al., 2010). Note that machine learning has been used for a seemingly similar but actually different task of predicting Library of Congress Classification (LCC) (Frank and Paynter, 2004). However, despite the similarity in their names, LCC and LCSH are completely different vocabularies.

Semantic indexing with other vocabularies has gained traction recently (Mirowski et al., 2010; Salakhutdinov and Hinton, 2009; Wu et al., 2014). Most notably, predicting Medical Subject Headings (MeSH) for biomedical literature using machine

[1] https://scholarworks.montana.edu/

Proceedings of the 16th Conference of the European Chapter of the Associationfor Computational Linguistics: Student Research Workshop, pages 43–49
April 19 - 23, 2021. ©2021 Association for Computational Linguistics

learning and deep learning techniques has seen significant recent interest (Mao and Lu, 2017; Jin et al., 2018; Kehoe et al., 2017; Rios and Kavuluru, 2015; Kosmopoulos et al., 2015; Yan et al., 2016) thanks to the BioASQ challenge on Biomedical Semantic Indexing (Tsatsaronis et al., 2015).

In this work, we explore the feasibility of developing an automated pipeline for predicting LCSH for scholarly articles using machine learning. As a case study, we leverage an extensive collection of scholarly articles from RAMP and generate a gold-standard dataset by assigning Biology-related LCSH concepts to each article through web scraping and string matching techniques. Using this gold-standard data, we develop predictive models that can predict LCSH by modeling this as a multi-label classification problem. Our experimental results indicate the effectiveness of the proposed approach.

2 Methodology

2.1 Data

In this approach, we build a gold-standard dataset by scraping RAMP data from 27 institutional repositories (IRs). A high-level overview of our approach is shown in Figure 1.

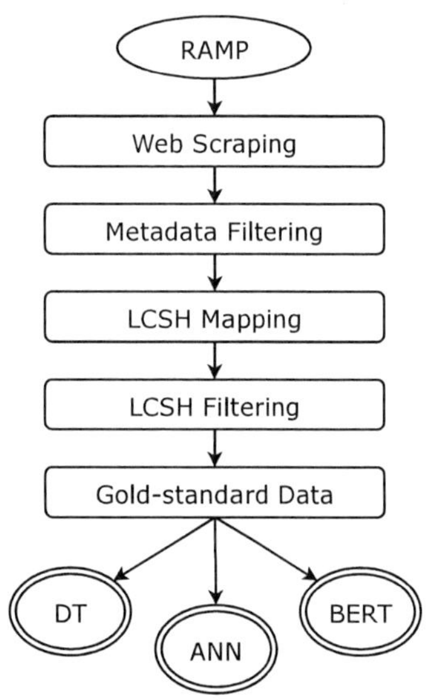

Figure 1: A high-level overview of our approach.

We identify the citable content downloads (CCD) from each institutional repository (IR) between July 2017 and July 2018 . Then, we scrape all metadata of each CCD from RAMP for the subset that includes all unique CCDs.

The raw data (scraped from RAMP) contains 457,879 articles and 270 different metadata types. However, we use only *title* concatenated with *abstract*, *article type*, and *keywords* for this study, and discard other metadata. There are many reasons why some of the metadata are empty. For example, items such as newspapers do not include abstracts, and sometimes IR managers add items into repositories without populating metadata. Therefore, we first discard articles without a title, an abstract, or keywords, which reduces the dataset to 126,655 articles that have a title, an abstract, and at least one keyword. Then, we map each keyword to the subject names from the 41st edition of LCSH[2] using full string matching (case insensitive). If a keyword does not match with any subject, we ignore that keyword.

Any article without at least one assigned subject heading is discarded. This results in a smaller set of articles with annotated subject headings. Then, we filter out any subjects not related to Biology by only retaining the concept *Biology* (sh85014203)[3] and its descendants. Finally, we remove subject headings that are annotated to less than 100 articles. After all the above, we have a dataset composed of 17,367 articles with 66 Biology-related subject headings. This LCSH-annotated dataset is used as the gold-standard dataset for developing predictive models. Note that while the string matching technique used in this study itself can potentially be used for "predicting" LCSH terms, we are assuming that unseen items that need to be annotated with LCSH in real-life may not necessarily come with keywords (and hence we resort to developing predictive machine learning models). The distribution of articles across IRs in this dataset is shown in Table 1.

2.2 Models

We model the task of predicting LCSH concepts as a multi-label classification problem and develop three supervised machine learning models using the above generated gold-standard data. These models are 1) Decision Tree (DT), 2) Artificial Neural Networks (ANN), and 3) Bidirectional Encoder Representations from Transformers (BERT). All the models are implemented using scikit-learn[4], Ten-

[2]https://loc.gov/aba/publications/FreeLCSH/freelcsh.html
[3]http://id.loc.gov/authorities/subjects/sh85014203.html
[4]https://scikit-learn.org/

	IR Name	# Articles
1	Deep Blue	7,820
2	DRUM	1,578
3	EASP	1,171
4	UWSpace	1,063
5	OpenBU	960
6	MacSphere	917
7	Texas ScholarWorks	849
8	Mountain Scholar	631
9	Epsilon Open Archive	576
10	K-REx	464
11	MSU ScholarWorks	405
12	OAKTrust	380
13	MD-SOAR	245
14	SHAREOK	192
15	Others	116
	Total:	17,367

Table 1: Number of articles per institute in the gold-standard dataset.

sorFlow[5], Transformers[6] and PyTorch[7] libraries. In our preliminary work, We also train models using Support Vector Machines and Random Forest classifiers, but none of them perform better than the models reported in this paper (data not shown).

We choose standard but varying pre-processing steps independently for each model since certain pre-processing techniques work well for some models over the others. For example, removing stopwords is a common practice for Decision Tree models but not for BERT since stopwords typically can act as noise for the former.

2.2.1 Decision Tree (DT) model

We apply the Decision Tree classifier to develop a tree-based one-vs-rest classification model. We use TF-IDF (term frequency-inverse document frequency) vectorizer with a word-based analyzer for feature extraction. We use lemmatization and stop word removal as standard pre-processing steps. We include both uni-grams and bi-grams as features and train our model over the top 10,000 features. Our model returns a binary value, i.e., either 0 or 1, as the prediction.

2.2.2 Artificial Neural Network (ANN) model

For the shallow artificial neural network model, we use the TF-IDF scores as input. These are generated using scikit-learn's TfidfVectorizer class. All stop words (common words such as "the" or "and") are removed before vectorization, and only the terms that appear in a minimum of 1% of all documents are kept.

Our artificial neural network has four layers: an input layer with 2,251 nodes, a dropout layer with a rate of 0.1, a hidden layer with 132 nodes, and an output layer with 66 nodes (one for each label) with a sigmoid activation function. We initially experimented with many different network structures but ultimately find that a single hidden layer with 132 nodes, double the number in the output, produces the best results (data not shown). We use 5-fold nested cross-validation to find the optimal epoch for training the networks. We train the largest network with 100 epochs and find 10 epochs as optimal as the learning curve reaches convergence. We use this optimal epoch to train all networks.

2.2.3 Bidirectional Encoder Representations from Transformers (BERT) model

We use the pre-trained BERT-Base (uncased) model (Devlin et al., 2018) and fine-tune it for multi-label text classification. The base model has 12 transformer blocks, i.e., hidden layers, a hidden size of 768, 12 attention heads, and 110 million parameters (Devlin et al., 2018). The model is pre-trained for English on uncased Wikipedia and BooksCorpus. For fine-tuning the model, we use *Adam* optimizer with a learning rate of $2e-5$, $\epsilon = 1e-8$, L2 weight decay of 0.01, learning rate warmup over the first 500 steps with linear decay and Cross-Entropy Loss function. We observe the learning curve over 5-fold nested cross-validation and find 6 epochs as the optimal number. Any example longer than the 512 token length restriction enforced by the BERT-Base model is truncated.

2.3 Experimental Setup and Metrics

In order to obtain unbiased estimations of model performance, we evaluate our models using 5-times 5-fold stratified cross-validation (Sechidis et al., 2011; Szymański and Kajdanowicz, 2017). We primarily report the performances of our models using Maximum F1-score (F_{max}), Precision at F_{max} and Recall at F_{max}. Precision reports the percentage of true samples among the samples that have been predicted as true, whereas Recall reports the percentage of true samples retrieved by the model. F1-score is the harmonic mean of precision and re-

[5]https://www.tensorflow.org/

[6]https://huggingface.co/transformers/

[7]https://pytorch.org/

Subject Frequency	# subjects	DT			ANN			BERT		
		P	R	F1	P	R	F_{max}	P	R	F_{max}
$[100, 200)$	35	0.36	0.35	0.36	0.48	0.40	0.43	0.51	0.43	0.43
$[200, 300)$	15	0.40	0.39	0.39	0.48	0.46	0.47	0.56	0.51	0.49
$[300, 400)$	6	0.31	0.30	0.30	0.42	0.44	0.43	0.55	0.55	0.54
$[400, 900)$	7	0.41	0.41	0.41	0.48	0.57	0.52	0.59	0.70	0.64
$[1700, 2600]$	3	0.40	0.40	0.40	0.46	0.67	0.54	0.57	0.71	0.63
	Macro average:	0.38	0.37	0.37	0.46	0.51	0.48	0.56	0.58	0.55

Table 2: Model performance per subject frequency range. # subjects: Number of unique subjects within the range, P: precision, R: recall.

Article Type	Freq.	Length		Average Number of		F_{max}		
		Avg	Std	Keywords	Subjects	DT	ANN	BERT
Thesis	6,765	379.89	191.32	30.24	1.15	0.31	0.38	0.41
Article	1,077	225.80	99.52	21.25	1.29	0.19	0.23	0.24
Report	880	442.89	280.80	15.80	1.09	0.14	0.18	0.19
Paper	364	207.68	111.74	22.29	1.17	0.10	0.12	0.16
Book	48	221.31	194.41	20.27	1.08	0.02	0.03	0.04
Others	383	164.54	116.59	24.53	1.30	0.12	0.14	0.19
NA	7,850	253.99	147.47	21.52	1.27	0.30	0.38	0.41

Table 3: Model performance per article type. NA: Not Available, Freq: number of articles in type, Length: number of words in title and abstract, P: precision, and R: recall.

Subject	Freq	F_{max}		
		DT	ANN	BERT
Commencement ceremonies	141	0.99	1.00	1.00
Discrimination	227	0.83	0.88	0.88
Irrigation	125	0.72	0.66	0.89
Machine Learning	260	0.68	0.71	0.75
Nanoparticles	174	0.67	0.67	0.78
Self-efficacy	112	0.64	0.69	0.71
Animal ecology	520	0.56	0.67	0.79
Autism	103	0.68	0.51	0.75
Feminism	113	0.63	0.52	0.76
Planning	245	0.50	0.65	0.69

Table 4: Top ten easiest to predict subjects. Freq: Frequency of subject in the dataset.

Subject	Freq	F_{max}		
		DT	ANN	BERT
Social psychology	157	0.05	0.14	0.02
Clinical psychology	196	0.10	0.22	0.00
Metabolism	104	0.14	0.19	0.00
Molecular biology	185	0.07	0.15	0.11
Developmental psychology	174	0.14	0.20	0.00
Cognition	109	0.18	0.20	0.00
Epidemiology	224	0.17	0.20	0.04
Zoology	242	0.13	0.24	0.05
Physiology	190	0.12	0.20	0.11
Neurology	176	0.23	0.25	0.00

Table 5: Top ten hardest to predict subjects. Freq: Frequency of subject in the dataset.

call. Unlike F1, F_{max}, which is computed across a range of thresholds, is threshold independent. More specifically, let threshold $t \in [0, 1]$, then

$$F_{max} = \max_t \left\{ \frac{2 \cdot \text{precision}(t) \cdot \text{recall}(t)}{\text{precision}(t) + \text{recall}(t)} \right\}$$

For this study, we use a step size of 0.05 for thresholds and Macro-averaging (arithmetic mean) for aggregating the performance across classes.Note that since the DT model returns binary predictions directly, without class probabilities, we report the performance of this model only using F1 instead of F_{max}.

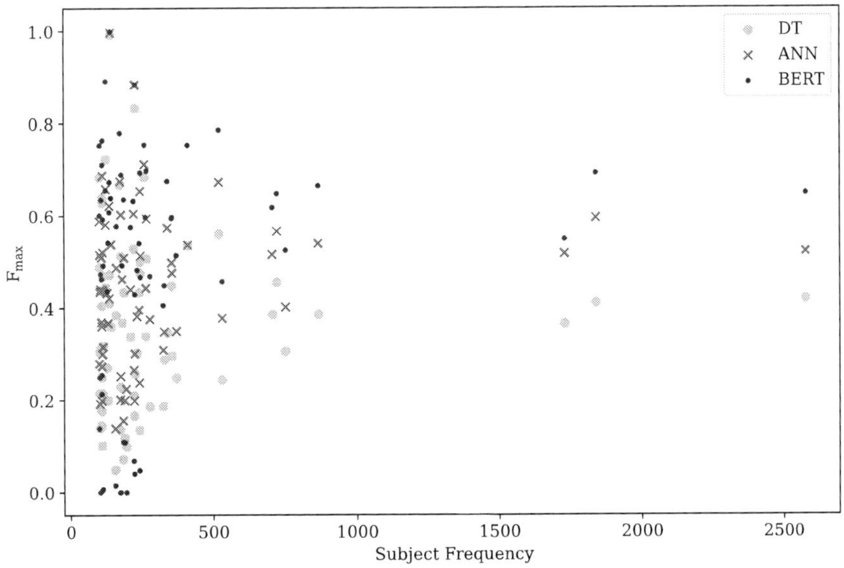

Figure 2: Model performance against subject frequency. DT: Decision Tree, ANN: Artificial Neural Network.

3 Results and Discussion

The overall performance for all our models is depicted in Table 2. Overall, the BERT model performs the best, and the DT model performs the worst among the three models. The DT model achieves an average F1 score of 0.37, whereas the lowest F1 score (0.30) is observed for frequency range $[300, 400)$. The performance of the DT model is seemingly immune to the frequency of subjects. The ANN model notably outperforms the DT model with an average F_{max} of 0.48. The ANN model also struggles for frequency range $[300, 400)$. However, the lowest F_{max} (0.43) of ANN is higher than the best F1 score (0.40) achieved by DT in any frequency range. Except for frequency range $[300, 400)$, we can see an increase in F_{max} of ANN as the frequency range increases. The BERT model significantly outperforms both DT and ANN models with an average F_{max} of 0.55 and shows a positive correlation between F_{max} and frequency range.

Figure 2 shows variation of performance of all three against the frequency. The subjects between range $[100, 200)$ are widely spread across the y-axis (F_{max}) for each model, which indicates that the easiest and the hardest subject to predict have similar subject frequencies. Top ten easiest and hardest subjects across all three models are listed in Table 4 and Table 5, respectively. We use macro-averaged F-score from all three models to compile these rankings. All three models show their best performance for the same subject, *Commencement ceremonies*. Both DT and ANN have a non-zero F-score for each subject. Despite being the best model, BERT shows zero F_{max} for several subjects, e.g., *Clinical psychology*.

We also assess the performance of each model per document type, as reported in Table 3. For the following analysis, we exclude the document type denoted as NA for which the corresponding metadata was missing. Same as before, BERT performs the best, and ANN outperforms DT. All three models show their best and worst performance for the same article types across all models, Thesis and Book, respectively. The frequency of each type may have played a significant role in these extremes. This is further supported by the fact that the performance across all three models follows the same trend: as the frequency decreases, the performance decreases as well.

4 Conclusions and Future Work

In this work, we explore the feasibility of using machine learning for predicting LCSH for scholarly articles. We first generate a gold-standard dataset annotated with LCSH subjects by web scraping/ string matching and utilize this data for developing multi-label classification models. Our results indicate the feasibility of our approach. We believe our approach is applicable to other data similar to LCSH concepts. This automated pipeline should be extremely valuable to librarians for expediting the manual cataloging process. We plan to measure the efficiency gains of this method through the Montana State University Library.

While our approach displays promising results, there are many different avenues for future investigation. First, in this work, we map the web scraped keywords to subject names (instead of identifiers or IDs). However, some subject names may map to more than one identifier (e.g., Psychology: sh85108459 or sh2002011487). So, we plan to explore two different solutions to this. One approach is to develop a chain-classifier that can predict the LCSH IDs using the already predicted subjects (i.e., a second classifier for disambiguation). Another option is the improve the web scraping/ string matching pipeline so that we can generate a gold-standard dataset directly annotated with IDs.

To improve the performance of our traditional machine learning models, we plan to investigate the inclusion of hand-engineered features, other resources such as MeSH terms, metadata fields that were ignored in this study, and the hierarchical information from the LCSH. Besides, using larger more sophisticated language models (e.g., Megatron-LM), using the complete set of LCSH terms (without restricting to Biology-related), and structured output models that explicitly use the hierarchy information will likely improve performance. Moreover, Extreme Multi-Label (XML) models that are equipped to handle very large sets of classes (Kumar et al., 2019) will also likely provide better performance.

5 Acknowledgement

We would like to thank Patrick OBrien and Kenning Arlitsch from Montana State University Library and Jonathan Wheeler from University of New Mexico for providing us with the data and guidance for this project. This work was supported in part by NSF awards CNS-1730158, ACI-1540112, ACI-1541349, OAC-1826967, the University of California Office of the President, and the University of California San Diego's California Institute for Telecommunications and Information Technology/Qualcomm Institute. Thanks to CENIC for the 100Gpbs networks.

References

Rosa Tsegaye Aga, Christian Wartena, and Michael Franke-Maier. 2016. Automatic recognition and disambiguation of library of congress subject headings. In *International Conference on Theory and Practice of Digital Libraries*, pages 442–446. Springer.

Jacob Devlin, Ming-Wei Chang, Kenton Lee, and Kristina Toutanova. 2018. Bert: Pre-training of deep bidirectional transformers for language understanding. *arXiv preprint arXiv:1810.04805*.

Leslie Engelson. 2013. Correlations between title keywords and lcsh terms and their implication for fast-track cataloging. *Cataloging & classification quarterly*, 51(6):697–727.

Eibe Frank and Gordon W Paynter. 2004. Predicting library of congress classifications from library of congress subject headings. *Journal of the American Society for Information Science and Technology*, 55(3):214–227.

Qiao Jin, Bhuwan Dhingra, William Cohen, and Xinghua Lu. 2018. Attentionmesh: Simple, effective and interpretable automatic mesh indexer. In *Proceedings of the 6th BioASQ Workshop A challenge on large-scale biomedical semantic indexing and question answering*, pages 47–56.

Adam K Kehoe, Vetle I Torvik, Matthew B Ross, and Neil R Smalheiser. 2017. Predicting mesh beyond medline. In *Proceedings of the 1st Workshop on Scholarly Web Mining*, pages 49–56.

Aris Kosmopoulos, Ion Androutsopoulos, and Georgios Paliouras. 2015. Biomedical semantic indexing using dense word vectors in bioasq. *J BioMed Semant Suppl BioMedl Inf Retr*, 3410:959136040–1510456246.

P. Kumar, V. K. Dubey, and M. I. H. Showrov. 2019. A comparative analysis on various extreme multi-label classification algorithms. In *2019 4th International Conference on Electrical, Electronics, Communication, Computer Technologies and Optimization Techniques (ICEECCOT)*, pages 265–268.

Yuqing Mao and Zhiyong Lu. 2017. Mesh now: automatic mesh indexing at pubmed scale via learning to rank. *Journal of biomedical semantics*, 8(1):15.

Piotr Mirowski, M Ranzato, and Yann LeCun. 2010. Dynamic auto-encoders for semantic indexing. In *Proceedings of the NIPS 2010 Workshop on Deep Learning*, volume 2.

Patrick OBrien, Kenning Arlitsch, Jeff Mixter, Jonathan Wheeler, and Leila Belle Sterman. 2017. Ramp–the repository analytics and metrics portal. *Library Hi Tech*.

Patrick Obrien, Kenning Arlitsch, Leila Sterman, Jeff Mixter, Jonathan Wheeler, and Susan Borda. 2016. Undercounting file downloads from institutional repositories. *Journal of Library Administration*, 56(7):854–874.

Gordon W Paynter. 2005. Developing practical automatic metadata assignment and evaluation tools for internet resources. In *Proceedings of the 5th ACM/IEEE-CS Joint Conference on Digital Libraries (JCDL'05)*, pages 291–300. IEEE.

Anthony Rios and Ramakanth Kavuluru. 2015. Analyzing the moving parts of a large-scale multi-label text classification pipeline: Experiences in indexing biomedical articles. In *2015 International Conference on Healthcare Informatics*, pages 1–7. IEEE.

Ruslan Salakhutdinov and Geoffrey Hinton. 2009. Semantic hashing. *International Journal of Approximate Reasoning*, 50(7):969–978.

Konstantinos Sechidis, Grigorios Tsoumakas, and Ioannis Vlahavas. 2011. On the stratification of multi-label data. *Machine Learning and Knowledge Discovery in Databases*, pages 145–158.

Piotr Szymański and Tomasz Kajdanowicz. 2017. A network perspective on stratification of multi-label data. In *Proceedings of the First International Workshop on Learning with Imbalanced Domains: Theory and Applications*, volume 74 of *Proceedings of Machine Learning Research*, pages 22–35, ECML-PKDD, Skopje, Macedonia. PMLR.

George Tsatsaronis, Georgios Balikas, Prodromos Malakasiotis, Ioannis Partalas, Matthias Zschunke, Michael R Alvers, Dirk Weissenborn, Anastasia Krithara, Sergios Petridis, Dimitris Polychronopoulos, et al. 2015. An overview of the bioasq large-scale biomedical semantic indexing and question answering competition. *BMC bioinformatics*, 16(1):138.

Diane Vizine-Goetz, Carol Hickey, Andrew Houghton, and Roger Thompson. 2004. Vocabulary mapping for terminology services. *Journal of digital information*, 4(4):2004.

John Walsh. 2011. The use of library of congress subject headings in digital collections. *Library review*.

Christian Wartena, Rogier Brussee, and Wout Slakhorst. 2010. Keyword extraction using word co-occurrence. In *2010 Workshops on Database and Expert Systems Applications*, pages 54–58. IEEE.

Jill A Work. 2016. Legislating librarianship. *The Political Librarian*, 2(2):7.

Hao Wu, Martin Renqiang Min, and Bing Bai. 2014. Deep semantic embedding. In *SMIR@ SIGIR*.

Yan Yan, Xu-Cheng Yin, Bo-Wen Zhang, Chun Yang, and Hong-Wei Hao. 2016. Semantic indexing with deep learning: a case study. *Big Data Analytics*, 1(1):1–13.

Kwan Yi. 2010. A semantic similarity approach to predicting library of congress subject headings for social tags. *Journal of the American Society for Information Science and Technology*, 61(8):1658–1672.

Model Agnostic Answer Reranking System for Adversarial Question Answering

Sagnik Majumder **Chinmoy Samant** **Greg Durrett**
Department of Computer Science
The University of Texas at Austin
{sagnik, chinmoy, gdurrett}@cs.utexas.edu

Abstract

While numerous methods have been proposed as defenses against adversarial examples in question answering (QA), these techniques are often model specific, require retraining of the model, and give only marginal improvements in performance over vanilla models. In this work, we present a simple model-agnostic approach to this problem that can be applied directly to any QA model without any retraining. Our method employs an explicit answer candidate reranking mechanism that scores candidate answers on the basis of their content overlap with the question before making the final prediction. Combined with a strong base QA model, our method outperforms state-of-the-art defense techniques, calling into question how well these techniques are actually doing and strong these adversarial testbeds are.

1 Introduction

As reading comprehension datasets (Richardson et al., 2013; Weston et al., 2015; Hermann et al., 2015a; Rajpurkar et al., 2016; Joshi et al., 2017) and models (Sukhbaatar et al., 2015; Seo et al., 2016; Devlin et al., 2019) have advanced, QA research has increasingly focused on out-of-distribution generalization (Khashabi et al., 2020; Talmor and Berant, 2019) and robustness. Jia and Liang (2017) and Wallace et al. (2019) show that appending unrelated distractors to contexts can easily confuse a deep QA model, calling into question the effectiveness of these models. Although these attacks do not necessarily reflect a real-world threat model, they serve as an additional testbed for generalization: models that perform better against such adversaries might be expected to generalize better in other ways, such as on contrastive examples (Gardner et al., 2020).

In this paper, we propose a simple method for adversarial QA that explicitly reranks candidate answers predicted by a QA model according to a notion of content overlap with the question. Specifically, by identifying contexts where more named entities are shared with the question, we can extract answers that are more likely to be correct in adversarial conditions.

The impact of this is two-fold. First, our proposed method is model agnostic in that it can be applied post-hoc to any QA model that predicts probabilities of answer spans, without any retraining. Second but most important, we demonstrate that even this simple named entity based question-answer matching technique can be surprisingly useful. We show that our method outperforms state-of-the-art but more complex adversarial defenses with both BiDAF (Seo et al., 2016) and BERT (Devlin et al., 2019) on two standard adversarial QA datasets (Jia and Liang, 2017; Wallace et al., 2019). The fact that such a straightforward technique works well calls into question how reliable current datasets are for evaluating actual robustness of QA models.

2 Related Work

Over the years, various methods have been proposed for robustness in adversarial QA, the most prominent ones being adversarial training (Wang and Bansal, 2018; Lee et al., 2019; Yang et al., 2019b), data augmentation (Welbl et al., 2020) and posterior regularization (Zhou et al., 2019). Among these, we compare our method only with techniques that train on clean SQuAD (Wu et al., 2019; Yeh and Chen, 2019) for fairness. Wu et al. (2019) use a syntax-driven encoder to model the syntactic match between a question and an answer. Yeh and Chen (2019) use a prior approach (Hjelm et al., 2019) to maximize mutual information among contexts, questions, and answers to avoid overfitting to surface cues. In contrast, our technique is more

Proceedings of the 16th Conference of the European Chapter of the Associationfor Computational Linguistics: Student Research Workshop, pages 50–57
April 19 - 23, 2021. ©2021 Association for Computational Linguistics

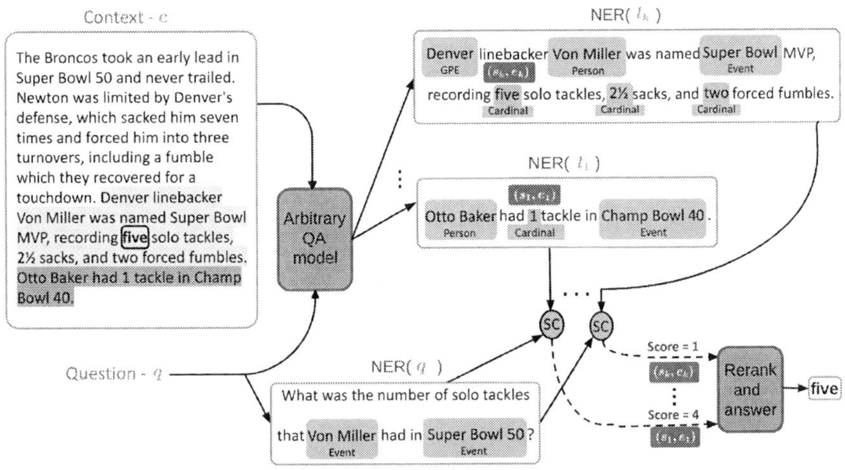

Figure 1: Our model agnostic answer reranking system (MAARS). Given each answer option (right column), we extract named entities and compare them to named entities in the question. The overlap is used as a reranking feature to choose the final answer. The ground truth answer containing sentence is highlighted in green, the ground truth answer is boxed and the distractor sentence is highlighted in red.

closely related to retrieval-based methods for open-domain QA (Chen et al., 2017; Yang et al., 2019a) and multi-hop QA (Welbl et al., 2018; De Cao et al., 2019): we show that shallow matching can improve the reliability of deep models against adversaries in addition to these more complex settings.

Methods for (re)ranking of candidate passages/answers have often been explored in the context of information retrieval (Severyn and Moschitti, 2015), content-based QA (Kratzwald et al., 2019) and open-domain QA (Wang et al., 2018; Lee et al., 2018). Similar to our approach, these methods also exploit some measure of coverage of the query by the candidate answers or their supporting passages to decide the ranks. However, the main motive behind ranking in such cases is usually to narrow down the area of interest within the text to look for the answer. On the contrary, we use a reranking mechanism that allows our QA model to ignore distractors in adversarial QA and can also provide model- and task-agnostic behavior unlike the commonly used learning-based (re)ranking mechanisms.

In yet another related line of research, (Chen et al., 2016; Kaushik and Lipton, 2018) reveal the simplistic nature and certain important shortcomings of popular QA datasets. Chen et al. (2016) conclude that the simple nature of the questions in the CNN/Daily Mail reading comprehension dataset (Hermann et al., 2015b) allows a QA model to perform well by extracting single-sentence relations. Kaushik and Lipton (2018) perform an extensive study with multiple well-known QA benchmarks to show several troubling trends: basic model ablations, such as making the input *question*- or *passage*-only, can beat the state-of-the-art performance, and the answers are often localized in the last few lines, even in very long passages, thus possibly allowing models to achieve very strong performance through learning trivial cues. Although we also question the efficacy of well-known adversarial QA datasets in this work, our core focus is on exposing certain issues specifically with the design of the adversarial distractors rather than the underlying datasets.

3 Approach

Neural QA models are usually trained in a supervised fashion on labeled examples of contexts, questions, and answers to predict answer spans; we represent these as (s, e) tuples, where s represents the sentence and e the candidate span. Prior work (Lewis and Fan, 2019; Mudrakarta et al., 2018; Yeh and Chen, 2019; Chen and Durrett, 2019) has noted that the end-to-end paradigm can overfit superficial biases in the data causing learning to stop when simple correlations are sufficient for the model to answer a question confidently. By explicitly enforcing content relevance between the predicted answer-containing sentence and the question, we can combat this poor generalization.

Specifically, we explicitly score the candidate sentences as per the word-level overlap in named entities common to both the question and a sen-

Model	Original	AddSent		AddOneSent	
		Adversarial	Mean	Adversarial	Mean
BERT-S	**89.4/82.1**	40.9/35.9	68.0/61.7	54.6/48.4	74.1/67.2
BERT-S + QAInfoMax	87.7/82.1	41.8/37.2	67.5/62.3	55.5/49.7	73.5/67.8
BERT-S + MAARS	80.2/71.1	**61.2/53.6**	**71.8/63.4**	**71.3/63.5**	**76.3/67.8**

Table 1: AddSent and AddOneSent results with BERT-S. MAARS outperforms the vanilla and baseline models on adversarial data but its performance drops a bit on the original data due to constrained reranking of answers.

tence. We refer to our method as Model Agnostic Answer Reranking System (MAARS).

Figure 1 illustrates the workflow of MAARS. MAARS can be applied to any arbitrary QA model that predicts answer span probabilities. First, we use the base QA model to compute the n best answer spans $\mathcal{A} = \{(s_1, e_1), \ldots, (s_n, e_n)\}$ for a context-question pair (c, q) where n is a hyperparameter. Any answer span not lying in a single sentence is broken into subspans that lie in separate sentences and $\mathcal{A}$ is updated accordingly.

Next, we extract the set of candidate sentences $\mathcal{L}$ from the context containing these n answer spans. For the question and each sentence, we compute a set of named entity chunks using an open-source AllenNLP (Gardner et al., 2017) NER model. We then compute the set of words inside named entity chunks from each candidate sentence $\text{NER}(l_k)\ \forall\, l_k \in \mathcal{L}$ and the question $\text{NER}(q)$; note that $\text{NER}(\cdot)$ refers to a set of words and not a set of named entities. Each candidate sentence l_k is then given a score $\text{SC}(l_k) = \text{NER}(l_k) \cap \text{NER}(q)$ and the answer spans are reranked per the scores of the sentences containing them. In the case of ties or if there are multiple spans in the same candidate sentence, they are reranked among themselves according to the original ordering as per the QA model. Finally, the span with the highest rank after reranking is chosen as the final answer.

Compared to the base QA model, this approach only relies on an additional NER model that can be used without any retraining of the base model. Note that the architecture doesn't depend on any specific tagger, and the other content matching models like word matching could also be used in the system here.

4 Experiments

4.1 Evaluation settings

Datasets and baselines. We evaluate MAARS on two well-known adversarial QA datasets built on top of SQuAD v1.1: Adversarial SQuAD (Jia and Liang, 2017) and Universal Adversarial Triggers (Wallace et al., 2019). For brevity, we don't include the adversarial distraction generation process for either of the datasets and point the interested reader to the original papers for exact details. For Adversarial SQuAD, we test MAARS with both BiDAF and BERT and compare against state-of-the-art baselines on adversary types used in the original papers. To the best of our knowledge, there is no pre-existing literature that proposes a defense technique for Universal Triggers. We also find that it fails to degrade the performance of our vanilla BERT model, probably because the attacks were originally generated for BiDAF. Thus, we only evaluate on this dataset in the BiDAF setting, using all four triggers *Who*, *When*, *Where* and *Why*.

Model	Original	AddSent	
		Adv.	Mean
BiDAF	72.4/62.4	21.4/16.0	49.9/42.0
BiDAF + SLN	72.3/62.4	22.8/17.2	50.5/42.5
BiDAF + MAARS	**72.3/62.9**	**45.4/38.0**	**60.4/51.9**

Table 2: AddSent results with BiDAF. Here, MAARS beats the vanilla and baseline models across all metrics.

For BiDAF, we compare MAARS against the Syntactic Leveraging Network (SLN) by Wu et al. (2019) on *AddSent*. SLN encodes predicate-argument structures from the context and question, a conceptually similar structure matching approach as MAARS but trained end-to-end with many more parameters. For BERT, we benchmark MAARS against QAInfoMax (Yeh and Chen, 2019) on *AddSent* and *AddOneSent*. In addition to the standard loss for training QA models, QAInfoMax adds a loss to maximize the mutual information between the learned representations of words in context and their neighborhood, and also between those of the answer spans and the question.

Implementation details. We use the uncased base (single) pretrained BERT from HuggingFace (Wolf et al., 2019) and finetune it using Adam with weight decay (Loshchilov and Hutter, 2019) optimizer and an initial learning rate of $3e^{-5}$ on SQuAD (Rajpurkar et al., 2016) v1.1 for 2 epochs for both vanilla BERT and BERT + QAInfoMax. We set the training batch size to 5 and the propor-

Adv. type	BiDAF	BiDAF + MAARS
Who	74.4/67.3	**76.3/68.9**
When	80.1/75.5	**81.8/77.1**
Where	63.5/52.8	**68.8/56.7**
Why	**51.9/34.1**	51.6/34.1

Table 3: Results on Universal Triggers with BiDAF (BERT-specific triggers unavailable publicly). MAARS is better than the vanilla model for most adversaries but with smaller performance gains than Adversarial SQuAD.

tion of linear learning rate warmup for the optimizer to 10%.

Our BiDAF (Seo et al., 2016) model has a hidden state of size 100 and takes 100 dimensional GloVe (Pennington et al., 2014) embeddings as input. For character-level embedding, it uses 100 one-dimensional convolutional filters, each with a width of 5. A uniform dropout (Srivastava et al., 2014) of 0.2 is applied at the CNN layer for character embedding, all LSTM (Hochreiter and Schmidhuber, 1997) layers and at the layer before the logits. We train it with AdaDelta (Zeiler, 2012) and an initial learning rate of 0.5 for 50 epochs. We set the training batch size to 128. For our Syntactic Leveraging Network, we follow the exact hyperparameter settings of (Wu et al., 2019).

Other hyperparameters common to both BERT and BiDAF include an input sequence length of 400, maximum query length of 64, and 40 predicted answer spans per context-question pair. For NER tagging, we use an ELMo-based implementation from AllenNLP (Gardner et al., 2017) that has been finetuned on CoNLL-2003 (Tjong Kim Sang and De Meulder, 2003). Finally, we set the value of n (the number of candidates considered for reranking) in MAARS to 10 across all our experiments.

4.2 Results

In all our results tables, we report the macro-averaged F1 and exact match (EM) scores separated by a slash in each cell. In Tables 1 and 2, **Original** and **Adversarial** (**Adv.**) refer to a model's performance on only clean and only adversarial data respectively. **Mean** denotes the weighted mean of the **Original** and **Adversarial** scores, weighted by the respective number of samples in the dataset. Both *AddSent* and *AddOneSent* have 1000 clean and 787 adversarial instances.

Adversarial SQuAD. Table 1 shows the results with BERT-single (-S) on *AddSent* and *AddOneSent*. MAARS outperforms both the vanilla model and QAInfoMax on both **Adversarial** and **Mean** metrics. The performance gains are also substantial, especially on **Adversarial** where MAARS improves F1 over QAInfoMax by about 20 points on *AddSent* and 16 points on *AddOneSent*. This clearly shows that our method is much more capable of avoiding distractors in data and it is a much stronger defense technique in this setting. For both QAInfoMax and MAARS there is a drop in performance on clean data, but the drop for MAARS is larger. This drop naturally arises from the simplicity of the heuristic: matching words in named entities with the question sometimes assigns a higher score to a candidate sentence which has a higher overlap in terms of named entities with the question but doesn't contain the right answer. One such example where MAARS fails to pick the correct top candidate after reranking is shown in fig. 2a.

Table 2 details the results with BiDAF on *AddSent*.[1] Here, we also see significant performance gains over the vanilla model and the SLN baseline. MAARS results in an increase in adversarial F1 by 24 points over vanilla BiDAF and about 22 points over BiDAF + SLN. Interestingly, the performance on clean data doesn't drop as in the case of BERT. This difference may be a result of BiDAF using more surface word matching itself, leading to a closer alignment between its predictions and the reranker's choices. However, note that our simple heuristic still performs well even with a complex model like BERT.

Discussion. Overall, our results on this dataset look promising for both BERT and BiDAF despite our method's inherent simplicity. This raises two questions. First, how effective is the Adversarial SQuAD dataset as a testbed for adversarial attacks? When a simple method can achieve large gains, we cannot be sure that more complex methods are truly working as advertised rather than learning such heuristics. Second, how effective are these current defenses? They underperform a simple heuristic in this setting; however, because the full breadth of possible adversarial settings has not been explored, it's hard to get a holistic sense of which methods are effective. Additional settings are needed to fully contrast these techniques.

Universal Adversarial Triggers. We create a dataset that has purely adversarial instances using the open-source code from Wallace et al. (2019)

[1]BiDAF + MAARS gives a similar F1/EM trend on *AddOneSent* (**Adversarial**: 46.1/38.5, **Mean**: 60.8/52.1).

Context: In Europe, the North American theater ... separate name. The entire international conflict is known as the **Seven Years' War**. "Seven Years" ... 1763. These dates do not correspond with the fighting on mainland North America, where the fighting between the two colonial powers was largely concluded in **six years**, from the Battle of Jumonville Glen in 1754 to the capture of Montreal in 1760. The bloody fighting lasted throughout the Five Years War.

Question: How long did the fighting last in Seven Years War?

(a) Wrong top candidate picked

Context: Under the terms of the Scotland Act 1978, ... total electorate. The 1979 **Scottish devolution referendum** to establish a devolved Scottish Assembly **failed**. Although the vote ... to, vote. The Scottish Assembly learned about the news when it was established in 1975.

Question: How did trying to establish a devolved Scottish Assembly go in 1979?

(b) Lack of attention to question type

Context: By the opening of the 2008 General Conference, total UMC membership was estimated at **11.4 million**, with about **7.9 million in the U.S.** and 3.5 million overseas. Significantly, about ... United States. u.s. total by total total by opening was membership 15.

Question: By the opening of the 2008 General Conference, what was the total UMC membership in the US?

(c) Multiple similar spans co-occur

Figure 2: Common failure cases for MAARS. The distractor sentence is highlighted in red, the predicted answer is underlined and the ground truth answer is boxed.

and present the results in Table 3. In particular, we append the following distractors for different adversary types. The target answers in the distractors have been bolded.

- *Who*: how]] there **donald trump** ; who who did
- *When*: ; its time about **january 2014** when may did british
- *Where*: ; : ' where **new york** may area where they
- *Why*: why how ; known because : **to kill american people** .

Due to unavailability of prior work on trigger-specific defense and BERT-specific triggers, we report only vanilla BiDAF and BiDAF with MAARS. F1 drops by a small amount (0.3 points) from BiDAF to BiDAF with MAARS while the EM score doesn't change at all for *Why*. The scores improve by around 1-2 points for the other adversary types. However, the gains are much lower in comparison to Adversarial SQuAD. These results indicate the promise of simple defenses, but more exhaustive evaluation of defenses on different types of attacks is needed to draw a more complete picture of the methods' generalization abilities.

4.3 Failure cases

Besides the instances where the primary error source is picking a wrong top candidate (refer to Fig. 2a), we notice two other common failure case types with MAARS. One directly stems from MAARS' inability to attend to the question type during reranking. In Fig. 2b, the question word is *How* but MAARS picks *Scottish devolution referendum* which is not the appropriate type of answer here. The other type of failure occurs when multiple similar span types are present in the same candidate, thus creating ambiguity for the base QA model. In the example shown in Fig. 2c, the QA model fails to distinguish between the two spans and retrieve specific information about *the US*. Better base QA models may resolve these issues, or a more powerful reranker could also be used. However, rerankers learned end-to-end would suffer from the same issues as BERT and require additional engineering to avoid overfitting the training data.

5 Conclusion

In this work, we introduce a simple and model agnostic post-hoc technique for adversarial question answering (QA) that predicts the final answer after re-ranking candidate answers from a generic QA model as per their overlap in relevant content with the question. Our results show the potential of our method through large performance gains over vanilla models and state-of-the-art methods. We also analyze common failure points in our method. Finally, we reiterate that our main contribution is not the heuristic defense itself but rather its ability to paint a more complete picture of the current state of affairs in adversarial QA. We seek to illustrate that our current adversaries are not strong and generic enough to attack a wide variety of QA methods, and we need a broader evaluation of our defenses to meaningfully gauge our progress in adversarial QA research.

References

Danqi Chen, Jason Bolton, and Christopher D. Manning. 2016. A thorough examination of the CNN/daily mail reading comprehension task. In *Proceedings of the 54th Annual Meeting of the Association for Computational Linguistics (Volume 1: Long Papers)*, pages 2358–2367, Berlin, Germany. Association for Computational Linguistics.

Danqi Chen, Adam Fisch, Jason Weston, and Antoine Bordes. 2017. Reading Wikipedia to answer open-domain questions. In *Proceedings of the 55th Annual Meeting of the Association for Computational Linguistics (Volume 1: Long Papers)*, pages 1870–1879, Vancouver, Canada. Association for Computational Linguistics.

Jifan Chen and Greg Durrett. 2019. Understanding dataset design choices for multi-hop reasoning. In *Proceedings of the 2019 Conference of the North American Chapter of the Association for Computational Linguistics: Human Language Technologies, Volume 1 (Long and Short Papers)*, pages 4026–4032, Minneapolis, Minnesota. Association for Computational Linguistics.

Nicola De Cao, Wilker Aziz, and Ivan Titov. 2019. Question answering by reasoning across documents with graph convolutional networks. In *Proceedings of the 2019 Conference of the North American Chapter of the Association for Computational Linguistics: Human Language Technologies, Volume 1 (Long and Short Papers)*, pages 2306–2317, Minneapolis, Minnesota. Association for Computational Linguistics.

Jacob Devlin, Ming-Wei Chang, Kenton Lee, and Kristina Toutanova. 2019. BERT: Pre-training of deep bidirectional transformers for language understanding. In *Proceedings of the 2019 Conference of the North American Chapter of the Association for Computational Linguistics: Human Language Technologies, Volume 1 (Long and Short Papers)*, pages 4171–4186, Minneapolis, Minnesota. Association for Computational Linguistics.

Matt Gardner, Yoav Artzi, Victoria Basmova, Jonathan Berant, Ben Bogin, Sihao Chen, Pradeep Dasigi, Dheeru Dua, Yanai Elazar, Ananth Gottumukkala, et al. 2020. Evaluating nlp models via contrast sets. *arXiv preprint arXiv:2004.02709*.

Matt Gardner, Joel Grus, Mark Neumann, Oyvind Tafjord, Pradeep Dasigi, Nelson F. Liu, Matthew Peters, Michael Schmitz, and Luke S. Zettlemoyer. 2017. Allennlp: A deep semantic natural language processing platform.

Karl Moritz Hermann, Tomas Kocisky, Edward Grefenstette, Lasse Espeholt, Will Kay, Mustafa Suleyman, and Phil Blunsom. 2015a. Teaching machines to read and comprehend. In C. Cortes, N. D. Lawrence, D. D. Lee, M. Sugiyama, and R. Garnett, editors, *Advances in Neural Information Processing Systems 28*, pages 1693–1701. Curran Associates, Inc.

Karl Moritz Hermann, Tomas Kocisky, Edward Grefenstette, Lasse Espeholt, Will Kay, Mustafa Suleyman, and Phil Blunsom. 2015b. Teaching machines to read and comprehend. In *Advances in Neural Information Processing Systems*, volume 28, pages 1693–1701. Curran Associates, Inc.

R Devon Hjelm, Alex Fedorov, Samuel Lavoie-Marchildon, Karan Grewal, Phil Bachman, Adam Trischler, and Yoshua Bengio. 2019. Learning deep representations by mutual information estimation and maximization. In *International Conference on Learning Representations*.

Sepp Hochreiter and Jürgen Schmidhuber. 1997. Long short-term memory. *Neural Computation*, 9(8):1735–1780.

Robin Jia and Percy Liang. 2017. Adversarial examples for evaluating reading comprehension systems. In *Proceedings of the 2017 Conference on Empirical Methods in Natural Language Processing*, pages 2021–2031, Copenhagen, Denmark. Association for Computational Linguistics.

Mandar Joshi, Eunsol Choi, Daniel Weld, and Luke Zettlemoyer. 2017. TriviaQA: A large scale distantly supervised challenge dataset for reading comprehension. In *Proceedings of the 55th Annual Meeting of the Association for Computational Linguistics (Volume 1: Long Papers)*, pages 1601–1611, Vancouver, Canada. Association for Computational Linguistics.

Divyansh Kaushik and Zachary C. Lipton. 2018. How much reading does reading comprehension require? a critical investigation of popular benchmarks. In *Proceedings of the 2018 Conference on Empirical Methods in Natural Language Processing*, pages 5010–5015, Brussels, Belgium. Association for Computational Linguistics.

Daniel Khashabi, Tushar Khot, Ashish Sabharwal, Oyvind Tafjord, Peter Clark, and Hannaneh Hajishirzi. 2020. Unifiedqa: Crossing format boundaries with a single qa system. *arXiv preprint arXiv:2005.00700*.

Bernhard Kratzwald, Anna Eigenmann, and Stefan Feuerriegel. 2019. RankQA: Neural question answering with answer re-ranking. In *Proceedings of the 57th Annual Meeting of the Association for Computational Linguistics*, pages 6076–6085, Florence, Italy. Association for Computational Linguistics.

Jinhyuk Lee, Seongjun Yun, Hyunjae Kim, Miyoung Ko, and Jaewoo Kang. 2018. Ranking paragraphs for improving answer recall in open-domain question answering. In *Proceedings of the 2018 Conference on Empirical Methods in Natural Language Processing*, pages 565–569, Brussels, Belgium. Association for Computational Linguistics.

Seanie Lee, Donggyu Kim, and Jangwon Park. 2019. Domain-agnostic question-answering with adversarial training. In *Proceedings of the 2nd Workshop on Machine Reading for Question Answering*. Association for Computational Linguistics.

Mike Lewis and Angela Fan. 2019. Generative question answering: Learning to answer the whole question. In *International Conference on Learning Representations*.

Ilya Loshchilov and Frank Hutter. 2019. Decoupled weight decay regularization. In *International Conference on Learning Representations*.

Pramod Kaushik Mudrakarta, Ankur Taly, Mukund Sundararajan, and Kedar Dhamdhere. 2018. Did the model understand the question? In *Proceedings of the 56th Annual Meeting of the Association for Computational Linguistics (Volume 1: Long Papers)*, pages 1896–1906, Melbourne, Australia. Association for Computational Linguistics.

Jeffrey Pennington, Richard Socher, and Christopher Manning. 2014. Glove: Global vectors for word representation. In *Proceedings of the 2014 Conference on Empirical Methods in Natural Language Processing (EMNLP)*, pages 1532–1543, Doha, Qatar. Association for Computational Linguistics.

Pranav Rajpurkar, Jian Zhang, Konstantin Lopyrev, and Percy Liang. 2016. SQuAD: 100,000+ questions for machine comprehension of text. In *Proceedings of the 2016 Conference on Empirical Methods in Natural Language Processing*, pages 2383–2392, Austin, Texas. Association for Computational Linguistics.

Matthew Richardson, Christopher J.C. Burges, and Erin Renshaw. 2013. MCTest: A challenge dataset for the open-domain machine comprehension of text. In *Proceedings of the 2013 Conference on Empirical Methods in Natural Language Processing*, pages 193–203, Seattle, Washington, USA. Association for Computational Linguistics.

Min Joon Seo, Aniruddha Kembhavi, Ali Farhadi, and Hannaneh Hajishirzi. 2016. Bidirectional attention flow for machine comprehension. *CoRR*, abs/1611.01603.

Aliaksei Severyn and Alessandro Moschitti. 2015. Learning to rank short text pairs with convolutional deep neural networks. In *Proceedings of the 38th International ACM SIGIR Conference on Research and Development in Information Retrieval*, SIGIR '15, page 373–382, New York, NY, USA. Association for Computing Machinery.

Nitish Srivastava, Geoffrey Hinton, Alex Krizhevsky, Ilya Sutskever, and Ruslan Salakhutdinov. 2014. Dropout: A simple way to prevent neural networks from overfitting. *Journal of Machine Learning Research*, 15(56):1929–1958.

Sainbayar Sukhbaatar, arthur szlam, Jason Weston, and Rob Fergus. 2015. End-to-end memory networks. In C. Cortes, N. D. Lawrence, D. D. Lee, M. Sugiyama, and R. Garnett, editors, *Advances in Neural Information Processing Systems 28*, pages 2440–2448. Curran Associates, Inc.

Alon Talmor and Jonathan Berant. 2019. MultiQA: An empirical investigation of generalization and transfer in reading comprehension. In *Proceedings of the 57th Annual Meeting of the Association for Computational Linguistics*, pages 4911–4921, Florence, Italy. Association for Computational Linguistics.

Erik F. Tjong Kim Sang and Fien De Meulder. 2003. Introduction to the CoNLL-2003 shared task: Language-independent named entity recognition. In *Proceedings of the Seventh Conference on Natural Language Learning at HLT-NAACL 2003*, pages 142–147.

Eric Wallace, Shi Feng, Nikhil Kandpal, Matt Gardner, and Sameer Singh. 2019. Universal adversarial triggers for attacking and analyzing NLP. In *Proceedings of the 2019 Conference on Empirical Methods in Natural Language Processing and the 9th International Joint Conference on Natural Language Processing (EMNLP-IJCNLP)*, pages 2153–2162, Hong Kong, China. Association for Computational Linguistics.

Shuohang Wang, Mo Yu, Jing Jiang, Wei Zhang, Xiaoxiao Guo, Shiyu Chang, Zhiguo Wang, Tim Klinger, Gerald Tesauro, and Murray Campbell. 2018. Evidence aggregation for answer re-ranking in open-domain question answering. In *International Conference on Learning Representations*.

Yicheng Wang and Mohit Bansal. 2018. Robust machine comprehension models via adversarial training. In *Proceedings of the 2018 Conference of the North American Chapter of the Association for Computational Linguistics: Human Language Technologies, Volume 2 (Short Papers)*, pages 575–581, New Orleans, Louisiana. Association for Computational Linguistics.

Johannes Welbl, Pasquale Minervini, Max Bartolo, Pontus Stenetorp, and Sebastian Riedel. 2020. Undersensitivity in neural reading comprehension. *arXiv preprint arXiv:2003.04808*.

Johannes Welbl, Pontus Stenetorp, and Sebastian Riedel. 2018. Constructing datasets for multi-hop reading comprehension across documents. *Transactions of the Association for Computational Linguistics*, 6:287–302.

Jason Weston, Antoine Bordes, Sumit Chopra, and Tomas Mikolov. 2015. Towards ai-complete question answering: A set of prerequisite toy tasks. *CoRR*, abs/1502.05698.

Thomas Wolf, Lysandre Debut, Victor Sanh, Julien Chaumond, Clement Delangue, Anthony Moi, Pierric Cistac, Tim Rault, R'emi Louf, Morgan Funtowicz, and Jamie Brew. 2019. Huggingface's transformers: State-of-the-art natural language processing. *ArXiv*, abs/1910.03771.

Bowen Wu, Haoyang Huang, Zongsheng Wang, Qihang Feng, Jingsong Yu, and Baoxun Wang. 2019. Improving the robustness of deep reading comprehension models by leveraging syntax prior. In *Proceedings of the 2nd Workshop on Machine Reading for Question Answering*, pages 53–57, Hong Kong, China. Association for Computational Linguistics.

Wei Yang, Yuqing Xie, Aileen Lin, Xingyu Li, Luchen Tan, Kun Xiong, Ming Li, and Jimmy Lin. 2019a. End-to-end open-domain question answering with BERTserini. In *Proceedings of the 2019 Conference of the North American Chapter of the Association for Computational Linguistics (Demonstrations)*, pages 72–77, Minneapolis, Minnesota. Association for Computational Linguistics.

Ziqing Yang, Yiming Cui, Wanxiang Che, Ting Liu, Shijin Wang, and Guoping Hu. 2019b. Improving machine reading comprehension via adversarial training. *arXiv preprint arXiv:1911.03614*.

Yi-Ting Yeh and Yun-Nung Chen. 2019. QAInfomax: Learning robust question answering system by mutual information maximization. In *Proceedings of the 2019 Conference on Empirical Methods in Natural Language Processing and the 9th International Joint Conference on Natural Language Processing (EMNLP-IJCNLP)*, pages 3370–3375, Hong Kong, China. Association for Computational Linguistics.

Matthew D. Zeiler. 2012. ADADELTA: an adaptive learning rate method. *CoRR*, abs/1212.5701.

Mantong Zhou, Minlie Huang, and Xiaoyan Zhu. 2019. Robust reading comprehension with linguistic constraints via posterior regularization. *arXiv preprint arXiv:1911.06948*.

BERT meets Cranfield: Uncovering the Properties of Full Ranking on Fully Labeled Data

Negin Ghasemi
Radboud University, Nijmegen
N.Ghasemi@cs.ru.nl

Djoerd Hiemstra
Radboud University, Nijmegen
Hiemstra@cs.ru.nl

Abstract

Recently, various information retrieval models have been proposed based on pre-trained BERT models, achieving outstanding performance. The majority of such models have been tested on data collections with partial relevance labels, where various potentially relevant documents have not been exposed to the annotators. Therefore, evaluating BERT-based rankers may lead to biased and unfair evaluation results, simply because a relevant document has not been exposed to the annotators while creating the collection. In our work, we aim to better understand a BERT-based ranker's strengths compared to a BERT-based re-ranker and the initial ranker. To this aim, we investigate BERT-based rankers performance on the Cranfield collection, which comes with full relevance judgment on all documents in the collection. Our results demonstrate the BERT-based full ranker's effectiveness, as opposed to the BERT-based re-ranker and BM25. Also, analysis shows that there are documents that the BERT-based full-ranker finds that were not found by the initial ranker.

1 Introduction

Transformers-based pre-trained language representations, such as ELMo (Peters et al., 2018), BERT (Devlin et al., 2019), and T5 (Raffel et al., 2020) have been counted as a promising approaches to various information retrieval tasks, such as document ranking (Nogueira and Cho, 2019) and question answering (Yang et al., 2019a).

Prior work argued that utilizing BERT for ranking can achieve state-of-the-art results on popular ad-hoc retrieval collections such as Robust04 (MacAvaney et al., 2019; Akkalyoncu Yilmaz et al., 2019; Yang et al., 2019b; Dai and Callan, 2019), ClueWeb09-B (Dai and Callan, 2019), and MS MARCO (Padigela et al., 2019; Nogueira and Cho, 2019; Nogueira et al., 2019). However, two major limitations make these collections unfair to BERT.

One of the limitations of these collections is that they have not been created to reflect BERT's superiority to its best (Yilmaz et al., 2020). As BERT-based models did not contribute to their assessment pool, testing a BERT-based ranking system with these collections can lead to unfair and biased results (Yilmaz et al., 2020). There may be relevant documents that traditional methods could not find, hence assumed irrelevant in the pooling process. Therefore, new collections are needed or collections with full relevant judgments.

The second limitation is that although reusable test collections play an important role in IR, conducting a lot of research on a single collection can direct the results to an outstanding value by chance (Carterette, 2015).

To avoid these two limitations, we use a previously unused collection with characteristics such as containing a relatively large number of queries in the form of short, full questions. Also, to address the first mentioned limitation, the collection contains a full set of judgments for each query.

The Cranfield[1] collection has all the mentioned features. Unlike other collections, Cranfield's main feature is a complete judgment, so documents uniquely found by a BERT-based ranker can be fairly assessed. This collection is built using abstracts of aerospace-related documents such as papers, research reports and articles from the collection of the College of Aeronautics, Cranfield, England. (Richmond, 1963). The documents' authors were asked to provide a set of related terms for their documents which were turned into natural language queries (Robertson, 2008). The collection contains 225 queries and 1400 documents. The collection has not been used for document ranking

[1] http://ir.dcs.gla.ac.uk/resources/test_collections/cran/

Proceedings of the 16th Conference of the European Chapter of the Associationfor Computational Linguistics: Student Research Workshop, pages 58–64
April 19 - 23, 2021. ©2021 Association for Computational Linguistics

with BERT before and can also address the second limitation. Furthermore, queries and most of the documents are short, which seems to be a good fit for BERT due to the BERT's token limitation.

Using the Cranfield collection, we address the following research questions:

- **RQ1**: Can we replicate a BERT-based re-ranker on a previously unused collection?
- **RQ2**: Does BERT only learn how to re-rank, or can it learn to find relevant documents that are not found by a bag-of-words baseline?

Our work to answer these research questions includes two steps: first, we provide experimental results on the Cranfield collection for document re-ranking with BERT, following the BERT-based re-ranker of Nogueira and Cho (2019) using BM25 (Robertson et al., 1995) as the initial ranker. Second, we study BERT's behavior as a *full*-ranker. In the paper, We refer to a ranker without any initial filtering method as a full-ranker. The code to reproduce our results is available at `https://gitlab.science.ru.nl/nghasemi/bert-meets-cranfield`.

The contributions of this work are as follows:

- We show that document re-ranking with BERT significantly improves the BM25 baseline on an unseen collection, although different hyperparameter settings may be needed.
- Our Analysis of the BERT-based full-ranker reveals better results than the re-ranker. Moreover, the BERT-based full-ranker retrieved documents are quite different from BM25, demonstrating BERT's ability to find relevant documents not found by a bag-of-words approach.

The rest of the paper is structured as follows: Section 2 reviews the related works on BERT and its usage in ranking problems. In Section 3, we describe the model used for document ranking with BERT in more detail. Experimental results and analysis are presented in Section 4. The final Section 5 concludes the paper and discusses potential research questions for future work.

2 Related Work

2.1 BERT

BERT's architecture is mostly designed based on several transformer blocks introduced by Vaswani et al. (2017); however, these blocks only consist of encoders. The authors introduce two differently sized BERT models. BERT-base and BERT-large consist of 12 and 24 transformer blocks, respectively. BERT is trained on two different unsupervised tasks. Train loss is the sum of the mean of both tasks' likelihood. The first task is the Masked Language Model, which trains to predict all the masked words. The second task is Next Sentence Prediction: This task aims to find if the second half of the input is the following sentence of the first half, or a random sentence.

BERT is not limited to the discussed pre-trained tasks. The self-attention mechanism in the transformers block makes BERT capable of modeling many tasks as long as the task inputs are appropriately processed with BERT's desired setups, namely using proper special tokens ($[CLS]$, $[SEP]$) and BERT's specialized tokenizer. Fine-tuning the BERT pre-trained model helps to gain better performance on a specific task. Adding one additional output layer to a BERT pre-trained model is suggested in the fine-tuning phase to minimize the number of learning parameters. We refer readers to Devlin et al. (2019) for more details.

2.2 Collections and BERT-based Rankers

Many valuable collections in the information retrieval community, such as MS MARCO, Robust, and Clueweb, are standard collections for ranking tasks. Robust and Clueweb are popular TREC collections. TREC extensively uses the pooling method to create each collection. They assume that each participant system's top-k ranked items are likely to cover most of the collection's relevant documents; therefore, judging this pool would make a decent collection. The k number for Robust04 is 100 (Voorhees, 2004) and for Clueweb12 is 20 or less (Collins-Thompson et al., 2014). The MS MARCO dataset is formed based on Bing's query samples and related human-generated answers. The corpus was initially formed by retrieving the top-10 passages from the Bing search engine. On average, each query has one relevant passage. However, there are queries with no relevant passages as well (Nguyen et al., 2016).

A recent work proposed by Yilmaz et al. (2020) analyzes the reusability of the collections for information retrieval ranking tasks when a deep neural approach is being used, especially when the collection is created solely using traditional methods.

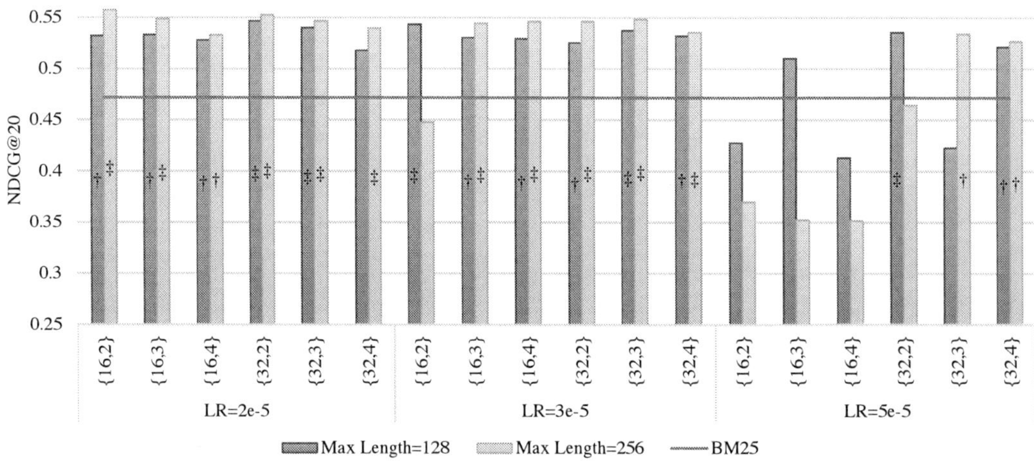

Figure 1: BERT re-ranker results for different hyperparameters. LR shows the value of the Learning Rate. Different batch sizes and epochs are shown as {Batch Size, Epoch}. Max Length shows the BERT token limitation.

The analysis argues that collections created without having neural rankers in their assessment pool should be used cautiously. They may lead to biased results for neural models compared to traditional methods. This work inspired us to use Cranfield, which contains a full set of relevant judgments.

Nogueira and Cho (2019) propose a common re-ranking approach to enhance the top results retrieved by BM25. In their method, a pre-trained BERT model is tuned to find the representation of a concatenated sequence, including query and document tokens.

Experiments by Padigela et al. (2019) show that a BERT-based re-ranker generally achieves higher performance as BM25 is more biased towards higher query term frequency than BERT. Also, the BERT-based re-ranker retrieves documents with more novel words.

Although BERT has shown to be very successful in all the described re-ranking models and many approaches have been proposed to improve the re-ranker, investigating a BERT-based full-ranker performance is still an open question. Of course, BERT-based models use re-ranking for efficiency reasons; however, if the full-ranker outperforms the re-ranker, it can be considered for offline systems and, more importantly, as an essential baseline to create high-quality search collections.

3 Method

Although BERT pre-trained models were trained on large corpora, fine-tuning is necessary for using BERT effectively. Inspired by the work proposed by Nogueira and Cho (2019), we fine-tuned the BERT model and used it to find the representation of the query and document pairs. Due to limited resources, we use the BERT-base, uncased, pre-trained model. This model produces 768-dimensional representation vectors.

Our input vector to BERT is similar to the next sentence prediction task's input vector used in pre-training BERT. Following the BERT's standard input format (Devlin et al., 2019), we converted each query Q and document D to a pair $[CLS] + Q + [SEP] + D + [SEP]$. The query always remains unchanged, but as BERT has a limitation on the number of tokens, we truncate documents that were longer than the model's maximum length.

We use a pre-trained BERT model with an added single linear classification layer on top of the $[CLS]$ output vector to suit the ad-hoc retrieval task. In this case, Each input's $[CLS]$ output vector would be fed to the classification layer, and both the pre-trained BERT model and the additional untrained classification layer is tuned on training samples of queries and documents from the Cranfield collection.

As mentioned in Section 1, the Cranfield collection contains 225 queries and 1400 documents. All queries in the Cranfield collection have full, graded relevance judgments. There are five different relevancy grades. Grades one to four are known to be relevant, and five shows irrelevant documents.

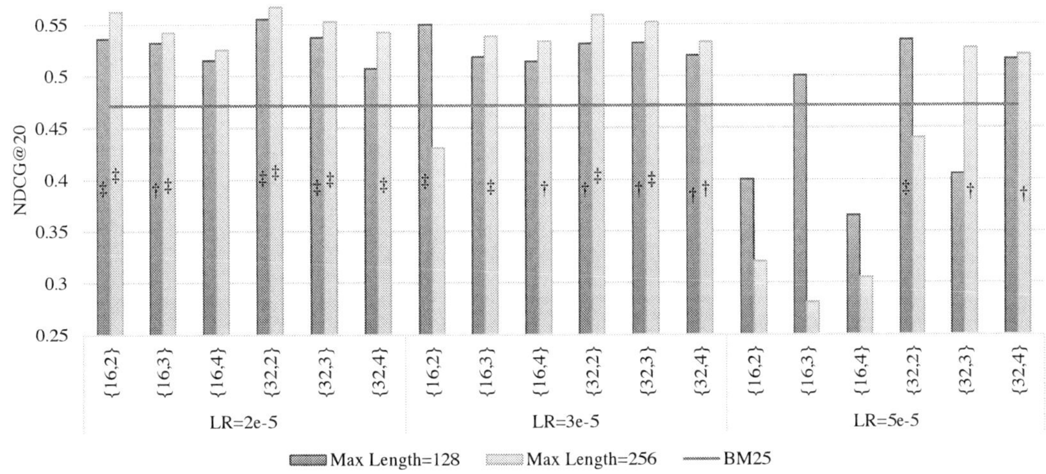

Figure 2: BERT full-ranker results for different hyperparameters. LR shows the value of the Learning Rate. Different batch sizes and epochs are shown as {Batch Size, Epoch}. Max Length shows the BERT token limitation.

To use judgments in classifier tuning, we turn them to binary labels despite its relevance grade. We assumed all the documents with grades one to four to be relevant.

We follow the many methods mentioned in Section 2 that fine-tune BERT on a re-ranking task using the top-k BM25 results. Tuning and testing process is performed using 5-fold cross-validation and the top-100 selection of BM25 results for each query. Folds are split by queries and are available in the code repository.

We test a BERT-based re-ranker and a BERT-based full-ranker, using the same fine-tuning method and hyperparameters. After tuning the BERT model, we use the top-100 BM25 results to do re-ranking, but we use all documents for full-ranking. We evaluate the results using MAP@100, and NDCG@20 (Järvelin and Kekäläinen, 2002) for both models.

4 Results

4.1 Re-ranker Analysis

For our experiments, we use BM25 and a BERT-based re-ranker to address **RQ1**, and we use a BERT-based full-ranker to investigate **RQ2**. We train both models following the hyperparameter value ranges recommended by Devlin et al. (2019).

For the initial ranker, BM25 parameters are as follows: $k1 = 1.5$ and $b = 0.75$. To fine-tune BERT, we use the ADAM optimizer with three different learning rate values of $2e-5$, $3e-5$, and $5e-5$ without the recommended learning rate warmup. Also, we use two batch size values of 16 and 32 and three epoch values of 2, 3, and 4. As the Cranfield collection does not include large documents (the average document length is 118 tokens), we limit the input token length with two different values of 128 and 256. We did not test 512 tokens because we had limited resources available. Results for the BERT-based re-ranker and full-ranker on NDCG@20 are shown in Figure 1 and Figure 2 respectively.

In all demonstrated and tabulated results, † marks a statistically significant difference between the proposed model and the BM25 baseline at $p < 0.05$ based on a two-tailed paired t-test, and ‡ shows highly statistical significance at $p < 0.01$ based on a two-tailed paired t-test.

Experiments show that a lower learning rate is more effective in fine-tuning for the Cranfield collection. The same applies to the number of epochs. We perform our analysis on the model with the learning rate of $2e-5$, batch size of 32, epoch numbers of 2, and the maximum length of input tokens limited to 256. We only report NDCG@20 due to space limitations; however, similar trends were observed with MAP@100.

4.2 Full-ranker Analysis

Table 1 shows the results of two BERT-based ranker models, namely re-ranker and full-ranker. Comparing the full-ranker with the same re-ranker results shows more improvement over the BM25 baseline. In this section, we provide more detail comparing

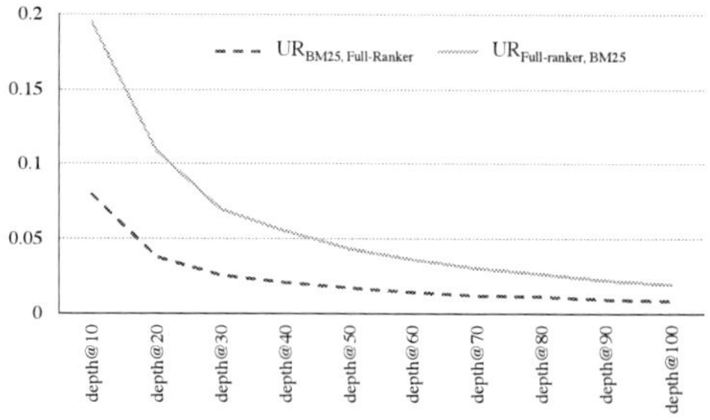

Figure 3: Unique Relevant (UR) percent of documents found by BM25 and the Full-ranker at different depths

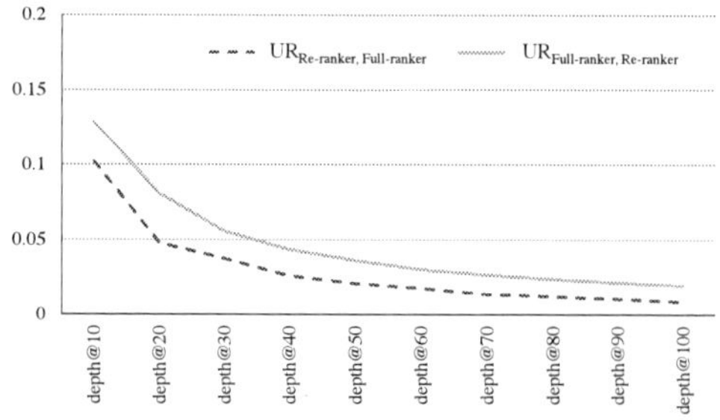

Figure 4: Unique Relevant (UR) percent of documents found by the Re-ranker and the Full-ranker at different depths

the BERT-based full-ranker with the BM25 initial ranker to address **RQ2**.

We observe performance improvement using full-ranking. We believe this behavior is rooted in two possible reasons: (1) The number of unique, relevant documents, which BERT-based ranker finds, that BM25 does not consider; (2) the BERT-based full-ranker can find more highly-ranked new documents.

Method	MAP@100	NDCG@20
BM25	0.3274	0.4714
Re-ranker	0.4198‡	0.5525‡
Full-ranker	0.4404‡	0.5670‡

Table 1: Results for Learning Rate=$2e-5$, Epoch=2, Batch Size=32, Max Length=256

To investigate these possible reasons, we went through the unique documents each model retrieves. Table 2 presents the results for the percentage of retrieved relevant documents that BM25 found that were not found by the full-ranker, and vice versa, for different depths. We are interested in comparing two different types of retrieved relevant documents: $UR_{BM25,Full-ranker}$ and $UR_{Full-ranker,BM25}$ which are defined as follows:

- $UR_{BM25,Full-ranker}$ (Unique Relevant found by BM25): the relevant documents retrieved by BM25 but not retrieved by the Full-ranker
- $UR_{Full-ranker,BM25}$ (Unique Relevant found by Full-ranker): the relevant documents retrieved by the Full-ranker but not retrieved by the BM25

Figure 3 demonstrates these results in more detail, showing the full-ranker's power to find more relevant documents than BM25, especially in the top results. Besides, We investigated another types of retrieved relevant documents: $UR_{Re-ranker,Full-ranker}$ and $UR_{Full-ranker,Re-ranker}$ which are defined as follows:

- $UR_{Re-ranker,Full-ranker}$ (Unique Relevant found by Re-ranker): the relevant documents retrieved by the Re-ranker but not retrieved by the Full-ranker
- $UR_{Full-ranker,Re-ranker}$ (Unique Relevant found by Full-ranker): the relevant documents retrieved by the Full-ranker but not retrieved by the Re-ranker

Table 3, and Figure 4 show the full-ranker's power in comparison with the re-ranker. It is worth mentioning that the re-ranker and the BM25 retrieved documents are the same in depth@100, but they have different rankings as the re-ranker changes the documents' ranking scores. Although there is a lower difference rate as the re-ranker itself outperforms BM25, the full-ranker still finds more unique, relevant documents than the re-ranker.

As shown in the results, (1) is a correct assumption. The BERT-based full-ranker can find more new relevant documents compared to BM25 and re-ranker, which confirms the **RQ2** hypothesis. It is also worth mentioning that there are 67.6% new documents in the BERT-based full-ranker model in total (both relevant and irrelevant) at top-100 results, which makes it a substantially different ranker than BM25.

Table 4 investigates the relevance degree (RD) of the unique, relevant documents found by each model at their top-100 results. The collection has four different grades indicating the relevancy of

Method	depth@10	depth@20	depth@100
$UR_{BM25,Full-ranker}$	0.08	0.04	0.009
$UR_{Full-ranker,BM25}$	0.19	0.11	0.02

Table 2: Unique Relevant (UR) percent of documents found by BM25 and the full-ranker at different depths

Method	depth@10	depth@20	depth@100
$UR_{Re-ranker,Full-ranker}$	0.1	0.05	0.009
$UR_{Full-ranker,Re-ranker}$	0.13	0.08	0.02

Table 3: Unique Relevant (UR) percent of documents found by the re-ranker and the full-ranker at different depths

Method	RD1	RD2	RD3	RD4
BM25/Re-ranker	0.26	0.45	0.22	0.07
Full-ranker	0.22	0.4	0.23	0.15

Table 4: Percentage of relevant documents per Relevance Degree (RD). RD4 indicates the highest relevance degree.

the document to a query. In this collection, RD4 indicates the highest relevance degree. The observations confirm (2). Results show that the BERT-based full-ranker is more likely to retrieve highly relevant documents.

5 Conclusion

This paper investigates BERT for document ranking. In our experiments, we explore the Cranfield collection, which has not been used on BERT-based ranking approaches and gives new insights because of its characteristics, such as full relevance judgments and a large number of queries. In addition to the document re-ranking with BERT, we considered using a full-ranker under the same experimental settings. The results show that the re-ranker and the full-ranker improve a BM25 baseline significantly. Furthermore, the BERT-based full-ranker outperforms the BERT-based re-ranker. Based on our studies, the BERT-based full-ranker is a different model than the BM25 ranker as it retrieves a notable number of new documents that were not found by BM25. This is especially true for highly relevant documents.

References

Zeynep Akkalyoncu Yilmaz, Wei Yang, Haotian Zhang, and Jimmy Lin. 2019. Cross-domain modeling of sentence-level evidence for document retrieval. In *Proceedings of the 2019 Conference on Empirical Methods in Natural Language Processing and the 9th International Joint Conference on Natural Language Processing (EMNLP-IJCNLP)*, pages 3490–3496, Hong Kong, China. Association for Computational Linguistics.

Ben Carterette. 2015. The best published result is random: Sequential testing and its effect on reported effectiveness. In *Proceedings of the 38th International ACM SIGIR Conference on Research and Development in Information Retrieval*, SIGIR '15, page 747–750, New York, NY, USA. Association for Computing Machinery.

Kevyn Collins-Thompson, Paul Bennett, Fernando Diaz, Charles L. A. Clarke, and Ellen M. Voorhees. 2014. Trec 2013 web track overview. In *Proceedings of the 22nd Text REtrieval Conference (TREC 2013)*.

Zhuyun Dai and Jamie Callan. 2019. Deeper text understanding for ir with contextual neural language modeling. In *Proceedings of the 42nd International ACM SIGIR Conference on Research and Development in Information Retrieval*, SIGIR'19, page 985–988, New York, NY, USA. Association for Computing Machinery.

Jacob Devlin, Ming-Wei Chang, Kenton Lee, and Kristina Toutanova. 2019. BERT: Pre-training of deep bidirectional transformers for language understanding. In *Proceedings of the 2019 Conference of the North American Chapter of the Association for Computational Linguistics: Human Language Technologies, Volume 1 (Long and Short Papers)*, pages 4171–4186, Minneapolis, Minnesota. Association for Computational Linguistics.

Kalervo Järvelin and Jaana Kekäläinen. 2002. Cumulated gain-based evaluation of ir techniques. *ACM Trans. Inf. Syst.*, 20(4):422–446.

Sean MacAvaney, Andrew Yates, Arman Cohan, and Nazli Goharian. 2019. Cedr: Contextualized embeddings for document ranking. In *SIGIR*.

Tri Nguyen, Mir Rosenberg, Xia Song, Jianfeng Gao, Saurabh Tiwary, Rangan Majumder, and Li Deng. 2016. Ms marco: A human generated machine reading comprehension dataset. *arXiv preprint arXiv:1611.09268 (2016)*.

Rodrigo Nogueira and Kyunghyun Cho. 2019. Passage re-ranking with bert. *arXiv preprint arXiv:1901.04085*.

Rodrigo Nogueira, Wei Yang, Kyunghyun Cho, and Jimmy Lin. 2019. Multi-stage document ranking with bert. *arXiv preprint arXiv:1910.14424*.

Harshith Padigela, Hamed Zamani, and W. Bruce Croft. 2019. Investigating the successes and failures of bert for passage re-ranking. *ArXiv*.

Matthew Peters, Mark Neumann, Mohit Iyyer, Matt Gardner, Christopher Clark, Kenton Lee, and Luke Zettlemoyer. 2018. Deep contextualized word representations. In *Proceedings of the 2018 Conference of the North American Chapter of the Association for Computational Linguistics: Human Language Technologies, Volume 1 (Long Papers)*, pages 2227–2237, New Orleans, Louisiana. Association for Computational Linguistics.

Colin Raffel, Noam Shazeer, Adam Roberts, Katherine Lee, Sharan Narang, Michael Matena, Yanqi Zhou, Wei Li, and Peter J. Liu. 2020. Exploring the limits of transfer learning with a unified text-to-text transformer. *Journal of Machine Learning Research*, 21(140):1–67.

Phyllis A. Richmond. 1963. Review of the cranfield project. *American Documentation*, 14(4):307–311.

Stephen Robertson. 2008. On the history of evaluation in ir. *Journal of Information Science*, 34:439–456.

Stephen Robertson, Steve Walker, Susan Jones, Micheline Hancock-Beaulieu, and Mike Gatford. 1995. Okapi at trec-3. In *Overview of the Third Text REtrieval Conference (TREC-3)*.

Ashish Vaswani, Noam Shazeer, Niki Parmar, Jakob Uszkoreit, Llion Jones, Aidan N. Gomez, undefinedukasz Kaiser, and Illia Polosukhin. 2017. Attention is all you need. In *Proceedings of the 31st International Conference on Neural Information Processing Systems*, NIPS'17, page 6000–6010. Curran Associates Inc.

Ellen M. Voorhees. 2004. Overview of the trec 2004 robust retrieval track. In *Proceedings of the 13nd Text REtrieval Conference (TREC 2004)*.

Wei Yang, Yuqing Xie, Aileen Lin, Xingyu Li, Luchen Tan, Kun Xiong, Ming Li, and Jimmy Lin. 2019a. End-to-end open-domain question answering with bertserini. In *NAACL-HLT*.

Wei Yang, Haotian Zhang, and Jimmy Lin. 2019b. Simple applications of bert for ad hoc document retrieval. *ArXiv*, abs/1903.10972.

Emine Yilmaz, Nick Craswell, Bhaskar Mitra, and Daniel Campos. 2020. On the reliability of test collections for evaluating systems of different types. In *Proceedings of the 43rd International ACM SIGIR Conference on Research and Development in Information Retrieval*, SIGIR '20, page 2101–2104, New York, NY, USA. Association for Computing Machinery.

Siamese Neural Networks for Detecting Complementary Products

Marina Angelovska
KTH Royal Institute of Technology
angelovs@kth.se

Sina Sheikholeslami
KTH Royal Institute of Technology
sinash@kth.se

Bas Dunn
bol.com
bas@dunn.nl

Amir H. Payberah
KTH Royal Institute of Technology
payberah@kth.se

Abstract

Recommender systems play an important role in e-commerce websites as they improve the customer journey by helping the users find what they want at the right moment. In this paper, we focus on identifying a complementary relationship between the products of an e-commerce company. We propose a content-based recommender system for detecting complementary products, using *Siamese Neural Networks (SNN)*. To this end, we implement and compare two different models: *Siamese Convolutional Neural Network (CNN)* and *Siamese Long Short-Term Memory (LSTM)*. Moreover, we propose an extension of the SNN approach to handling millions of products in a matter of seconds, and we reduce the training time complexity by half. In the experiments, we show that Siamese LSTM can predict complementary products with an accuracy of $\sim 85\%$ using only the product titles.

1 Introduction

As much as the diverse and rich offers on e-commerce websites help the users find what they need at one market place, the online catalogs are sometimes too overwhelming. Recommender systems play a significant role in making this process convenient for users. A specific case for recommender systems is *complementary products* (also known as *add-ons*), which are the products that are sold separately but are used together, each creating a demand for the other. Figure 1 shows some examples of complementary products.

Detecting complementary products in many of the current platforms is mainly based on co-purchase history and business rules. In this approach, if two items have been bought together more than a certain number of times, they are assumed to complement one another with a high probability. However, complementarity among products cannot be accurately detected using only the purchase history because (i) identical items having different sizes or colors are likely to be bought together and are pure substitutes instead of complementary products (e.g., a user buys three flower vases in different sizes), and (ii) if there are no purchases made yet, the ground truth is missing (it is known as the cold-start problem). One solution to overcome these problems is to introduce human labeling for accurate validation. The problem of this approach lies in the time and scalability limitations. Moreover, these approaches focus on popular items; thus, unpopular (less frequently bought) products will stay undiscovered.

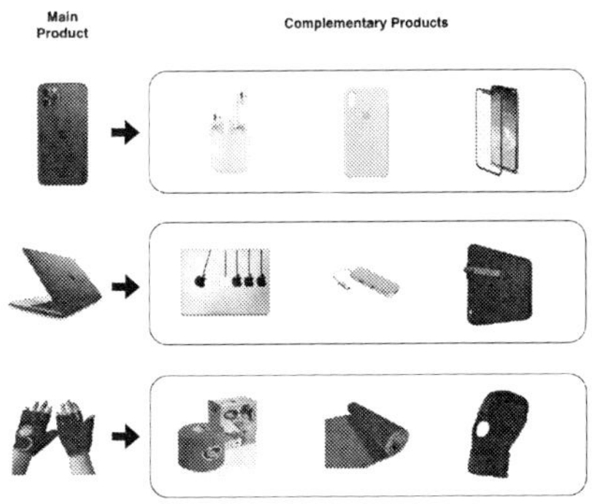

Figure 1: Complementary product examples.

To address the aforementioned problems, we propose a supervised deep learning approach based on *Siamese Neural Networks (SNN)* (Chicco, 2021), and in particular *Siamese Convolutional Neural Network (CNN)* and *Siamese Long Short-Term Memory (LSTM)*. To train the model, we give the input dataset in the format of `MainProduct`, `AddOnProduct`, and `Label(Y/N)` that identifies if two products are complementary. Using this data, the SNN creates embeddings and generates vector outputs that show the actual distance between the two given products in terms of their complementarity. For each product, we consider the title, the

Proceedings of the 16th Conference of the European Chapter of the Associationfor Computational Linguistics: Student Research Workshop, pages 65–70
April 19 - 23, 2021. ©2021 Association for Computational Linguistics

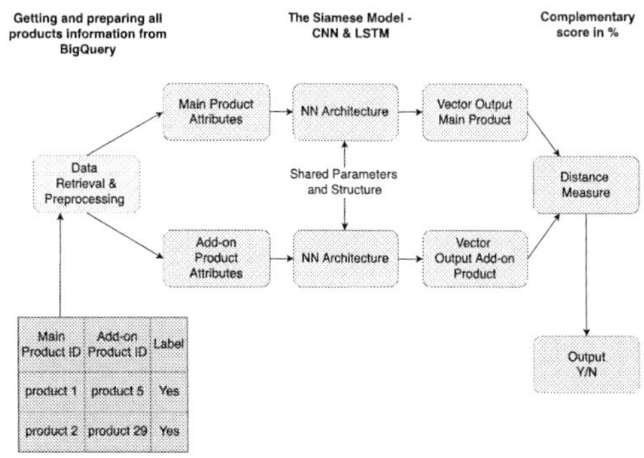

Figure 2: The proposed model pipeline using SNN.

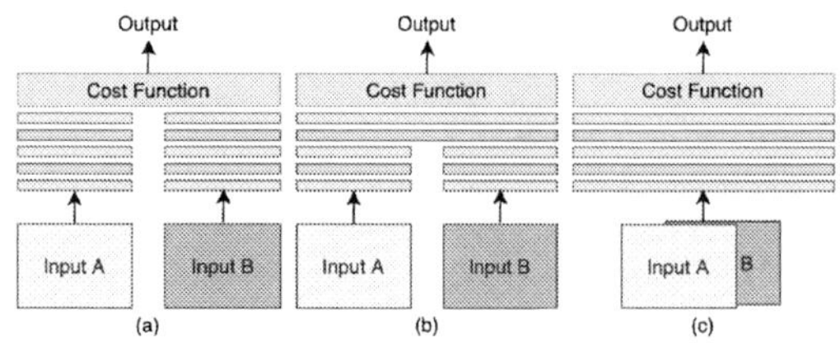

Figure 3: Three types of SNNs (a) late merge, (b) intermediate merge, and (c) early merge (Fiaz et al., 2019).

description, and the brand as its attributes. Figure 2 shows the pipeline of the proposed model.

The objectives of this work are three-fold:

1. Studying the performance of Siamese CNN and Siamese LSTM in predicting complementary products using textual attributes.

2. Studying the impact of different product attributes (such as the product title, the description, and the brand) on predicting complementary products.

3. Transforming the problem into a K-Nearest-Neighbour (KNN) solution to predict complementarity among millions of products in a matter of seconds.

Our work builds upon the Siamese CNN introduced by Zhao et al. (2017) by comparing Siamese CNN and Siamese LSTM models and showing how Siamese architecture can be transformed to handle massive data. Through the experiments we show that Siamese LSTM outperforms Siamese CNN in predicting complementary products using textual product attributes with an accuracy of $\sim 85\%$. We also observe that among different attributes of products, the product title produces results with a higher accuracy. Moreover, we show that we can extend the proposed Siamese LSTM approach to a KNN problem that reduces the time complexity by half. The source code of our model is available on GitHub[1].

2 Preliminary

In this section, we briefly present the SNN architecture and explain how it works. SNN (Chicco, 2021) is a twin neural network (NN) composed of two separate NNs sharing the same architecture and the same weights, with no limitation on the NN architecture (Figure 2). In other words, SNN is an NN architecture capable of learning similarity between data samples by receiving pairs of samples and analyzing the differences between their features to map them to a multidimensional feature space (Martin et al., 2017). By receiving two different inputs, the main goal of such networks is to develop similarity knowledge between the two produced outputs.

Fiaz et al. (2019) categorize SNNs in three groups based on the time of merging the layers: *late merge* (LM), *intermediate merge* (IM), and *early merge* (EM), which are shown in Figure 3. In LM, the output vectors of each network are merged at the last dense layer. IM suggests to merge the outputs of the two networks in the middle of the network and process them as one output in the last layers. In EM, the two inputs are merged right before the actual network, resulting in a single-like NN architecture.

One of the benefits of using SNN is its scalability. It processes each data sample once and then computes each pair's compatibility score, which results in a significantly lower complexity than iterating through the whole model for each pair of products. In a real-life scenario, we are usually given target products set $Q = \{q_1, q_2, \cdots, q_n\}$ and candidate set for the add-ons $C = \{c_1, c_2, \cdots, c_m\}$ where n and m have values larger than 10^6, indicating a few millions of products. Thus, to train a NN, we need to create $n \times m$ pairs of products to make input samples to the NN. However, usually, we are interested in the top k candidate add-ons for a given target product, and SNNs enable us to do so.

3 Method

We now discuss the network architectures used in our Siamese CNN and Siamese LSTM models.

[1] https://github.com/marinaangelovska /complementary_products_suggestions

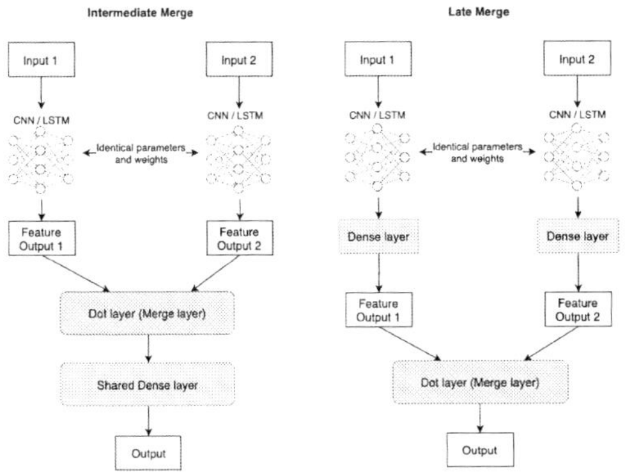

Figure 4: The difference between IM and LM in the implementation of the proposed model.

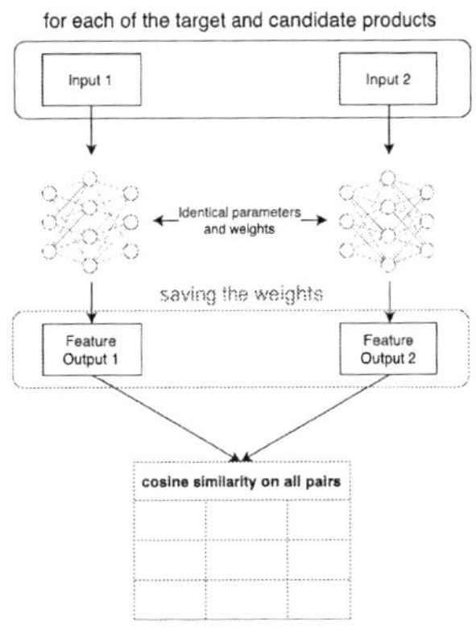

Figure 5: The place where we save the weights in the SNN architecture.

The input to these networks is the pair of any two product attributes (e.g., title and description).

CNN Architecture. The CNN network has 11 layers. The first layer is an *embedding* layer to create embeddings for each of the words in the product's attributes. The output dimension is set to 300, so that each word will be represented in 300 different features in the multi-dimensional space. Then, the *ZeroPadding1D*, the *Conv1D*, and the *MaxPooling1D* layers follow one after each other. We repeat these three layers by only reducing their filter length and pooling size. Finally, after flattening we use a *dense* layer with 100 neurons and ReLU activation. We use the *dot layer* to combine the two products from the Siamese input and compute their similarity. By normalizing the input given to the *dot layer* we compute the cosine proximity between the products.

LSTM Architecture. The LSTM network has seven layers in total. Like the CNN architecture, the *embedding layer* is the first layer with the output dimension of 300. The *LSTM* layer with 150 neurons and ReLU activation is the core part of this pipeline that learns the sequential characteristics of the words in the product titles or descriptions. After the *flatten* layer, for the same reasons as in the CNN architecture we use *dot* layer to merge the two inputs and obtain their similarity score. Then, we have a *dense* layer, which is a fully-connected layer with 100 neurons.

In both CNN and LSTM models, we use the Sigmoid activation in the output layer for the binary classification problem. Figure 4 illustrates the difference between IM and LM in our implementation. In IM, we apply the *dot* layer right after the *flatten* layer, meaning that one *dense* layer is available after the merging and before the final output layer. LM represents the architecture when the *dot* layer is implemented right before the final output layer. For comparing both Siamese architectures (IM and LM), we apply exactly the same layers just in a different order.

In both CNN or LSTM implementations, the Siamese approach can efficiently find the top K most complementary products for a given product over massive data (Martin et al., 2017). For a target product q and a candidate add-on product c from the sets of Q and C, we first generate their vector representations. However, we are only interested in the weights that the network produces before applying the dot product. The Siamese setup treats each product separately until the merge point in the model, thus for each of the products in sets Q and C, we can get the weights as shown on Figure 5. This means that the embeddings part is done only once for each product separately.

Once we have the vector representations X_Q and X_C for each product from Q and C, respectively, we can compute the similarity. From this point on, we have a KNN problem. Then, we save those weights in the forms of matrices and apply the normalized dot product between the two matrices having the weights for each target and candidate product (we calculate the *cosine similarity*), representing their complementarity.

4 Experiments

In this section, we first explain the dataset and the preprocessing step to make it ready to be given to the models, and then present the experiments.

4.1 Dataset

To train the models, we use manually labeled data points from an e-commerce company[2]. We consider the product title, description, and brand as the attributes for each product. We get pairs of positive matches for each product, which has at least one add-on, meaning that if a product has multiple add-ons, it will appear multiple times as the `MainProduct` in the dataset. Also, a product might be an add-on for multiple different main products.

Initially, there are 18346 pairs of complementary products. We assume that two products are non-complementary if they were never bought together and are not included in our initial dataset. Moreover, we want each product to have the same number of positive and negative samples, so that the model is able to generalize well. We achieve this by iterating through the add-ons list, and for each add-on, we make sure that we generate as many negative samples as there are positive.

For example, given `Product5`, which is an add-on to 10 different products, we find another 10 products for which product `Product5` will not be an add-on. After making sure that we have $50 - 50$ ratio in terms of the labels for each add-on in our dataset, we repeat the same process for the main products. In the end, we end up having 60442 total pairs of products, out of which 35978 are unique products.

Before giving the data to the models we: lowercase all letters, remove punctuation signs, digits, measurements (e.g., cm, m), and stop words. We observe that excluding the digits from the products in the dataset improves the performance by 10%. We consider 80% of the dataset for training the models and the rest for testing them. We also use 10% of the training data for validation during training. To make sure that the model's performance is calculated on new unseen data, we use *Group Shuffle Split* so that each product that will appear as an add-on in the train set will not appear as an add-on in the test set. We train the embeddings using Word2Vec (Mikolov et al., 2013) before the embedding layer in the models. Word2vec was trained using the whole corpus of titles in the category of interest. Once we have the embeddings for each of the words in the corpus, we add those weights to the weights parameter in the embedding layer.

[2]Due to the company's policy we do not reveal the company's name. It is an e-commerce company that offers various products in multiple categories.

Table 1: Comparative results showing the performance of Siamese CNN and Siamese LSTM based on the place of merging the two product outputs.

Siamese model	AUC	Accuracy
CNN - IM	72%	65%
CNN - LM	82%	78%
LSTM - IM	93%	85%
LSTM - LM	80%	75%

4.2 Results

Before conducting the experiments, we measure the impact of the merging location in the two Siamese models. Table 1 shows that Siamese CNN performs better with LM. However, Siamese LSTM performs better with IM and outperforms all other models' architectures, thus that is the architecture we will use in the rest of the experiments.

We first compare the performance of Siamese LSTM with three frequently used methods: *Random Forest (RF)*, *Single LSTM* network, and *Vanilla NN*. The RF baseline, which is used in Martin et al. (2017), combines the inputs from each sample in the dataset and tokenizes the product titles using *Bag of Words representation*. The single LSTM is the second baseline we consider.

The main difference between the single and the Siamese LSTM is in the way the input is processed. In the single LSTM model's input, we concatenate the two products' attributes in the form of `MainProductTitle_AddonProductTitle`. On the other hand, in the Siamese approach the two input products are treated separately until the moment of merging the two vector outputs. This enables us to later transform the Siamese approach to a KNN model. Lastly, we also implement and test a vanilla NN with six layers: *input*, *emedding*, *flatten*, *dense*, *dropout* and *output* layer. The *dense* layer has 100 neurons and ReLU activation.

Figure 6 shows the accuracy and AUC score for each of these models. Although Siamese LSTM and the Single LSTM perform with the same accuracy, Siamese LSTM can be transformed to a KNN model and used with massive data. To pair 13000 unique products from the test dataset with each other, we would get roughly $170M$ pairs of products for which we want to know their complementary relationship. However, in this work, due to the hardware limitations, we only take $1M$ pairs

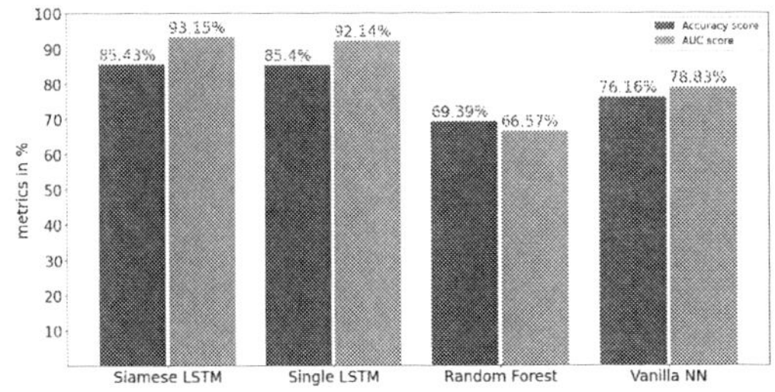

Figure 6: Comparative results showing the accuracy and AUC for Siamese LSTM, Single LSTM, Vanilla NN and Random Forest.

Table 2: Comparing the time needed for predicting complementarity among $1M$ pairs of products and the time complexity for creating the embeddings in the NN.

Model	Prediction time	Time complexity
Single LSTM	11min	$O(N^2)$
Siamese LSTM	8min	$O(N^2)$
Transformed Siamese LSTM	10sec	$O(N)$

of products in the following experiments. Both, the single and Siamese LSTM network are traversed $1M$ times, once for creating the embeddings for each pair of products.

The Siamese LSTM has a slightly better time performance due to the ability to learn faster. In the transformed Siamese LSTM, we calculate the embeddings for each product only once by using the Siamese LSTM model and we save those embeddings before the *dot* layer. This means that the Siamese LSTM will be traversed only 13000 times, once for each product. Once we have these embeddings for each of the 13000 products, the complementarity score for the $1M$ pairs is calculated very fast, as we do simple matrix multiplication operation using *cosine similarity*.

Here we use cosine similarity as it is basically a normalized dot product. If we were using single LSTM approach, we would not have been able to achieve this because in that setup we cannot get embeddings for a single product, but only for a pair of products. Table 2 shows the time analysis for the three approaches, where N represents the number of unique products.

Using the transformed Siamese LSTM (the KNN approach), we compute the complementarity score between all possible products from the test set within seconds. Table 3 shows the complementarity score (cosine similarity) of the top five add-ons

Table 3: Complementarity score for five add-on suggestions using the the initial Siamese LSTM model and the transformed Siamese LSTM.

Target product: 	Suggested add-on products		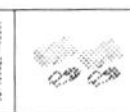	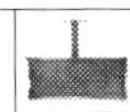	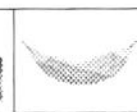	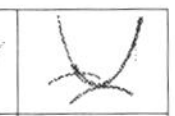
	Transformed Siamese LSTM	83%	72%	69%	68%	66%

Table 4: Comparing accuracy, AUC score and training time for Siamese LSTM using different product attributes when the training was done on 10 epochs.

Product attribute(s)	Accuracy	AUC	Training time
Title	85%	93%	13min
Title + Description	89%	95%	58min
Description	72%	81%	58min
Title + Brand	80%	83%	14min

suggested by the KNN approach for a randomly selected product. The third and fifth products from Table 3 are newly detected add-ons, while the second product is a correctly detected add-on already present in the ground truth. The first and fourth products are substitutes to the target product, hence false positives. Our KNN approach suggests substitute products because, in some cases, in the ground truth, the add-on products can be similar/substitute products to the target product. Ideally, we would not want to have this in our training set.

Table 4 shows the results from including different textual attributes (e.g., the title, the description, and the brand) in the Siamese LSTM. Although the description, as an addition to the title, increases the accuracy and AUC score, we conclude that speed-accuracy trade-off needs to be made since including the description slows down the training process for about four times.

5 Related Work

We split the available methods for measuring similarity and complementarity into two groups: *unsupervised* and *supervised* learning approaches.

One of the most common unsupervised learning methods using co-purchase history is the *Frequent Pattern (FP) Growth* (Han et al., 2004) algorithm. Other groups of research focus on using the paradigm of *Word2Vec* (Mikolov et al., 2013). Grbovic et al. (2015) propose a *Prod2Vec* model that learns product representations from sequences of past orders by considering the purchase sequence as a sentence and products within the sequence as words. The *Meta-Prod2Vec* model by Vasile et al. (2016) extends the *Prod2Vec* model by taking into account products' metadata. The *BB2Vec* model (Trofimov, 2018) eliminates the cold-start problem by using browsing and purchase session data, and is a combination of several *Prod2Vec* models.

Zhao et al. (2017) introduce the Siamese CNN approach, which this work is based on. Other supervised learning approaches focus on image data, text attributes, or both. *SCEPTRE* is a model introduced by McAuley et al. (2015), and its main goal is topic modeling using Latent Dirichlet Allocation (LDA) (Blei et al., 2003) and edge detection of related topics. Zhang et al. (2018) suggest *ENCORE*, a three-step algorithm: (i) detecting the complementarity among products based on their embedding distances of image and text attributes, (ii) taking into account user preferences for detecting validity of each complementarity distance, and (iii) training a NN with the outcomes of the previous two steps (Yu et al., 2019). Kalchbrenner et al. (2014) explore Dynamic CNN (DCNN) for semantic modeling of sentences using CNNs.

6 Conclusion

In this paper, we present a supervised learning approach for complementary product recommendations. We take manually labelled pairs of complementary products from an e-commerce company and propose a scalable solution. To this end, we design and compare Siamese CNN and Siamese LSTM architectures to create embeddings for products' features and compute a complementarity score for a given pair of products. We conclude that Siamese LSTM outperforms Siamese CNN and its baselines. We show that the product title is the most valuable attribute. Lastly, we show that our model can be transformed into a KNN solution to handle big data scenarios.

This work can be extended by introducing user click history to include items that have been viewed in the same session (items which are very similar) in the negative training sample, thus teaching the model the difference between substitute and complementary relationships. Furthermore, including more product attributes (such as the price or subcategory) could improve the model's performance.

References

D. Blei et al. 2003. Latent dirichlet allocation. *the Journal of machine Learning research*, 3:993–1022.

F. Vasile et al. 2016. Meta-prod2vec: Product embeddings using side-information for recommendation. In *Proceedings of the 10th ACM Conference on Recommender Systems*, pages 225–232.

H. Yu et al. 2019. Complementary recommendations: A brief survey. In *2019 International Conference on High Performance Big Data and Intelligent Systems (HPBD&IS)*, pages 73–78. IEEE.

J. Han et al. 2004. Mining frequent patterns without candidate generation: A frequent-pattern tree approach. *Data mining and knowledge discovery*, 8(1):53–87.

J. McAuley et al. 2015. Inferring networks of substitutable and complementary products. In *Proceedings of the 21th ACM SIGKDD international conference on knowledge discovery and data mining*, pages 785–794.

K. Martin et al. 2017. A convolutional siamese network for developing similarity knowledge in the selfback dataset. CEUR Workshop Proceedings.

K. Zhao et al. 2017. Deep style match for complementary recommendation. In *AAAI Workshops*.

M. Grbovic et al. 2015. E-commerce in your inbox: Product recommendations at scale. In *Proceedings of the 21th ACM SIGKDD international conference on knowledge discovery and data mining*, pages 1809–1818.

M. Fiaz et al. 2019. Deep siamese networks toward robust visual tracking. In *Visual Object Tracking with Deep Neural Networks*. IntechOpen.

N. Kalchbrenner et al. 2014. A convolutional neural network for modelling sentences. In *52nd Annual Meeting of the Association for Computational Linguistics*. Association for Computational Linguistics.

T. Mikolov et al. 2013. Efficient estimation of word representations in vector space. pages 1–12.

Y. Zhang et al. 2018. Quality-aware neural complementary item recommendation. In *Proceedings of the 12th ACM Conference on Recommender Systems*, pages 77–85.

Davide Chicco. 2021. Siamese neural networks: An overview. *Artificial Neural Networks*, pages 73–94.

I. Trofimov. 2018. Inferring complementary products from baskets and browsing sessions. *arXiv preprint arXiv:1809.09621*.

Contrasting distinct structured views to learn sentence embeddings

Antoine Simoulin[1,2] **Benoît Crabbé**[1]
[1]University of Paris, LLF [2]Quantmetry
asimoulin@quantmetry.com
benoit.crabbe@linguist.univ-paris-diderot.fr

Abstract

We propose a self-supervised method that builds sentence embeddings from the combination of diverse explicit syntactic structures of a sentence. We assume structure is crucial to building consistent representations as we expect sentence meaning to be a function of both syntax and semantic aspects. In this perspective, we hypothesize that some linguistic representations might be better adapted given the considered task or sentence. We, therefore, propose to learn individual representation functions for different syntactic frameworks jointly. Again, by hypothesis, all such functions should encode similar semantic information differently and consequently, be complementary for building better sentential semantic embeddings. To assess such hypothesis, we propose an original contrastive multi-view framework that induces an explicit interaction between models during the training phase. We make experiments combining various structures such as dependency, constituency, or sequential schemes. Our results outperform comparable methods on several tasks from standard sentence embedding benchmarks.

1 Introduction

We propose a self-supervised method that builds sentence embeddings from the combination of diverse explicit syntactic structures. The method aims at improving the ability of models to yield compositional sentence embeddings. We evaluate the embedding potential to solve downstream tasks.

Building generic sentence embeddings remains an open problem. Many training methods have been explored: generating past and previous sentences (Kiros et al., 2015; Hill et al., 2016), discriminating context sentences (Logeswaran and Lee, 2018), predicting specific relations between pairs of sentences (Conneau et al., 2017; Nie et al., 2019). While all these methods propose efficient training objectives, they all rely on a similar Recurrent Neural Network (RNN) as encoder architecture. Nonetheless, model architectures have been subject to extensive work as well (Tai et al., 2015; Zhao et al., 2015; Arora et al., 2017; Lin et al., 2017), and in supervised frameworks, many encoder structures outperform standard RNN networks.

We hypothesize structure is a crucial element to perform compositional knowledge. In particular, the heterogeneity of performances across models and tasks makes us assume that some structures may be better adapted for a given example or task. Therefore, combining diverse structures should be more robust for tasks requiring complex word composition to derive their meaning. Hence, we aim here to evaluate the potential benefit from interactions between pairs of encoders. In particular, we propose a training method for which distinct encoders are learned jointly. We conjecture this association might improve our embeddings' power of generalization and propose an experimental setup to corroborate our hypothesis.

We take inspiration from multi-view learning, which is successfully applied in a variety of domains. In such a framework, the model learns representations by aligning separate observations of the same object. Such observations are referred to as *views*. In our case, we consider a view for a given sentence as the association of the plain sentence with a syntactic structure.

As proposed in image processing (Tian et al., 2019; Bachman et al., 2019), we aim to align the different views using a contrastive learning framework. Indeed, contrastive learning is broadly used in NLP (Mikolov et al., 2013b,a; Logeswaran and Lee, 2018). We intend to enhance the sentence embedding framework proposed in Logeswaran and Lee (2018) with a multi-view paradigm.

Combining different structural views has already been proven to be successful in many NLP applica-

Proceedings of the 16th Conference of the European Chapter of the Associationfor Computational Linguistics: Student Research Workshop, pages 71–79
April 19 - 23, 2021. ©2021 Association for Computational Linguistics

tions. Kong and Zhou (2011) provide a heuristic to combine dependency and constituency analysis for coreference resolution. Zhou et al. (2016); Ahmed et al. (2019) combine Tree LSTM and standard sequential LSTM with a cross-attention method and observe improvements on a semantic textual similarity task. Chen et al. (2017a) combine CNN and Tree LSTM using attention methods and outperform both models taken separately on a sentiment classification task. Finally, Chen et al. (2017b) combine sequential LSTM and Tree LSTM for natural language inference tasks.

The novelty here is to combine distinct structured models to build standalone sentence embeddings, which has not yet been explored. This paradigm benefits from several structural advantages. It pairs nicely with contrastive learning, as already mentioned. It might thus be trained in a self-supervised manner that does not require data annotation. Moreover, contrary to models presented in Section 2.2, our method is not specific to a certain kind of encoder architecture. It does not require, for example, the use of attention layers or tree-structured models. Our setup could therefore be extended with any encoding function. Finally, our training method induces an interaction between models during inference and, paramountly, during the training phase.

2 Method

Given a sentence s, the model aims at discriminating the sentences s^+ in the neighborhood of s from sentences s^- outside of this neighborhood. This is contrastive learning (Section 2.1). The representation of each sentence is acquired by using multiple views (Section 2.2).

2.1 Contrastive learning

Contrastive learning is successfully applied in a variety of domains including audio (van den Oord et al., 2018), image (Wu et al., 2018; Tian et al., 2019), video or natural language processing for word embedding (Mikolov et al., 2013b) or sentence embedding (Logeswaran and Lee, 2018). Some mathematical foundations are detailed in (Saunshi et al., 2019). The idea supposes to build a dataset such that each sample x is combined with another sample x^+, which is somehow *close*. For word or sentence embeddings, the close samples are the words or the sentences appearing in the given textual context. For image processing, close samples might be two different parts of the same image. Systems are trained to bring close samples together while dispersing negative examples.

In particular, a sentence embedding framework is proposed by Logeswaran and Lee (2018). The method takes inspiration from the distributional hypothesis successfully applied for word, but this time, to identify context sentences. The network is trained using a contrastive method. Given a sentence s, a corresponding context sentence s^+ and a set of K negative samples $s_1^- \cdots s_K^-$, the training objective is to maximize the probability of discriminate the correct sentence among negative samples: $p(s^+|S)$ with $S = \{s, s^+, s_1^- \cdots s_K^-\}$.

The algorithm architecture used to estimate p is close to *word2vec* (Mikolov et al., 2013b,a). As illustrated in Figure 1, two sentences encoders f and g are defined and the conditional probability is estimated as follow[1]:

$$p(s^+|S) = \frac{e^{c\left(f(s),g(s^+)\right)}}{e^{c(f(s),g(s^+))} + \sum_{i=1}^{N} e^{c\left(f(s),g(s_i^-)\right)}}$$

At inference time, the sentence representation is obtained as the concatenation of the two encoders f and g such as $s \rightarrow [f(s); g(s)]$, as illustrated in Figure 2. In Logeswaran and Lee (2018), f and g use the same RNN encoder. However, the authors observe that the encoders might learn redundant features. To limit this effect, they propose to use a distinct set of embeddings for each encoder.

We propose addressing this aspect by enhancing the method with a multi-view framework and using a distinct structured model for the encoders f and g. We hypothesize that some structures may be better adapted for a given example or task. For example, dependency parsing usually sets the verb as the root node. Whereas in constituency parsing, subject and verb are often the right and left child from the root node. Therefore, the combination of different structures should be more robust for tasks requiring complex word composition and be less sensitive to lexical variations. Consequently, we propose a training procedure that allows the model to benefit from the interaction of various syntactic structures. The choice for the encoder architecture is detailed in the following section.

[1] Logeswaran and Lee (2018) simply use an inner product for c such as $c(x, y) = x^T y$. In our case, as the encoders f and g are distincts, we choose a bilinear function defined as $c(x, y) = x^T W y$ (Tschannen et al., 2020).

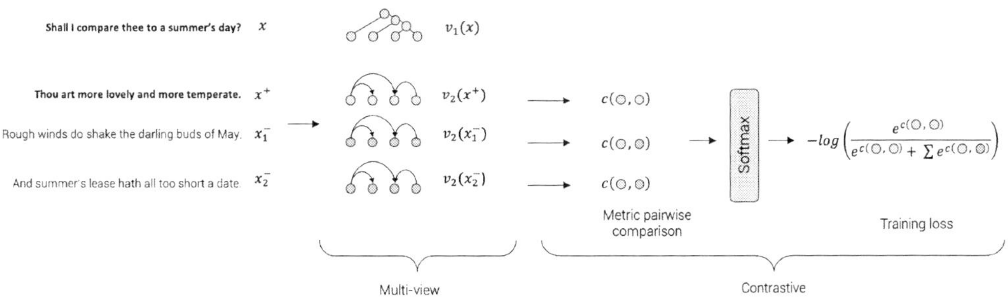

Figure 1: **Contrastive training method**. The objective is to reconstruct the storyline. Sentences are presented in their original order. Given an anchor sentence x, the model should identify the context sentence x^+ out of negative samples x_1^-, x_2^-. Sentences are encoded using separate views, which are composed within a pairwise distance matrix.

2.2 Language views

Multi-view aims as learning representations from data represented by multiple independent sets of features. As depicted in Section 1, we generalize the notion of view for a sentence as the application of a specific syntactic framework. For each view, we use an ad-hoc algorithm that maps the structured sentence into an embedding space.

We consider structures including sequence and trees detailed below. Although equivalences might be derived between the two representations schemes, we hypothesize that, in our context, the corresponding sequence of operations might allow capturing rather distinct linguistic properties. The various models may, therefore, be complementary and their combination allows for more fine-grained analysis.

Vanilla GRU (SEQ) assumes a sequential structure where each word depends on the previous words in the sentence. The framework is a bidirectional sequential GRU (Cho et al., 2014). The concatenation of the forward and backward last hidden state of the model is used as sequence embedding.

Dependency tree (DEP) In the dependency tree model, words are connected through dependency edges. A word might have an arbitrary number of dependents. The sentence can be represented as a tree where nodes corresponding to words and edges indicate whether or not the words are connected in the dependency tree. In our case, the dependency tree is obtained using the deep biaffine parser from Dozat and Manning (2017). The details of the parsing operations are detailed in Appendix A.1. For this view, we compute sentence embeddings with the Child-Sum Tree LSTM model described in Tai et al. (2015): Each node is assigned an embedding given its dependent with a recursive function. The recursive node function is derived from standard LSTM formulations but adapted for tree inputs. In particular, the hidden state is computed as the sum of all children hidden states. Here, we consider an Attentive Child-Sum Tree LSTM and we compute $\tilde{h}_j$ as the weighted sum of children vectors as in Zhou et al. (2016). The computation of $\tilde{h}_j$ in Equation 1 allows the model to filter semantically less relevant children.

$$\tilde{h}_j = \sum_{k \in C(j)} \alpha_{kj} h_k \quad (1)$$

With $C(j)$, the set of children of node j. All equations are detailed in Tai et al. (2015). The parameters α_{kj} are attention weights computed using a *soft attention layer*. Given a node j, we consider $h_1, h_2, \ldots, h_n$ the corresponding children hidden states. the soft attention layer produces a weight α_k for each child's hidden state. We did not use any external query to compute the attention but instead use a projection from the current node embedding. The attention equations are detailed below:

$$q_j = W^{(q)} x_j + b^{(q)}; \quad p_k = W^{(p)} h_k + b^{(p)} \quad (2)$$

$$a_{kj} = \frac{q_j \cdot p_k^{\intercal}}{\|q_j\|_2 \cdot \|p_k\|_2} \quad (3)$$

$$\alpha_{kj} = \text{softmax}_k(a_{1j} \cdots a_{nj}) \quad (4)$$

The embedding at the root of the tree is used as the sentence embedding as the Tree LSTM model computes representations bottom up.

Constituency tree (CONST) Constituent analysis describes the sentence as a nested multi-word structure. In this framework, words are grouped recursively in constituents. In the resulting tree, only leaf nodes correspond to words, while internal nodes encode recursively word sequences. The structure is obtained using the constituency neural parser from Kitaev and Klein (2018). The framework is associated with the N-Ary Tree LSTM, which is defined in Tai et al. (2015). Similarly to the original article, we binarize the trees to ensure that every node has exactly two dependents. The binarization is performed using a left markovization and unary productions are collapsed in a single node. Again the representation is computed bottom-up and the embedding of the tree root node is used as sentence embedding. The equations detailed in Tai et al. (2015) make the distinction between right and left nodes. Therefore we do not propose to enhance the original architecture with a weighted sum as on the DEP view.

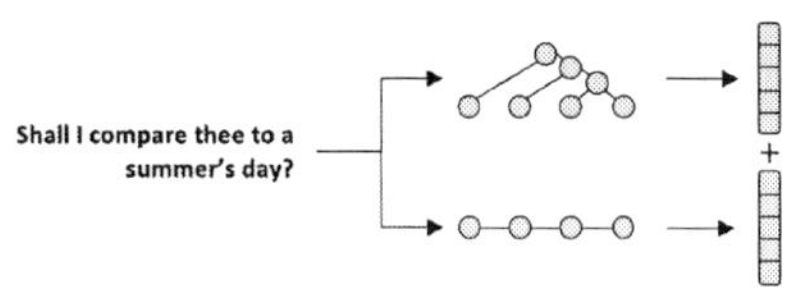

Figure 2: **Multi-view sentence embedding**. At inference, embeddings are the concatenation from both views.

3 Experiments

3.1 Training configuration

We train our models on the UMBC dataset [2,3] (Han et al., 2013). We limited our corpus to the first 40M sentences from the tokenized corpus. Indeed, Logeswaran and Lee (2018) already analyze the effect of the corpus size, and we focus here on the impact of our multi-view setting. We build batches from successive sentences. Given a sentence in a batch, other sentences not in the context are considered as negatives samples as presented in Section 2.1. Hyperparameters of the models such as the hidden size and the optimization procedure such as learning rate are detailed in Appendix A.2.

3.2 Evaluation on downstream tasks

As usual for models aiming to build generic sentence embeddings (Kiros et al., 2015; Hill et al., 2016; Arora et al., 2017; Conneau et al., 2017; Logeswaran and Lee, 2018; Nie et al., 2019), we use tasks from the SentEval benchmark (Conneau and Kiela, 2018)[4]. SentEval is specifically designed to assess the quality of the embeddings themselves rather than the quality of a model specifically targeting a downstream task, as is the case for the GLUE and SuperGLUE benchmarks (Wang et al., 2019b,a). Indeed, the evaluation protocol prevents for fine-tuning the model during inference and the architecture to tackle the downstream tasks is kept minimal. Moreover, the embedding is kept identical for all tasks, thus assessing their properties of generalization.

Therefore, classification tasks from the SentEval benchmark are usually used for evaluation of sentence representations (Conneau and Kiela, 2018): the tasks include sentiment and subjectivity analysis (**MR, CR, SUBJ, MPQA**), question type classification (**TREC**), paraphrase identification (**MRPC**) and semantic relatedness (**SICK-R**). Contrasting the results of our model on this set of tasks will help to better understand its properties.

The MR, CR, SUBJ, MPQA tasks are binary classification tasks with no pre-defined train-test split. We therefore use a 10-fold cross validation. For the other tasks we use the proposed train/dev/test splits. We follow the linear evaluation protocol of Kiros et al. (2015), where a logistic regression or softmax classifier is trained on top of sentence representations. The dev set is used for choosing the regularization parameter and results are reported on the test set.

For the vocabulary, we follow the setup proposed in Kiros et al. (2015); Logeswaran and Lee (2018) and we train two models in each configuration. One initialized with pre-trained embedding vectors. The vectors are not updated during training and the vocabulary includes the top 2M cased words from the 300-dimensional GloVe vectors[5] (Pennington et al., 2014). The other is limited to 50K words initialized with a Xavier distribution and updated during training. For inference, the vocabulary is expanded to 2M words using a linear projection.

[2] `https://ebiquity.umbc.edu/blogger/2013/05/01/umbc-webbase-corpus-of-3b-english-words/`

[3] The bookcorpus introduced in Zhu et al. (2015) and traditionally used for sentence embedding is no longer distributed for copyright reasons. Therefore, we prefer a corpus freely available. The impact of the training dataset choice is analyzed in Appendix A.3.

[4] Senteval is posterior to most of the references. However, these studies do evaluate on tasks later included in the benchmark.

[5] `https://nlp.stanford.edu/projects/glove/`

Model	Dim	Hrs	MR	CR	SUBJ	MPQA	TREC	MRPC Acc	MRPC F1	SICK-R r	SICK-R ρ	SICK-R MSE
Context sentences prediction												
FastSent	≤ 500	2	70.8	78.4	88.7	80.6	76.8	72.2	80.3	—	—	—
FastSent + AE	≤ 500	2	71.8	76.7	88.8	81.5	80.4	71.2	79.1	—	—	—
Skipthought	4800	336	76.5	80.1	93.6	87.1	92.2	73.0	82.0	85.8	79.2	26.9
Skipthought + LN	4800	672	79.4	83.1	93.7	89.3	—	—	—	85.8	78.8	27.0
Quickthoughts	4800	11	**80.4**	**85.2**	**93.9**	**89.4**	**92.8**	**76.9**	**84.0**	**86.8**	**80.1**	**25.6**
Sentence relations prediction												
InferSent	4096	—	**81.1**	**86.3**	92.4	90.2	88.2	**76.2**	**83.1**	**88.4**	—	—
DisSent Books 5	4096	—	80.2	85.4	93.2	90.2	91.2	76.1	—	84.5	—	—
DisSent Books 8	4096	—	79.8	85.0	**93.4**	**90.5**	**93.0**	76.1	—	85.4	—	—
Pre-trained transformers												
BERT-base [CLS]	768	96	78.7	84.9	94.2	88.2	**91.4**	71.1	—	75.7†	—	—
BERT-base [NLI]	768	96	**83.6**	**89.4**	**94.4**	**89.9**	89.6	**76.0**	—	**84.4**†	—	—
Our models (GloVe & Pretrained Embeddings)												
SEQ, CONST†	4800	41	79.8	82.9	94.6	88.5	90.4	76.4	83.7	86.1	78.9	26.3
DEP, SEQ†	4800	27	79.7	82.2	94.4	88.6	91.0	**77.9**	**84.4**	86.6	79.8	25.5
DEP, CONST†	4800	39	**80.7**	**83.6**	**94.9**	**89.2**	**92.6**	76.8	83.6	**87.0**	**80.3**	**24.8**

Table 1: **SentEval Task Results Using Fixed Sentence Encoder.** We divided the table into sections. The first range of models is directly comparable to our model as the training objective is to identify context sentences. The second section objective is to identify the correct relationship between a pair of sentences. The third section reports pre-trained transformers based-models. The last section reports the results from our models. FastSent is reported from Hill et al. (2016). Skipthoughts results from Kiros et al. (2015) Skipthoughts + LN which includes layer normalization method from Ba et al. (2016). We considered the Quickthoughts results (Logeswaran and Lee, 2018) with a pre-training on the bookcorpus dataset. DisSent and Infersent are reported from Nie et al. (2019) and Conneau et al. (2017) respectively. Pre-trained transformers results are reported from Reimers and Gurevych (2019). The **Hrs** column indicates indicative training time, the **Dim** column corresponds to the sentence embedding dimension. † indicates models that we had to re-train. Best results in each section are shown in **bold**, best results overall are underlined. Performance for **SICK-R** results are reported by convention as ρ and $r \times 100$.

3.3 Results analysis

We compare the properties of distinct views combination on downstream tasks. Results are compared with state of the art methods in Table 1. The first set of methods (*Context sentences prediction*) are trained to reconstruct books storyline. The second set of models (*Sentence relations prediction*) is pre-trained on a supervised task. Infersent (Conneau et al., 2017) is trained on the SNLI dataset, which proposes to predict the entailment relation between two sentences. DisSent (Nie et al., 2019) proposes a generalization of the method and builds a corpus of sentence pairs with more possible relations between them. Finally, we include models relying on transformer architectures (Pre-trained transformers) for comparison. In particular, BERT-base model and a BERT-model fine-tuned on the SNLI dataset (Reimers and Gurevych, 2019). In Table 1, we observe that our models expressing a combination of views such as (DEP, SEQ) or (DEP, CONST) give better results than the use of the same view (SEQ, SEQ) used in Quick-Thought model. It seems that the entanglement of views benefits the sentence embedding properties. In particular, we obtain state-of-the-art results for almost every metric from **MRPC** and **SICK-R** tasks, which focus on paraphrase identification. For the **MRPC** task, we gain a full point in accuracy and outperform BERT models. We hypothesize structure is important for achieving this task, especially as the dataset is composed of rather long sentences. The **SICK-R** dataset is structurally designed to discriminate models that rely on compositional operations.

This also explains the score improvement on this task. Tasks such as **MR**, **CR** or **MPQA** consist in sentiment or subjectivity analysis. We hypothesize that our models are less relevant in this case: such tasks are less sensitive to structure and depend more on individual word or lexical variation.

3.4 Impact of the multi-view

We aim to measure the impact of multi-view specifically. Table 2 compares all possible view pairs out of DEP, CONST and SEQ views. For each multi-view model, we report the average score from SentEval tasks[6]. The first section of the Table corresponds to *single-view* models, for which both views from the pair are identical. The second section reports multi-view models.

Multi-view models outperform those using a single view. Given our experiment, it is advantageous to use multiple views instead of one. It also confirms our hypothesis that combining multiple structured models or views yield richer sentence embeddings.

Model	Avg. SentEval Score
Single-view models	
CONST, CONST	84.4
DEP, DEP	84.6
SEQ, SEQ	84.9
Multi-view models	
SEQ, CONST	85.1
SEQ, DEP	85.3
DEP, CONST	**86.0**

Table 2: **Impact of the multi-view.** The first section corresponds to single-view setups for which f and g are the same views. The second section reports multi-view models. For each model, we report the average score on the SentEval benchmark.

4 Conclusion and future work

Inspired from linguistic insights and supervised learning, we hypothesize that structure is a central element to build sentence embeddings. The novelty here is detailed in Section 2 and consists in jointly learning structured models in a contrastive framework. In Section 3 we evaluate the standalone sentence embeddings and use them as a feature for the dedicated SentEval benchmark. We obtain state-of-the-art results on tasks which are expected, by hypothesis, to be more sensitive to sentence structure. We show in Section 3.4 that multi-view embeddings yield better downstream task results. Our setup confirms our hypothesis that combining diverse structures should be more robust for tasks requiring to perform complex compositional knowledge.

[6]We scale all metrics as percentages. In particular, we use 100 - MSE for the **SICK-R** task. The final score corresponds to the average of all tasks. We average the scores for tasks with multiple metrics (**MRPC** and **SICK-R**).

References

Mahtab Ahmed, Muhammad Rifayat Samee, and Robert E. Mercer. 2019. Improving tree-lstm with tree attention. In *13th IEEE International Conference on Semantic Computing, ICSC 2019, Newport Beach, CA, USA, January 30 - February 1, 2019*, pages 247–254.

Sanjeev Arora, Yingyu Liang, and Tengyu Ma. 2017. A simple but tough-to-beat baseline for sentence embeddings. In *5th International Conference on Learning Representations, ICLR 2017, Toulon, France, April 24-26, 2017, Conference Track Proceedings*.

Lei Jimmy Ba, Jamie Ryan Kiros, and Geoffrey E. Hinton. 2016. Layer normalization. *CoRR*, abs/1607.06450.

Philip Bachman, R. Devon Hjelm, and William Buchwalter. 2019. Learning representations by maximizing mutual information across views. In *Advances in Neural Information Processing Systems 32: Annual Conference on Neural Information Processing Systems 2019, NeurIPS 2019, 8-14 December 2019, Vancouver, BC, Canada*, pages 15509–15519.

Liu Chen, Guangping Zeng, Qingchuan Zhang, and Xingyu Chen. 2017a. Tree-lstm guided attention pooling of DCNN for semantic sentence modeling. In *5G for Future Wireless Networks - First International Conference, 5GWN 2017, Beijing, China, April 21-23, 2017, Proceedings*, pages 52–59.

Qian Chen, Xiaodan Zhu, Zhen-Hua Ling, Si Wei, Hui Jiang, and Diana Inkpen. 2017b. Enhanced LSTM for natural language inference. In *Proceedings of the 55th Annual Meeting of the Association for Computational Linguistics, ACL 2017, Vancouver, Canada, July 30 - August 4, Volume 1: Long Papers*, pages 1657–1668.

Kyunghyun Cho, Bart van Merrienboer, Çaglar Gülçehre, Dzmitry Bahdanau, Fethi Bougares, Holger Schwenk, and Yoshua Bengio. 2014. Learning phrase representations using RNN encoder-decoder for statistical machine translation. In *Proceedings of the 2014 Conference on Empirical Methods in Natural Language Processing, EMNLP 2014, October 25-29, 2014, Doha, Qatar, A meeting of SIGDAT, a Special Interest Group of the ACL*, pages 1724–1734. ACL.

Alexis Conneau and Douwe Kiela. 2018. Senteval: An evaluation toolkit for universal sentence representations. In *Proceedings of the Eleventh International Conference on Language Resources and Evaluation, LREC 2018, Miyazaki, Japan, May 7-12, 2018*.

Alexis Conneau, Douwe Kiela, Holger Schwenk, Loïc Barrault, and Antoine Bordes. 2017. Supervised learning of universal sentence representations from natural language inference data. In *Proceedings of the 2017 Conference on Empirical Methods in Natural Language Processing, EMNLP 2017, Copenhagen, Denmark, September 9-11, 2017*, pages 670–680.

Timothy Dozat and Christopher D. Manning. 2017. Deep biaffine attention for neural dependency parsing. In *5th International Conference on Learning Representations, ICLR 2017, Toulon, France, April 24-26, 2017, Conference Track Proceedings*.

Steffen Eger, Andreas Rücklé, and Iryna Gurevych. 2019. Pitfalls in the evaluation of sentence embeddings. In *Proceedings of the 4th Workshop on Representation Learning for NLP, RepL4NLP@ACL 2019, Florence, Italy, August 2, 2019*, pages 55–60. Association for Computational Linguistics.

Lushan Han, Abhay L. Kashyap, Tim Finin, James Mayfield, and Jonathan Weese. 2013. Umbc_ebiquity-core: Semantic textual similarity systems. In *Proceedings of the Second Joint Conference on Lexical and Computational Semantics, *SEM 2013, June 13-14, 2013, Atlanta, Georgia, USA*, pages 44–52.

Felix Hill, Kyunghyun Cho, and Anna Korhonen. 2016. Learning distributed representations of sentences from unlabelled data. In *NAACL HLT 2016, The 2016 Conference of the North American Chapter of the Association for Computational Linguistics: Human Language Technologies, San Diego California, USA, June 12-17, 2016*, pages 1367–1377.

Ryan Kiros, Yukun Zhu, Ruslan Salakhutdinov, Richard S. Zemel, Raquel Urtasun, Antonio Torralba, and Sanja Fidler. 2015. Skip-thought vectors. In *Advances in Neural Information Processing Systems 28: Annual Conference on Neural Information Processing Systems 2015, December 7-12, 2015, Montreal, Quebec, Canada*, pages 3294–3302.

Nikita Kitaev and Dan Klein. 2018. Constituency parsing with a self-attentive encoder. In *Proceedings of the 56th Annual Meeting of the Association for Computational Linguistics, ACL 2018, Melbourne, Australia, July 15-20, 2018, Volume 1: Long Papers*, pages 2676–2686.

Fang Kong and Guodong Zhou. 2011. Combining dependency and constituent-based syntactic information for anaphoricity determination in coreference resolution. In *Proceedings of the 25th Pacific Asia Conference on Language, Information and Computation, PACLIC 25, Singapore, December 16-18, 2011*, pages 410–419.

Zhouhan Lin, Minwei Feng, Cícero Nogueira dos Santos, Mo Yu, Bing Xiang, Bowen Zhou, and Yoshua Bengio. 2017. A structured self-attentive sentence embedding. In *5th International Conference on Learning Representations, ICLR 2017, Toulon, France, April 24-26, 2017, Conference Track Proceedings*.

Lajanugen Logeswaran and Honglak Lee. 2018. An efficient framework for learning sentence representations. In *6th International Conference on Learning Representations, ICLR 2018, Vancouver, BC, Canada, April 30 - May 3, 2018, Conference Track Proceedings*.

Tomas Mikolov, Kai Chen, Greg Corrado, and Jeffrey Dean. 2013a. Efficient estimation of word representations in vector space. In *1st International Conference on Learning Representations, ICLR 2013, Scottsdale, Arizona, USA, May 2-4, 2013, Workshop Track Proceedings*.

Tomas Mikolov, Ilya Sutskever, Kai Chen, Gregory S. Corrado, and Jeffrey Dean. 2013b. Distributed representations of words and phrases and their compositionality. In *Advances in Neural Information Processing Systems 26: 27th Annual Conference on Neural Information Processing Systems 2013. Proceedings of a meeting held December 5-8, 2013, Lake Tahoe, Nevada, United States.*, pages 3111–3119.

Allen Nie, Erin Bennett, and Noah Goodman. 2019. Dissent: Learning sentence representations from explicit discourse relations. In *Proceedings of the 57th Conference of the Association for Computational Linguistics, ACL 2019, Florence, Italy, July 28- August 2, 2019, Volume 1: Long Papers*, pages 4497–4510.

Aäron van den Oord, Yazhe Li, and Oriol Vinyals. 2018. Representation learning with contrastive predictive coding. *CoRR*, abs/1807.03748.

Jeffrey Pennington, Richard Socher, and Christopher D. Manning. 2014. Glove: Global vectors for word representation. In *Proceedings of the 2014 Conference on Empirical Methods in Natural Language Processing, EMNLP 2014, October 25-29, 2014, Doha, Qatar, A meeting of SIGDAT, a Special Interest Group of the ACL*, pages 1532–1543.

Nils Reimers and Iryna Gurevych. 2019. Sentence-BERT: Sentence embeddings using Siamese BERT-networks. In *Proceedings of the 2019 Conference on Empirical Methods in Natural Language Processing and the 9th International Joint Conference on Natural Language Processing (EMNLP-IJCNLP)*.

Nikunj Saunshi, Orestis Plevrakis, Sanjeev Arora, Mikhail Khodak, and Hrishikesh Khandeparkar. 2019. A theoretical analysis of contrastive unsupervised representation learning. In *Proceedings of the 36th International Conference on Machine Learning, ICML 2019, 9-15 June 2019, Long Beach, California, USA*, pages 5628–5637.

Kai Sheng Tai, Richard Socher, and Christopher D. Manning. 2015. Improved semantic representations from tree-structured long short-term memory networks. In *Proceedings of the 53rd Annual Meeting of the Association for Computational Linguistics and the 7th International Joint Conference on Natural Language Processing of the Asian Federation of Natural Language Processing, ACL 2015, July 26-31, 2015, Beijing, China, Volume 1: Long Papers*, pages 1556–1566.

Yonglong Tian, Dilip Krishnan, and Phillip Isola. 2019. Contrastive multiview coding. *CoRR*, abs/1906.05849.

Michael Tschannen, Josip Djolonga, Paul K. Rubenstein, Sylvain Gelly, and Mario Lucic. 2020. On mutual information maximization for representation learning. In *8th International Conference on Learning Representations, ICLR 2020, Addis Ababa, Ethiopia, April 26-30, 2020*. OpenReview.net.

Alex Wang, Yada Pruksachatkun, Nikita Nangia, Amanpreet Singh, Julian Michael, Felix Hill, Omer Levy, and Samuel R. Bowman. 2019a. Superglue: A stickier benchmark for general-purpose language understanding systems. In *Advances in Neural Information Processing Systems 32: Annual Conference on Neural Information Processing Systems 2019, NeurIPS 2019, 8-14 December 2019, Vancouver, BC, Canada*, pages 3261–3275.

Alex Wang, Amanpreet Singh, Julian Michael, Felix Hill, Omer Levy, and Samuel R. Bowman. 2019b. GLUE: A multi-task benchmark and analysis platform for natural language understanding. In *7th International Conference on Learning Representations, ICLR 2019, New Orleans, LA, USA, May 6-9, 2019*.

John Wieting and Douwe Kiela. 2019. No training required: Exploring random encoders for sentence classification. In *7th International Conference on Learning Representations, ICLR 2019, New Orleans, LA, USA, May 6-9, 2019*. OpenReview.net.

Zhirong Wu, Yuanjun Xiong, Stella Yu, and Dahua Lin. 2018. Unsupervised feature learning via non-parametric instance-level discrimination. *CoRR*, abs/1805.01978.

Han Zhao, Zhengdong Lu, and Pascal Poupart. 2015. Self-adaptive hierarchical sentence model. In *Proceedings of the Twenty-Fourth International Joint Conference on Artificial Intelligence, IJCAI 2015, Buenos Aires, Argentina, July 25-31, 2015*, pages 4069–4076.

Yao Zhou, Cong Liu, and Yan Pan. 2016. Modelling sentence pairs with tree-structured attentive encoder. In *COLING 2016, 26th International Conference on Computational Linguistics, Proceedings of the Conference: Technical Papers, December 11-16, 2016, Osaka, Japan*, pages 2912–2922.

Yukun Zhu, Ryan Kiros, Richard S. Zemel, Ruslan Salakhutdinov, Raquel Urtasun, Antonio Torralba, and Sanja Fidler. 2015. Aligning books and movies: Towards story-like visual explanations by watching movies and reading books. In *2015 IEEE International Conference on Computer Vision, ICCV 2015, Santiago, Chile, December 7-13, 2015*, pages 19–27.

A Appendices

A.1 Parsing procedure

We use an open-source implementation[7] of the dependency parser (Dozat and Manning, 2017) and replace the pos-tags features with features obtained with BERT. Therefore we do not need pos-tags annotations to parse our corpus. Regarding the inference speed, The constituency parser is the bottleneck in this case and parse around 500 sentences/second. In our case, the parsing of the entire corpus (40M sentences) take about a day to complete. Regarding the model, we implemented tree models using an efficient batching method which allows us to keep training in a reasonable range (maximum 41 hours.)

A.2 Hyper parameters

Model hyper parameters are fixed given literature on comparable work (Tai et al., 2015; Logeswaran and Lee, 2018). All models are trained using a batch size of 400 and the Adam optimizer with a $5e^{-4}$ learning rate. Regarding the infrastructure, we use a Nvidia GTX 1080 Ti GPU. All model weights are initialized with a Xavier distribution and biases set to 0. We do not apply any dropout.

A.3 Impact of the training dataset

We train our model on the UMBC dataset. We have chosen to make use of a distinct corpus as the BookCorpus dataset is no longer distributed for copyright reasons. We have run QuickThought scripts (Logeswaran and Lee, 2018) using our dataset based on the UMBC corpus to compare both setups. Results are detailed in the first Section from Table 3 and are rather close in both configurations. Indeed, except for the **SUBJ** and **MR** task, the use of our dataset penalizes the results. Our corpus is indeed restricted to 40M sentences, in comparison with 74M for the Bookcorpus. Regarding the dataset size and the SentEval results, we have considered the comparison holds.

A.4 Biases toward embedding size

SentEval evaluation framework is suspected to suffers from biases toward the embedding size (Eger et al., 2019). Moreover, some works on sentence embedding evaluation methods points surprising good results may be achieved using randomly initialized encoders (Wieting and Kiela, 2019). We

[7]`https://github.com/yzhangcs/biaffine-parser`

Model	MR	CR	SUBJ	MPQA	TREC	MRPC Acc	MRPC F1	SICK-R r	SICK-R ρ	SICK-R MSE
Impact of the pretraining corpus on QuickThought										
Quickthoughts (results from paper)	80.4	**85.2**	93.9	**89.4**	**92.8**	**76.9**	84.0	**86.8**	**80.1**	**25.6**
Quickthoughts (UMCB 40M)†	**80.9**	84.4	**95.1**	88.9	92.2	75.8	—	86.0	—	—
Impact of the embedding size										
BERT-base [CLS] †	**77.3**	81.3	92.7	85.0	80.2	69.9	—	61.0	—	—
BERT-base [CLS] /w random projection †	77.1	**82.6**	**93.1**	**85.9**	**80.8**	**71.3**	—	**71.0**	—	—
Impact of pre-training										
DEP, CONST†	**80.7**	**83.6**	**94.9**	**89.2**	**92.6**	**76.8**	**83.6**	**87.0**	**80.3**	**24.8**
Rand LSTM	77.2	78.7	91.9	87.9	86.5	74.1	—	86.0	—	—

Table 3: **Ablation study on SentEval task results.** The first section compares the impact of the training dataset for QuickToughts. The next section focuses on the impact of the embedding size. To this end, hidden representations are projected into a larger embedding space using a random, fully connected layer. The final Section compares models randomly initialized with those pre-trained on our self-supervised task. † indicates models that we had to re-train.

provide extra analysis to discuss these potential pitfalls.

Regarding the dependency on the embedding size, we run experiments to analyze if such bias could explain BERT low performances on SentEval since the output hidden size is only of 768. Following the protocol from Wieting and Kiela (2019), we project the embedding from the CLS token using a random matrix initialized with a glorot distribution. This setup expands BERT embedding into 4096 dimensions. We reported the results in Table 3. We observe expanding the embedding size seems to slightly improve the results. However, the results are still below Quickthought vectors by a large margin.

Regarding the effect of randomly initialized encoders (Wieting and Kiela, 2019), we reported the results in Table 3. Although randomly initialized encoders achieve surprisingly good results, they are still below our results obtained with pre-training.

Discrete Reasoning Templates for Natural Language Understanding

Hadeel Al-Negheimish **Pranava Madhyastha** **Alessandra Russo**

Department of Computing
Imperial College London
{halnegheimish,pranava,a.russo}@imperial.ac.uk

Abstract

Reasoning about information from multiple parts of a passage to derive an answer is an open challenge for reading-comprehension models. In this paper, we present an approach that reasons about complex questions by decomposing them to simpler subquestions that can take advantage of single-span extraction reading-comprehension models, and derives the final answer according to instructions in a predefined reasoning template. We focus on subtraction based arithmetic questions and evaluate our approach on a subset of the DROP dataset. We show that our approach is competitive with the state of the art while being interpretable and requires little supervision.

1 Introduction

Automated reading comprehension (RC) is an important natural language understanding task, where a model is presented with a passage and is asked to answer questions about that passage. While models have excelled at single-span extraction questions, they still struggle with reasoning over distinct parts of a passage (Dua et al., 2019). Several multi-hop reasoning benchmarks have been proposed (Yang et al., 2018; Khashabi et al., 2018; Dua et al., 2019), of which, in this paper, we focus on the DROP (Discrete Reasoning Over the content of Paragraphs) dataset. Inspired by the semantic parsing literature, the dataset contains questions that involve possibly multiple steps of discrete reasoning over the contents of paragraphs, including numerical reasoning.

Recent work has proposed several novel approaches to tackle DROP (Ran et al., 2019; Hu et al., 2019; Andor et al., 2019; Gupta et al., 2020; Chen et al., 2020). However, most approaches provide little evidence of their reasoning process, especially with regards to *why* specific operands are chosen for a reasoning task. With the exception of (Gupta et al., 2020; Chen et al., 2020), they also suffer from limited compositionality.

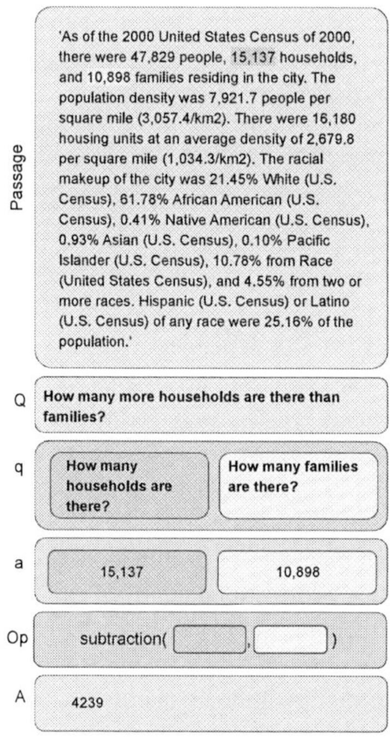

Figure 1: Subtraction Template: Original question is decomposed to two simpler subquestions that find the values associated with the two compared entities as span-extraction, and the final answer is calculated by finding the absolute difference of the two partial answers.

In this paper, we present a first attempt at building an interface between discrete reasoning and unstructured natural language. We propose decomposing a question to simpler subquestions that can more easily be solved by single-span extraction RC models. Such decomposition is defined by Reasoning Templates, which also determine how to assemble the computed partial answers. We demonstrate the feasibility of our approach with the *subtraction* based questions (illustrated in Figure 1). We show that our approach is competitive with the state of the art models on a subset of DROP's subtraction

Proceedings of the 16th Conference of the European Chapter of the Associationfor Computational Linguistics: Student Research Workshop, pages 80–87
April 19 - 23, 2021. ©2021 Association for Computational Linguistics

questions while requiring much less training data and providing visibility of the model's decision-making process.

2 Related Work

There has been a recent resurgence in research on automated reading comprehension (RC) where an automated system is capable of reading a document in order to answer the questions pertaining to the document. This has led to the creation of several RC datasets to facilitate the research (Rajpurkar et al., 2016, 2018; Yang et al., 2018; Reddy et al., 2019; Dua et al., 2019; Huang et al., 2019). Among these, SQuAD (Rajpurkar et al., 2016) is a popular *single-hop question answering* dataset where a question can be answered by relying on a single sentence from the document. SoTA models have achieved near-human performance on such single-hop question answering tasks.[1] However, answering a question by only identifying the most relevant span leaves models prone to exploiting advanced pattern matching algorithms.

On the other hand, multi-hop questions make reading-comprehension more challenging, as they require integrating information from multiple parts in a passage (Yang et al., 2018; Khashabi et al., 2018; Dua et al., 2019). DROP (Dua et al., 2019) is one such dataset that contains questions covering many types of reasoning, such as counting, sorting, or arithmetic. The dataset was constructed by adversarially crowdsourcing questions on a set of Wikipedia passages known to have many numbers. Special model architectures have been built to tackle DROP, and these fall into two general directions: the first direction augments reading comprehension models that were successful on single-span extraction questions with specialized modules that tackle more complex questions. These include NAQANet (Dua et al., 2019), NumNet (Ran et al., 2019) , and MTMSN (Hu et al., 2019). The second direction works on predicting programs that would solve the question, CalBERT (Andor et al., 2019) defines a set of derivations and scoring functions for each of them, while more recent work NMN (Gupta et al., 2020) and NeRd (Chen et al., 2020) utilize LSTMs to decode variable-length programs from question and passage embeddings.

By definition, models with specialized modules have limited compositional reasoning abilities. The two directions vary in their interpretability; the first shows which module has been used, and the second shows the resulting programs which have been generated to compute the answer. However, none of these directions indicate why operands in the passage were selected. For all approaches, the dataset is augmented with all possible derivations that lead to the gold answer, by performing an exhaustive search. Moreover, all approaches assume a preprocessing step that extracts all numbers in the passage and their indices, which massively reduces the search space for arithmetic questions.

In this work, we build upon DecompRC (Min et al., 2019) for question decomposition, where a model is trained to extract key parts of content from the question which are then used for decomposition. Arithmetic questions, which we focus on in this work, are a known limitation of DecompRC. An alternative approach to decomposition is QDMR (Wolfson et al., 2020), a recently proposed formalism for decomposing questions into a series of simpler steps based on predefined query operators. QDMR breaks down a question to its atomic parts directly, whereas we propose recursively decomposing questions to simpler ones. While (Wolfson et al., 2020) provides a dataset of annotated questions, QDMR parsing remains an open challenge. In the following section we present our approach that focuses on answering arithmetic questions.

3 Approach

We propose a pipelined approach that focuses on breaking down complex questions that require reasoning over multiple parts in the passage to simpler single-hop questions. The latter can be resolved by taking advantage of state of the art single-hop reading comprehension models. The main building block of our approach is a *reasoning template*. Each reasoning type is associated with a single template, which contains instructions on how to decompose a question and how to combine partial answers to arrive at the final answer.

Figure 2 illustrates our pipeline. First, the question and passage are fed to our system, which selects a template depending on the reasoning type required (classification task). The template decomposes the question to simpler subquestions that are then passed on to a single-hop RC model. Partial answers are used to arrive at an answer according to the instructions provided by the template. Some questions need further decomposition, and the appropriate template will be chosen for the sub-

[1]https://rajpurkar.github.io/SQuAD-explorer/

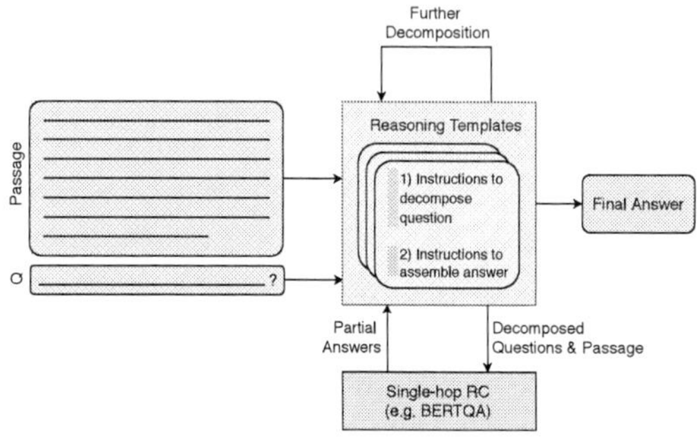

Figure 2: Model Overview: Given a question, decompose it into simpler questions according to a template such that they can be answered by a single-hop RC model, and assemble the final answer by applying the operation associated with the template.

question.[2]

For the question decomposition component, our approach closely follows and builds upon DecompRC (Min et al., 2019), originally proposed for multihop, multidocument question answering. We repurpose the model for multihop arithmetic questions. DecompRC uses a two step approach to decompose questions. First, a pointer model is trained to identify a key part of the question that is used to formulate the sub-questions. Second, the predicted pointers are used to procedurally change the original question into two or three sub-questions. The approach is defined for three types of questions: Bridging, Intersection, and Comparison; each of them uses a different pointer model and a different heuristic procedure to generate the sub-questions.

In this paper, we propose the discrete reasoning template framework and demonstrate its potential by defining a single template: *subtraction*. We describe in detail our approach in the following subsections.

3.1 Question Decomposition

Question decomposition is a two-step process that includes identifying relevant information in the text of the original question (span extraction), and then using those spans for heuristic generation of subquestions. The output of this step are simpler subquestions, see 'q' in Figure 1.

Span Extraction For subtraction questions, the spans we are interested in identify two entities whose associated values are to be subtracted. Consider '$_0$How $_1$many $_2$more $_3$*households* $_4$are $_5$there $_6$than $_7$*married* $_8$*couples* $_9$*living* $_{10}$*together*$_{11}$?'. We need to extract the start and end indices of the first entity *households*, and the start and end indices of the second entity *married couples living together*, which are $[3, 3, 7, 10]$.

The pointer model is trained to predict 4 pointers, the start and end indices of the first and second entity respectively. Concretely, the model extracts 4 indices, $p_1 \leq p_2 \leq p_3 \leq p_4$, that surround the two spans of interest, maximizing the joint probability:

$$p_1, \cdots, p_4 = \underset{\{i_1 \leq \cdots \leq i_4\}}{\arg\max} \prod_{j=1}^{4} \mathbb{P}(i_j = ind_j)$$

where $\mathbb{P}(i_j = ind_j) = Y_{ij}$ is the probability that the ith word is the jth index produced by the pointer, and

$$Y = \text{softmax}(UW) \in \mathbb{R}^{n \times 4}$$

where W is a learned weight matrix of size $h \times 4$ and U is the contextualized embeddings of length h produced by pre-trained BERT(Devlin et al., 2019) of the n tokens in the original question:

$$U = \text{BERT}(S) \in \mathbb{R}^{n \times h}$$

We then train this model using cross entropy loss until convergence.

Subquestion Generation We find that the subquestions needed in our approach have a high degree of overlap with the original question, making them amenable to heuristic decomposition as in DecompRC (Min et al., 2019). While DecompRC is defined for bridging, intersection and comparison type questions, we extend it with a separate procedure to handle *subtraction* type questions as described below. We outline in Algorithm 1 how subquestions can be generated for subtraction questions, given the pointers that have been predicted by the previous step. The algorithm keeps words that are common for both subquestions and then places each of the entities in the center of the generated questions. First, we chunk the original question into parts using the pointers as in lines 2-6. In lines 7-9, we remove comparative adjectives and adverbs from the first part. Before concatenating the different parts again, we remove the extra words from the middle part, utilizing the dependency parse of the original question.

[2]Further decomposition and template selection modules are left for future research.

Algorithm 1: Subquestion generation for subtraction questions

```
Data: Original question q: string, pointers P_4: array
      of length 4
Result: subquestions q_1, q_2: strings
dep_parse= dependency_parse(q);
part1 ← q[0:p_1];
ent1←q[p_1:p_2 + 1];
middle←q[p_2 + 1:p_3];
ent2←q[p_3:p_4 + 1];
part2← q[p_4 + 1:end];
for word in part1 do
    if word.pos_tag in [ 'JJR',  'RBR' ] then
        remove word from part1;
head ← dep_parse.parent(ent2);
i ← head.i;
prev_i ← i;
while (head in middle) AND (prev_i-i ≤ 1) do
    new_head ← dep_parse.parent(head) ;
    remove head from middle;
    head ← new_head;
    prev_i ← i;
    i ← head.i;
q1← part1+ent1+middle+part2;
q2← part1+ent2+middle+part2;
```

3.2 Single-hop question answering

Once we have decomposed questions into simpler, single-hop questions, we can use the subquestions to extract the appropriate operands for reasoning from the passage. We opt to make use of a pre-trained off-the-shelf single-span extraction model, details provided in section 4. This is one possible instantiation for the model, and we can use any robust span-extraction model in its place.

3.3 Operation

A reasoning template includes instructions on how to perform two main steps; the first step decomposes a question to simpler subquestions as we have described in section 3.1. The second step, operation, is designed to derive the final answer given partial answers to decomposed questions. In the case of subtraction, it is simply the absolute difference between the two retrieved values, see '*Op*' in Figure 1. In the case where a span retrieved for a decomposed question contains more than a single number, we use the first number in the span.

4 Experiments

We start with a single template to demonstrate our approach: *subtraction*. Subtraction questions rely on finding the difference between two numbers to find the answer, they are usually in the form of *'How many more..?'* or *'How many fewer..?'*.

Dataset For evaluation, we collect two sets of subtraction questions from the DROP development set. The first, *clean*, is a subset of 52 questions curated by filtering the original dataset to find questions that contain words with 'JJR' or 'RBR' pos-tags (comparative adjective and comparative adverb respectively), and from those we randomly sample 10 questions at a time and manually identify subtraction questions. We also annotate each of these questions with gold decompositions, two subquestions for each complex question. The other evaluation set, *noisy*, is a larger dataset that has been heuristically generated, this is intended to support generalizability of results on the smaller evaluation set. It contains 892 questions that have been filtered using trigrams at the beginning of the question: *'How many more'* or *'How many fewer'*.

There are two learning components in our pipeline: a pointer model to extract relevant entities from the question and a single-hop RC model to answer decomposed questions. For the latter, we use an off-the-shelf pre-trained BERT (Devlin et al., 2019) question answering model, which has been fine-tuned on SQuAD (Rajpurkar et al., 2016), a single-hop reading comprehension dataset. Specifically, we use the one provided by the huggingface transformer library (Wolf et al., 2020). As for the former, to train the pointer model we follow (Min et al., 2019) and annotate 200 examples. The data for this was gathered from the DROP training set in the same way we curated the *clean* evaluation set, for this step we simply identify the compared entities and delimit them with '#'.

4.1 Results and Discussion

Evaluating Question Decomposition In Table 1 we report the accuracy of the pointer model on the *clean* subtraction evaluation set, and in Table 2 we measure the overlap between the resulting spans and the annotated entities. While getting all pointers to match label succeeds for 73% of the data, we note that the accuracy of each of the pointers is much higher. We find that the pointer delimiting the start of the first entity is seemingly the most difficult to predict, which is also seen in lower F1 score for the first entity. We conjecture this to be the likely case as the second entity is usually preceded by words such as 'than' or 'compared to'.

We also measure the similarity between decomposed questions generated by our approach and the manually annotated gold decompositions. Table 3

	p1	p2	p3	p4	all
Acc	84.0 ± 0.9	88.5 ± 1.6	98.1	94.9 ± 0.9	73.1

Table 1: Accuracy of Pointer_4 model, we list the accuracy of individual pointers separately and accuracy of all pointers for each example. Results are reported as an average of 3 runs of the model with different random seeds.

	First Entity	Second Entity
F1	0.89 ± 0.02	0.97 ± 0.003
Precision	0.91 ± 0.018	0.96
Recall	0.90 ± 0.023	0.99 ± 0.006

Table 2: Measured overlap between resulting spans of the predicted pointers and the annotated entities, averaged over all questions in *clean* evaluation set.

Similarity Measure	q1	q2
WMD_{max}	3.56	4.43
WMD_{avg}	0.2266	0.6714
WMD_{median}	0.0	0.0
$cos(\theta)_{min}$	0.9538	0.9476
$cos(\theta)_{avg}$	0.9959	0.9913
$cos(\theta)_{median}$	1.0	1.0

Table 3: Reported similarities between manually decomposed questions (gold) and decompositions generated by our approach. We use word mover's distance (WMD) and cosine similarity of average word embeddings. For the former we report *max* distance, while in the latter we report *min* similarity as these highlight the worst-case of all subquestions. For most examples, the gold decompositions and generated subquestions overlap perfectly, as indicated by *median* score.

displays the Word Mover's Distance metric (Kusner et al., 2015) and cosine similarity, based on the GloVe word embeddings shipped with SpaCy's (Honnibal et al., 2020) `en_core_web_lg` model. For most questions, the two subquestions match perfectly between the gold annotations and the generated ones. However, upon manual inspection, we find that the generated subquestion might sometimes omit the final verb. This is because of our traversal of the dependency parse in Algorithm 1. We found BERTQA was robust to these differences when extracting the related span from the passage.

Evaluating the Approach Table 4 shows the accuracy of each of the models on the subtraction evaluation sets. Since the result is a number, accuracy is evaluated as an exact match between the predicted answer and its label. We compare our approach with the state-of-the-art; MTMSN (Hu et al., 2019), the best performing model with specialized modules; and NeRd (Chen et al., 2020), the most recent work based on program induction. These were evaluated on the original questions in subtraction evaluation set. For our work, we evaluate two different variations: We run the pipeline on the gold decompositions that have been manually rewritten, and automatically-decomposed questions generated by our approach, using BERT single-hop RC described in section 4. For both gold-decompositions and learned-decompositions we get promising results that are on par with the state-of-the-art on this dataset.

When investigating the mistakes that our approach makes on the *clean* set, we find that many

	Model	Acc_c	Acc_c^-	# MM	Acc_n
SoTA	MTMSN	86.5	89.4	3	81.3
SoTA	NeRd	73	76.6	2	62.3
Ours	Decomp_G	78.8	85.1	1	-
Ours	Decomp_L	74.4 ± 2.4	79.9 ± 2.6	1	64

Table 4: Accuracy of models for subtraction questions. We report accuracy on *clean* evaluation set (52 questions) in Acc_c, accuracy after omitting 5 mislabeled questions in the second column (Acc_c^-) and specify how many of these Mislabeled questions Match the prediction in the #MM. The last column (Acc_n) reports accuracy on the *noisy* evaluation set (892 questions). Learned Decompositions (Decomp_L) are averaged over 3 random seeds in pointer model training.

of the mistakes are actually due to incorrect labels. The gold answer (or label) does not match the correct answer for a certain question. To validate this, we check the entire *clean* evaluation set and manually label each question. We find that 5 of the 52 questions are incorrectly annotated, one of these questions is actually invalid as the information needed to answer it does not exist in the passage. To better understand the effect of this, we discard incorrectly labeled examples and report accuracy in the second column of Table 4. We also report the number of predictions matching the incorrect label. The primary set of *true* mistakes our model makes are due to some questions needing further decomposition, eliciting commonsense knowledge, or because they are not *subtraction* questions, i.e. can be classified as MTMSN's `Negation` rather than `Diff` module.

NeRd fails on 3 questions that MTMSN and our approach got correctly because it could not produce a valid program to be evaluated. It also failed on 2 of the `Negation` question that our approach failed on, not because it was not able to address those kinds of question, but because the attention mechanism ignored a condition in the question "18 or over". Surprisingly, NeRd failed on both questions that necessitate nested processing, even though the architecture allows for compositionality. The remaining failure cases are due to choosing incorrect operands for the difference, but it is not clear why the model made those choices.

Discussion We find that our approach is promising; it is interpretable and requires little training data when compared to previous approaches, without compromising performance. Steps to arrive at an answer are explicit, and we can interpret each of the retrieved operands by their associated subquestions. Figure 1 shows an example of this for subtraction questions. MTMSN indicates which module was used, but it does not show what led to this particular choice of the arithmetic expression. Likewise, NeRD shows the program necessary to find the answer, but there is no indication on why the operands of each function were chosen.

The only training data needed was a small subset (200 examples) to train the pointer model, and in the future we need some data to train reasoning type classifier and other templates' pointer models. This comes in contrast to the exhaustive search needed to find all possible derivations to reach an answer for all questions in the training set (77.4k examples). Reasoning Templates retrieve operands for the subtraction operation by answering subquestions that refer to a particular number, making it more robust to noise in the annotation. We started by focusing on the subtraction template, because it is the most prevalent numerical reasoning type (with an estimated proportion of 29% of all questions (Dua et al., 2019)). However, this approach can be similarly extended to other reasoning types by defining a template for each, such as *date-difference* or *addition*.

We believe that such reasoning templates would be able to answer compositional questions with its recursive *decomposition* component. While this exploration is left for future research, we believe it is useful it outline how we expect it to handle compositionality. Recall from Figure 1 that input questions are passed to a classifier that selects which template to apply, one of the classes decides if the question is single-span and should be passed on to single-hop RC directly. Decomposed questions should also be passed through this classifier to determine if they need further decomposition.

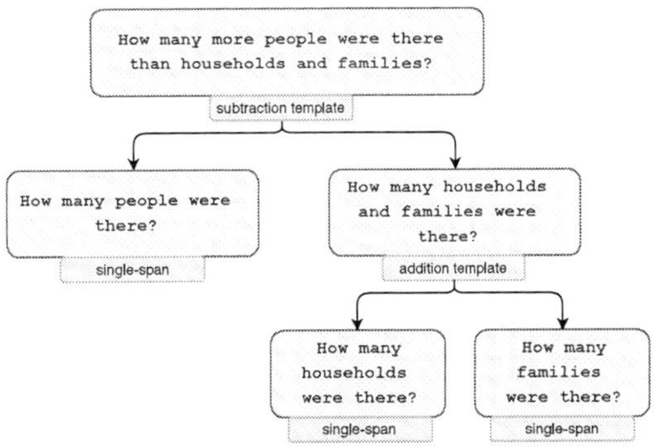

Figure 3: An example of how questions are further decomposed to facilitate compositionality.

Figure 3 shows an example where the second subquestion involves another reasoning task. After further decomposing it to single-span extraction questions and finding the solution to the addition operation, that answer would be passed to the previous task. This recursive processing should ideally allow for compositionality.

After building the entire pipeline we expect mistakes like nested operations and mis-classified `Negation` types to be rectified, boosting performance further. One challenge we wish to overcome is the engineering bottleneck involved in crafting each of the templates. Future work would explore methods that learn to construct these the templates.

5 Conclusion

We propose using Reasoning Templates for tackling reading comprehension tasks that involve reasoning over multiple paragraphs. We show that this approach is competitive with state of the art models on a subset of DROP's subtraction questions, while requiring much less training data and providing better visibility of the model's decision making. In future work, we plan on extending to further templates and investigate how to learn templates instead of working from a predefined set.

Acknowledgements

This research has been supported by a scholarship from King Saud University. We thank our anonymous mentor and reviewers for their constructive comments and suggestions.

References

Daniel Andor, Luheng He, Kenton Lee, and Emily Pitler. 2019. Giving BERT a calculator: Finding operations and arguments with reading comprehension. In *Proceedings of the 2019 Conference on Empirical Methods in Natural Language Processing and the 9th International Joint Conference on Natural Language Processing (EMNLP-IJCNLP)*, pages 5947–5952, Hong Kong, China. Association for Computational Linguistics.

Xinyun Chen, Chen Liang, Adams Wei Yu, Denny Zhou, Dawn Song, and Quoc V. Le. 2020. Neural symbolic reader: Scalable integration of distributed and symbolic representations for reading comprehension. In *International Conference on Learning Representations*.

Jacob Devlin, Ming-Wei Chang, Kenton Lee, and Kristina Toutanova. 2019. BERT: Pre-training of deep bidirectional transformers for language understanding. In *Proceedings of the 2019 Conference of the North American Chapter of the Association for Computational Linguistics: Human Language Technologies, Volume 1 (Long and Short Papers)*, pages 4171–4186, Minneapolis, Minnesota. Association for Computational Linguistics.

Dheeru Dua, Yizhong Wang, Pradeep Dasigi, Gabriel Stanovsky, Sameer Singh, and Matt Gardner. 2019. DROP: A reading comprehension benchmark requiring discrete reasoning over paragraphs. In *Proc. of NAACL*.

Nitish Gupta, Kevin Lin, Dan Roth, Sameer Singh, and Matt Gardner. 2020. Neural module networks for reasoning over text. In *International Conference on Learning Representations*.

Matthew Honnibal, Ines Montani, Sofie Van Landeghem, and Adriane Boyd. 2020. spaCy: Industrial-strength Natural Language Processing in Python.

Minghao Hu, Yuxing Peng, Zhen Huang, and Dongsheng Li. 2019. A multi-type multi-span network for reading comprehension that requires discrete reasoning. In *Proceedings of the 2019 Conference on Empirical Methods in Natural Language Processing and the 9th International Joint Conference on Natural Language Processing (EMNLP-IJCNLP)*, pages 1596–1606, Hong Kong, China. Association for Computational Linguistics.

Lifu Huang, Ronan Le Bras, Chandra Bhagavatula, and Yejin Choi. 2019. Cosmos QA: Machine reading comprehension with contextual commonsense reasoning. In *Proceedings of the 2019 Conference on Empirical Methods in Natural Language Processing and the 9th International Joint Conference on Natural Language Processing (EMNLP-IJCNLP)*, pages 2391–2401, Hong Kong, China. Association for Computational Linguistics.

Daniel Khashabi, Snigdha Chaturvedi, Michael Roth, Shyam Upadhyay, and Dan Roth. 2018. Looking beyond the surface: A challenge set for reading comprehension over multiple sentences. In *Proceedings of the 2018 Conference of the North American Chapter of the Association for Computational Linguistics: Human Language Technologies, Volume 1 (Long Papers)*, pages 252–262, New Orleans, Louisiana. Association for Computational Linguistics.

Matt J. Kusner, Yu Sun, Nicholas I. Kolkin, and Kilian Q. Weinberger. 2015. From word embeddings to document distances. In *Proceedings of the 32nd International Conference on International Conference on Machine Learning - Volume 37*, ICML'15, page 957–966. JMLR.org.

Sewon Min, Victor Zhong, Luke Zettlemoyer, and Hannaneh Hajishirzi. 2019. Multi-hop reading comprehension through question decomposition and rescoring. In *Proceedings of the 57th Annual Meeting of the Association for Computational Linguistics*, pages 6097–6109, Florence, Italy. Association for Computational Linguistics.

Pranav Rajpurkar, Robin Jia, and Percy Liang. 2018. Know what you don't know: Unanswerable questions for SQuAD. In *Proceedings of the 56th Annual Meeting of the Association for Computational Linguistics (Volume 2: Short Papers)*, pages 784–789, Melbourne, Australia. Association for Computational Linguistics.

Pranav Rajpurkar, Jian Zhang, Konstantin Lopyrev, and Percy Liang. 2016. SQuAD: 100,000+ questions for machine comprehension of text. In *Proceedings of the 2016 Conference on Empirical Methods in Natural Language Processing*, pages 2383–2392, Austin, Texas. Association for Computational Linguistics.

Qiu Ran, Yankai Lin, Peng Li, Jie Zhou, and Zhiyuan Liu. 2019. NumNet: Machine reading comprehension with numerical reasoning. In *Proceedings of the 2019 Conference on Empirical Methods in Natural Language Processing and the 9th International Joint Conference on Natural Language Processing (EMNLP-IJCNLP)*, pages 2474–2484, Hong Kong, China. Association for Computational Linguistics.

Siva Reddy, Danqi Chen, and Christopher D. Manning. 2019. CoQA: A conversational question answering challenge. *Transactions of the Association for Computational Linguistics*, 7:249–266.

Thomas Wolf, Lysandre Debut, Victor Sanh, Julien Chaumond, Clement Delangue, Anthony Moi, Pierric Cistac, Tim Rault, Rémi Louf, Morgan Funtowicz, Joe Davison, Sam Shleifer, Patrick von Platen, Clara Ma, Yacine Jernite, Julien Plu, Canwen Xu, Teven Le Scao, Sylvain Gugger, Mariama Drame, Quentin Lhoest, and Alexander M. Rush. 2020. Transformers: State-of-the-art natural language processing. In *Proceedings of the 2020 Conference on Empirical Methods in Natural Language Processing: System Demonstrations*, pages 38–45, Online. Association for Computational Linguistics.

Tomer Wolfson, Mor Geva, Ankit Gupta, Matt Gardner, Yoav Goldberg, Daniel Deutch, and Jonathan Berant. 2020. Break it down: A question understanding benchmark. *Transactions of the Association for Computational Linguistics*.

Zhilin Yang, Peng Qi, Saizheng Zhang, Yoshua Bengio, William W. Cohen, Ruslan Salakhutdinov, and Christopher D. Manning. 2018. HotpotQA: A dataset for diverse, explainable multi-hop question answering. In *Conference on Empirical Methods in Natural Language Processing (EMNLP)*.

A Experimental Settings

A.1 Model Settings

We use the final layer of $\text{BERT}_{\text{LARGE}}$ (Devlin et al., 2019) to produce contextualized embeddings used for span extraction fine-tuned to extract 4 pointers.[3] We use Adam optimizer with learning rate of $5e-5$ and warm-up over the first 10% steps to train. Loss function is calculated with cross-entropy. Training batch size is 20 examples. We train three models with different random seeds and report average performance over these.

A.2 SoTA Comparison

We report the accuracy of MTMSN (Hu et al., 2019) and NeRd (Chen et al., 2020) on the two subtraction evaluation sets in Table 4. For MTMSN, we use the pre-trained `MTMSN_LARGE` model published on their github page. Code and model checkpoints for NeRd were shared in email communication with the authors in June, 2020.

B Evaluating on a larger dataset

We started evaluating this work on the smaller, *clean*, dataset of 52 questions that has been manually curated. To validate that this sample is representative of subtraction questions in the DROP devset, we worked to heuristically identify relevant questions. We started with the same 2 steps involved in the manual curation, filter the devset (9536 questions) for questions that have 'number' as answer type (leaves 5850 questions) and contain comparative adjectives or adverbs. This leaves us with a subset of 1386 questions. The above conditions cover more questions than we are interested in, e.g. 'How many people are 18 or older?'. We refine the second condition to exclude sentences where the `JJR | RBR` tokens are preceded with an *or*, this omits 146 more samples. We proceed by passing these through our pipeline. Below is a summary of failure cases of the different components of our approach:

a. 1 sample did not produce valid pointers (used [SEP] token which is BERT-specific).

b. 22 samples did not produce valid decomposition. This is due to issues in mismatching tokenization between the pointer model and the subquestion generation function. The function used to map pointers between the two tokenizers did not generalize to the cases here. Examples of these are ['80', '-', 'yard'] and ['80-yard'].

c. 28 samples did not pass through BERTQA successfully, as they exceeded the sequence length (512).

Of the remaining 1189 questions that were processed successfully, we get 55.9% correctly. This still includes questions which are not covered by our subtraction template. We proceed in two ways: First, we filter out questions that MTMSN predicted not to be `addition_subtraction`. This leaves 1106 questions with 59.3% accuracy. The alternative is to filter questions based on their start trigrams, which gives a more relevant set of questions. Of the 1189 questions, 892 start with the phrases 'How many more', 'How many fewer', and 'How many less'. Our model answers 64% of these correctly.

[3] We build upon the implementation of Min et al. (2019)

Multilingual Email Zoning

Bruno Jardim
Cleverly, Lisbon, Portugal
NOVA-IMS, Lisbon, Portugal
bjardim@novaims.unl.pt

Ricardo Rei
NOVA-IMS, Lisbon, Portugal
Unbabel, Lisbon, Portugal
rrei@novaims.unl.pt

Mariana S.C. Almeida
Cleverly, Lisbon, Portugal
mariana.almeida@cleverly.ai

Abstract

The segmentation of emails into functional zones (also dubbed **email zoning**) is a relevant preprocessing step for most NLP tasks that deal with emails. However, despite the multilingual character of emails and their applications, previous literature regarding email zoning corpora and systems was developed essentially for English.

In this paper, we analyse the existing email zoning corpora and propose a new multilingual benchmark composed of 625 emails in Portuguese, Spanish and French. Moreover, we introduce OKAPI, the first multilingual email segmentation model based on a language agnostic sentence encoder. Besides generalizing well for unseen languages, our model is competitive with current English benchmarks, and reached new state-of-the-art performances for domain adaptation tasks in English.

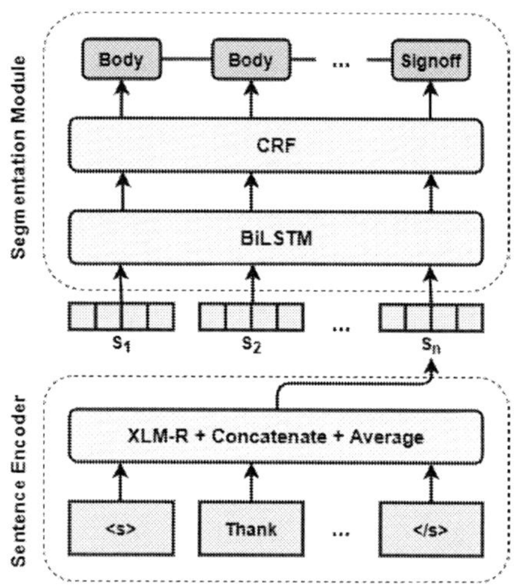

Figure 1: OKAPI is composed of two building blocks: 1) a multilingual sentence encoder (XLM-RoBERTa) to derive sentence embeddings; and 2) a segmentation module that uses a BiLSTM with a CRF on top to classify each sentence into an email zone.

1 Introduction

Worldwide, email is a predominant means of social and business communication. Its importance has attracted studies in areas of Machine Learning (ML) and Natural Language Processing (NLP), impacting a wide range of applications, from spam filtering (Qaroush et al., 2012) to network analysis (Christidis and Losada, 2019).

The email body is commonly perceived as unstructured textual data with multiple possible formats. However, it is possible to discern a level of formal organization in the way most emails are formed. Different functional parts can be identified such as greetings, signatures, quoted content, legal disclaimers, etc. The segmentation of email text into zones, also known as **email zoning** (Lampert et al., 2009), has since become a prevalent preprocessing task for a diversity of downstream applications, such as author profiling (Estival et al., 2007), request detection (Lampert et al., 2010), uncover of technical artifacts (Bettenburg et al., 2011), automated template induction (Proskurnia et al., 2017), email classification (Kocayusufoglu et al., 2019) or automated email response suggestion (Kannan et al., 2016; Chen et al., 2019).

Since email communication is a worldwide phenomenon, all previous applications are in fact highly multilingual. Despite this, email zoning literature remains English-centric and without a standardize zone taxonomy. To mitigate those problems, we make the following research contributions:

1. We discuss the existing zoning taxonomies and their limitations.

2. We release Cleverly zoning corpus, the first multilingual corpus for email zoning. This

Proceedings of the 16th Conference of the European Chapter of the Associationfor Computational Linguistics: Student Research Workshop, pages 88–95
April 19 - 23, 2021. ©2021 Association for Computational Linguistics

corpus consists of 625 emails in 3 languages rather than English (Portuguese, Spanish and French), and encompasses 15 email zones as defined in (Bevendorff et al., 2020)

3. We introduce OKAPI, a multilingual email segmentation system built on top of XLM-RoBERTa (Conneau et al., 2020) that can be easily extended to 100 languages.

To the best of our knowledge, OKAPI is the first end-to-end multilingual system exploring pre-trained transformer models (Vaswani et al., 2017) to perform email zoning. Besides having multilingual capabilities, OKAPI is competitive with existing approaches for English email zoning, and attained state-of-the-art performance in domain adaptation tasks for English email zoning.

The rest of the paper is organized as follows: Section 2 presents an overview of the related literature. Section 3 provides a comprehensive review of existing email zoning corpora, and introduces Cleverly zoning corpus, our new multilingual email zoning corpus. Section 4 describes the OKAPI model architecture. Section 5 reports and discusses the results achieved. Finally, Section 6 concludes the paper.

2 Literature Review

Chen et al. (1999) were one of the pioneers in the topic of email segmentation. Looking at linguist and geometrical patterns, their work focuses on the identification of email signature. Similarly, Carvalho and Cohen (2004) developed JANGADA, a supervised learning system that classifies each line using a Conditional Random Field (CRF) (Lafferty et al., 2001) and a sequence-aware perceptron (Collins, 2002), that identifies signature blocks and quoted text from previous emails. Tang et al. (2005) proposed an email data cleansing system based on a Support Vector Machine (SVM) (Cortes and Vapnik, 1995) model that aimed at filtering the non-textual noisy content from emails independently of downstream text mining applications, based on hand-coded features.

Estival et al. (2007) were the first to introduce a general segmentation schema for email text. Segmentation of emails is a crucial part on their work, which aims at identifying the author's basic demographic and psychometric traits. In that work, the authors compared a range of ML algorithms together with feature selection to classify email segments into five functional parts, attaining improvements in the end task of auto profiling. Later, Lampert et al. (2009) formally defined the functional parts as email zones, describing the different segments inside email messages based on graphic, orthographic, and lexical features. Lampert et al. (2009) also proposed ZEBRA, an email zoning system based on a SVM. In a posterior work towards detecting emails containing requests for action, Lampert et al. (2010) used ZEBRA to "zone" emails, considering only the zones that had relevant patterns to increase the accuracy of their request detection task.

As email zoning surpassed its original purpose of signature identification and text cleansing into a more general task, Repke and Krestel (2018) extended its utility to thread reconstruction. Inspired by ZEBRA (Lampert et al., 2009), the authors proposed QUAGGA (Repke and Krestel, 2018), a neural system with a Convolutional Neural Network (CNN) (LeCun et al., 1989) to produce sentence representations followed by a Recurrent Neural Network (RNN) (Elman, 1990). QUAGGA was trained and evaluated on English emails from both the Enron (Klimt and Yang, 2004) corpus and the public mail archives of the Apache Software Foundation (ASF)[1], outperforming JANGADA and ZEBRA.

Until very recently, email zoning resorted to small samples of mailing lists or newsgroup corpus and was limited to the English language. Bevendorff et al. (2020) were the first to crawl email at scale, extracting 153 million emails from the Gmane email-to-newsgroup gateway[2] in different languages such as English, Spanish, French and Portuguese[3]. The authors annotated email zones for a subset of Gmane English emails and, due to the idiosyncratic characteristics of the corpora, they developed a more fine-grained zone classification schema with 15 zones. Moreover, Bevendorff et al. (2020) introduced an email zoning system, named CHIPMUNK, that combines a Bidirectional Gated Recurrent Unit (BiGRU) (Cho et al., 2014) with a CNN. When compared to other models in the literature, CHIPMUNK achieved better performance.

[1] http://mail-archives.apache.org/mod_mbox/

[2] https://news.gmane.io/

[3] https://webis.de/data.html?q=Webis-Gmane-19

Authors	Source	emails	zones	Language
(Carvalho and Cohen, 2004)[4]	20 Newsgroup[5]	617	2	English
(Estival et al., 2007)[6]	Donated[6]	9,836	5	English
(Lampert et al., 2009)[7]	Enron[8]	400	3/9	English
(Repke and Krestel, 2018)[9]	Enron[8]	800	2/5	English
	ASF[1]	500	2/5	English
Bevendorff et al. (2020)[10]	Gmane[3]	3,033	15	Multilingual*
	Enron[8]	300	15	English
Ours	Gmane[3]	625	15	Multilingual

Table 1: Summary of existing email zoning corpora. *Note that, although Bevendorff et al. (2020)'s Gmane corpus is technically multilingual, it only has 38 non-English test emails that are spread over 13 different languages.

3 Email Zoning Corpora

Several corpora and zoning schemes have been proposed in the literature under different contexts. This section provides an overview of the existing corpora, hoping to make it easier to develop and compare new email zoning methods in the future.

Table 1 compiles the information of existing email zoning corpus. To the best of our knowledge, Carvalho and Cohen (2004) released the first email zoning corpus. The corpus consists of 617 emails[4] from the 20 Newsgroup corpus[5] identified with two zones: *signature* and *quotation*. Despite the usefulness of identifying those zones for email cleansing, this level of detail is still insufficient for a general email segmentation.

Estival et al. (2007) released a corpus of 9,836 recruited respondents donated email messages[6] and introduced a wider annotation schema focusing on more email parts: *author text*, *signature*, *advertisement*, *quoted text*, and *reply* lines. However, Estival et al. (2007) still did not divide the email text into some other relevant zones, such as greetings, closings nor identify attachments and code lines.

Lampert et al. (2009) were arguably the first to conceptualize the email zoning task and fully define the characteristics of each identified zone, as well as dividing the authored text into different zones. They annotated 400 English emails[7] from the Enron email corpus database dump, identifying 3 email zones: *sender*, *quoted conversation* and *boilerplate* zones, each containing a different set of sub-zones, within a total of 9 sub-zones.

Repke and Krestel (2018) also resorted to the Enron database[8], annotating a total of 800 emails[9]. Reconsidering the task as thread reconstruction, they produced a new annotation schema, considering a 2-level and a 5-level approach (the latter being a refinement of the 2-level segmentation). Repke and Krestel (2018) also annotated 500 ASF emails[7] using both the 2-level and 5-level taxonomies. Their 5-level annotation schema consists of segmenting emails into: *body* (typically comprising ~80% of the lines), *header*, *signoff*, *signature* and *greetings*.

Bevendorff et al. (2020) introduced the Gmane corpus for email zoning[10]. Even though the corpus is composed of 31 languages, the annotated emails are mostly in English, and their test set only contains a residual number of non-English emails (38 emails covering 13 different languages), which is insufficient for a consistent multilingual evaluation. Due to the richness of the Gmane conversations on technical topics, Bevendorff et al. (2020) developed a more fine grained classification schema, considering the segmentation of blocks of code, log data and technical data. Whilst also preserving most of the common zones introduced in previous works, they ended up with a total of 15 zones: *closing*, *inline headers*, *log data*, *MUA signature*, *paragraph*, *patch*, *personal signature*, *quotation*, *quotation marker*, *raw code*, *salutation*, *section heading*, *tabular*, *technical*, *visual separator*. Following the same zone taxonomy they also released a set of 300 English emails from the Enron database dump. In both Enron and Gmane

[4]http://www.cs.cmu.edu/~vitor/codeAndData.html

[5]http://qwone.com/~jason/20Newsgroups/

[6]available upon contact with the authors.

[7]http://zebra.thoughtlets.org/

[8]http://www.cs.cmu.edu/~enron/

[9]https://github.com/HPI-Information-Systems/Quagga

[10]https://github.com/webis-de/acl20-crawling-mailing-lists

emails, the majority of the email segments belong to the *paragraph* and *quotation* zones. This being said, Gmane has much more lines of *quotation* than *paragraph*, while Enron is the other way around.

Overall, email zoning corpora show a great variability of zone taxonomies and most works have introduced new zones to face the nature of each email source or downstream task. The Enron database dump has been the most used source to retrieve emails to build new corpus. On the other hand, the recent Gmane raw dump of emails is multilingual and it contains various functional zones, which opens the door to new challenges in email zoning and multilingual methodologies.

3.1 Cleverly Zoning Corpus

	pt	es	fr
# zones	15	14	14
# emails	210	200	215
# lines	12366	9824	6958
# lines / email	58.9	49.1	32.4
# zones /email	8.6	6.5	5.9
# unique zones / email	5.8	5.1	4.9

Table 2: Some statistics of the Cleverly zoning corpus.

This section presents Cleverly zoning corpus, the first multilingual email zoning corpus. To create the corpus, we searched the Gmane raw corpus (Bevendorff et al., 2020) for Portuguese (pt), Spanish (es) and French (fr) emails. Then, following the classification schema proposed by Bevendorff et al. (2020), we produced a total of 625 annotated emails.

Table 2 compiles a brief description of the email statistics for each of the languages. While French is the language with more emails, Portuguese and Spanish emails tend to be longer, resulting in a greater amount of lines and an overall higher number of zones per email. The distribution of zones is similar between the three languages, as detailed in Table 3.

The annotation was carried out by two annotators. The first annotator was a native Portuguese speaker and the second annotator a native Spanish speaker, both with academical background in French and fluent in the third language. Each email was annotated by both annotators using the tagtog[11] annotation tool.

[11]https://www.tagtog.net

Zone	pt (%)	es (%)	fr (%)
Quotation	52.43	59.02	46.20
Paragraph	16.33	17.36	27.61
MUA Sig.	12.04	3.84	9.04
Personal Sig.	3.93	4.47	2.00
Visual Sep.	2.94	2.29	2,60
Quot. Mark.	2.72	1.54	2.10
Closing	2.63	2.00	3.73
Log Data	1.04	3.79	1.82
Raw Code	1.28	2.45	2.07
Inl. Head.	2.96	0,82	1.33
Salutation	0,96	0.81	1,35
Tabular	0.32	0.42	0.27
Technical	0.30	1.00	0.38
Patch	0.02	0.20	0.02
Sec. Head.	0.15	0.04	0.03

Table 3: Distribution, for each language, of the number of lines per zone in the Cleverly zoning corpus. The distributions were obtained by averaging statistics from both annotators.

measure	pt	es	fr
accuracy	0.93	0.92	0.96
F_1 A_1A_2	0.93	0.92	0.96
F_1 A_2A_1	0.94	0.92	0.96
k	0.90	0.87	0.94

Table 4: Inter-annotator agreement for each language in the Cleverly zoning corpus, using Cohen's kappa (k), accuracy and F_1 between annotators A_1 and A_2.

Table 4 shows the inter-annotator agreement scores for each language using the Cohen's kappa coefficient (k) (McHugh, 2012), accuracy and F_1 of one annotator versus the other. All annotations and required information to compile the original emails are freely available at https://github.com/cleverly-ai/multilingual-email-zoning.

4 OKAPI Architecture

We propose OKAPI, an email segmentation model composed of two building blocks: a multilingual sentence encoder and a segmentation module. Figure 1 shows the OKAPI architecture.

4.1 Multilingual Sentence Encoder

To address the multilingual nature of emails we developed a language agnostic sentence encoder that turns each email line into an embedding. Figure 2 illustrates the encoding process.

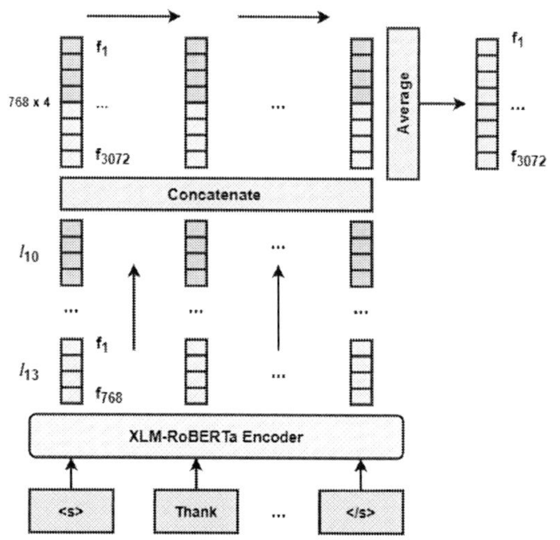

Figure 2: To derive a cross-lingual line embedding we use XLM-RoBERTa (Conneau et al., 2020) to extract word-level embeddings, and then we apply average pooling to the last 4 layers. This leads to a final 3072 features embedding.

Given an email line $x = [x_0, x_1, ..., x_n]$, our encoder module uses XLM-RoBERTa (base) (Conneau et al., 2020) to produce an embedding $e_j^{(\ell)}$ for each token x_j and each layer $\ell \in \{0, 1, ..., 13\}$. Since it has been shown that BERT-like models capture within the network layers diverse linguistic information, and, particularly, the last layers preserve most of the semantic information (Tenney et al., 2019), we keep, for each sentence, only the word embeddings from the last 4 layers. Lastly, as in (Reimers and Gurevych, 2019), these word embedding are turned into a 3072 sentence embedding s_k by averaging the concatenation of the 4 word layer embeddings.

4.2 Segmentation Module

After passing each email line into the previous sentence encoder we get a cross-lingual line embedding s_k. After that, we pass all line embeddings of an email into a Bidirectional Long Short-Term Memory (BiLSTM) (Graves and Schmidhuber, 2005), with 1 layer and 64 hidden units, to derive compact line representations that encompass information from the entire structure of the email. Finally, as in Huang et al. (2015), we use a CRF output layer to predict the zone of each line in the document. Preliminary experiments showed that not using CRF either slightly deteriorates model performance or does not have an impact on the results.

4.3 Training setup

During training, XLM-RoBERTa's weights were kept frozen and only the BiLSTM and CRF layers were updated. We experimented BiLSTM with $16, 32, 64, 128, 256$ and 512 hidden units and more layers, but in the end, having a small segmentation module, with 64 hidden units and 1 layer, generically yielded the best performances in the validation splits. We used a dropout layer of value 0.25 between the BiLSTM and the CRF, and the RMSprop optimizer with a fixed learning rate of 0.001.

5 Results and Discussion

In this section, we analyse both multilingual and monolingual capabilities of OKAPI, considering various zoning corpora and annotation schemas.

5.1 Multilingual Email Zoning

zone	pt	es	fr
All	0.91	0.93	0.93
Quotation	0.99	0.99	0.99
Paragraph	0.91	0.96	0.92
MUA Sig.	0.95	0.82	0.91
Personal Sig.	0.81	0.87	0.79
Visual Sep.	0.92	0.90	0.96
Quot. Mark.	0.55	0.97	0.97
Closing	0.59	0.58	0.69
Log Data	0.56	0.53	0.57
Raw Code	0.54	0.74	0.84
Inl. Head.	0.78	0.77	0.58
Salutation	0.65	0.69	0.89
Tabular	0.30	0.00	0.60
Technical	0.67	0.56	0.48
Patch	0.00	0.00	0.00
Sec. Head.	0.34	0.00	0.00

Table 5: Multilingual zero-shot evaluation of OKAPI, using Cleverly zoning corpus. Global accuracy and recall of each zone, computed by averaging the scores regarding both annotators.

We evaluate the multilingual capabilities of OKAPI in a zero-shot fashion. For that, we trained the model with the Gmane English corpus released by Bevendorff et al. (2020), and tested it with the Cleverly multilingual corpus that we annotated for Portuguese, Spanish and French.

Table 5 presents the performances of OKAPI in our multilingual corpus for each zone. Comparing with the typical performance of email zoning and the Gmane corpus (see next Tables), OKAPI achieves quite reasonable performances, confirming its multilingual character. As expected, zone recall seems to be dependent on the total number of lines per zone.

5.2 English Email Zoning

Model	Zones	Enron	ASF
JANGADA	2	0.88	0.97
ZEBRA	2	0.25	0.18
QUAGGA	2	0.98	0.98
OKAPI	2	**0.99**	**0.99**
JANGADA	5	0.85	0.91
ZEBRA	5	0.24	0.20
QUAGGA	5	0.93	**0.95**
OKAPI	5	**0.96**	**0.95**

Table 6: Email zoning accuracy of various models, for the corpus of Repke and Krestel (2018).

Model	Zones	Gmane	Enron
Tang et al. (2005)	15	0.80	0.73
QUAGGA	15	0.94	0.83
CHIPMUNCK	15	**0.96**	**0.88**
OKAPI	15	**0.96**	**0.88**

Table 7: Zoning accuracy of various models, under the 15-level zoning schema of Bevendorff et al. (2020).

Resorting to the numbers reported in the literature for email zoning, we compared OKAPI with existing monolingual methods using various English corpora and zoning taxonomies. In particular, Table 6 compares OKAPI with other zoning systems on the corpora annotated by Repke and Krestel (2018) with 2 and 5 types of zones; and Table 7 shows the results obtained with the most recent and fine-grained annotation schema with 15 zones proposed by Bevendorff et al. (2020). For all those combination of corpora and zoning strategies, OKAPI achieved competitive, and sometimes better results when compared with state-of-the-art methods for English email zoning, being simultaneously able to perform well on different languages.

Finally, we analyse how OKAPI adapts to new domains. For that, Table 8 shows the performance of both OKAPI and QUAGGA (Repke and Krestel, 2018), when evaluated in a different corpus then

Model	Corpus Train/Test	Accuracy 2 zones	Accuracy 5 zones
QUAGGA	Enron/ASF	0.94	0.86
OKAPI	Enron/ASF	**0.98**	**0.93**
QUAGGA	ASF/Enron	0.86	0.80
OKAPI	ASF/Enron	**0.97**	**0.88**

Table 8: Comparison between OKAPI and QUAGGA for domain adaptation, considering Repke and Krestel (2018) 2 and 5 zoning schema.

the one they were trained on. In these experiments, OKAPI clearly outperformed QUAGGA, indicating a superior ability to generalize to unseen domains.

6 Conclusion

To overcome the English-centric email zoning literature we propose OKAPI. Besides having multilingual capabilities, the proposed model is competitive with existing approaches for English email zoning, and attained state-of-the-art performance in domain adaptation tasks of English email zoning. Futhermore, to evaluate our model and to foster future research into multilingual email zoning, we release Cleverly zoning corpus – a corpus with 625 emails annotated in Portuguese, Spanish and French.

7 Acknowledgments

This project has received funding from the European Union's Horizon 2020 research and innovation program under grant agreement No 873904.

References

Nicolas Bettenburg, Bram Adams, Ahmed E. Hassan, and Michel Smidt. 2011. A lightweight approach to uncover technical artifacts in unstructured data. In International Conference on Program Comprehension, pages 185–188, Los Alamitos, CA, USA. IEEE Computer Society.

Janek Bevendorff, Khalid Al Khatib, Martin Potthast, and Benno Stein. 2020. Crawling and preprocessing mailing lists at scale for dialog analysis. In Proceedings of the 58th Annual Meeting of the Association for Computational Linguistics, pages 1151–1158, Online. Association for Computational Linguistics.

Vitor R. Carvalho and William W. Cohen. 2004. Learning to extract signature and reply lines from email. In CEAS - 2004 (Conference on Email and Anti-Spam), Mountain View, CA, USA.

Hao Chen, Jianying Hu, and Richard W. Sproat. 1999. Integrating geometrical and linguistic analysis for email signature block parsing. ACM Transactions on Information Systems, 17(4):343–366.

Mia Xu Chen, Benjamin N. Lee, Gagan Bansal, Yuan Cao, Shuyuan Zhang, Justin Lu, Jackie Tsay, Yinan Wang, Andrew M. Dai, Zhifeng Chen, Timothy Sohn, and Yonghui Wu. 2019. Gmail smart compose: Real-time assisted writing. In Proceedings of the 25th ACM SIGKDD International Conference on Knowledge Discovery & Data Mining, KDD '19, page 2287–2295, New York, NY, USA. Association for Computing Machinery.

Kyunghyun Cho, Bart van Merriënboer, Caglar Gulcehre, Dzmitry Bahdanau, Fethi Bougares, Holger Schwenk, and Yoshua Bengio. 2014. Learning phrase representations using RNN encoder–decoder for statistical machine translation. In Proceedings of the 2014 Conference on Empirical Methods in Natural Language Processing (EMNLP), pages 1724–1734, Doha, Qatar. Association for Computational Linguistics.

Panayotis Christidis and Álvaro G. Losada. 2019. Email based institutional network analysis: Applications and risks. The Social Sciences, 8(11):306.

Michael Collins. 2002. Discriminative training methods for hidden markov models: Theory and experiments with perceptron algorithms. In Proceedings of the ACL-02 Conference on Empirical Methods in Natural Language Processing - Volume 10, EMNLP '02, page 1–8, USA. Association for Computational Linguistics.

Alexis Conneau, Kartikay Khandelwal, Naman Goyal, Vishrav Chaudhary, Guillaume Wenzek, Francisco Guzmán, Edouard Grave, Myle Ott, Luke Zettlemoyer, and Veselin Stoyanov. 2020. Unsupervised cross-lingual representation learning at scale. In Proceedings of the 58th Annual Meeting of the Association for Computational Linguistics, pages 8440–8451, Online. Association for Computational Linguistics.

Corinna Cortes and Vladimir Vapnik. 1995. Support-vector networks. Machine Learning, 20:273–297.

Jeffrey L. Elman. 1990. Finding structure in time. Cognitive Science, 14(2):179 - 211.

Dominique Estival, Tanja Gaustad, Son Bao Pham, Will Radford, and Ben Hutchinson. 2007. Author profiling for english emails. In Proceedings of the 10th Conference of the Pacific Association for Computational Linguistics, pages 263–272.

Alex Graves and Jürgen Schmidhuber. 2005. Framewise phoneme classification with bidirectional LSTM and other neural network architectures. Neural Networks, 18(5):602–610.

Zhiheng Huang, Wei Xu, and Kai Yu. 2015. Bidirectional LSTM-CRF models for sequence tagging. CoRR, abs/1508.01991.

Anjuli Kannan, Karol Kurach, Sujith Ravi, Tobias Kaufmann, Andrew Tomkins, Balint Miklos, Greg Corrado, Laszlo Lukacs, Marina Ganea, Peter Young, and Vivek Ramavajjala. 2016. Smart reply: Automated response suggestion for email. In Proceedings of the 22nd ACM SIGKDD International Conference on Knowledge Discovery and Data Mining, KDD '16, page 955–964, New York, NY, USA. Association for Computing Machinery.

Bryan Klimt and Yiming Yang. 2004. The enron corpus: A new dataset for email classification research. In Proceedings of the 15th European Conference on Machine Learning, ECML'04, page 217–226, Berlin, Heidelberg. Springer-Verlag.

Furkan Kocayusufoglu, Ying Sheng, Nguyen Vo, James Wendt, Qi Zhao, Sandeep Tata, and Marc Najork. 2019. Riser: Learning better representations for richly structured emails. In The World Wide Web Conference, WWW '19, page 886–895, New York, NY, USA. Association for Computing Machinery.

John D. Lafferty, Andrew McCallum, and Fernando C. N. Pereira. 2001. Conditional random fields: Probabilistic models for segmenting and labeling sequence data. In Proceedings of the Eighteenth International Conference on Machine Learning, ICML '01, page 282–289, San Francisco, CA, USA. Morgan Kaufmann Publishers Inc.

Andrew Lampert, Robert Dale, and Cécile Paris. 2009. Segmenting email message text into zones. In Proceedings of the 2009 Conference on Empirical Methods in Natural Language Processing: A Meeting of SIGDAT, EMNLP 2009, pages 919–928. Association for Computational Linguistics (ACL).

Andrew Lampert, Robert Dale, and Cecile Paris. 2010. Detecting emails containing requests for action. In Human Language Technologies: The 2010 Annual Conference of the North American Chapter of the Association for Computational Linguistics, pages 984–992, Los Angeles, California. Association for Computational Linguistics.

Yann LeCun, Bernhard E. Boser, John S. Denker, Donnie Henderson, Richard E. Howard, Wayne E. Hubbard, and Lawrence D. Jackel. 1989. Backpropagation applied to handwritten zip code recognition. Neural Computation, 1(4):541–551.

M. McHugh. 2012. Interrater reliability: the kappa statistic. Biochemia Medica, 22:276 - 282.

Julia Proskurnia, Marc-Allen Cartright, Lluis Garcia-Pueyo, Ivo Krka, James B. Wendt, Tobias Kaufmann, and Balint Miklos. 2017. Template induction over unstructured email corpora. In Proceedings of the 26th International Conference on World Wide Web, WWW '17, page 1521–1530, Republic and Canton of Geneva, CHE. International World Wide Web Conferences Steering Committee.

Aziz Qaroush, Ismail M. Khater, and Mahdi Washaha. 2012. Identifying spam e-mail based-on statistical header features and sender behavior. In Proceedings of the CUBE International Information Technology Conference, page 771–778, NY, USA. Association for Computing Machinery.

Nils Reimers and Iryna Gurevych. 2019. Sentence-BERT: Sentence embeddings using Siamese BERT-networks. In Proceedings of the 2019 Conference on Empirical Methods in Natural Language Processing and the 9th International Joint Conference on Natural Language Processing (EMNLP-IJCNLP), pages 3982–3992, Hong Kong, China. Association for Computational Linguistics.

Tim Repke and Ralf Krestel. 2018. Bringing back structure to free text email conversations with recurrent neural networks. In European Conference on Information Retrieval, pages 114–126. Springer.

Jie Tang, Hang Li, Yunbo Cao, and Zhaohui Tang. 2005. Email data cleaning. In Proceedings of the Eleventh ACM SIGKDD International Conference on Knowledge Discovery in Data Mining, KDD '05, page 489–498, New York, NY, USA. Association for Computing Machinery.

Ian Tenney, Dipanjan Das, and Ellie Pavlick. 2019. BERT rediscovers the classical NLP pipeline. In Proceedings of the 57th Annual Meeting of the Association for Computational Linguistics, pages 4593–4601, Florence, Italy. Association for Computational Linguistics.

Ashish Vaswani, Noam Shazeer, Niki Parmar, Jakob Uszkoreit, Llion Jones, Aidan N Gomez, Ł ukasz Kaiser, and Illia Polosukhin. 2017. Attention is all you need. In Advances in Neural Information Processing Systems, volume 30, pages 5998–6008. Curran Associates, Inc.

Familiar words but strange voices: Modeling the influence of speech variability on word recognition

Alexandra Mayn[1] **Badr M. Abdullah**[2] **Dietrich Klakow**[2]

[1]Department of Information and Computing Sciences
Utrecht University, The Netherlands
[2]Department of Language Science and Technology (LST)
Saarland University, Germany

a.mayn@uu.nl, {babdullah|dietrich}@lsv.uni-saarland.de

Abstract

We present a deep neural model of spoken word recognition which is trained to retrieve the meaning of a word (in the form of a word embedding) given its spoken form, a task which resembles that faced by a human listener. Furthermore, we investigate the influence of variability in speech signals on the model's performance. To this end, we conduct a set of controlled experiments using word-aligned read speech data in German. Our experiments show that (1) the model is more sensitive to dialectical variation than gender variation, and (2) recognition performance of word cognates from related languages reflect the degree of relatedness between languages in our study. Our work highlights the feasibility of modeling human speech perception using deep neural networks.

1 Introduction

Human speech is highly complex and variable. The sources underlying this variability include speaker-related factors such as vocal tract shape, gender, age, and dialect as well as context-related factors such as word surprisal and phonological prominence. As a result, two acoustic realizations of the same word are unlikely to be identical even if produced by the same speaker. Nevertheless, listeners can reliably recognize spoken words despite the lack of acoustic-phonetic invariance in speech (Pisoni and Levi, 2007). The robust human ability to decode the intended message from a highly variable, noisy speech signal enables speakers of different but related languages to communicate with each other using their own mother tongue — a phenomenon that has been referred to as *receptive multilingualism* (Gooskens, 2019).

To gain a better understanding of human speech processing, a vast body of research at the intersection of speech perception and cognitive modeling has been dedicated to developing computational models of spoken word recognition (cf. Weber and Scharenborg (2012) for an overview). In a nutshell, models of spoken word recognition aim to simulate and explain the process of accessing the mental lexicon given a representation of an auditory word stimulus (McClelland and Elman, 1986; Marslen-Wilson, 1987; Norris, 1994; Gaskell and Marslen-Wilson, 1997). Despite the considerable differences in the representational specificity of the proposed models in the literature, there is a consensus among them with respect to the activation of multiple word candidates which leads to competition for lexical access (Weber and Scharenborg, 2012). One model of word recognition that we take inspiration from in this paper is the Distributed Cohort Model (DCM) (Gaskell and Marslen-Wilson, 1997), which is a connectionist model that defines the process of spoken word recognition as a mapping of low-level acoustic features onto the stored semantic and phonological representations, allowing efficient lexical access. A computational model of spoken word recognition allows researchers to simulate the conditions of behavioral experiments on human listeners and investigate whether the predictions of the model show human-like behavior.

Although deep neural networks (DNNs) have become the dominant paradigm for automatic speech recognition (ASR) research in the last decade (Graves et al., 2006; Mohamed et al., 2009; Hinton et al., 2012), using DNN-based ASR components to model human speech processing has only been explored recently with the EARSHOT model (Magnuson et al., 2020). EARSHOT is an incremental model based a long short-term memory (LSTM) that captures the temporal structure of speech. The training data for the EARSHOT model are spoken words produced using a speech synthesizer and each word is associated into a sparse vector that represents the word semantics. The authors

Proceedings of the 16th Conference of the European Chapter of the Associationfor Computational Linguistics: Student Research Workshop, pages 96–102
April 19 - 23, 2021. ©2021 Association for Computational Linguistics

use a unique but arbitrary sparse vector for each word, thus the semantic relatedness of words is not encoded in their representations. EARSHOT is trained to map each acoustic word form onto its semantic vector.

In this paper, we attempt to bridge between the connectionist view of word recognition and the recent advances in spoken language learning using deep neural networks. We also address some of the modeling limitations in the EARSHOT model. Precisely, our contribution is two-fold: (1) we propose a model of spoken word recognition based on a deep neural network that maps a spoken word form onto a distributed meaning representation. Our model is trained on naturalistic data that consists of actual acoustic realizations of spoken words extracted from the German portion of the Spoken Wikipedia Corpus. And (2) we investigate the degree to which the emergent representations from the model can generalize with respect to two sources of variability in speech signals — inter-speaker variability and cross-lingual variability.

2 A neural model of spoken word recognition

Our proposed model can be described at the high level as a function that maps the acoustic form of a word onto its lexical meaning. In the following, we describe the different representation schemes of our model.

2.1 Acoustic form representation

Human speech is modeled with various low-level signal representations. In this paper, we adopt the conventional approach in automatic speech recognition (ASR) which converts a time-domain speech waveform into a time-frequency frame-based representation using a standard signal processing pipeline. In particular, we convert each acoustic segment of a spoken word into a sequence of MFCC vectors $\mathbf{x}_{1:T} = (\mathbf{x}_1, \ldots, \mathbf{x}_T)$, where $\mathbf{x}_t \in \mathbb{R}^k$ is a spectral feature vector, or a frame, at timestep t and T is the number of frames.

2.2 Meaning representation

Following previous studies that adopted the distributional approach to represent lexical meaning (Pimentel et al., 2019; Williams et al., 2020), we use pre-trained distributed word representations, or word embeddings, as a proxy for the stored lexical representations of word forms. This modeling

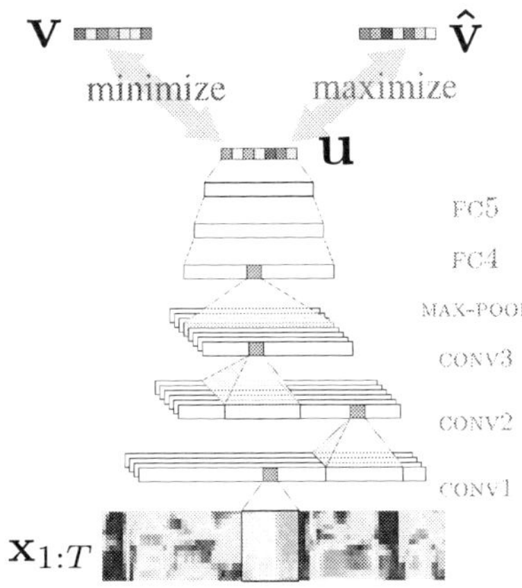

Figure 1: A schematic view of our proposed model for spoken word recognition.

choice can be justified since word embeddings have been shown to reliably encode lexical features such as taxonomic information (Rubinstein et al., 2015).

2.3 Proposed model

Architecture. Similar to the architecture presented in work of Maas et al. (2012), our proposed spoken word recognition model is based on a multilayer convolutional neural network that maps an acoustic input onto a meaning representation (depicted in Figure 1). However, instead of vector regression as the objective function, the training procedure of our model builds on the ideas of visually-grounded learning of spoken language (Harwath et al., 2016; Chrupała et al., 2017a). While in previous work models have been trained to project an image and its corresponding spoken caption onto a shared representation space, we train our model to project an acoustic segment of a word onto its word embedding. This process can be formalized as a mapping function using a deep neural network as follows:

$$\mathbf{u} = \boldsymbol{f}(\mathbf{x}_{1:T};\ \boldsymbol{\theta})$$

where $\mathbf{u}$ is the meaning representation computed by the model, $\boldsymbol{f}(.)$ is the model presented as a parametric function, $\mathbf{x}_{1:T}$ is the observed acoustic word segment, and $\boldsymbol{\theta}$ are the model's parameters learned in a supervised approach.

Training. Given a training dataset of N tuples $\{(\mathbf{x}^1_{1:T}, \mathbf{v}^1), (\mathbf{x}^2_{1:T}, \mathbf{v}^2), \ldots, (\mathbf{x}^N_{1:T}, \mathbf{v}^N)\}$, our model is trained to take an acoustic word token $\mathbf{x}_{1:T}$ as input, build up a meaning representation $\mathbf{u}$, and then minimize the distance between the computed representation $\mathbf{u}$ and the embedding of the word $\mathbf{v}$. This learning objective can be realized by projecting the acoustic word token into the word embedding space in such a way that an acoustic segment and embedding of the same word type are encouraged to end up closer in space than mismatched word embeddings. Concretely, we use a triplet margin loss function as follows:

$$\mathcal{L} = \sum_{i=1}^{N} \max\big(0, \alpha + d(\mathbf{u}^i, \mathbf{v}^i) - d(\hat{\mathbf{u}}^i, \mathbf{v}^i)\big) + \max\big(0, \alpha + d(\mathbf{u}^i, \mathbf{v}^i) - d(\mathbf{u}^i, \hat{\mathbf{v}}^i)\big)$$

where $d(.)$ is the cosine distance metric and $\mathbf{u}^i$ and $\mathbf{v}^i$ are the matching computed representation and embedding of a word, while $\hat{\mathbf{u}}^i$ and $\hat{\mathbf{v}}^i$ are the unmatched computed representation and embedding that are sampled from the mini-batch of N samples. α is the margin hyperparameter of the loss function.

3 Experimental setup

3.1 Experimental data

We use the multilingual Spoken Wikipedia Corpus (SWC), which consists of recordings of Wikipedia articles read by volunteers in German, Dutch, and English (Köhn et al., 2016). A large portion of the dataset has been word-aligned and each article is associated with a metadata file that optionally includes (self-identified) information about the speaker's gender and dialect. Therefore, this resource is highly suitable for our experimental aims concerning speech variability.

3.2 Model hyperparameters

Low-level speech features. We use 39-dimensional MFCC feature vectors as well as frame-level averaged energy as low-level speech features. Frames are extracted from speech segment of 25ms with 10ms overlap between frames. Each speech sample is then scaled with word-level zero mean and unit variance.

Speech encoder. We employ three convolutional layers over the temporal dimension with 128, 128, and 256 channels respectively and strides of 1 step for each layer. Batch normalization and ReLU nonlinearity are applied after each convolutional operation. The speech representation is down-sampled by applying a single max pooling operation at the end of the convolution block. Then, the resulting vector from the convolutional layers is fed into two fully-connected layers with dropout ($p = 0.5$) and ReLU non-linearity, followed by a linear projection that outputs a representation in the same dimensionality as the word embedding.

	dim	R@1	R@5	R@10
GloVe	300	0.159	0.451	0.608
FastText (FT)	300	0.176	0.461	0.610
Flair	4096	0.216	0.530	0.665
FT + Flair	4396	**0.227**	**0.557**	**0.696**

Table 1: Comparison of the model's retrieval performance using different word embeddings.

Training details. The triplet margin loss is used with $\alpha = 0.2$ for all presented experiments. We use the Adam optimizer with a learning rate of 1×10^{-3} and train our models with a batch size of 32 samples for 60 epochs.

4 Experiments

We present and discuss the results of our experiments in this section. We first investigate the effect of different pre-trained word embeddings on the model performance. In the variability experiments, we aim to probe the model's ability to generalize to unheard speaker types as well as to recognize spoken word cognates in two languages that are phylogenetically related to German: Dutch and English. Following Chrupała et al. (2017b), we use the R @ N metric to evaluate our models for $N = \{1, 5, 10\}$.

4.1 Choice of word embeddings

In this experiment, we train our model on a subset of the SWC consisting of 1500 word types, 20 tokens per type, with each of the following word embeddings: GloVe (Pennington et al., 2014), FastText (Bojanowski et al., 2017), bidirectional Flair (Akbik et al., 2018), and stacked Flair and FastText.

The retrieval scores of the model with different word embeddings are reported in Table 1. Although the difference is not dramatic, the best-performing model is the one that uses stacked FastText and Flair embeddings. It seems that stacking the embeddings provides richer semantic representations that benefit the model during training. Therefore, we proceed to the variability experiments with stacked Flair and FastText word embeddings as meaning representations.

	R@1	R@5	R@10	med. R
heard	0.473	0.850	0.970	2
speaker	0.348	0.688	0.812	3
gender	0.297	0.615	0.756	3
dialect	0.240	0.515	0.643	5

Table 2: Retrieval performance across speaker types.

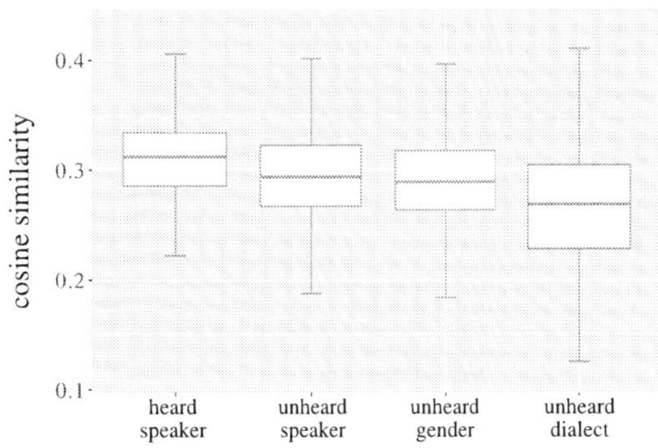

Figure 2: Average cosine similarity of utterance-embedding pairs by speaker type.

4.2 Speaker variability

In this experiment, we aim to probe the model's robustness against speaker variability by comparing its performance on various speaker groups: unheard utterances by heard speakers, unheard speakers, unheard gender (female speakers), and unheard dialect (speakers who self-identified as native speakers of the Swiss German variety). To this end, we train a separate model on a subset of the German portion of the SWC consisting of 2500 word types, 10-100 tokens per type, which were produced by native male speakers of standard German. This training set size is chosen as a trade-off between having a representative training set that includes a variety of words with different lexical properties and practical considerations such as training time and scalability of the model. The test sets we use for evaluation are matched at the token level, the only difference being the speaker characteristics.

Retrieval scores, including median rank of the correct embeddings, are reported in Table 2, and average cosine similarity of the computed meaning representation from the input signal to the corresponding embedding is displayed in Figure 2. Overall, one can observe that signal variability due to speaker-related factors that are unobserved during training degrades the model's performance. A one-way ANOVA test on the cosine similarities revealed significant differences between speaker types ($\chi^2(3) = 230.2, p < 0.001$).[1] Post-hoc Tukey HSD revealed significant differences between all groups except *unheard speaker* and *unheard gender* ($p > 0.5$).

The model performs best at recognizing words when they are spoken by a speaker heard during training, suggesting that the representations learned by the model are not entirely speaker invariant. Interestingly, the model is quite good at generalizing to unheard gender, performing on a par with unheard speakers of the same gender. We hypothesize that the model learns to abstract from pitch variations because there was pitch variability present in the training data. Finally, spoken words from an unheard dialect (i.e., Swiss German) are more challenging for the model to correctly recognize, which suggests that the representations induced by the model are more sensitive to fine-grained acoustic-phonetic variations in the signal than pitch variations.

4.3 Cross-lingual variability

Speakers of related languages are often able to decode some information from each other's speech without ever having had to explicitly learn the correspondences because related languages exhibit prelexical as well as lexical similarities. Gooskens et al. (2018) have shown that the comprehension ability of speakers of related languages correlates very strongly with the degree of language relatedness from a phylogenetic point of view. In this experiment, we explore whether and to what extent the model which has only been exposed to German will be able to recognize cognates in two related languages, English and Dutch. We also ask the question: does the cross-lingual performance reflect the degree of language relatedness? Since German and Dutch are a part of the continental West Germanic dialect continuum, while English is not, we hypothesize that the model should be better at recognizing spoken Dutch words than spoken English words.

To this end, we use the same model as for the speaker variability experiment. The test sets contain cognates in German, English and Dutch, aligned at the token level. Words in the German and Dutch test sets are produced by unheard male speakers of the standard language variety, while

[1] We used cosine similarities for statistical testing because ranks are not normally distributed; most words have low rank.

	R@1	R@5	R@10	med. R
German	0.388	0.715	0.819	2
Dutch	0.041	0.138	0.203	133.5
English	0.011	0.064	0.111	177.5
chance	≈ 0.0004	≈ 0.002	≈ 0.04	—

Table 3: Retrieval performance on cognates.

words in the English test set are produced by male native speakers of American English.[2] Spoken word representations for Dutch and English are obtained via a forward pass through the speech encoder, the same way as for German, and the model receives no explicit information that the cognates are in a different language.

Retrieval scores @1, 5 and 10, as well as median rank, for all three languages are reported in Table 3. Average cosine similarities of matching utterance-embedding pairs for the three languages are reported in Figure 3. The standard error is relatively high for the two related languages, especially for Dutch, because the model's guess for some cognates was quite poor. One-way repeated measures ANOVA reveals unsurprising significant differences between groups ($\chi^2(2)$=362.3, p<0.0001): the model is much better at recognizing German since this is the language that the model was trained on. If we compare the retrieval scores for Dutch and English to chance performance,[3] we observe that the model is relatively good at recognizing cognates in the two related languages, with 20% and 11% of words in Dutch and English respectively within the top 10 retrieved word embeddings. The difference in performance on the two related languages is shown to be significant in post-hoc Tukey HSD (p=0.004), supporting our hypothesis that cross-lingual word recognition performance reflects language relatedness.

We look more closely at the model's recognition performance on cognates (a selection is reported in Figure 4). Cognates which are well-recognized are mostly identical word forms, except for vowel length or slightly different consonant quality (e.g., the Dutch *jaar* (/jaːr/) and the German *Jahr* (/jaːɐ̯/). However, other interesting correspondences are apparent. For example, we observe that for the word *ship* (/ʃɪp/), the model is better at recognizing the English word, which is different from the German *Schiff* (/ʃɪf/) only in the final consonant, than the Dutch *schip* (/sxɪp/), where the word onset is different. This finding suggests that the model might have learned to pay closer attention to the beginnings of words. Future work could explore systematically which sound correspondences make it easy or difficult to recognize cognates.

[2]We would have favoured to include British English in the study as well but that was not feasible since not enough data of that kind is available in the SWC.

[3]We approximate chance performance by assuming that the probability of a word ending up at each of the 2500 positions is equally high. This approximation is not perfect since it does not take into account the fact that more frequent words are relatively more likely to end up in the top positions. However, this is very computationally expensive to calculate.

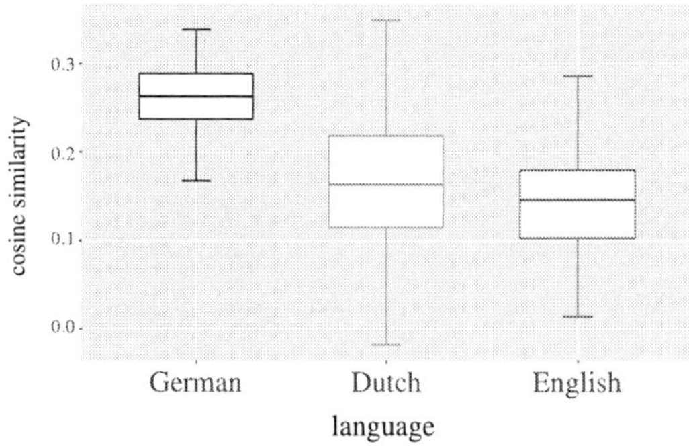

Figure 3: Average cosine similarity of utterance-embedding pairs by language.

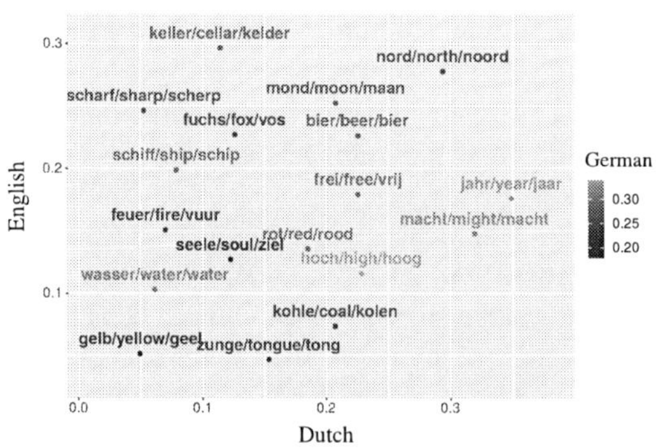

Figure 4: Average cosine similarity between matching utterance-pair embeddings for cognates in the three languages (words depicted as German/English/Dutch). Higher cosine similarity corresponds to a more accurate acoustic representation and, in turn, better recognition. For example, the word *cellar* is recognized better in English than in Dutch (reflected in a relatively higher cosine similarity). Lighter shades of blue correspond to higher cosine similarity for German utterances.

5 Discussion and future work

We observe that the representations produced by the model seem to be largely gender-invariant since the model's performance on unheard female speakers is on a par with its performance on unheard male speakers. On the other hand, dialect variability seems to have a stronger impact than gender which suggests that the model is sensitive to low-level acoustic-phonetic variance in the speech signal. We would expect a human listener to exhibit similar patterns in case of little exposure to dialectical variability.

Our model operates by creating a general representation of a word, which it uses to generalize to unheard speakers. However, there is evidence in psycholinguistics which suggests that we adapt to individuals' pronunciation and create speaker-specific representations (Kleinschmidt and Jaeger, 2015). This could be simulated by fine-tuning the trained model on more data by a particular speaker.

When tested on cognates in related languages in a zero-shot fashion, the model shows reasonably good cognate recognition performance. There is also a significant difference in the model's performance on Dutch and on English, reflecting the closer phylogenetic relationship between German and Dutch. One could imagine using the proposed model to test mutual intelligibility: if trained on Dutch, would such a model be better at recognizing German cognates than the other way around? This would be a test of intelligibility that eliminates extra-linguistic factors that cannot be isolated in behavioral experiments (van Heuven et al., 2012).

Since this is a word-level model of word recognition, there is no facilitatory effect of context, which human listeners are known to rely on to a large extent when there is uncertainty as to which word was uttered. In the cross-lingual experiment, too, we would expect that a model which is able to benefit from context would show much better performance. Such sentence-level models of related language comprehension are an exciting avenue to pursue in future work.

Acknowledgments

We would like to thank the anonymous reviewers of the student research workshop at EACL for their comments and suggestions. Badr M. Abdullah is supported by funding from the Deutsche Forschungsgemeinschaft (DFG, German Research Foundation), Project ID 232722074, SFB 1102.

References

Alan Akbik, Duncan Blythe, and Roland Vollgraf. 2018. Contextual string embeddings for sequence labeling. In *Proceedings of the 27th International Conference on Computational Linguistics*, pages 1638–1649, Santa Fe, New Mexico, USA. Association for Computational Linguistics.

Piotr Bojanowski, Edouard Grave, Armand Joulin, and Tomas Mikolov. 2017. Enriching word vectors with subword information. *Transactions of the Association for Computational Linguistics*, 5:135–146.

Grzegorz Chrupała, Lieke Gelderloos, and Afra Alishahi. 2017a. Representations of language in a model of visually grounded speech signal. *arXiv preprint arXiv:1702.01991*.

Grzegorz Chrupała, Lieke Gelderloos, and Afra Alishahi. 2017b. Representations of language in a model of visually grounded speech signal. In *Proceedings of the 55th Annual Meeting of the Association for Computational Linguistics (Volume 1: Long Papers)*, pages 613–622, Vancouver, Canada. Association for Computational Linguistics.

Gareth M Gaskell and William D Marslen-Wilson. 1997. Integrating form and meaning: A distributed model of speech perception. *Language and cognitive Processes*, 12(5-6):613–656.

Charlotte Gooskens. 2019. 8 receptive multilingualism. *Multidisciplinary Perspectives on Multilingualism: The Fundamentals*, 19:149.

Charlotte Gooskens, Vincent J van Heuven, Jelena Golubović, Anja Schüppert, Femke Swarte, and Stefanie Voigt. 2018. Mutual intelligibility between closely related languages in europe. *International Journal of Multilingualism*, 15(2):169–193.

Alex Graves, Santiago Fernández, Faustino Gomez, and Jürgen Schmidhuber. 2006. Connectionist temporal classification: labelling unsegmented sequence data with recurrent neural networks. In *Proceedings of the 23rd international conference on Machine learning*, pages 369–376.

David Harwath, Antonio Torralba, and James Glass. 2016. Unsupervised learning of spoken language with visual context. In *Advances in Neural Information Processing Systems*, pages 1858–1866.

Vincent J van Heuven, Charlotte Gooskens, and Renée van Bezooijen. 2012. Mutual intelligibility of dutch and german cognates.

Geoffrey Hinton, Li Deng, Dong Yu, George E Dahl, Abdel-rahman Mohamed, Navdeep Jaitly, Andrew Senior, Vincent Vanhoucke, Patrick Nguyen, Tara N Sainath, et al. 2012. Deep neural networks for acoustic modeling in speech recognition: The shared views of four research groups. *IEEE Signal processing magazine*, 29(6):82–97.

Dave F Kleinschmidt and Florian T Jaeger. 2015. Robust speech perception: recognize the familiar, generalize to the similar, and adapt to the novel. *Psychological review*, 122(2):148.

Arne Köhn, Florian Stegen, and Timo Baumann. 2016. Mining the spoken wikipedia for speech data and beyond.

Andrew L Maas, Stephen D Miller, Tyler M O'neil, Andrew Y Ng, and Patrick Nguyen. 2012. Word-level acoustic modeling with convolutional vector regression. In *Proc. ICML Workshop Representation Learn.*

James S Magnuson, Heejo You, Sahil Luthra, Monica Li, Hosung Nam, Monty Escabi, Kevin Brown, Paul D Allopenna, Rachel M Theodore, Nicholas Monto, et al. 2020. Earshot: A minimal neural network model of incremental human speech recognition. *Cognitive science*, 44(4):e12823.

William Marslen-Wilson. 1987. Functional parallelism in spoken word-recognition. *Cognition*, 25:71–102.

James L McClelland and Jeffrey L Elman. 1986. The TRACE model of speech perception. *Cognitive Psychology*, 18(1):1 – 86.

Abdel-rahman Mohamed, George Dahl, and Geoffrey Hinton. 2009. Deep belief networks for phone recognition. In *NIPS workshop on deep learning for speech recognition and related applications*, volume 1, page 39. Vancouver, Canada.

Dennis Norris. 1994. Shortlist: a connectionist model of continuous speech recognition. *Cognition*, 52(3):189 – 234.

Jeffrey Pennington, Richard Socher, and Christopher D Manning. 2014. Glove: Global vectors for word representation. In *Proceedings of the 2014 conference on empirical methods in natural language processing (EMNLP)*, pages 1532–1543.

Tiago Pimentel, Arya D McCarthy, Damian Blasi, Brian Roark, and Ryan Cotterell. 2019. Meaning to form: Measuring systematicity as information. In *Proceedings of the 57th Annual Meeting of the Association for Computational Linguistics*, pages 1751–1764.

David B Pisoni and Susannah Levi. 2007. Some observations on representations and representational specificity in speech perception and spoken word recognition. In *The Oxford Handbook of Psycholinguistics*, pages 3–18. Oxford University Press.

Dana Rubinstein, Effi Levi, Roy Schwartz, and Ari Rappoport. 2015. How well do distributional models capture different types of semantic knowledge? *Volume 2: Short Papers*.

Andrea Weber and Odette Scharenborg. 2012. Models of spoken-word recognition. *Wiley Interdisciplinary Reviews: Cognitive Science*, 3(3):387–401.

Adina Williams, Tiago Pimentel, Arya McCarthy, Hagen Blix, Eleanor Chodroff, and Ryan Cotterell. 2020. Predicting declension class from form and meaning. In *Proceedings of the 58th Annual Meeting for the Association of Computational Linguistics*. York.

Emoji-Based Transfer Learning for Sentiment Tasks

Susann Boy
Saarland University

Dana Ruiter
Saarland University

Dietrich Klakow
Saarland University

{sboy,druiter,dietrich.klakow}@lsv.uni-saarland.de

Abstract

Sentiment tasks such as hate speech detection and sentiment analysis, especially when performed on languages other than English, are often low-resource. In this study, we exploit the emotional information encoded in emojis to enhance the performance on a variety of sentiment tasks. This is done using a transfer learning approach, where the parameters learned by an emoji-based source task are transferred to a sentiment target task. We analyse the efficacy of the transfer under three conditions, i.e. i) the emoji content and ii) label distribution of the target task as well as iii) the difference between monolingually and multilingually learned source tasks. We find i.a. that the transfer is most beneficial if the target task is balanced with high emoji content. Monolingually learned source tasks have the benefit of taking into account the culturally specific use of emojis and gain up to F1 $+0.280$ over the baseline.

1 Introduction

Many natural language processing (NLP) tasks suffer from a lack of available data. This is especially true for sentiment tasks, such as hate speech (HS) detection, which depend on the availability of manually annotated data. When moving to languages other than English, many sentiment tasks quickly become very low-resourced.

On the other hand, noisy social media content is available in abundance and many sentiment tasks are based on user comments on such platforms. Emojis can be a valuable source for the distant supervision of sentiment tasks, as they correlate with the underlying emotion of a comment. In this study, we aim to exploit the emotional information encoded in emojis to improve the performance on various sentiment tasks using a transfer learning approach from an emoji-based **source task** (ST) to a sentiment **target task** (TT). Previous work has focused on the transfer from predicting single emojis (Felbo et al., 2017) or strictly pre-defined emoji-clusters (Deriu et al., 2016). However, pre-defined emoji clusters do not take into account the culturally diverse usage of emojis (Park et al., 2012; Kaneko et al., 2019). We therefore introduce data-driven supervised and unsupervised emoji clusters and compare these with single emoji prediction tasks. Specifically, we analyze the efficacy of the transfer from a single emoji or (un)supervised emoji cluster prediction ST to a sentiment TT under three conditions, i.e. *i)* low vs. high amount of **emoji content** present in TT, *ii)* balanced vs. unbalanced **label distribution** in TT and *iii)* **monolingually** or **multilingually** learned ST. The first two conditions are based on typical qualities of sentiment corpora, which tend to be unbalanced in their label distribution with varying degrees of emoji content depending on the source of the data. The third condition is relevant for languages for which a TT is low-resource and which might benefit from a multilingually learned ST.

In Section 2 we give an outline of related work, followed by the introduction of our method (Section 3). The experimental setup in Section 4 details the data and models used as well as the (un)supervised clusters generated. In Section 5 we describe our results and conclude in Section 6.

2 Related Work

Emojis have been used as a type of distant supervision using pre-defined emotion classes based on psychological models (Suttles and Ide, 2013), binary (*positive/negative*) classes (Deriu et al., 2016) or a set of single emojis (Felbo et al., 2017). However, such pre-defined emoji classes often do not account for the culturally diverse use of emojis (Park et al., 2012; Kaneko et al., 2019). In contrast, our

Proceedings of the 16th Conference of the European Chapter of the Associationfor Computational Linguistics: Student Research Workshop, pages 103–110
April 19 - 23, 2021. ©2021 Association for Computational Linguistics

work does not pre-define the emotion classes found in emojis and instead learns these classes, or clusters, from the data itself. While our and the above approaches focus on exploiting emojis as additional labelled data, e.g. in a transfer setting, emoji embeddings (Eisner et al., 2016) have been used as additional features in downstream tasks such as sarcasm detection (Subramanian et al., 2019).

Transfer learning has recently been driven by transformer-based (Vaswani et al., 2017) language models (LM) such as BERT (Devlin et al., 2019) or XLM-R (Conneau et al., 2020). When learning a source task on these models, the representations in the encoder change to become informative to the task at hand. In a parameter transfer setting, a new but related target task then profits from the learned representations in the encoder. Transfer learning has been applied to sentiment analysis (SA) using parameter transfer methods such as pre-trained sentiment embeddings (Dong and de Melo, 2018) or machine translation-based context vectors (McCann et al., 2017). Our approach forms part of the parameter transfer approach, as we use encoder representations learned using emoji-based source tasks and transfer these to sentiment target tasks.

Hate speech classification and **sentiment analysis** have in recent years been the object of many shared tasks (Rosenthal et al., 2017; Wiegand, 2018; Basile et al., 2019; Mandl et al., 2019; Ogrodniczuk and Łukasz Kobyliński, 2019). Classification models for these tasks often rely on feature engineering and statistical methods such as naive-bayes (Saleem et al., 2016), logistic regression over subwords (Waseem and Hovy, 2016) or neural approaches including convolutional neural networks (Park and Fung, 2017) or, as in our case, the representations of large LMs (Yang et al., 2019).

3 Method: Emoji-Prediction

For our parameter transfer, we rely on a single transformer-based LM which is shared among different tasks. A sequence $x \in X$ is featurized by reading it into the encoder of the LM and retrieving its last hidden state. A linear layer is then used as a predictive function $f : X \rightarrow Y$ to predict labels $y \in Y$. A task $\mathcal{T} = \{Y, f(x)\}$ is then a set of labels Y and the predictive function f over the instances in X.

We follow a **transfer learning** approach, where source task $\mathcal{T}_S$ is an emoji-based classification task, i.e. given a sequence, predict the emoji (class) that it originally contained. Target task $\mathcal{T}_T$ is a downstream task such as SA or HS (Section 4.1). Each task has its own set of instances X, labels Y and predictive function f, while the feature-generating LM stays the same. The error of predictor f is back-propagated to the LM, which allows us to transfer learned parameters from $\mathcal{T}_S$ to $\mathcal{T}_T$.

3.1 Source Tasks (ST)

We focus on 5 different emoji-based STs, that can be divided into two types, emoji prediction (EP) and emoji cluster prediction. To sample emojis for EP or create clusters, we rely on a large collection of user generated comments. **EP** is a multi-class prediction task over the 64 most common emojis identified in the collection of comments. Concretely, given a tweet with all emojis removed, the classifier has to predict which of the 64 emojis was originally contained within it.

The **emoji cluster prediction** tasks can be supervised (PMI-{Target,Swear}) or unsupervised (KMeans-{2,3}). In this case the task is simplified: Given a tweet with all emojis removed, predict the cluster to which the emoji originally contained in the tweet belonged.

Unsupervised Clusters In order to account for the cultural differences in the use of emojis, we learn emoji clusters directly from the user generated data. We generate 50-dimensional vector representations over the tokens in the collection of user comments using the continuous bag of words (Mikolov et al., 2013) approach. We then perform k-means clustering with 6 target clusters on the representations of emojis that occurred ≥ 1000 times. These clusters are manually merged into 2 (*positive/negative*) and 3 (*positive/negative/neutral*) clusters to create the binary **KMeans-2** and ternary **KMeans-3** emoji cluster prediction STs respectively. Below a comment to be classified as *positive* according to the KMeans-{2,3} tasks, as it originally contained an emoji that belonged to the *positive* cluster:

So beautiful and great advice →positive

Supervised Clusters As an alternative to the completely unsupervised clusters, we exploit the mutual information between emojis and swear words as a type of distant supervision for HS tasks. We calculate the pointwise mutual information (PMI) between comments in our collection of user content (not) containing slurs and the emojis that appear. An emoji is in the slur cluster if its PMI is larger to comments containing swearwords, otherwise it is in the neutral cluster. **PMI-Swear** is then a binary classification task based on the resulting slur/neutral emoji clusters.

While the unsupervised emoji cluster prediction STs and PMI-Swear are source-oriented, i.e. learned on user generated content, we also explore target-oriented clusters that rely on the shared information between emojis and the labels in each of the TTs. Concretely, we calculate the PMI between the label of an instance in the respective TT training data and the emojis it contains. The emoji is placed into the cluster of the label to which its PMI value is largest. **PMI-Target** is the ST based on these target-oriented emoji clusters.

3.2 Target Tasks (TT)

Once the classifier has been fully trained on the ST, and thus has adapted the underlying LMs representations to fit the ST at hand, we discard it and train a new classifier on top of the enriched LM to predict the TT. We evaluate this transfer from the various STs on two main categories of TTs, namely Hate Speech Detection and Sentiment Analysis. Given a user generated comment, **Hate Speech** Detection is the task of classifying the comment as either *hate* or *none*. Note, however, that concrete label names (e.g. *offense*, *hate*, *harmful*) may differ across specific HS tasks.

While HS in our case is a binary classification task, **Sentiment Analysis** is a ternary classification task which takes as input a user generated comment and classifies it as either *positive*, *neutral* or *negative*. In the following an example from the Sentiment Analysis in Twitter (Rosenthal et al., 2017) task:

> *Finally starting the 5th season of Dexter.*
> *See ya later, weekend! →positive*

Both HS and SA are sentiment-based tasks, e.g. *hate* towards a group of people or *positive* sentiment towards a product etc. We therefore take these two types of tasks to have the potential to benefit from the emotion information encoded in emojis. In the following sections we explore the conditions under which the transfer from an emoji-based ST to a sentiment-based TT is beneficial for the TT.

4 Experimental Setup

We describe the data used for the STs and TTs respectively (Section 4.1), followed by the specifications of the encoding LM (Section 4.2) and the emoji cluster creation (Section 4.3).

Corpus	# Tweets Train	Test	# Emojis
Target Tasks (TT)			
HS-DE	1158/2439	970/2061	853 (7.2%)
SA-DE	1346/900/3676	83/49/197	166 (2%)
HS-ES	1857/2643	660/940	957 (14.5%)
SA-EN	18481/7551/21542	2375/3972/5937	1211 (1.9%)
SA-AR	653/1022/1336	1514/2222/2364	2126 (22.5%)
HS-PL	812/8726	134/866	1733 (13.7%)
Source Tasks (ST)			
TW-DE	16M	–	3M (10%)
TW-EN	323M	–	82M (17%)
TW-ES	320M	–	43M (9%)
TW-PL	7M	–	1M (12%)
TW-AR	183M	–	56M (20%)

Table 1: Number of train, test (for TT) and collected (for ST) tweets as well as number of (non-unique) emojis contained in each corpus. Percentage of training tweets containing emojis in brackets. TTs with label distribution for HS (*hate/none*) and SA (*positive/negative/neutral*) tasks.

4.1 Data

Source Tasks We use a collection[1] of tweets that has been collected from the Twitter stream between 2011 and 2019 as our corpus needed to sample emojis and create emoji clusters for the STs. We perform language identification using the `polyglot`[2] library over the tweets to create a corpus for German, English, Spanish, Polish and Arabic (TW-{DE,EN,ES,PL,AR}) respectively.

To automatically identify swear words for PMI-Swear, we use a German and a multilingual swear word collection, namely `WoltLab`[3] and `Hatebase`[4]. In total, we collected 785 slurs for German, and 1531, 140, 306, 79 for English, Spanish, Polish and Arabic respectively.

Target Tasks We work with 6 target tasks in total, 3 HS and 3 SA tasks, taking into account their emoji content, class (im)balance and language.

For German, we use GermEval 2018 (Wiegand, 2018) Task 1 (*offense/other*) (HS-DE) and SB10k (Cieliebak et al., 2017) (*positive/negative/neutral*) (SA-DE). For English, we use Sentiment Analysis in Twitter (Rosenthal et al., 2017) (*positive/negative/neutral*) (SA-EN). Sentiment Anal-

[1] www.archive.org/details/twitterstream
[2] www.github.com/aboSamoor/polyglot
[3] www.woltlab.com/attachment/3615-schimpfwortliste-txt/
[4] www.hatebase.org/

ysis in Twitter is also used for Arabic (SA-AR). For Spanish we use HatEval (Basile et al., 2019) (*hate/none*) (HS-ES) and for Polish, we use PolEval (Ogrodniczuk and Łukasz Kobyliński, 2019) Task 6 (*harmful/none*) (HS-PL). For all of the above, we use the original train/test splits. While the HA tasks have different label names, we normalize these to be *hate/none* across all tasks. For all SA, the labels to be predicted are *positive/negative/neutral*.

In Table 1, we report the label distribution, *hate/none* for HS and *positive/negative/neutral* for SA, across all TT training and test sets, as well as ST Twitter corpora sizes. For both ST and TT corpora, we also report the percentage as well as total number of tweets containing emojis.

Preprocessing All data sets undergo the same preprocessing. Tweets are tokenized using the NLTK (Bird and Loper, 2004) `TweetTokenizer` and user mentions, retweets and punctuation are removed. Repeated characters are shortened. We use token frequencies to determine the standard orthography of a word (e.g. *coooool* $\rightarrow$ *cool* instead of *col*).

4.2 Model Specifications

For the monolingual (German) experiments, we use the German BERT[5] (BERT-DE) and for multilingual experiments we use `Bert-Base-Multilingual-Cased` (BERT-M) as the LM to encode the tweets. We base our code[6] on the `simpletransformers`[7] sequence classification implementations of the above models. Each classification task is trained for a maximum of 10 epochs using early stopping over the validation accuracy with $\delta = 0.01$ and patience 3. Training was performed on a single Titan-X GPU, which took between 1 and 6 hours depending on the data size. We evaluate the resulting classifiers using the Macro F1 measure.

4.3 Clusters

We describe the creation of the emoji clusters used for the emoji cluster STs.

Unsupervised The unsupervised clusters (Section 3) were trained on TW-DE and the concatenation of TW-{DE,EN,ES,PL,AR} for the mono- and multilingual experiments respectively. In both cases, this yielded clusters that can be manually categorized as *happy, love, fun, nature, unhappy, other* (Figure 1). For KMeans-3, {*happy, fun, love*} were merged to *positive*, {*other, nature*} to *neutral* and {*unhappy*} was used as the *negative* class. For KMeans-2, the *neutral* class is ignored.

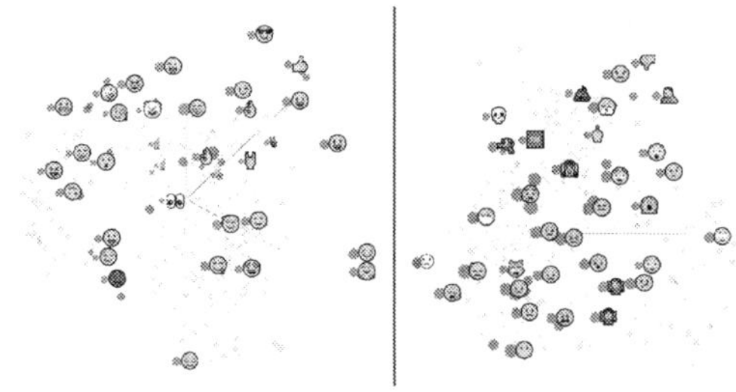

Figure 1: *Happy* (left) and *unhappy* (right) emoji clusters obtained by KMeans on TW-DE.

Supervised The PMI-Target clusters are trained on the respective TT training data. The slur lists are used to identify the slurs in the twitter corpora. PMI-Swear is then trained on TW-DE and the concatenation of TW-{DE,EN,ES,PL,AR} for the mono- and multilingual experiments respectively.

5 Results

We train each model over 10 seeded runs and report the averaged Macro F1 with standard error (Figure 2). For each TT, we train a **baseline**, which is the same pre-trained BERT-{DE,M} model that is now fine-tuned directly on the TT classification task at hand, without prior training on the ST. We compare these baselines with those models that have undergone a transfer from ST to TT. We use the term *equivalent* to signify that two models lie within each others error bounds.

5.1 Condition 1: Emoji Content

We evaluate the effect that STs have on TTs with different amounts of emoji content. We focus on the TTs with the lowest and highest amount of emoji content, namely SA-EN (1.9% emoji content) and SA-AR (22.5%). This is the multilingual case. For the monolingual case, we evaluate the effect on SA-DE (2%) and HS-DE (7.2%). All of these TTs are unbalanced, i.e. the minority class makes up 15.2–32.2% of the training data.

The **monolingual**, low emoji content SA-DE task does not profit from the transfer. Rather, the

[5] www.deepset.ai/german-bert

[6] https://github.com/uds-lsv/emoji-transfer

[7] www.github.com/ThilinaRajapakse/simpletransformers

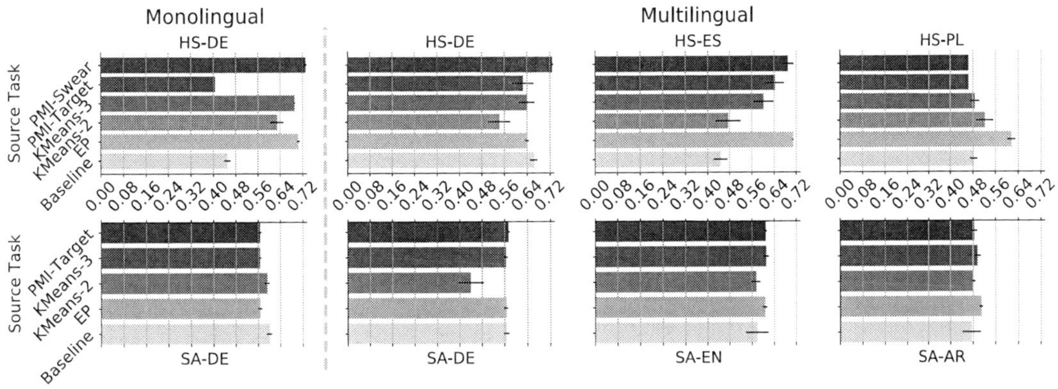

Figure 2: Macro F1 of the HS and SA target tasks transferred from monolingual (left) and multilingual (right) STs.

training on most STs leads to a slight drop in F1-Macro compared to the baseline (F1 0.600). On the other hand, high emoji content HS-DE greatly benefits from the transfer, with PMI-Swear (F1 0.730) being especially beneficial for the performance on the TT, yielding a gain of F1 +0.280 over the baseline. This shows that the shared information in emojis and slurs is relevant to the HS task at hand. Also beneficial are EP (F1 0.705), and the unsupervised KMeans-3 (F1 0.690) and KMeans-2 (F1 0.629) cluster prediction tasks. Only the supervised PMI-Target (F1 0.405) does no seem to be beneficial for the performance on the TT, leading to a drop in performance, which is due to the unbalanced nature of the TT (Section 5.2).

The **multilingual** case shows a slightly mixed trend. Low emoji content SA-EN does not benefit from the transfer, but unlike in the monolingual setting, it is not harmed by it either. All STs lead to a TT performance that is equivalent to the baseline (F1 0.578). High emoji content SA-AR only barely profits from the transfer, with EP (F1 0.509) leading to a small gain of F1 (+0.034) over the baseline (F1 0.475), while all other STs lead to an equivalent performance to the baseline. The overall trend is similar to the monolingual case but the positive and negative effects are dimmed down, which may be due to the multilingual aspect (Section 5.3).

The **general trend** shows that a decent amount of emoji content in the TT training data is crucial for the transfer to be beneficial.

5.2 Condition 2: Label Distribution

To analyze the effect that the STs have on differently (un)balanced TTs, we focus on HS-PL (the minority class makes up 8.5% of training data) and HS-ES (41.3%), as they are the two most (un)balanced TTs, while being comparable in terms of emoji content (13.7% and 14.5% respectively).

For **unbalanced** HS-PL, EP (F1 0.617) and unsupervised KMeans-2 (F1 0.522) lead to an improvement of F1 +0.134 and F1 +0.039 over the baseline, respectively. All other STs are equivalent to the baseline. **Balanced** HS-ES benefits from all TTs, with EP (F1 0.708) leading to a gain of F1 +0.261 over the baseline (F1 0.447), followed by PMI-Swear (F1 0.690) and PMI-Target (F1 0.643). The unsupervised clusters are beneficial but less effective, with F1 0.602 and F1 0.475 for KMeans-3 and KMeans-2 respectively, which likely stems from the multilingual aspect (Section 5.3).

PMI-Target performs poorly on unbalanced HS-PL (and HS-DE etc.) due to its use of mutual information between emojis and the TT labels. This leads to it reproducing the class imbalance, making it less effective on unbalanced TTs.

The difference in impact of **PMI-Swear** on HS-PL (none) and HS-ES (and HS-DE) (gain) can be explained by the composition of the ST dataset. TW-PL is the smallest corpus in the multilingual collection of user comments, and this sparsity is further driven by the morphological complexity of Polish, such that the 306 slurs from the Polish slur list only resulted in $65k$ Polish training samples in PMI-Swear, as opposed to 1.8M and 3M for German and Spanish respectively.

Overall, if the label distribution in TT is balanced, the TT easily benefits from the transfer. Otherwise other conditions such as the multilinguality or emoji content become more relevant.

5.3 Condition 3: Multilinguality

We analyze the effectiveness of the transfer in a monolingual and multilingual setting. For this, we focus on the effect that the monolingually and multilingually learned STs have on HS-DE and SA-DE. Both TTs are unbalanced, while HS-DE has a high emoji content and SA-DE has a low emoji content.

The different effects of the emoji-content in HS-DE and SA-DE has been discussed in Section 5.1, showing that in the **monolingual** setting, high emoji content HS-DE benefits from the transfer, while low emoji content SA-DE does not. In the **multilingual** case, we see a similar, but dimmed, trend. SA-DE does not benefit from the transfer, with all TTs leading to an equivalent performance as the baseline (F1 0.566), except KMeans-2 (F1 0.439) which is below the baseline. The STs have a similar performance on HS-DE, being equivalent or below the baseline (F1 0.663). Only PMI-Swear (F1 0.678) is beneficial for the TT performance.

The effect of ST-oriented clusters KMeans-{2,3} was beneficial in the monolingual case (HS-DE), but this benefit is lost in the multilingual setting. This underlines our original idea that ST-oriented unsupervised emoji clusters learned on large amounts of user generated text have the advantage of accounting for **cultural differences** in the usage of emojis. When learned multilingually, this advantage is lost. An example of the culturally diverse use of emojis is ♻, which is rather infrequent in Europe and might be used to point towards the importance of *recycling*. In TW-AR, this emoji is among the top 5 most frequent emojis, and is used to motivate other users to *share* their content.

The **overall trend** thus shows that monolingually learned STs are more beneficial than multilingual STs. However, if the training data of a TT is balanced, this effect is less pronounced.

5.4 Comparison to Benchmark Results

To put the results into a broader perspective, we compare to state-of-the-art (SOTA) models for each of the shared-tasks/datasets that our TTs are based on (Table 2). For two of the **Hate Speech** benchmarks, the performance of our transfer approach is close to the SOTA, namely with a difference of F1 -0.038 (HS-DE) and F1 -0.03 (HS-ES). For HS-PL, we were able to achieve a gain of $+0.031$ over the SOTA. Across all three **Sentiment Analysis** benchmarks, our models are below the SOTA. This indicates that SA, in general, is a more difficult task to our transfer approach than HS, possibly due to its ternary, rather than binary, classification objective. This is another factor causing the transfer to be overall more beneficial for HS rather than SA, next to the unbalanced (SA-{EN,AR}) and low-emoji content (SA-DE) nature of the SA tasks.

TT	Method	F1	SOTA
HS-DE	PMI-Swear (monolingual)	0.730	**0.768**
HS-ES	EP	0.708	**0.730**
HS-PL	EP	**0.617**	0.586
SA-DE	Baseline (monolingual)	0.600	**0.651**
SA-AR	EP	0.509	**0.610**
SA-EN	KMeans-3	0.611	**0.677**

Table 2: Macro F1 comparison of top-scoring transfer method (*F1*) with SOTA results on the different TT test sets. Best scores in **bold**. See (Montani and Schüller, 2018) (HS-DE), (Basile et al., 2019) (HS-ES), (Ogrodniczuk and Łukasz Kobyliński, 2019) (HS-PL), (Cieliebak et al., 2017) (SA-DE) and (Rosenthal et al., 2017) (HS-{AR,EN}) for SOTA method descriptions.

6 Summary

We have evaluated and identified conditions under which the transfer from an emoji-based ST is beneficial for a sentiment TT. In the experiments in Section 5 we observed three major trends, namely *i*) TTs with high amounts of emoji content benefit more from the transfer, *ii*) PMI-Target tends to be detrimental to unbalanced TTs and *iii*) monolingually learned STs tend to perform better than their multilingual counterparts, due to their improved representation of culturally unique emoji usages. The latter underlines the importance of taking into account cultural differences when exploiting the information encoded in emojis.

From these results, we can draw conclusions about the conditions under which a given emoji-based ST is beneficial. Due to the shared information between emojis and slurs, **PMI-Swear** is beneficial to HS tasks when the data that can be generated from the swear word list is decently large. **PMI-Target** is beneficial when the TT is balanced, otherwise it replicates the already existing class imbalance. Unsupervised **KMeans-{2,3}** should be learned monolingually to be beneficial and **EP** is a safe choice for TTs with high emoji content.

Acknowledgments

We want to thank the anonymous reviewers as well as Thomas Kleinbauer for their valuable feedback. The project on which this paper is based is funded by the DFG under funding code WI 4204/3-1.

References

Valerio Basile, Cristina Bosco, Elisabetta Fersini, Debora Nozza, Viviana Patti, Francisco Manuel Rangel Pardo, Paolo Rosso, and Manuela Sanguinetti. 2019. SemEval-2019 task 5: Multilingual detection of hate speech against immigrants and women in Twitter. In *Proceedings of the 13th International Workshop on Semantic Evaluation*, pages 54–63, Minneapolis, Minnesota, USA. Association for Computational Linguistics.

Steven Bird and Edward Loper. 2004. NLTK: The natural language toolkit. In *Proceedings of the ACL Interactive Poster and Demonstration Sessions*, pages 214–217, Barcelona, Spain. Association for Computational Linguistics.

Mark Cieliebak, Jan Milan Deriu, Dominic Egger, and Fatih Uzdilli. 2017. A twitter corpus and benchmark resources for German sentiment analysis. In *Proceedings of the Fifth International Workshop on Natural Language Processing for Social Media*, pages 45–51, Valencia, Spain. Association for Computational Linguistics.

Alexis Conneau, Kartikay Khandelwal, Naman Goyal, Vishrav Chaudhary, Guillaume Wenzek, Francisco Guzmán, Edouard Grave, Myle Ott, Luke Zettlemoyer, and Veselin Stoyanov. 2020. Unsupervised cross-lingual representation learning at scale. In *Proceedings of the 58th Annual Meeting of the Association for Computational Linguistics*, pages 8440–8451, Online. Association for Computational Linguistics.

Jan Deriu, Maurice Gonzenbach, Fatih Uzdilli, Aurelien Lucchi, Valeria De Luca, and Martin Jaggi. 2016. SwissCheese at SemEval-2016 task 4: Sentiment classification using an ensemble of convolutional neural networks with distant supervision. In *Proceedings of the 10th International Workshop on Semantic Evaluation (SemEval-2016)*, pages 1124–1128, San Diego, California. Association for Computational Linguistics.

Jacob Devlin, Ming-Wei Chang, Kenton Lee, and Kristina Toutanova. 2019. BERT: Pre-training of deep bidirectional transformers for language understanding. In *Proceedings of the 2019 Conference of the North American Chapter of the Association for Computational Linguistics: Human Language Technologies, Volume 1 (Long and Short Papers)*, pages 4171–4186, Minneapolis, Minnesota. Association for Computational Linguistics.

Xin Dong and Gerard de Melo. 2018. A helping hand: Transfer learning for deep sentiment analysis. In *Proceedings of the 56th Annual Meeting of the Association for Computational Linguistics (Volume 1: Long Papers)*, pages 2524–2534, Melbourne, Australia. Association for Computational Linguistics.

Ben Eisner, Tim Rocktäschel, Isabelle Augenstein, Matko Bošnjak, and Sebastian Riedel. 2016. emoji2vec: Learning emoji representations from their description. In *Proceedings of The Fourth International Workshop on Natural Language Processing for Social Media*, pages 48–54, Austin, TX, USA. Association for Computational Linguistics.

Bjarke Felbo, Alan Mislove, Anders Søgaard, Iyad Rahwan, and Sune Lehmann. 2017. Using millions of emoji occurrences to learn any-domain representations for detecting sentiment, emotion and sarcasm. In *Proceedings of the 2017 Conference on Empirical Methods in Natural Language Processing*, pages 1615–1625, Copenhagen, Denmark. Association for Computational Linguistics.

Daisuke Kaneko, Alexander Toet, Shota Ushiama, Anne-Marie Brouwer, Victor Kallen, and Jan B.F. van Erp. 2019. Emojigrid: A 2d pictorial scale for cross-cultural emotion assessment of negatively and positively valenced food. *Food Research International*, 115:541 – 551.

Thomas Mandl, Sandip Modha, Prasenjit Majumder, Daksh Patel, Mohana Dave, Chintak Mandlia, and Aditya Patel. 2019. Overview of the hasoc track at fire 2019: Hate speech and offensive content identification in indo-european languages. In *Proceedings of the 11th Forum for Information Retrieval Evaluation*, FIRE '19, page 14–17, New York, NY, USA. Association for Computing Machinery.

Bryan McCann, James Bradbury, Caiming Xiong, and Richard Socher. 2017. Learned in translation: Contextualized word vectors. In *Advances in Neural Information Processing Systems*, volume 30, pages 6294–6305. Curran Associates, Inc.

Tomas Mikolov, Kai Chen, Greg Corrado, and Jeffrey Dean. 2013. Efficient estimation of word representations in vector space.

Joaquín Padilla Montani and Peter Schüller. 2018. Tuwienkbs at germeval 2018: German abusive tweet detection. In *Proceedings of GermEval 2018, 14th Conference on Natural Language Processing (KONVENS 2018)*, pages 45–50.

Maciej Ogrodniczuk and Łukasz Kobyliński, editors. 2019. *Proceedings of the PolEval 2019 Workshop*. Institute of Computer Science, Polish Academy of Sciences, Warsaw, Poland.

Jaram Park, Young Min Baek, and Meeyoung Cha. 2012. Cross-Cultural Comparison of Nonverbal Cues in Emoticons on Twitter: Evidence from Big Data Analysis. *Journal of Communication*, 64(2):333–354.

Ji Ho Park and Pascale Fung. 2017. One-step and two-step classification for abusive language detection on twitter. In *Proceedings of the First Workshop on Abusive Language Online*, pages 41–45.

Sara Rosenthal, Noura Farra, and Preslav Nakov. 2017. Semeval-2017 task 4: Sentiment analysis in twitter. In *Proceedings of the 11th international workshop on semantic evaluation (SemEval-2017)*, pages 502–518.

Haji Mohammad Saleem, Kelly P. Dillon, Susan Benesch, and Derek Ruths. 2016. A web of hate: tackling hateful speech in online social spaces. In *First Workshop on text Analytics for Cybersecurity and Online Safety at LREC 2016*.

Jayashree Subramanian, Varun Sridharan, Kai Shu, and Huan Liu. 2019. Exploiting emojis for sarcasm detection. In *International Conference on Social Computing, Behavioral-Cultural Modeling and Prediction and Behavior Representation in Modeling and Simulation*, pages 70–80. Springer.

Jared Suttles and Nancy Ide. 2013. Distant supervision for emotion classification with discrete binary values. In *International Conference on Intelligent Text Processing and Computational Linguistics*, pages 121–136. Springer.

Ashish Vaswani, Noam Shazeer, Niki Parmar, Jakob Uszkoreit, Llion Jones, Aidan N Gomez, Ł ukasz Kaiser, and Illia Polosukhin. 2017. Attention is all you need. In *Advances in Neural Information Processing Systems*, volume 30, pages 5998–6008. Curran Associates, Inc.

Zeerak Waseem and Dirk Hovy. 2016. Hateful symbols or hateful people? predictive features for hate speech detection on twitter. In *Proceedings of the NAACL student research workshop*, pages 88–93.

Michael Wiegand. 2018. Overview of the germeval 2018 shared task on the identification of offensive language. pages 1–10, Wien. Verlag der Österreichischen Akademie der Wissenschaften.

Zhilin Yang, Zihang Dai, Yiming Yang, Jaime Carbonell, Russ R Salakhutdinov, and Quoc V Le. 2019. Xlnet: Generalized autoregressive pretraining for language understanding. In *Advances in neural information processing systems*, pages 5753–5763.

A Little Pretraining Goes a Long Way: A Case Study on Dependency Parsing Task for Low-resource Morphologically Rich Languages

Jivnesh Sandhan[1], Amrith Krishna[2], Ashim Gupta[3], Laxmidhar Behera[1,4] and Pawan Goyal[5]

[1]Dept. of Electrical Engineering, IIT Kanpur,
[2]Dept. of Computer Science and Technology, University of Cambridge,
[3]School of Computing, University of Utah, [4]Tata Consultancy Services,
[5]Dept. of Computer Science and Engineering, IIT Kharagpur

jivnesh@iitk.ac.in, ak2329@cam.ac.uk, pawang@cse.iitkgp.ac.in

Abstract

Neural dependency parsing has achieved remarkable performance for many domains and languages. The bottleneck of massive labeled data limits the effectiveness of these approaches for low resource languages. In this work, we focus on dependency parsing for morphological rich languages (MRLs) in a low-resource setting. Although morphological information is essential for the dependency parsing task, the morphological disambiguation and lack of powerful analyzers pose challenges to get this information for MRLs. To address these challenges, we propose simple auxiliary tasks for pretraining. We perform experiments on 10 MRLs in low-resource settings to measure the efficacy of our proposed pretraining method and observe an average absolute gain of 2 points (UAS) and 3.6 points (LAS).[1]

1 Introduction

Dependency parsing has greatly benefited from neural network-based approaches. While these approaches simplify the parsing architecture and eliminate the need for hand-crafted feature engineering (Chen and Manning, 2014; Dyer et al., 2015; Kiperwasser and Goldberg, 2016; Dozat and Manning, 2017; Kulmizev et al., 2019), their performance has been less exciting for several morphologically rich languages (MRLs) and low-resource languages (More et al., 2019; Seeker and Çetinoğlu, 2015). In fact, the need for large labeled treebanks for such systems has adversely affected the development of parsing solutions for low-resource languages (Vania et al., 2019). Zeman et al. (2018) observe that data-driven parsing on 9 low resource treebanks resulted not only in low scores but those outputs "are hardly useful for downstream applications".

Several approaches have been suggested for improving the parsing performance of low-resource languages. This includes data augmentation strategies, cross-lingual transfer (Vania et al., 2019) and using unlabelled data with semi-supervised learning (Clark et al., 2018) and self-training (Rotman and Reichart, 2019). Further, incorporating morphological knowledge substantially improves the parsing performance for MRLs, including low-resource languages (Vania et al., 2018; Dehouck and Denis, 2018). This aligns well with the linguistic intuition of the role of morphological markers, especially that of case markers, in deciding the syntactic roles for the words involved (Wunderlich and Lakämper, 2001; Sigursson, 2003; Kittilä et al., 2011). However, obtaining the morphological tags for input sentences during run time is a challenge in itself for MRLs (More et al., 2019) and use of predicted tags from taggers, if available, often hampers the performance of these parsers. In this work, we primarily focus on one such morphologically-rich low-resource language, Sanskrit.

We propose a simple pretraining approach, where we incorporate encoders from simple auxiliary tasks by means of a gating mechanism (Sato et al., 2017). This approach outperforms multitask training and transfer learning methods under the same low-resource data conditions ($\sim$500 sentences). The proposed approach when applied to Dozat et al. (2017), a neural parser, not only obviates the need for providing morphological tags as input at runtime, but also outperforms its original configuration that uses gold morphological tags as input. Further, our method performs close to DCST (Rotman and Reichart, 2019), a self-training based extension of Dozat et al. (2017), which uses gold morphological tags as input for training.

To measure the efficacy of the proposed method, we further perform a series of experiments on 10 MRLs in low-resource settings and show 2 points

[1]Code and data available at: https://github.com/jivnesh/LCM

Proceedings of the 16th Conference of the European Chapter of the Associationfor Computational Linguistics: Student Research Workshop, pages 111–120
April 19 - 23, 2021. ©2021 Association for Computational Linguistics

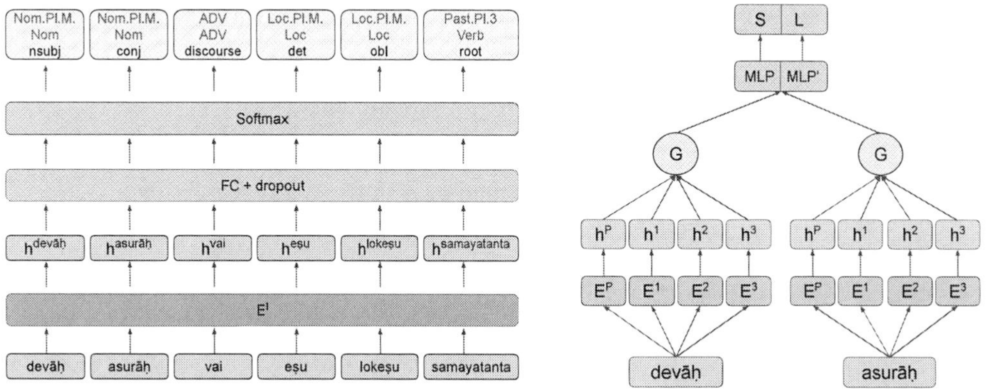

(a) (b)

Figure 1: Illustration of proposed architecture for a Sanskrit sequence. English translation: "Demigods and demons had tried with equal effort for these planets". (a) Pretraining step: For an input word sequence, tagger predicts labels as per three proposed auxiliary tasks, namely, Morphological Tag (green), Case Tag (red) and Label Tag (black). (b) Parser with gating: $E^{(P)}$ is encoder of a neural parser like Dozat and Manning (2017) and $E^{(1)-(3)}$ are the encoders pre-trained with proposed auxiliary tasks. Gating mechanism combines representations of all the encoders which, for each word pair, is passed to two MLPs to predict the probability of arc score (S) and label (L).

and 3.6 points average absolute gain (§ 3.1) in terms of UAS and LAS, respectively. Our proposed method also outperforms multilingual BERT (Devlin et al., 2019, mBERT) based multi-task learning model (Kondratyuk and Straka, 2019, Udify) for the languages which are not covered in mBERT (§ 3.4).

2 Pretraining approach

Our proposed pretraining approach essentially attempts to combine word representations from encoders trained on multiple sequence level supervised tasks, as auxiliary tasks, with that of the default encoder of the neural dependency parser. While our approach is generic and can be used with any neural parser, we use BiAFFINE parser (Dozat and Manning, 2017), hence forth referred to as BiAFF, in our experiments.This is a graph-based neural parser that makes use of biaffine attention and a biaffine classifier.[2] Figure 1 illustrates the proposed approach using an example sequence from Sanskrit. Our pipeline-based approach consists of two steps: (1) Pretraining step (2) Integration step. Figure 1a describes the pretraining step with three auxiliary tasks to pretrain the corresponding encoders $E^{(1)-(3)}$. Finally, in the integration step, these pretrained encoders along with the encoder for the BiAFF model $E^{(P)}$ are then combined using a gating mechanism (1b) as employed in Sato et al. (2017). [3]

All the auxiliary tasks are trained independently as separate models, but using the same architecture and hyperparameter settings which differ only in terms of the output label they use. The models for the pretraining components are trained using BiLSTM encoders, similar to the encoders in Dozat and Manning (2017) and then decoded using two fully connected layers, followed by a softmax layer (Huang et al., 2015). These sequential tasks involve prediction of the morphological tag **(MT)**, dependency label (relation) that each word holds with its head **(LT)** and further we also consider task where the case information of each nominal forms the output label **(CT)**. Other grammatical categories did not show significant improvements over the case (§ 3.2). This aligns well with the linguistic paradigm that the case information plays an important role in deciding the syntactic role that a nominal can be assigned in the sentence. For words with no case-information, we predict their coarse POS tags. Here, the morphological information is automatically leveraged using the pre-trained encoders, and thus during runtime the morphological tags need not be provided as inputs. It also helps in reducing the gap between UAS and LAS (§ 3.1).

[2]More details can be found in supplemental (§ A.1).

[3]Our proposed approach is inspired from Rotman and Reichart (2019).

3 Experiments

Data and Metric: We use 500, 1,000 and 1,000 sentences from the Sanskrit Treebank Corpus (Kulkarni et al., 2010, STBC) as the training, dev and test data respectively for all the models. For the proposed auxiliary tasks, all the sequence taggers are trained with additional previously unused 1,000 sentences from STBC along with the training sentences used for the dependency parsing task. For the Label Tag (LT) prediction auxiliary task, we do not use gold dependency information; rather we use predicted tags from BiAFF parser. For the remaining auxiliary tasks, we use gold standard morphological information.

For all the models, input representation consists of FastText (Grave et al., 2018)[4] embedding of 300-dimension and convolutional neural network (CNN) based 100-dimensional character embedding (Zhang et al., 2015). For character level CNN architecture, we use following setting: 100 number of filters with kernel size equal to 3. We use standard Unlabelled and Labelled Attachment Scores (UAS, LAS) to measure the parsing performance and use t-test for statistical significance (Dror et al., 2018).

For STBC treebank, the original data does not have morphological tag entry, so the Sanskrit Heritage reader (Huet and Goyal, 2013; Goyal and Huet, 2016) is used to obtain all the possible morphological analysis and only those sentences are chosen which do not have any word showing homonymy or syncretism (Krishna et al., 2020). For other MRLs, we restrict to the same training setup as Sanskrit and use 500 annotated sentences as labeled data for training. Additionally, we use 1000 sentences with morphological information as unlabelled data for pretraining sequence taggers.[5] We use all the sentences present in original development and test split data for development and test data. For languages where multiple treebanks are available, we chose only one available treebank to avoid domain shift. Note that STBC adopts a tagging scheme based on the grammatical tradition of Sanskrit, specifically based on Kāraka (Kulkarni and Sharma, 2019; Kulkarni et al., 2010), while the other MRLs including Sanskrit-Vedic use UD.

[4]https://fasttext.cc/docs/en/crawl-vectors.html

[5]The predicted relations on unlabelled data by the model trained with 500 samples are used for Label Tagging task.

Hyper-parameters: We utilize the BiAFFINE parser (BiAFF) implemented by Ma et al. (2018). We employ the following hyper-parameter setting for pretraining sequence taggers and base parser BiAFF: the batch size of 16, number of epochs as 100, and a dropout rate of 0.33 with a learning rate equal to 0.002. The hidden representation generated from n-Stacked-LSTM layers of size 1,024 is passed through two fully connected layers of size 128 and 64. Note that LCM and MTL models use 2-Stacked LSTMs. We keep all the remaining parameters the same as that of Ma et al. (2018).

For all TranSeq variants, one BiLSTM layer is added on top of three augmented pretrained layers from an off-the-shelf morphological tagger (Gupta et al., 2020) to learn task-specific features. In TranSeq-FEA, the dimension of the non-linearity layer of the adaptor module is 256, and in TranSeq-UF, after every 20 epochs, one layer is unfrozen from top to down fashion. In TranSeq-DL, the learning rate is decreased from top to down by a factor of 1.2. We have used default parameters to train Hierarchical Tagger [6] and baseline models.

Models: All our experiments are performed as augmentations on two off the shelf neural parsers, BiAFF (Dozat and Manning, 2017) and Deep Contextualized Self-training (DCST), which integrates self-training with BiAFF (Rotman and Reichart, 2019).[7] Hence their default configurations become the baseline models (**Base**). We also use a system that simultaneously trains the BiAFF (and DCST) model for dependency parsing along with the sequence level case prediction task in a multi task setting (**MTL**). For MTL model, we also experiment with morphological tagging, as an auxiliary task. However, we do not find significant improvement in performance compared to case tagging. Hence, we consider case tagging as an auxiliary task to avoid sparsity issue due to the monolithic tag scheme for morphological tagging. As a transfer learning variant (**TranSeq**), we extract first three layers from a hierarchical multi-task morphological tagger (Gupta et al., 2020), trained on 50k examples from DCS (Hellwig, 2010). Here each layer corresponds to different grammatical categories, namely, number, gender and case. Note that number of randomly initialised encoder layers in BiAFF (and DCST) are now reduced from 3 to

[6]https://github.com/ashim95/sanskrit-morphological-taggers

[7]We describe the baseline models in supplemental (§ A).

1. We fine-tune these layers with default learning rate and experiment with four different fine-tuning schedules.[8] Finally, our proposed configuration (in §2) is referred to as the **LCM** model.[9] We also train a version each of the base models which expects morphological tags as input and is trained with gold morphological tags. During runtime, we report two different settings, one which uses predicted tags as input (**Predicted MI**) and other that uses gold tag as input (**Oracle MI**). We obtain the morphological tags from a Neural CRF tagger (Yang and Zhang, 2018) trained on our training data. Oracle MI will act as an upper-bound on the reported results.

3.1 Results

Table 6 presents results for dependency parsing on Sanskrit. We observe that BiAFF + LCM outperforms all corresponding BiAFF models including Oracle MI. This is indeed a serendipitous outcome as one would expect Oracle MI to be an upper bound owing to its use of gold morphological tags at runtime. The DCST variant of our pretraining approach is also the best among its peers, although the performance of Oracle MI model in this case is indeed the upper bound.

	BiAFF		DCST	
Model	UAS	LAS	UAS	LAS
Base	70.67	56.85	73.23	58.64
Predicted MI	69.02	53.11	71.15	51.75
MTL	70.85	57.93	73.04	59.12
TranSeq	71.46	60.58	74.58	62.70
LCM	**75.91**	**64.87**	**75.75**	**64.28**
Oracle MI	*74.08*	*62.48*	*76.66*	*66.35*

Table 1: Results on Sanskrit dependency parsing. Oracle MI is an upper bound and is not comparable.

On the other hand, using predicted morphological tags instead of gold tags at run time degrades results drastically, especially for LAS, possibly due to the cascading effect of incorrect morphological information (Nguyen and Verspoor, 2018). This shows that morphological information is essential in filling the UAS-LAS gap and substantiates the need for pretraining to incorporate such knowledge even when it is not available at run time. Interestingly, both MTL, and TranSeq, show improvements as compared to the base models, though do

Training Size	BiAFF UAS/LAS	DCST UAS/LAS	BiAFF+LCM UAS/LAS
100	58.0/42.3	64.0/44.0	**70.4/59.9**
500	70.7/56.9	73.2/58.6	**75.9/64.9**
750	74.0/61.8	75.2/62.3	**77.3/66.8**
1000	74.4/62.9	76.0/64.1	**77.9/67.3**
1250	75.6/64.7	76.7/65.2	**78.5/68.3**

Table 2: Performance as a function of training set size.

not match with that of our pretraining approach. In our experiments, the pretraining approach, even with *a little training data*, clearly outperforms the other approaches.

Ablation: We perform further analysis on Sanskrit to study the effect of training set size as well as the impact of various tagging schemes as auxiliary tasks. First, we evaluate the impact on performance as a function of the training size (Table 2). Noticeably, for training size 100, we observe a 12 (UAS) and 17 (LAS) points increase for BiAFF+LCM over BiAFF, demonstrating the effectiveness of our approach in a very low-resource setting. This improvement is consistent for larger training sizes, though the gain reduces.

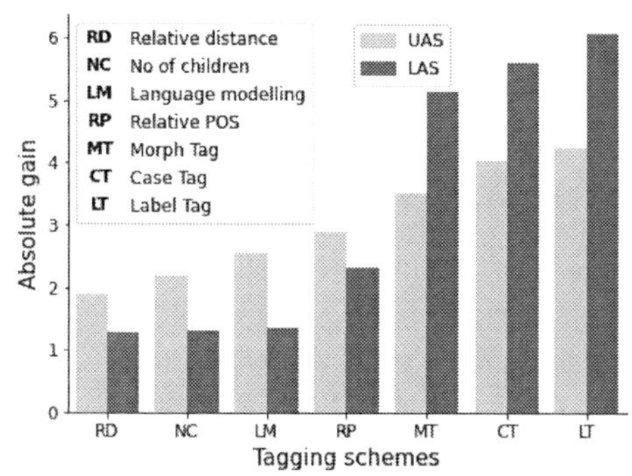

Figure 2: Comparison of proposed tagging schemes (MT, CT, LT) with those in DCST (RD, NC, LM, RP).

In Figure 2, we compare our tagging schemes with those used in self-training of DCST, namely, Relative Distance from root (RD), Number of Children for each word (NC), Language Modeling (LM) objective where task is to predict next word in sentence, and Relative POS (RP) of modifier from root word. Here, we integrate each pretrained model (corresponding to each tagging scheme) individually on top of the BiAFF baseline using the gating mechanism and report the absolute gain over the BiAFF in terms of UAS and LAS metric. Inter-

[8]Refer supplemental (§ B) for variations of TranSeq.

[9]LCM denotes Label, Case and Morph tagging schemes.

	eu		el		sv		pl		ru		avg	
Model	UAS	LAS	UAS	LAS	UAS	LAS	UAS	LAS	UAS	LAS	UAS	LAS
BiAFF	63.18	54.52	79.64	75.01	71.73	64.83	78.33	70.83	73.98	67.42	73.37	66.52
DCST	69.60	60.65	83.48	78.61	77.03	69.62	81.40	73.09	78.61	72.07	78.02	70.81
DCST+MTL	70.38	61.52	83.74	79.31	76.70	69.88	81.25	73.34	78.46	72.08	78.11	71.23
DCST+TranSeq	70.70	62.96	84.69	80.37	77.30	70.85	82.84	75.02	78.95	73.18	78.90	72.48
BiAFF+LCM	**72.40**	**65.50**	**86.56**	**83.18**	77.95	72.20	**84.08**	**77.65**	79.97	74.47	80.20	74.60
DCST+LCM	72.01	65.33	85.94	82.22	**78.72**	**73.04**	83.83	77.63	**80.62**	**75.26**	**80.22**	**74.70**
BiAFF+Oracle MI	*72.16*	*66.08*	*83.05*	*79.81*	*76.50*	*71.17*	*83.27*	*77.83*	*77.83*	*73.13*	*78.56*	*73.60*
DCST+Oracle MI	*77.47*	*71.55*	*85.99*	*82.72*	*80.33*	*75.00*	*86.03*	*80.46*	*82.21*	*77.54*	*82.41*	*77.45*

	ar		hu		fi		de		cs		avg	
Model	UAS	LAS	UAS	LAS	UAS	LAS	UAS	LAS	UAS	LAS	UAS	LAS
BiAFF	76.24	68.07	70.00	62.81	60.93	50.68	67.77	59.94	65.75	57.43	70.30	62.62
DCST	79.05	71.18	74.62	67.00	66.04	54.76	73.22	65.18	74.15	65.52	75.61	67.70
DCST+Predicted MI	77.17	66.63	61.55	36.18	56.48	39.67	65.31	47.12	72.03	58.37	68.72	52.61
DCST+MTL	79.35	71.37	74.49	66.70	66.30	55.29	73.98	66.05	74.66	65.95	75.84	67.99
DCST+TranSeq-FT	79.66	72.17	75.22	68.25	67.04	56.57	74.66	67.27	**75.15**	67.02	76.40	69.11
BiAFF+LCM	**79.68**	**72.55**	**76.15**	**69.53**	69.05	59.41	75.85	68.80	74.94	**67.58**	76.91	70.13
DCST+LCM	79.60	72.38	75.71	68.93	**69.15**	**60.06**	**76.12**	**69.20**	74.81	67.54	**76.99**	**70.22**
BiAFF+Oracle MI	*77.52*	*71.46*	*75.89*	*70.63*	*70.80*	*64.64*	*72.63*	*66.53*	*72.39*	*66.22*	*74.99*	*69.20*
DCST+Oracle MI	*80.43*	*74.79*	*78.43*	*73.19*	*75.30*	*68.90*	*77.70*	*71.66*	*78.54*	*72.38*	*79.09*	*73.40*

Table 3: Evaluation on 10 MRLs. Results of BiAFF+LCM and DCST+LCM are statistically significant compared to strong baseline DCST as per t-test ($p < 0.01$). Last two columns denote the average performance. Models using Oracle MI are not comparable.

estingly, our proposed tagging schemes, with an improvement of 3-4 points (UAS) and 5-6 points (LAS), outperform those of DCST and help bridge the gap between UAS-LAS.

3.2 Additional auxiliary tasks

With our proposed pretraining approach, we experiment with using the prediction of different grammatical categories as auxiliary tasks, namely, Number Tagging (NT), Person Tagging (PT), and Gender Tagging (GT). As the results in table **??** demonstrate, the improvements observed in these cases are much smaller than those for our proposed auxiliary tasks. Similar results are observed when considering other auxiliary tasks (see table **??**). We find that combining these auxiliary tasks with our proposed ones did not provide any notable improvements. One possible reason for under performance of these tagging schemes compared to the proposed ones could be that either when the training set is small, sequence taggers are not able to learn discriminative features only from surface form of words (F-score is less than 40 in all such cases in table **??**) or the learned features are not helpful for the dependency parsing task.

3.3 Experiments on other MRLs

We choose 10 additional MRLs from Universal Dependencies (UD) dataset (McDonald et al., 2013; Nivre et al., 2016), namely, Arabic (ar), Czech (cs), German (de), Basque (eu), Greek (el), Finnish (fi), Hungarian (hu), Polish (pl), Russian (ru) and Swedish (sv).[10] Then we train them in low-resource setting (500 examples) to investigate the applicability of our approach for these MRLs.

For all MRLs, the trend is similar to what is observed for Sanskrit. While all four models improve over both the baselines, BiAFF+LCM and DCST+LCM consistently turn out to be the best configurations. Note that these models are not directly comparable to Oracle MI models since Oracle MI models use gold morphological tags instead of the predicted ones. The performance of BiAFF+LCM and DCST+LCM is also comparable. Across all 11 MRLs, BiAFF+LCM shows the average absolute gain of 2 points (UAS) and 3.6 points (LAS) compared to the strong baseline DCST.

[10]We choose MRLs that have the explicit morphological information with following grammatical categories: case, number, gender, and tense.

Auxiliary Task	F-score	Gain
Relative Distance (RD)	58.71	1.9/1.3
No of children (NC)	52.82	2.2/1.3
Relative POS (RP)	46.52	2.9/2.3
Lang Model (LM)	41.54	2.6/1.4
Coarse POS (CP)	13.02	1.6/0.8
Head Word (HW)	40.12	1.5/0.4
POS Head Word (PHW)	38.98	2.0/1.2
Number Tagging (NT)	13.33	1.9/0.9
Person Tagging (PT)	12.27	1.6/0.7
Gender Tagging (GT)	0.28	1.3/0.2
Morph Tagging (MT)	62.84	3.5/5.1
Case Tagging (CT)	73.51	4.0/5.6
Label Tagging (LT)	71.51	4.2/6.0

Table 4: Comparison of different auxiliary tasks. F-score: Task performance, Gain: Absolute gain (when integrated with BiAFF) in terms of UAS/LAS score compared to BiAFF scores.

3.4 Comparison with mBERT Pretraining

We compare the proposed method with multilingual BERT (Devlin et al., 2019, mBERT) based multi-task learning model (Kondratyuk and Straka, 2019, Udify). This single model trained on 124 UD treebanks covers 75 different languages and produces state of the art results for many of them. Multilingual BERT leverages large scale pretraining on wikipedia for 104 languages.

Lang	BiAFF	BiAFF+LCM	Udify
Basque	63.2/54.5	72.4/65.5	**76.6/69.0**
German	67.7/60.0	75.8/68.8	**83.7/77.5**
Hungarian	70.0/62.8	76.2/69.5	**84.4/76.7**
Greek	69.6/75.0	86.6/83.2	**90.6/87.0**
Polish	78.3.70.8	84.1/77.7	**90.7/85.0**
Sanskrit	70.7/56.8	**75.9/64.9**	69.4/53.2
Sanskrit-Vedic	56.0/42.3	**61.6/48.0**	47.4/28.3
Wolof	75.3/67.8	**78.4/71.3**	70.9/60.6
Gothic	61.7/53.3	**69.6/61.4**	63.4/52.2
Coptic	84.3/80.2	**86.2/82.7**	32.7/14.3

Table 5: The proposed method outperforms Udify for the languages (down) not covered in mBERT and under performs for the languages (top) which are covered in mBERT.

In our experiments, we find that Udify outperforms the proposed method for languages covered during mBERT's pretraining. Notably, not only the proposed method but also a simple BiAFF parser with randomly initialized embedding outperforms Udify (Table 5) for languages which not available in mBERT. Out of 7,000 languages, only a handful of languages can take advantage of mBERT pretraining (Joshi et al., 2020) which substantiates the need of our proposed pretraining scheme.

4 Conclusion

In this work, we focused on dependency parsing for low-resource MRLs, where getting morphological information itself is a challenge. To address low-resource nature and lack of morphological information, we proposed a simple pretraining method based on sequence labeling that does not require complex architectures or massive labelled or unlabelled data. We show that little supervised pretraining goes a long way compared to transfer learning, multi-task learning, and mBERT pretraining approaches (for the languages not covered in mBERT). One primary benefit of our approach is that it does not rely on morphological information at run time; instead this information is leveraged using the pretrained encoders. Our experiments across 10 MRLs showed that proposed pretraining provides a significant boost with an average 2 points (UAS) and 3.6 points (LAS) absolute gain compared to DCST.

Acknowledgements

We thank Amba Kulkarni for providing Sanskrit dependency treebank data and the anonymous reviewers for their constructive feedback towards improving this work. The work of the first author is supported by the TCS Fellowship under the Project TCS/EE/2011191P.

References

Danqi Chen and Christopher Manning. 2014. A fast and accurate dependency parser using neural networks. In *Proceedings of the 2014 Conference on Empirical Methods in Natural Language Processing (EMNLP)*, pages 740–750, Doha, Qatar. Association for Computational Linguistics.

Kevin Clark, Minh-Thang Luong, Christopher D. Manning, and Quoc Le. 2018. Semi-supervised sequence modeling with cross-view training. In *Proceedings of the 2018 Conference on Empirical Methods in Natural Language Processing*, pages 1914–1925, Brussels, Belgium. Association for Computational Linguistics.

Mathieu Dehouck and Pascal Denis. 2018. A framework for understanding the role of morphology in universal dependency parsing. In *Proceedings of the 2018 Conference on Empirical Methods in Natural Language Processing*, pages 2864–2870, Brussels, Belgium. Association for Computational Linguistics.

Jacob Devlin, Ming-Wei Chang, Kenton Lee, and Kristina Toutanova. 2019. BERT: Pre-training of deep bidirectional transformers for language understanding. In *Proceedings of the 2019 Conference of the North American Chapter of the Association for Computational Linguistics: Human Language Technologies, Volume 1 (Long and Short Papers)*, pages 4171–4186, Minneapolis, Minnesota. Association for Computational Linguistics.

Timothy Dozat and Christopher D. Manning. 2017. Deep biaffine attention for neural dependency parsing. In *5th International Conference on Learning Representations, ICLR 2017, Toulon, France, April 24-26, 2017, Conference Track Proceedings*. OpenReview.net.

Timothy Dozat, Peng Qi, and Christopher D Manning. 2017. Stanford's graph-based neural dependency parser at the conll 2017 shared task. In *Proceedings of the CoNLL 2017 Shared Task: Multilingual Parsing from Raw Text to Universal Dependencies*, pages 20–30.

Rotem Dror, Gili Baumer, Segev Shlomov, and Roi Reichart. 2018. The hitchhiker's guide to testing statistical significance in natural language processing. In *Proceedings of the 56th Annual Meeting of the Association for Computational Linguistics (Volume 1: Long Papers)*, pages 1383–1392, Melbourne, Australia. Association for Computational Linguistics.

Chris Dyer, Miguel Ballesteros, Wang Ling, Austin Matthews, and Noah A. Smith. 2015. Transition-based dependency parsing with stack long short-term memory. In *Proceedings of the 53rd Annual Meeting of the Association for Computational Linguistics and the 7th International Joint Conference on Natural Language Processing (Volume 1: Long Papers)*, pages 334–343, Beijing, China. Association for Computational Linguistics.

Jack Edmonds. 1967. Optimum branchings. *Journal of Research of the national Bureau of Standards B*, 71(4):233–240.

Bjarke Felbo, Alan Mislove, Anders Søgaard, Iyad Rahwan, and Sune Lehmann. 2017. Using millions of emoji occurrences to learn any-domain representations for detecting sentiment, emotion and sarcasm. In *Proceedings of the 2017 Conference on Empirical Methods in Natural Language Processing*, pages 1615–1625, Copenhagen, Denmark. Association for Computational Linguistics.

Robert M French. 1999. Catastrophic forgetting in connectionist networks. *Trends in cognitive sciences*, 3(4):128–135.

Pawan Goyal and Gérard Huet. 2016. Design and analysis of a lean interface for sanskrit corpus annotation. *Journal of Language Modelling*, 4(2):145–182.

Edouard Grave, Piotr Bojanowski, Prakhar Gupta, Armand Joulin, and Tomas Mikolov. 2018. Learning word vectors for 157 languages. In *Proceedings of the Eleventh International Conference on Language Resources and Evaluation (LREC 2018)*, Miyazaki, Japan. European Language Resources Association (ELRA).

Ashim Gupta, Amrith Krishna, Pawan Goyal, and Oliver Hellwig. 2020. Evaluating neural morphological taggers for sanskrit. In *Proceedings of the 17th SIGMORPHON Workshop on Computational Research in Phonetics, Phonology, and Morphology*, Seattle, USA. Association for Computational Linguistics.

Oliver Hellwig. 2010. Dcs-the digital corpus of sanskrit. *Heidelberg (2010-2020). URL http://www.sanskrit-linguistics.org/dcs/index.php*.

Neil Houlsby, Andrei Giurgiu, Stanislaw Jastrzebski, Bruna Morrone, Quentin De Laroussilhe, Andrea Gesmundo, Mona Attariyan, and Sylvain Gelly. 2019. Parameter-efficient transfer learning for NLP. In *Proceedings of the 36th International Conference on Machine Learning*, volume 97 of *Proceedings of Machine Learning Research*, pages 2790–2799, Long Beach, California, USA. PMLR.

Jeremy Howard and Sebastian Ruder. 2018. Universal language model fine-tuning for text classification. In *Proceedings of the 56th Annual Meeting of the Association for Computational Linguistics (Volume 1: Long Papers)*, pages 328–339, Melbourne, Australia. Association for Computational Linguistics.

Zhiheng Huang, Wei Xu, and Kai Yu. 2015. Bidirectional lstm-crf models for sequence tagging. *arXiv preprint arXiv:1508.01991*.

Gérard Huet and Pawan Goyal. 2013. Design of a lean interface for sanskrit corpus annotation. *Proceedings of ICON*, pages 177–186.

Pratik Joshi, Sebastin Santy, Amar Budhiraja, Kalika Bali, and Monojit Choudhury. 2020. The state and fate of linguistic diversity and inclusion in the NLP world. In *Proceedings of the 58th Annual Meeting of the Association for Computational Linguistics*, pages 6282–6293, Online. Association for Computational Linguistics.

Eliyahu Kiperwasser and Yoav Goldberg. 2016. Simple and accurate dependency parsing using bidirectional LSTM feature representations. *Transactions of the Association for Computational Linguistics*, 4:313–327.

Seppo Kittilä, Katja Västi, and Jussi Ylikoski. 2011. Introduction to case, animacy and semantic roles. *Case, animacy and semantic roles*, 99:1–26.

Dan Kondratyuk and Milan Straka. 2019. 75 languages, 1 model: Parsing Universal Dependencies universally. In *Proceedings of the 2019 Conference on Empirical Methods in Natural Language Processing and the 9th International Joint Conference on Natural Language Processing (EMNLP-IJCNLP)*, pages 2779–2795, Hong Kong, China. Association for Computational Linguistics.

Amrith Krishna, Bishal Santra, Ashim Gupta, Pavankumar Satuluri, and Pawan Goyal. 2020. A graph based framework for structured prediction tasks in sanskrit. *Computational Linguistics*, 46(4):1–63.

Amba Kulkarni, Sheetal Pokar, and Devanand Shukl. 2010. Designing a constraint based parser for sanskrit. In *International Sanskrit Computational Linguistics Symposium*, pages 70–90. Springer.

Amba Kulkarni and Dipti Sharma. 2019. Pāinian syntactico-semantic relation labels. In *Proceedings of the Fifth International Conference on Dependency Linguistics (Depling, SyntaxFest 2019)*, pages 198–208, Paris, France. Association for Computational Linguistics.

Artur Kulmizev, Miryam de Lhoneux, Johannes Gontrum, Elena Fano, and Joakim Nivre. 2019. Deep contextualized word embeddings in transition-based and graph-based dependency parsing - a tale of two parsers revisited. In *Proceedings of the 2019 Conference on Empirical Methods in Natural Language Processing and the 9th International Joint Conference on Natural Language Processing (EMNLP-IJCNLP)*, pages 2755–2768, Hong Kong, China. Association for Computational Linguistics.

Xuezhe Ma, Zecong Hu, Jingzhou Liu, Nanyun Peng, Graham Neubig, and Eduard Hovy. 2018. Stack-pointer networks for dependency parsing. In *Proceedings of the 56th Annual Meeting of the Association for Computational Linguistics (Volume 1: Long Papers)*, pages 1403–1414, Melbourne, Australia. Association for Computational Linguistics.

Michael McCloskey and Neal J. Cohen. 1989. Catastrophic interference in connectionist networks: The sequential learning problem. In Gordon H. Bower, editor, *Psychology of Learning and Motivation*, volume 24, pages 109 – 165. Academic Press.

Ryan McDonald, Joakim Nivre, Yvonne Quirmbach-Brundage, Yoav Goldberg, Dipanjan Das, Kuzman Ganchev, Keith Hall, Slav Petrov, Hao Zhang, Oscar Täckström, et al. 2013. Universal dependency annotation for multilingual parsing. In *Proceedings of the 51st Annual Meeting of the Association for Computational Linguistics (Volume 2: Short Papers)*, pages 92–97.

Amir More, Amit Seker, Victoria Basmova, and Reut Tsarfaty. 2019. Joint transition-based models for morpho-syntactic parsing: Parsing strategies for MRLs and a case study from modern Hebrew. *Transactions of the Association for Computational Linguistics*, 7:33–48.

Dat Quoc Nguyen and Karin Verspoor. 2018. An improved neural network model for joint POS tagging and dependency parsing. In *Proceedings of the CoNLL 2018 Shared Task: Multilingual Parsing from Raw Text to Universal Dependencies*, pages 81–91, Brussels, Belgium. Association for Computational Linguistics.

Joakim Nivre, Marie-Catherine De Marneffe, Filip Ginter, Yoav Goldberg, Jan Hajic, Christopher D Manning, Ryan McDonald, Slav Petrov, Sampo Pyysalo, Natalia Silveira, et al. 2016. Universal dependencies v1: A multilingual treebank collection. In *Proceedings of the Tenth International Conference on Language Resources and Evaluation (LREC'16)*, pages 1659–1666.

Matthew Peters, Mark Neumann, Mohit Iyyer, Matt Gardner, Christopher Clark, Kenton Lee, and Luke Zettlemoyer. 2018. Deep contextualized word representations. In *Proceedings of the 2018 Conference of the North American Chapter of the Association for Computational Linguistics: Human Language Technologies, Volume 1 (Long Papers)*, pages 2227–2237, New Orleans, Louisiana. Association for Computational Linguistics.

Guy Rotman and Roi Reichart. 2019. Deep contextualized self-training for low resource dependency parsing. *Transactions of the Association for Computational Linguistics*, 7:695–713.

Motoki Sato, Hitoshi Manabe, Hiroshi Noji, and Yuji Matsumoto. 2017. Adversarial training for cross-domain universal dependency parsing. In *Proceedings of the CoNLL 2017 Shared Task: Multilingual Parsing from Raw Text to Universal Dependencies*, pages 71–79, Vancouver, Canada. Association for Computational Linguistics.

Wolfgang Seeker and Özlem Çetinoğlu. 2015. A graph-based lattice dependency parser for joint morphological segmentation and syntactic analysis. *Transactions of the Association for Computational Linguistics*, 3:359–373.

Halldór Ármann Sigursson. 2003. Case: abstract vs. morphological. *New perspectives on case theory*, pages 223–268.

Asa Cooper Stickland and Iain Murray. 2019. BERT and PALs: Projected attention layers for efficient adaptation in multi-task learning. In *Proceedings of the 36th International Conference on Machine Learning*, volume 97 of *Proceedings of Machine Learning Research*, pages 5986–5995, Long Beach, California, USA. PMLR.

Clara Vania, Andreas Grivas, and Adam Lopez. 2018. What do character-level models learn about morphology? the case of dependency parsing. In *Proceedings of the 2018 Conference on Empirical Methods in Natural Language Processing*, pages 2573–2583, Brussels, Belgium. Association for Computational Linguistics.

Clara Vania, Yova Kementchedjhieva, Anders Søgaard, and Adam Lopez. 2019. A systematic comparison of methods for low-resource dependency parsing on genuinely low-resource languages. In *Proceedings of the 2019 Conference on Empirical Methods in Natural Language Processing and the 9th International Joint Conference on Natural Language Processing (EMNLP-IJCNLP)*, pages 1105–1116, Hong Kong, China. Association for Computational Linguistics.

Dieter Wunderlich and Renate Lakämper. 2001. On the interaction of structural and semantic case. *Lingua*, 111(4-7):377–418.

Jie Yang and Yue Zhang. 2018. Ncrf++: An open-source neural sequence labeling toolkit. In *Proceedings of the 56th Annual Meeting of the Association for Computational Linguistics*.

Daniel Zeman, Jan Hajič, Martin Popel, Martin Potthast, Milan Straka, Filip Ginter, Joakim Nivre, and Slav Petrov. 2018. CoNLL 2018 shared task: Multilingual parsing from raw text to universal dependencies. In *Proceedings of the CoNLL 2018 Shared Task: Multilingual Parsing from Raw Text to Universal Dependencies*, pages 1–21, Brussels, Belgium. Association for Computational Linguistics.

Xiang Zhang, Junbo Zhao, and Yann LeCun. 2015. Character-level convolutional networks for text classification. In C. Cortes, N. D. Lawrence, D. D. Lee, M. Sugiyama, and R. Garnett, editors, *Advances in Neural Information Processing Systems 28*, pages 649–657. Curran Associates, Inc.

Supplemental Material

A Baselines

A.1 BiAFFINE Parser (BiAFF)

BiAFF (Dozat and Manning, 2017) is a graph-based dependency parsing approach similar to Kiperwasser and Goldberg (2016). It uses biaffine attention instead of using a traditional MLP-based attention mechanism. For input vector $\vec{h}$, the affine classifier is expressed as $W\vec{h}+b$, while the biaffine classifier is expressed as $W'(W\vec{h}+b)+b'$. The choice of biaffine classifier facilitates the key benefit of representing the prior probability of word j to be head and the likelihood of word i getting word j as the head. In this system, during training, each modifier in the predicted tree has the highest-scoring word as the head. This predicted tree need not be valid. However, at test time, to generate a valid tree MST algorithm (Edmonds, 1967) is used on the arc scores.

A.2 Deep Contextualized Self-training (DCST)

Rotman and Reichart (2019) proposed a self-training method called Deep Contextualized Self-training (DCST).[11] In this system, the base parser BiAFF (Dozat and Manning, 2017) is trained on the labelled dataset. Then this trained base parser is applied to the unlabelled data to generate automatically labelled dependency trees. In the next step, these automatically-generated trees are transformed into one or more sequence tagging schemes. Finally, the ensembled parser is trained on manually labelled data by integrating base parser with learned representation models. The gating mechanism proposed by Sato et al. (2017) is used to integrate different tagging schemes into the ensembled parser. This approach is in line with the representation models based on language modeling related tasks (Peters et al., 2018; Devlin et al., 2019). In summary, DCST demonstrates a novel approach to transfer information learned on labelled data to unlabelled data using sequence tagging schemes such that it can be integrated into final ensembled parser via word embedding layers.

B Experiments on TranSeq Variants

In TranSeq variations, instead of pretraining with three auxiliary tasks, we use a hierarchical multi-task morphological tagger (Gupta et al., 2020) trained on 50k training data from DCS (Hellwig, 2010). In TranSeq setting, we extract the first three layers from this tagger and augment them in baseline models and experiment with five model sub-variants. To avoid catastrophic forget-

Model	BiAFF UAS	BiAFF LAS	DCST UAS	DCST LAS
Base	70.67	56.85	73.23	58.64
Base⋆	69.35	52.79	72.31	54.82
TranSeq-FE	66.54	55.46	71.65	60.10
TranSeq-FEA	69.50	58.48	73.48	61.52
TranSeq-UF	70.60	59.74	73.55	62.39
TranSeq-DL	71.40	60.58	74.52	62.73
TranSeq-FT	**71.46**	**60.58**	**74.58**	**62.70**
Oracle MI	*74.08*	*62.48*	*76.66*	*66.35*

Table 6: Ablation analysis for TranSeq variations. Oracle MI is not comparable. It can be considered as upper bound for TranSeq.

[11] `https://github.com/rotmanguy/DCST`

ting (McCloskey and Cohen, 1989; French, 1999), we gradually increase the capacity of adaptations for each variant. **TranSeq-FE:** Freeze the pre-trained layers and use them as Feature Extractors (FE). **TranSeq-FEA:** In the feature extractor setting, we additionally integrate adaptor modules (Houlsby et al., 2019; Stickland and Murray, 2019) in between two consecutive pre-trained layers. **TranSeq-UF:** Gradually Unfreeze (UF) these three pre-trained layers in the top to down fashion (Felbo et al., 2017; Howard and Ruder, 2018). **TranSeq-DL:** In this setting, we use discriminative learning (DL) rate (Howard and Ruder, 2018) for pre-trained layers, i.e., decreasing the learning rate as we move from top-to-bottom layers. **TranSeq-FT:** We fine-tune (FT), pre-trained layers with default learning rate used by Dozat and Manning (2017).

In the TranSeq setting, as we move down across its sub-variants in Table 6, performance improves gradually, and TranSeq-FT configuration shows the best performance with 1-2 points improvement over Base. The Base$\star$ has one additional LSTM layer compared to Base such that the number of parameters are same as that of TranSeq-FT variation. The performance of Base$\star$ decreases compared to Base but TranSeq-FT outperforms Base. This shows that transfer learning definitely helps to boost the performance.

Development of Conversational AI for Sleep Coaching Programme

Heereen Shim
KU Leuven, Campus Group T, eMedia Research Lab, Leuven, Belgium
KU Leuven, Department of Electrical Engineering (ESAT), STADIUS, Leuven, Belgium
heereen.shim@kuleuven.be

Abstract

Almost 30% of the adult population in the world is experiencing or has experience insomnia. Cognitive Behaviour Therapy for insomnia (CBT-I) is one of the most effective treatment, but it has limitations on accessibility and availability. Utilising technology is one of the possible solutions, but existing methods neglect conversational aspects, which plays a critical role in sleep therapy. To address this issue, we propose a PhD project exploring potentials of developing conversational artificial intelligence (AI) for a sleep coaching programme, which is motivated by CBT-I treatment. This PhD project aims to develop natural language processing (NLP) algorithms to allow the system to interact naturally with a user and provide automated analytic system to support human experts. In this paper, we introduce research questions lying under three phases of the sleep coaching programme: triaging, monitoring the progress, and providing coaching. We expect this research project's outcomes could contribute to the research domains of NLP and AI but also the healthcare field by providing a more accessible and affordable sleep treatment solution and an automated analytic system to lessen the burden of human experts.

1 Introduction

Insomnia is one of the most common sleep disorders with a high prevalence. Approximately one-third of adults experience one or more of the symptoms of insomnia (Roth, 2007). The consequences of insomnia include not only individual problems but also societal issues, such as daytime fatigue, low energy level, which can cause depression, and even increased risk of accidents(Leger et al., 2014). The cost associated with insomnia, including direct and indirect costs, in the US is around 92.5 to 107.5 billion USD per year (Stoller, 1994).

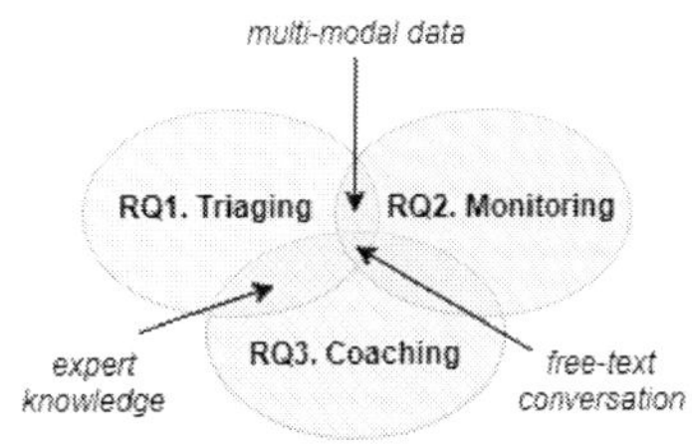

Figure 1: Overview of the proposed PhD research project: Three research questions (RQs) and the overlapped research topics.

Cognitive behaviour therapy for insomnia (CBT-I) is one of the most effective solutions to treat insomnia. During CBT-I process, a person who is suffering from symptoms of insomnia (patient) will consult with a CBT-I provider (therapist) who provides support to identify behaviours, thoughts, and feelings that are related to the symptoms. Since its goal is to change the potential causes, both behavioural and cognitive factors, it produces long-lasting improvement in the condition of insomnia, compared to the medication treatment (Morin et al., 2006).

Despite its effectiveness, CBT-I treatment has a limitation. From a patient's perspective, the treatment cost is high and, from clinician's perspectives, the number of patients that potentially can be treated is significantly large (Edinger and Means, 2005). Consequently, many researchers and engineers have been working on developing more accessible and affordable therapy solutions that can also lessen the burden of clinicians, such as internet- or mobile-based computerised therapy tools (Ström et al., 2004; Ritterband et al., 2009; Vincent and Lewycky, 2009; Lancee et al., 2012). These studies explored opportunities for applying technologies to automate treatment process. However, the conversational aspect, which is the core of the in-person treatment, has been neglected.

Proceedings of the 16th Conference of the European Chapter of the Associationfor Computational Linguistics: Student Research Workshop, pages 121–128
April 19 - 23, 2021. ©2021 Association for Computational Linguistics

In this study, we will explore the possibilities of developing conversational AI (artificial intelligence) to make a computerised sleep therapy tool to be more close to in-person therapy. Since this research field is still in its infancy, we consider a sleep coaching programme targeting healthy people who would like to optimise their sleep, rather than a sleep therapy for patients with the chronic sleep disorder. Also, the goal of this study is to provide a user-friendly interface for users and to support human experts, rather than to replace or eliminate human-in-the-loop. Therefore, we mainly focus on two things: 1) adding a conversational feature that allows users to provide inputs to enable a natural conversation between human and the system; and 2) adding an analytic feature that automates processing user inputs to support decision making. The main research questions of this project lie under three processes of the sleep coaching programme: triage, monitor the progress, and provide coaching. Overview of research questions and overlapped components are illustrated in Figure 1.

We start our research by analysing in-person sleep treatment and existing automated tools and identifying missing gaps to decide research questions (Section 2). Then we revisit the research questions and explain the methodology to address each question (Section 3). As the first step, we introduce a pilot study and present a preliminary result to discuss and provide next steps (Section 4). Finally, we conclude this paper by summarising research questions and research plan of this PhD project (Section 5).

2 Related Work

In this section, we will first provide a brief overview of sleep treatment of CBT-I made by a human expert. Secondly, we will review the existing methods of automated sleep treatment tools. Lastly, we will identify missing gaps and introduce research questions.

2.1 In-person treatment

CBT-I is a sleep treatment that focuses on investigating the relationship between how we behave, how we think, and how we sleep. To achieve this, the treatment consists of multiple components: stimulus control, sleep restriction, sleep hygiene education, relaxation training, and cognitive restructuring (Perlis et al., 2006; Morin and Espie, 2007; Belanger et al., 2006). Stimulus control aims to change associations between the bedroom with habits that make sleeping more difficult (Bootzin and Perlis, 2011). Sleep restriction treatment requires patients to limit time spent in bed in order to resolve the mismatch between the time in bed and sleep time (Spielman et al., 2011). Sleep hygiene focuses on educating the patient to avoid behaviours that influence sleep (Kleitman, 1987; Hauri, 1991). Relaxation training is given to help reduce the racing thoughts (Ong et al., 2014). Cognitive restructuring targets to break the vicious circle between inaccurate thoughts about sleep and behaviours that contribute to insomnia. Standard CBT-I treatment includes three or more of these components.

Conversation between patient and therapist plays a critical role in in-person sleep treatment. In the first session of treatment, the patient will provide complaints of their sleep and the therapist will determine whether the patient is appropriate for CBT-I treatment. To identify this, the therapist should assess the patient based on the clinical interview and the completed questionnaires. Once it is determined that the patient is appropriated for the treatment, the therapist will select the treatment components and structure plan tailored to the patient. The remaining sessions will be followed depending on the stage of treatment and the degree of patient compliance. Therefore, it is important that the therapist monitors the progress, identifies the patient's difficulties, provides personalised support, and encourages the patient to complete the treatment.

2.2 Computerised treatment

One of the earliest approaches is a research work by Ström et al. (2004) investigating the feasibility of an internet-based CBT-I. They proposed a self-help program that patients provide their information and progress by completing questions and questionnaires via the internet. However, their method does not provide automated analytic features to support monitoring process done by human experts.

Later on, Ritterband et al. (2009) proposed a fully automated sleep treatment tool. They proposed an automated algorithm that can produce a personalised recommendation for sleep restriction. It also automatically sends emails of reminders. All intervention was delivered without human support and the outcome was comparable to in-person treatment. Nevertheless, it still misses the interactive conversational feature that participants could report their specific concerns or difficulties of complying the treatment.

Later studies also did not explore the opportunity to get feedback or support. For example, both Vincent and Lewycky (2009) and Lancee et al. (2012) developed online treatment methods for insomnia, but neither of them offered automated support feature where the participants could contact when facing issues or difficulties to follow the sessions. Until recently, conversational aspects have been neglected (Kuhn et al., 2016; Werner-Seidler et al., 2017; Horsch et al., 2017).

2.3 Missing gaps and research questions

So far, conversational aspects, which plays a critical role in in-person sleep treatment, are less studied. Our main hypothesis is that conversational AI will enable natural interaction between users and a system, throughout the treatment process, to make a computerised treatment be more close to in-person treatment. To this end, we will focus on the following research questions:

RQ1. How to triage via conversation together with the completed questionnaires?

RQ2. How to monitor the progress during the sleep coaching programme?

RQ3. How to understand a user-specific situation for personalised coaching programme?

3 Research Plan

RQ1: How to triage via conversation together with the completed questionnaires?

Answer to this research question entails three subtasks: The first sub-task is to assess users' complaints and identify sleep-related issues and its impacts to identify potential causes. The second subtask is to ask follow-up questions to clarify ambiguous statements and differentiate causes that have similar impacts. The third sub-task is to explain the assessment result.

Complaints assessment

Assessing the users' complaints can be reformulated as a classification task. One of the most similar approaches is a recent study conducted by Shim et al. (2020). They used neural networks-based multi-label classifier to detect pre-defined sleep issues from free-text. What makes our study more challenging is that 1) we aim to assess not only sleep issues but also impacts to identify underlying causes. And 2) we aim to incorporate the completed questionnaire results, which is different modality from free-text. For the first challenge, a naive approach is to build three separate classifiers for sleep issues, impact, and causes. It is limited, however, because these three entities are connected, such as there are causal links between sleep issues to impacts. Therefore, as the first step, we will build a directed graph, such as a Bayesian Network (BN) that each node represents the observed results of each entity. Since each node can be either free-text classification results or questionnaire results, we can address the second challenge, too. We will also explain other benefits of implementing the BN in the following paragraphs.

Follow-up question

In this project, we will explore the potential of conversational environment that the system can interact with patients. One of the benefits is that the system can actively search for additional information when it is needed. For example, the free-text inputs from users can be ambiguous. Also, multiple sleep issues could result in similar impacts so that it requires further assessment that differentiates between two or more conditions. We hypothesise that asking follow-up questions will solve these challenges by clarifying and refining it. Then the real challenge becomes how to decide *'when to ask?'* and *'what to ask?'*. A study by Middleton et al. (2016) addressed these challenges by framing a triage as a sequence of questions and answers. To achieve this, they encoded expert knowledge into a graph structure; each possible questions is linked to the possible answers, each of which is linked to a follow-up question. Since this approach requires human resource, we foresee to work with experts in sleep domain to encode the domain knowledge into structured form, such as a graph. Also, we will investigate whether the BN can select the most appropriate follow-up question. We will describe a preliminary experimental result of this approach in Section 4.

Triage result

The end task of the first research question is to support triage via text-based conversation and by explaining the assessment result: what was the main complaint from the user and which habits were associated with the detected complaints. We plan to take a similar approach with Chen et al. (2020)

who implemented BN on top of neural networks to provide interpretability. However, compared to their task, our task is more challenging because not all information is given from the beginning. Therefore, we will model uncertainty to deal with unknown information to triage. For evaluation, we will follow a recent study by Razzaki et al. (2018) and evaluate our triage system both quantitatively and qualitatively: Quantitatively, we will calculate precision and recall of detecting sleep issues and underlying causes. Qualitatively, we will rate triage flows with the help of an expert in sleep domain.

RQ2: How to monitor the progress during the sleep coaching programme?

One of the fundamentals of sleep treatment is to monitor the progress of a participant. To monitor the progress and analyse sleep patterns, we will use a sleep diary that is a widely used method to access people's quality of sleep (Monk et al., 1994; Carney et al., 2012). The traditional sleep diary consists of a log of sleep-related activities, including bedtime, wake up time, and sleep time and heavily relies on objective values, such as total time in bed (TIB), total sleep time (TST), and sleep efficiency (SE). However, to monitor the progress and understand the user-specific condition, subjective values and context should be also considered. To achieve this, we will use a narrative sleep diary written in free-text that contains not only the time information of sleep-related events but also the rich information of context. For example, a user can describe her/his sleep in free-text to explain not only how long they slept and how many times they woke up during the night but also the quality of sleep or feeling after sleep and what disturbed their sleep. Recent work by Rick et al. (2019) takes a similar approach to obtain qualifiable insights about the subjective experience of sleep by incorporating free-text user inputs. During this project, we will investigate combine different modalities, objective and subjective values, extracted from the narrative sleep diary to assess the progress.

RQ3: How to understand a user-specific situation for personalised coaching programme?

During the sleep coaching programme that helps user change their behaviour to improve their sleep, it is critical to provide personalised coaching programme tailored to a user. To achieve this, understanding the experience of a user and identifying the user-specific issues and difficulties is essential. In this study, we will use free-text input from users that describe their experiences, thoughts, and feelings during the coaching programme. Specifically, we will consider a behaviour change programme and aim to build a model that performs aspect-based sentiment analysis on review comments from a user. Sentiment analysis (SA) is a widely used natural language processing (NLP) technique used to assess user experiences (Liu, 2012). Aspect-based sentiment analysis (ABSA) is a type of SA that aims to detect sentimental values expressed toward fine-grained aspects (Pontiki et al., 2014), rather than performing classification at the sentence level. Even though ABSA is widely studied, the majority of works are limited to the review of consumer products (Do et al., 2019). Recently, Barahona et al. (2018) conducted research on detecting mental health concepts for cognitive behaviour therapy from user inputs by reformulating it as sentiment analysis detecting negative sentiment. Similar to this, we will investigate using ABSA technique to detect concepts related to sleep health for providing personalised support and behaviour change programme by analysing user inputs during the sleep coaching programme.

4 Pilot study

We ran a pilot experiment to examine our assumptions for RQ1. The main goal of this pilot study as follows: 1) To build a model that classifies free-text user inputs. 2) To implement BN to select a follow-up question. Following subsections describes details of the experiments and results.

4.1 Dataset

Motivated by Shim et al. (2020), we collected free-text data via crowdsourcing platform. We also adapted their approach that asks participants *to imagine they are sitting at the doctor's office and being ask to describe three different topics: sleep issues, the impact of their issues, and factors that might contribute to the issues*. We cleaned the data by dropping invalid input texts and annotated to create three datasets named issues, causes, and impact, respectively. Table 1 summarises statistics of each dataset. More information about dataset can be found in Appendix A.

Dataset	#.class	Train	Test
Causes	19	10,430	1,155
Issues	11	12,928	1,437
Impact	11	10,733	1,142

Table 1: Statistics of datasets. #.class refers the number of class categories. The numbers in Train and Test columns refer the number of data points.

4.2 Experimental settings

For classification, we used the pre-trained language model (Devlin et al., 2019) initialised with pre-trained weights and fine-tuned on our datasets. Implementation details are given in Appendix B. To evaluate the classifiers, we calculated macro-averaged precision, recall, and F1-score for issues, impacts, and causes, separately.

For selecting a follow-up question, we created a simple BN with three layers, which are sleep causes, issues, and impact. Details of the model are described in Appendix C. Since this is a pilot study, we only considered a few entities and created conditional probability tables (CPT) based on our limited knowledge. Note that the structure and CPT of BN are not clinically proved; The goal of this pilot study is to demonstrate the concept. At each iteration of question and answering, the BN updates its probability distribution at each node given information and selects the entity node with the highest probability of the entity is true. We qualitatively evaluated this approach.

4.3 Preliminary result and next steps

Table 2 summarises the classification result. The result shows that the model performs better on causes dataset than both on issues and impact datasets, even though there are more class categories in causes dataset. We conducted error analysis and observed that the trained models tend to misclassify similar classes. It implies that further assessment is needed to differentiate semantically close texts.

Dataset	P (%)	R(%)	F-1 (%)
Causes	94.9	91.7	93.2
Issues	87.4	79.9	82.7
Impact	79.9	72.3	75.2

Table 2: Classification results. All measures are macro-averaged per each class.

Figure 2 shows demonstrations of triage flow with BN. Each sub-figure shows a sequence of follow-up questions and answers given condition: normal BMI[1] (2a) and high BMI (2b). It is worth noting that each flow selected different follow-up question after the classification model predicted the same results. It shows the possibility of using BN to select the most appropriate follow-up question given information.

Currently, we did not evaluate the system based on the final triage result and the appropriateness of follow-up question because our dataset contains only free-text describing sleep issues, causes, and impacts, seperately. In our future study, we plan to follow a similar data collection protocol of Razzaki et al. (2018). They asked doctors to play patients based on given vignettes containing simple demographics, complaint, and other information that can be obtained by either open-ended or closed-ended questions.

5 Conclusion

In this paper, we propose a PhD project exploring potentials of developing conversational AI for a sleep coaching programme, which is motivated by CBT-I treatment, targeting healthy people who would like to optimise their sleep. The main goal of this PhD project is to develop NLP algorithms for conversational AI to allow the system to interact naturally with a user and provide automated analytic. To this end, we identified three research questions lying under three phases of the sleep coaching programme: triage, monitor, and support. We expect this research project's outcomes could contribute to the research domains of NLP and AI but also the healthcare field by providing a more accessible and affordable sleep treatment solution and an automated analytic system to lessen the burden of human experts.

Acknowledgments

This project has received funding from the European Union's Horizon 2020 research and innovation programme under the Marie Skłodowska-Curie grant agreement No 766139. This article reflects only the author's view and the REA is not responsible for any use that may be made of the information it contains.

[1]Body Mass Index (BMI) is a value derived from the mass (m) and height of a person (h), defined as m/h^2.

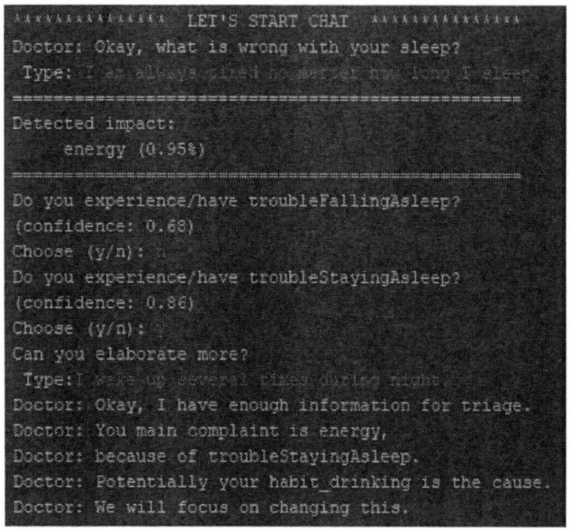

(a) When condition of 'high BMI' is given as *false*.

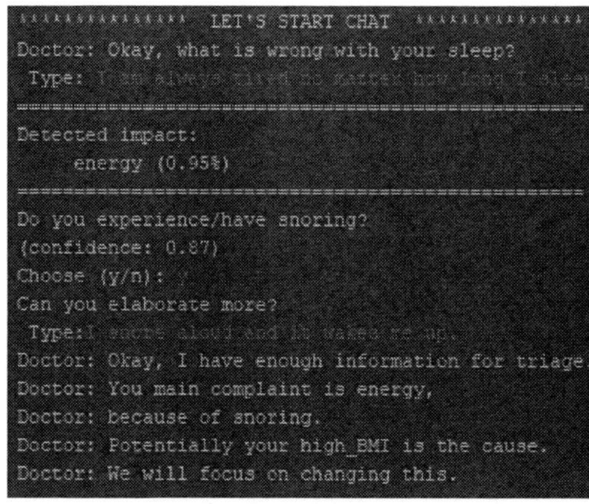

(b) When condition of 'high BMI' is given as *true*.

Figure 2: Examples of triage flow with BN and neural networks-based text-classifier. Green coloured texts show user-inputs while white coloured texts show system outputs.

References

Lina M Rojas Barahona, Bo-Hsiang Tseng, Yinpei Dai, Clare Mansfield, Osman Ramadan, Stefan Ultes, Michael Crawford, and Milica Gasic. 2018. Deep learning for language understanding of mental health concepts derived from cognitive behavioural therapy. In *Proceedings of the Ninth International Workshop on Health Text Mining and Information Analysis*, pages 44–54.

Lynda Belanger, Josee Savard, and Charles M Morin. 2006. Clinical management of insomnia using cognitive therapy. *Behavioral sleep medicine*, 4(3):179–202.

Richard R Bootzin and Michael L Perlis. 2011. Stimulus control therapy. In *Behavioral treatments for sleep disorders*, pages 21–30. Elsevier.

Colleen E Carney, Daniel J Buysse, Sonia Ancoli-Israel, Jack D Edinger, Andrew D Krystal, Kenneth L Lichstein, and Charles M Morin. 2012. The consensus sleep diary: standardizing prospective sleep self-monitoring. *Sleep*, 35(2):287–302.

Jun Chen, Xiaoya Dai, Quan Yuan, Chao Lu, and Haifeng Huang. 2020. Towards interpretable clinical diagnosis with bayesian network ensembles stacked on entity-aware cnns. In *Proceedings of the 58th Annual Meeting of the Association for Computational Linguistics*, pages 3143–3153.

Jacob Devlin, Ming-Wei Chang, Kenton Lee, and Kristina Toutanova. 2019. Bert: Pre-training of deep bidirectional transformers for language understanding. In *NAACL-HLT (1)*.

Hai Ha Do, PWC Prasad, Angelika Maag, and Abeer Alsadoon. 2019. Deep learning for aspect-based sentiment analysis: a comparative review. *Expert Systems with Applications*, 118:272–299.

Jack D Edinger and Melanie K Means. 2005. Cognitive–behavioral therapy for primary insomnia. *Clinical psychology review*, 25(5):539–558.

Peter J Hauri. 1991. Sleep hygiene, relaxation therapy, and cognitive interventions. In *Case studies in insomnia*, pages 65–84. Springer.

Corine HG Horsch, Jaap Lancee, Fiemke Griffioen-Both, Sandor Spruit, Siska Fitrianie, Mark A Neerincx, Robbert Jan Beun, and Willem-Paul Brinkman. 2017. Mobile phone-delivered cognitive behavioral therapy for insomnia: a randomized waitlist controlled trial. *Journal of medical Internet research*, 19(4):e70.

Nathaniel Kleitman. 1987. *Sleep and wakefulness.* University of Chicago Press.

Eric Kuhn, Brandon J Weiss, Katherine L Taylor, Julia E Hoffman, Kelly M Ramsey, Rachel Manber, Philip Gehrman, Jill J Crowley, Josef I Ruzek, and Mickey Trockel. 2016. Cbt-i coach: a description and clinician perceptions of a mobile app for cognitive behavioral therapy for insomnia. *Journal of clinical sleep medicine*, 12(4):597–606.

Jaap Lancee, Jan van den Bout, Annemieke van Straten, and Victor I Spoormaker. 2012. Internet-delivered or mailed self-help treatment for insomnia? a randomized waiting-list controlled trial. *Behaviour research and therapy*, 50(1):22–29.

Damien Leger, Virginie Bayon, Maurice M Ohayon, Pierre Philip, Philippe Ement, Arnaud Metlaine, Mounir Chennaoui, and Brice Faraut. 2014. Insomnia and accidents: cross-sectional study (equinox) on sleep-related home, work and car accidents in 5293 subjects with insomnia from 10 countries. *Journal of sleep research*, 23(2):143–152.

Bing Liu. 2012. Sentiment analysis and opinion mining. *Synthesis lectures on human language technologies*, 5(1):1–167.

Katherine Middleton, Mobasher Butt, Nils Hammerla, Steven Hamblin, Karan Mehta, and Ali Parsa. 2016. Sorting out symptoms: design and evaluation of the'babylon check'automated triage system. *arXiv preprint arXiv:1606.02041*.

Timothy H Monk, CHARLES F REYNOLDS III, David J Kupfer, Daniel J Buysse, Patricia A Coble, Amy J Hayes, Mary Ann Machen, Susan R Petrie, and Angela M Ritenour. 1994. The pittsburgh sleep diary. *Journal of sleep research*, 3(2):111–120.

Charles M Morin, Richard R Bootzin, Daniel J Buysse, Jack D Edinger, Colin A Espie, and Kenneth L Lichstein. 2006. Psychological and behavioral treatment of insomnia: update of the recent evidence (1998–2004). *Sleep*, 29(11):1398–1414.

Charles M Morin and Colin A Espie. 2007. *Insomnia: A clinical guide to assessment and treatment*. Springer Science & Business Media.

Jason C Ong, Rachel Manber, Zindel Segal, Yinglin Xia, Shauna Shapiro, and James K Wyatt. 2014. A randomized controlled trial of mindfulness meditation for chronic insomnia. *Sleep*, 37(9):1553–1563.

Michael L Perlis, Carla Jungquist, Michael T Smith, and Donn Posner. 2006. *Cognitive behavioral treatment of insomnia: A session-by-session guide*, volume 1. Springer Science & Business Media.

Maria Pontiki, Dimitris Galanis, John Pavlopoulos, Harris Papageorgiou, Ion Androutsopoulos, and Suresh Manandhar. 2014. SemEval-2014 task 4: Aspect based sentiment analysis. In *Proceedings of the 8th International Workshop on Semantic Evaluation (SemEval 2014)*, pages 27–35, Dublin, Ireland. Association for Computational Linguistics.

Salman Razzaki, Adam Baker, Yura Perov, Katherine Middleton, Janie Baxter, Daniel Mullarkey, Davinder Sangar, Michael Taliercio, Mobasher Butt, Azeem Majeed, et al. 2018. A comparative study of artificial intelligence and human doctors for the purpose of triage and diagnosis. *arXiv preprint arXiv:1806.10698*.

Steven R Rick, Aaron Paul Goldberg, and Nadir Weibel. 2019. Sleepbot: encouraging sleep hygiene using an intelligent chatbot. In *Proceedings of the 24th International Conference on Intelligent User Interfaces: Companion*, pages 107–108.

Lee M Ritterband, Frances P Thorndike, Linda A Gonder-Frederick, Joshua C Magee, Elaine T Bailey, Drew K Saylor, and Charles M Morin. 2009. Efficacy of an internet-based behavioral intervention for adults with insomnia. *Archives of general psychiatry*, 66(7):692–698.

Thomas Roth. 2007. Insomnia: definition, prevalence, etiology, and consequences. *Journal of clinical sleep medicine*, 3(5 suppl):S7–S10.

Heereen Shim, Stijn Luca, Dietwig Lowet, and Bart Vanrumste. 2020. Data augmentation and semi-supervised learning for deep neural networks-based text classifier. In *Proceedings of the 35th Annual ACM Symposium on Applied Computing*, pages 1119–1126.

Arthur J Spielman, Chien-Ming Yang, and Paul B Glovinsky. 2011. Sleep restriction therapy. In *Behavioral treatments for sleep disorders*, pages 9–19. Elsevier.

Melissa Kaleta Stoller. 1994. Economic effects of insomnia. *Clinical Therapeutics: The International Peer-Reviewed Journal of Drug Therapy*.

Lars Ström, Richard Pettersson, and Gerhard Andersson. 2004. Internet-based treatment for insomnia: a controlled evaluation. *Journal of consulting and clinical psychology*, 72(1):113.

Norah Vincent and Samantha Lewycky. 2009. Logging on for better sleep: Rct of the effectiveness of online treatment for insomnia. *Sleep*, 32(6):807–815.

Aliza Werner-Seidler, Bridianne O'Dea, Fiona Shand, Lara Johnston, Anna Frayne, Andrea S Fogarty, and Helen Christensen. 2017. A smartphone app for adolescents with sleep disturbance: development of the sleep ninja. *JMIR mental health*, 4(3):e28.

Thomas Wolf, Lysandre Debut, Victor Sanh, Julien Chaumond, Clement Delangue, Anthony Moi, Pierric Cistac, Tim Rault, Rémi Louf, Morgan Funtowicz, et al. 2019. Huggingface's transformers: State-of-the-art natural language processing. *ArXiv*, pages arXiv–1910.

A Dataset for pilot study

We collected three data sets for experiment: sleep causes, issues, and impact dataset. Class labels and label descriptions of causes, issues, and impact dataset are summarised in tables 3 to 5, respectively. Each data points annotated with either one or more class labels (max. 3 classes).

B Implementation and training settings

For experiment, PyTorch version (Wolf et al., 2019) of a Bidirectional embedding representations from transformers (BERT) model (Devlin et al., 2019) was used. We initialised the model with pre-trained weights (`bert-base-uncased`) obtained from language modelling with general copora (e.g., Wikicorpus, etc). For classification task, we added a

Class	Description
exercise	Work out/exercise
passivity	Physically not active
sleepEnvironment	Bad sleep environment
bedTimes	Irregular bed times
napping	Nap during the day
notTired	Not tired at night
breathingIssues	Stopped breathing
otherHealthIssues	Other health issues
obligationDuties	Too many duties
stressMoodAnxiety	Experience stress
media	Engage in screen-time
caffeine	Consume caffeine
pets	Sleep disturbance by pets
kids	Sleep disturbance by kids
eating	Eat heavy meals
drinking	Consume drink
alcohol	Consume alcohol drinks
nicotine	Smoke
noCause	No causes

Table 3: Class categories for causes dataset

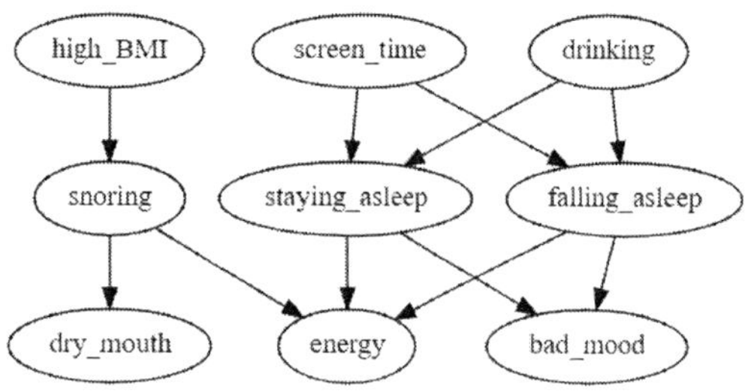

Figure 3: A simple Bayesian Network modelled connectivity between sleep causes, issues, and impact.

final dense layer with sigmoid activation function and used binary cross entropy loss to perform multi-label classification. Details of fine-tuning training are summarised in Table 6.

C Bayesian Network

A Bayesian Network used in a pilot study (Section 4) is illustrated in Figure 3.

Class	Description
snoringBothersMe	Snoring issue 1
snoringBothersOthers	Snoring issue 2
snoringStoppedBreathing	Stopped breathing
staysUpLate	Stay up late
troubleFallingAsleep	Lie in bed awake
troubleStayingAsleep	Wake up frequently
wakeUpTooEarly	Wake up too early
problemWakingUp	Trouble waking up
sleepsInLater	Sleep in late
otherIssue	Other issue
goodSleep	No issue

Table 4: Class categories for issues dataset

Class	Description
embarrassedBySnoring	Snoring impact
dryMouth	Cause dry mouth
energy	Feel tired or less energy
performance	Affect performance
appearance	Look tired
stressMoodAnxiety	Bad mood
lessPatience	Become less patience
socialImpact	Affect social life
otherHealthImmunity	Affect health
otherImpact	Other impact
noImpact	No impact

Table 5: Class categories for impacts dataset

Hyperparameter	Assignment
number of epochs	4
batch size	32
learning rate	$5e-5$
classificaiton layer	feedforward
drop out	0.1
optimaser	AdamW

Table 6: Hyperparameters for BERT text classifier

Relating Relations: Meta-Relation Extraction from Online Health Forum Posts

Daniel Stickley
University of Brighton
UK
d.stickley@brighton.ac.uk

Abstract

Relation extraction is a key task in knowledge extraction, and is commonly defined as the task of identifying relations that hold between entities in text. This thesis proposal addresses the specific task of identifying meta-relations, a higher order family of relations naturally construed as holding between other relations which includes temporal, comparative, and causal relations. More specifically, we aim to develop theoretical underpinnings and practical solutions for the challenges of (1) incorporating meta-relations into conceptualisations and annotation schemes for (lower-order) relations and named entities, (2) obtaining annotations for them with tolerable cognitive load on annotators, (3) creating models capable of reliably extracting meta-relations, and related to that (4) addressing the limited-data problem exacerbated by the introduction of meta-relations into the learning task. We explore recent works in relation extraction and discuss our plans to formally conceptualise meta-relations for the domain of user-generated health texts, and create a new dataset, annotation scheme and models for meta-relation extraction.

1 Introduction

The vast amounts of information now stored digitally in various forms e.g. social media and online forum posts, electronic health records, academic papers, etc., represent large amounts of unstructured data that contain useful information for a variety of purposes. Due to the scale of this data, automatic Knowledge Extraction (KE) holds the promise of allowing the automatic extraction of machine interpretable knowledge from these unstructured sources. Relation Extraction (RE) identifies relations that hold (typically) between entities in text; it is often an important and challenging subtask in KE - and is the primary focus of our thesis. Although there has been much work on RE and KE (Han et al., 2020; Manchanda and Phansalkar, 2019; Ma et al., 2019; Belz et al., 2019) there still remain considerable problems, including the high cost of creating high-quality annotated data, adequate conceptualisation of higher-order relationships that link events and/or cross sentence boundaries, and extraction from messy user-generated text.

In this research proposal we explore recent work in the field of RE, and identify some of the limitations that current research still faces. Next, we outline the specific problems that our research will address, before presenting a first outline of our approach based on meta-relations. We demonstrate the role of meta-relations with a worked example and outline how they will allow us to extract more richly structured data that more adequately captures the relationships between different types of information, as well as lowering the cognitive load on annotators. We then go on to discuss the data and methods we will use in our research, how these will progress our research, address our objectives, and conclude with a summary of the expected contributions of our thesis.

2 Research Context

This thesis will focus on relation extraction from natural language - with a particular focus on user generated text such as in online forum and social media posts. The task of relation extraction is typically approached by identifying named entities in the text, then identifying relations that hold between these entities. RE is often a very important component of KE systems, where these entities and relations are then used to populate a knowledge graph. This section will discuss recent RE approaches in order to establish the context our research will belong to.

Proceedings of the 16th Conference of the European Chapter of the Associationfor Computational Linguistics: Student Research Workshop, pages 129–136
April 19 - 23, 2021. ©2021 Association for Computational Linguistics

Relation extraction is a task that has seen much attention over the years, as Han et al.'s survey (2020) shows. Previous work has used statistical approaches, feature based methods, and graph-based approaches, but more recently neural machine learning models that use word embeddings as inputs have become the norm. Looking at shared tasks in RE, we can see particular language models and neural architectures that have been widely adopted and adapted for RE, such as the BERT language model (Devlin et al., 2018). A widely used architecture for RE is the Recurrent Neural Network (RNN), such as the Bi-LSTM (Huang et al., 2015) - a very popular model that has seen wide adoption and further developments such as using attention to enhance performance (Geng et al., 2020). BERT and Bi-LSTM based methods are the top performing models in various shared tasks, such as RuREBus (Ivanin et al., 2020), CCKS (Wang et al., 2019a), FewRel2.0 (Gao et al., 2019), and BioNLP 2019's AGAC and BB tasks (Wang et al., 2019b; Bossy et al., 2019). Han et al. (2020) also identify various challenges still faced by RE systems: current RE models often work in a simplified setting, but struggle with more complex tasks such as inter-sentence relations, and in few shot learning and open domain scenarios. Despite recent works attempting to overcome these challenges (Christopoulou et al., 2019; Gao et al., 2019; Cui et al., 2018; Wu et al., 2019) they can still be considered largely unsolved.

One challenge commonly faced in RE research is acquiring high quality labelled data to train and evaluate supervised models on. State-of-the-art models require a large amount of adequately varied, labelled data in order to be successfully trained, however RE is usually domain specific and so for each new task it can be difficult to acquire or create high quality gold standard training data. This is one of the main motivations for few-shot and cross-domain RE (Gao et al., 2019), as they both focus on learning with small amounts of labelled data. Belz et al. (2019) discuss the complexities that must be considered when creating labelled data for RE, and the difficulties that are encountered. They explore issues such as the high cognitive load that annotators can encounter with complex annotation schemes, and the resource intensive nature of annotating data with experts. In addition to few-shot learning and cross domain adaptation, there have been other methods attempting to mitigate the lack of data, such as initially training on coarse-grained labels (which are much quicker and cheaper to produce), then adopting a label-as-you-go approach whereby users create fine-grained labels as the system is used (Manchanda and Phansalkar, 2019).

Distant supervision has been used to increase usable data, and is applied to RE by using the basic assumption *"If two entities participate in a relation, any sentence that contains those two entities might express that relation"* (Mintz et al., 2009) to create weakly labelled data. This understandably leads to noisy data, with false positives and incomplete labels, however it has still shown to work reasonably well in practice (Smirnova and Cudré-Mauroux, 2018). Several approaches have attempted to address the shortcomings of distant supervision methods in RE, such as revising the basic assumption (that all sentences containing two entities with a known relation express that relation) to reduce the noise of the data (Riedel et al., 2010), creating undirected graphical models for distant supervision (Hoffmann et al., 2011; Surdeanu et al., 2012), allowing more than one relation to be predicted for two entities.

These models have since been further developed to introduce negative examples (of unrelated entity pairs) with an additional layer that denotes whether a relation holds for given entities (Min et al., 2013), leading to an increase in precision by between 1-4% (Smirnova and Cudré-Mauroux, 2018). Ritter et al. (2013) add a variable when aligning the text with the knowledge base, denoting whether a relation fact is present in the text. The model penalises disagreement between this variable and the variable that indicates whether the relation is present in the knowledge base. This allows us to encode certain intuitions about how likely certain relations are to be present or absent from the text, helping to reduce the issue of missing labels. Despite the continued development of distantly supervised approaches, noisy and incomplete data remains a problem that limits the performance of such systems (Smirnova and Cudré-Mauroux, 2018).

Current RE methods work best for relations that can be construed as holding between two named entities in text, e.g. [Margaret Hamilton, *worked_at*, NASA]. There has been less progress on relations that are inherently higher order, such as temporal relations which hold between events, e.g. *BEFORE*[[Margaret Hamilton, *worked_at*, NASA], [Margaret Hamilton, *founded*, Hamilton

Technologies]], or causal relations, which can hold between events, entities, and relations. Both temporal and causal RE are typically treated as separate tasks from general RE, which means they cannot take advantage of the mutually constraining nature of the general RE. A recent survey of temporal relation extraction (Alfattni et al., 2020) shows that extracting and classifying time expressions e.g. 'last week' and events e.g. 'pain has increased' are close to solved problems, but there still is much room for improvement in extracting relations that involve such time expressions. Causal relation extraction has seen much attention, with a recent focus on deep neural network approaches, however a recent survey shows that causal RE is also an open problem (Yang et al., 2021). Developing RE methods to better extract higher-order relations such as temporal and causal relations is still an important challenge for research to address.

From our review of the relation extraction literature, of which selected highlights were explored in this section, we have identified several key areas to address in our thesis. We will focus on the task of extracting a higher-order family of relations - specifically temporal, comparative, and causal - naturally construed as holding between other relations. We will develop theoretical underpinnings of and practical solutions for the challenges of (1) incorporating meta-relations into RE task conceptualisations, and annotation schemes for lower-order relations and named entities, (2) obtaining annotations for them with tolerable cognitive load on annotators, (3) creating models capable of reliably extracting meta-relations, and related to that (4) how to overcome the limited-data problem exacerbated by the introduction of meta-relations into the learning task.

3 Meta-Relations

The focus of the proposed thesis is a class of relations that are inherently *meta*, because they hold between (structured) relations, rather than monadic entities. This class includes temporal relations such as BEFORE and AFTER, comparative relations such as LONGER and SHORTER, and causal relations. As a starting point, we propose to incorporate meta-relations into the RE processes as follows, aiming to explore both sequential and joint modelling of the subtasks:

1. Named entity recognition (NER) is used to identify relevant entities in the text;
2. Relation extraction is performed, linking pairs of entities with a relation;
3. Meta-relation extraction is performed on the lower-level relations extracted in the previous step, linking pairs of relations with a meta-relation.

Let us break this down with a worked example - taken from the dataset presented by Belz et al. (2019), and using their annotation scheme:

I took Wellbutrin for a short period of time but it make me sick so I was given Zoloft

This sentence contains information that the user took - but subsequently stopped taking[1] - Wellbutrin, it made them feel sick, and they were then given Zoloft to take. As a human reader the temporal order in this information is easy to discern, however in order to extract this information in a machine readable format e.g. as relational triples, there are several steps that must be completed. First, named entities and other lowest-level units of information must be identified; in our case these would be drugs {*Wellbutrin, it, Zoloft*}, drug modification actions {*took, was given*}, and drug effects {*make me sick*}. Next there may be an entity linking step where the identified entities are linked to nodes in a knowledge graph. This is followed by the RE step, where the relations between pairs of entities will be identified: modification/drug relations will denote the user started or stopped taking a drug, and drug/effect relations will show effects associated with a drug.

With typical RE, this is where the process would end and the (unordered) extracted information would be: Wellbutrin started being taken, Wellbutrin stopped being taken, Wellbutrin caused nausea, and Zoloft started being taken. This information is useful but lacks important information such as the order of events and causality. Each relation is treated separately, and from this relation information we cannot infer the order of events as these same relations could be present in another order of events. e.g. if the user was taking Zoloft and Wellbutrin together, then they stopped taking Wellbutrin after feeling sick. This demonstrates that the temporal order of events is a crucial aspect to properly understanding the content in a sentence/document.

[1]We can make this assumption as these are both antidepressant medications, even though this may not be immediately clear solely from this text span.

It is crucial in a number of real world tasks such as automated Yellow Card filling,[2] for reporting unknown adverse side effects from drugs, where the temporal order of events - which drugs a person was taking, at what time, and in what order - must be reported as all of these factors may play a role in the adverse reaction (Belz et al., 2019).

Figure 1 shows how temporal meta-relations could be integrated with other extracted relations. In doing this we extract an unambiguous temporal order that shows Wellbutrin was taken, then the user felt sick, then they stopped taking Wellbutrin and started taking Zoloft. Temporal meta-relations are only one example, there are other types of meta-relations that could provide additional key pieces of information such as causal meta-relations. In our example in figure 1, we can see two event relations from Blez et al.'s (2019) annotation scheme: DRUG_MODIF[TYPE=START] and DRUG_EFFECT. Here we could use a causal meta-relation to show explicitly that starting to take the labelled drug (in this case Wellbutrin) is what caused the labelled effect (nausea).

4 Problem Addressed, Data, Methods

4.1 Problem addressed

Firstly, we will create a formal conceptualisation of the meta-relation extraction task and a new annotation scheme that incorporates meta-relations. We will use this to create a new large scale annotated dataset. As demonstrated by Belz et al. (2019), task conceptualisation is a complex and important task itself, and a crucial component in creating an annotation scheme and dataset, and in defining learning tasks. Therefore, creating a formal conceptualisation for meta-relation extraction will be an important first step in our research.

Meta-relations allow us to create methods for higher-order relation extraction, and to create more complete RE systems that develop a better understanding of the text, by extracting more richly structured information that more adequately captures the relationships between different types of information, as well as lowering the cognitive load on annotators. To achieve this, it will be important to address the different types of meta-relations and information we wish to extract when conceptualising the meta-relation task in the first instance.

[2]For information about the Yellow Card Scheme see https://yellowcard.mhra.gov.uk

So far our objectives will further the creation and performance of directly supervised methods using gold standard labelled data, however in order to make our novel conceptualisation of meta-relation extraction more generally applicable we will also develop less supervised methods. Approaches using distantly supervised and data augmentation methods allow the extension of existing datasets with meta-relations, whereas other methods such as bootstrapping and transfer learning enable the adoption of meta-relation extraction for neighbouring domains when data is limited. Utilising methods such as these will allow new meta-relation extraction models to be created with a reduced need for the resource intensive process of creating new data and models from scratch.

4.2 Data

We plan to use two existing data resources which we will adapt for our purposes. Belz et al. (2019) have collected 148,575 posts from online drug forums, and so far have annotated 2,000 posts for RE with the first phase of their annotation scheme described in their paper. We plan to adapt this annotation scheme, extending it to incorporate typed relations and meta-relations. The development of this annotation scheme will be a nontrivial task as it is important to properly consider how best to annotate the data to produce high quality labels whilst minimising cognitive load on workers during the annotation process.

Belz et al. describe the difficulty of maintaining a manageable cognitive strain on annotators. The goal of annotating the data is to produce labels that convey a complex level of information for the machine learning model to learn from, however if the labelling task is too difficult or convoluted it can lead to issues with slow turnaround time and low inter-annotator agreement, as well as annotators abandoning their work. Because of these potential issues, it is important that we consider the cognitive load annotators will experience when creating the annotation pipeline, for example by splitting annotation up into several simpler phases, and facilitating workshops to ensure the workers fully understand the annotation task and are able to use the required labelling tools.

The second resource we have identified that will be useful in this work is the MedNorm corpus and embeddings, created for cross-terminology medical concept normalisation (Belousov et al., 2019).

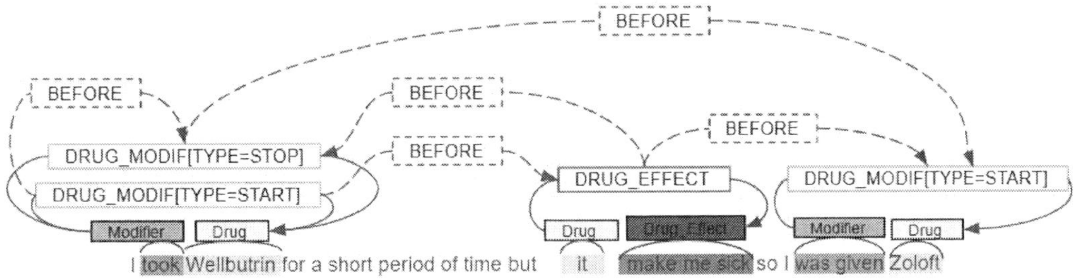

Figure 1: An example sentence taken from the dataset presented by Belz et al. (2019), annotated with meta-relations. Filled coloured boxes represent entities and lowest-level units of information, solid boxes and arrows represent lower order relations, dashed boxes with dashed arrows represent meta-relations.

This corpus is made up of five other datasets for medical concept normalisation, merged and annotated with a more uniform approach using two well known biomedical vocabularies and lexicons - SNOMED-CT and MedDRA (Stearns et al., 2001; Brown et al., 1999). This corpus will prove useful in developing RE systems for the medical domain, allowing us to leverage biomedical vocabularies and develop models that extract useful data for downstream tasks such as knowledge graph population.

4.3 Methods

As stated earlier, our research at the start aims to create a formal conceptualisation of meta-relation extraction, followed by creating an annotation scheme and dataset. Working from what we have already laid out in this paper, we will carefully consider what information can be represented by meta-relations. So far we have suggested temporal, causal, and comparative meta-relations, as they hold between relations, however more thorough exploration of the problem space is necessary to understand how to conceptualise the task of meta-relation extraction, and how best to create an annotation scheme incorporating these higher-order relations. To accomplish this, we will perform an in-depth investigation of how relations that we consider meta-relations have been treated in the literature and in existing annotation schemes. We will also consider a type system for lower-level (traditional) relations - in addition to named entities - in our conceptualisation. A type system would allow us to constrain the types of named entities a relation could apply to, and relations that meta-relations can apply to, meaning that not every entity/relation will need to be considered for every type of relation/meta-relation. This would also help in the development of distantly supervised methods for meta-relation extraction, similar to Xu et al. (2013) where they incorporate type constraints into their automatic labelling process.

We will use the annotation scheme presented by Belz et al. (2019) as the basis for our annotation scheme, revising as necessary to incorporate meta-relations, typed relations, and any additional entity labels in order to fit our conceptualisation. As mentioned earlier, asking workers to fully label the data in one step would be too cognitively demanding, so we plan to split the annotation process into several smaller phases. The presence of meta-relations will help when breaking the annotation down into smaller phases, as entities and lower level relations can be annotated separately, and should be relatively straightforward to label as they will represent the simplest units of information. Then, more complex higher-order information can be labeled as meta-relations in subsequent phases. Additionally, we will ensure annotators fully understand the labelling task by running an instructive course before they begin the labelling process. By splitting the process up into smaller tasks - paired with the instructive course - the annotators job will be more straightforward and less challenging, which should lead to both faster annotating and fewer mistakes made by annotators.

Our newly annotated dataset will then allow us to perform a series of experiments to explore the task of meta-RE. First, we will create a baseline approach for meta-RE, this will demonstrate how successful current state-of-the-art models are at extracting meta-relations, and show the accuracy with which different types of mental relations can be extracted using current methods. As we have described in Section 3, the task of meta-relation extraction can be framed as a pipelined extension of relation extraction, passing through the output of a traditional RE system (entities with corresponding relations) to another RE model, with some minor modification in order to perform relation extraction over the relations (as opposed to the entities). In this model we will follow the steps outlined in section 3: Use an NER model to identify the entities, before passing them into an RE model, and finally pass the entities and their corresponding relations through a modified RE model to extract meta-relations. This will be a very simple baseline model with little modification from the base RE model, meaning that we should be able to use most well performing RE models that take entities as input. We currently plan to use REDN (Li and Tian, 2020) due to its high performance on the popular shared task SemEval-2010 Task 8 (Hendrickx et al., 2009). The modifications we intend to make to the model for the final step in our baseline approach, are to treat extracted relations as entities. If we were to only input the relations (and text) in this step, the model will not be able to predict meta-relations that hold between relations and entities - instead only predicting meta-relations that hold between multiple relations; to avoid this, we will pass both the relations and entities through together, treating both as 'entities'.

We will then go on to explore alternative approaches and models developed specifically for meta-relations with the aim of achieving better results both quantitatively in the meta-relation extraction task, but also qualitatively in the quality of information the model can extract (in the form of entities, relations, and meta-relations). One alternative approach we will explore will be joint extraction of entities, relations, and meta-relations. It has been reported that jointly extracting entities and relations can lead to better overall performance as this reduces error propagation and allows more information to be leveraged from the text for both entity recognition and relation extraction (Cohen et al., 2020). In our experiments we will investigate how well meta-relations could be extracted jointly with entities and lower order relations; there are many RE models that jointly extract entities and relations, and one that we have identified for our experiments is TPLinker (Wang et al., 2020). The handshake tagging system used in the TPLinker model could be modified to also incorporate meta-relations which would enable the joint extraction of entities, relations and meta-relations.

5 Conclusion

In this paper we have provided the research context that our work will contribute to, identified various limitations in current work, including data collection/creation, cross domain adaptation, higher-order relation extraction, and distantly supervised relation extraction. We then proposed using meta-relations to extract more knowledge from text and discussed our plans to conceptualise the task of meta-relation extraction, and to incorporate meta-relations in an annotation scheme and dataset we will create. We also identified challenges we anticipate in addition to the data and methods we plan to use, and how we will utilise these methods in our work. Focusing on extraction of temporal, comparative, and causal relations in user-generated texts in the health domain, the expected contributions of our thesis are as follows:

- Formal conceptualisation of temporal, comparative, and causal meta-relation extraction.
- A new annotation scheme incorporating typed relations and meta-relations as well as lower-level relations.
- A new dataset for meta-relation extraction created with the above annotation scheme.
- A baseline pipelined approach and trained model for meta-relation extraction for drug effect and nonadherance information from user generated text.
- An alternative model for joint entity, relation and, meta-relation extraction for the above user generated text.
- Methods to address the dataset-creation problem capable of resulting in high quality relation extraction models trained on them, where access to data is limited.

Acknowledgements

We thank the anonymous reviewers for their very helpful comments.

References

Ghada Alfattni, Niels Peek, and Goran Nenadic. 2020. Extraction of temporal relations from clinical free text: A systematic review of current approaches. *Journal of Biomedical Informatics*, page 103488.

Maksim Belousov, William G Dixon, and Goran Nenadic. 2019. Mednorm: A corpus and embeddings for cross-terminology medical concept normalisation. In *Proceedings of the Fourth Social Media Mining for Health Applications (# SMM4H) Workshop & Shared Task*, pages 31–39.

Anya Belz, Richard Hoile, Elizabeth Ford, and Azam Mullick. 2019. Conceptualisation and annotation of drug nonadherence information for knowledge extraction from patient-generated texts. In *Proceedings of the 5th Workshop on Noisy User-generated Text (W-NUT 2019)*, pages 202–211.

Robert Bossy, Louise Deléger, Estelle Chaix, Mouhamadou Ba, and Claire Nédellec. 2019. Bacteria biotope at bionlp open shared tasks 2019. In *Proceedings of The 5th Workshop on BioNLP Open Shared Tasks*, pages 121–131.

Elliot G Brown, Louise Wood, and Sue Wood. 1999. The medical dictionary for regulatory activities (meddra). *Drug safety*, 20(2):109–117.

Fenia Christopoulou, Makoto Miwa, and Sophia Ananiadou. 2019. A walk-based model on entity graphs for relation extraction. *arXiv preprint arXiv:1902.07023*.

Amir DN Cohen, Shachar Rosenman, and Yoav Goldberg. 2020. Relation extraction as two-way span-prediction. *arXiv preprint arXiv:2010.04829*.

Lei Cui, Furu Wei, and Ming Zhou. 2018. Neural open information extraction. In *Proceedings of the 56th Annual Meeting of the Association for Computational Linguistics (Volume 2: Short Papers)*, pages 407–413, Melbourne, Australia. Association for Computational Linguistics.

Jacob Devlin, Ming-Wei Chang, Kenton Lee, and Kristina Toutanova. 2018. Bert: Pre-training of deep bidirectional transformers for language understanding. *arXiv preprint arXiv:1810.04805*.

Tianyu Gao, Xu Han, Hao Zhu, Zhiyuan Liu, Peng Li, Maosong Sun, and Jie Zhou. 2019. Fewrel 2.0: Towards more challenging few-shot relation classification. *arXiv preprint arXiv:1910.07124*.

ZhiQiang Geng, GuoFei Chen, YongMing Han, Gang Lu, and Fang Li. 2020. Semantic relation extraction using sequential and tree-structured lstm with attention. *Information Sciences*, 509:183–192.

Xu Han, Tianyu Gao, Yankai Lin, Hao Peng, Yaoliang Yang, Chaojun Xiao, Zhiyuan Liu, Peng Li, Maosong Sun, and Jie Zhou. 2020. More data, more relations, more context and more openness: A review and outlook for relation extraction. *arXiv preprint arXiv:2004.03186*.

Iris Hendrickx, Su Nam Kim, Zornitsa Kozareva, Preslav Nakov, Diarmuid Ó Séaghdha, Sebastian Padó, Marco Pennacchiotti, Lorenza Romano, and Stan Szpakowicz. 2009. Semeval-2010 task 8: Multi-way classification of semantic relations between pairs of nominals. In *Proceedings of the Workshop on Semantic Evaluations: Recent Achievements and Future Directions*, SEW '09, page 94–99, USA. Association for Computational Linguistics.

Raphael Hoffmann, Congle Zhang, Xiao Ling, Luke Zettlemoyer, and Daniel S Weld. 2011. Knowledge-based weak supervision for information extraction of overlapping relations. In *Proceedings of the 49th annual meeting of the association for computational linguistics: human language technologies*, pages 541–550.

Zhiheng Huang, Wei Xu, and Kai Yu. 2015. Bidirectional lstm-crf models for sequence tagging.

V Ivanin, E Artemova, T Batura, V Ivanov, V Sarkisyan, E Tutubalina, and I Smurov. 2020. Rurebus-2020 shared task: Russian relation extraction for business. In *Computational Linguistics and Intellectual Technologies: Proceedings of the International Conference "Dialog*.

Cheng Li and Ye Tian. 2020. Downstream model design of pre-trained language model for relation extraction task. *arXiv preprint arXiv:2004.03786*.

Yunshan Ma, Lizi Liao, and Tat-Seng Chua. 2019. Automatic fashion knowledge extraction from social media. In *Proceedings of the 27th ACM International Conference on Multimedia*, pages 2223–2224.

Sanjeev Manchanda and Ajeet Phansalkar. 2019. Automating knowledge extraction from unstructured knowledge articles. In *2019 IEEE Pune Section International Conference (PuneCon)*, pages 1–6. IEEE.

Bonan Min, Ralph Grishman, Li Wan, Chang Wang, and David Gondek. 2013. Distant supervision for relation extraction with an incomplete knowledge base. In *Proceedings of the 2013 Conference of the North American Chapter of the Association for Computational Linguistics: Human Language Technologies*, pages 777–782.

Mike Mintz, Steven Bills, Rion Snow, and Dan Jurafsky. 2009. Distant supervision for relation extraction without labeled data. In *Proceedings of the Joint Conference of the 47th Annual Meeting of the ACL and the 4th International Joint Conference on Natural Language Processing of the AFNLP*, pages 1003–1011.

Sebastian Riedel, Limin Yao, and Andrew McCallum. 2010. Modeling relations and their mentions without labeled text. In *Joint European Conference on Machine Learning and Knowledge Discovery in Databases*, pages 148–163. Springer.

Alan Ritter, Luke Zettlemoyer, Mausam, and Oren Etzioni. 2013. Modeling missing data in distant supervision for information extraction. *Transactions of the Association for Computational Linguistics*, 1:367–378.

Alisa Smirnova and Philippe Cudré-Mauroux. 2018. Relation extraction using distant supervision: A survey. *ACM Computing Surveys (CSUR)*, 51(5):1–35.

Michael Q Stearns, Colin Price, Kent A Spackman, and Amy Y Wang. 2001. Snomed clinical terms: overview of the development process and project status. In *Proceedings of the AMIA Symposium*, page 662. American Medical Informatics Association.

Mihai Surdeanu, Julie Tibshirani, Ramesh Nallapati, and Christopher D Manning. 2012. Multi-instance multi-label learning for relation extraction. In *Proceedings of the 2012 joint conference on empirical methods in natural language processing and computational natural language learning*, pages 455–465.

Haitao Wang, Zhengqiu He, Tong Zhu, Hao Shao, Wenliang Chen, and Min Zhang. 2019a. Ccks 2019 shared task on inter-personal relationship extraction. *arXiv preprint arXiv:1908.11337*.

Yucheng Wang, Bowen Yu, Yueyang Zhang, Tingwen Liu, Hongsong Zhu, and Limin Sun. 2020. Tplinker: Single-stage joint extraction of entities and relations through token pair linking. *arXiv preprint arXiv:2010.13415*.

Yuxing Wang, Kaiyin Zhou, Mina Gachloo, and Jingbo Xia. 2019b. An overview of the active gene annotation corpus and the bionlp ost 2019 agac track tasks. In *Proceedings of The 5th Workshop on BioNLP Open Shared Tasks*, pages 62–71.

Ruidong Wu, Yuan Yao, Xu Han, Ruobing Xie, Zhiyuan Liu, Fen Lin, Leyu Lin, and Maosong Sun. 2019. Open relation extraction: Relational knowledge transfer from supervised data to unsupervised data. In *Proceedings of EMNLP-IJCNLP 2019*, pages 219–228, Hong Kong, China. Association for Computational Linguistics.

Wei Xu, Raphael Hoffmann, Le Zhao, and Ralph Grishman. 2013. Filling knowledge base gaps for distant supervision of relation extraction. In *Proceedings of the 51st Annual Meeting of the Association for Computational Linguistics (Volume 2: Short Papers)*, pages 665–670.

Jie Yang, Soyeon Caren Han, and Josiah Poon. 2021. A survey on extraction of causal relations from natural language text. *arXiv preprint arXiv:2101.06426*.

Towards Personalised and Document-level Machine Translation of Dialogue

Sebastian T. Vincent
Department of Computer Science, University of Sheffield
Regent Court, 211 Portobello, Sheffield, S1 4DP, UK
stvincent1@sheffield.ac.uk

Abstract

State-of-the-art (SOTA) neural machine translation (NMT) systems translate texts at sentence level, ignoring context: intra-textual information, like the previous sentence, and extra-textual information, like the gender of the speaker. Because of that, some sentences are translated incorrectly. Personalised NMT (PersNMT) and document-level NMT (DocNMT) incorporate this information into the translation process. Both fields are relatively new and previous work within them is limited. Moreover, there are no readily available robust evaluation metrics for them, which makes it difficult to develop better systems, as well as track global progress and compare different methods. This thesis proposal focuses on PersNMT and DocNMT for the domain of dialogue extracted from TV subtitles in five languages: English, Brazilian Portuguese, German, French and Polish. Three main challenges are addressed: (1) incorporating extra-textual information directly into NMT systems; (2) improving the machine translation of cohesion devices; (3) reliable evaluation for PersNMT and DocNMT.

1 Introduction

Neural machine translation (NMT) represents state-of-the-art (SOTA) results in many domains (Sutskever et al., 2014; Vaswani et al., 2017; Lample et al., 2020), with some authors claiming human parity (Hassan et al., 2018). However, traditional methods process texts in short units like the utterance or sentence, isolating them from the entire dialogue or document, as well as ignoring extra-textual information (e.g. who is speaking, who they are talking to). This can result in a translation hypothesis' meaning or function being significantly different from the reference or make the text incohesive or illogical. For instance, the sentence in Polish *"Nie poszłam."* (*"I didn't go."*[1]) incorporates gender information in the word *poszłam* (*went$_{fem}$*) – as opposed to *poszedłem* (*went$_{masc}$*) – while the English verb does not incorporate such information. When translating *"I didn't go."* into Polish, the machine translation (MT) model must guess the gender of *I*, as this information is not rendered in the English sentence. Rescigno et al. (2020) show that when commercial MT engines need to "guess" the gender of a word, they do so by making implications based on its co-occurrence with other words in the training data. Since training data is often biased (Stanovsky et al., 2020), MT models will reproduce these biases, further propagating and reinforcing them. Clearly, research on context-aware machine translation is needed.

Sentence-level NMT (SentNMT) is especially harmful in the domain of dialogue, where most utterances rely on previously spoken ones, both in content and in style. The way in which an interlocutor chooses to express themselves depends on what they perceive as the easiest for the other person to understand (Pickering and Garrod, 2004). Dialogue is naturally cohesive (Halliday and Matthiessen, 2013), i.e. rid of redundancies, confusing redefinition of terms and unclear references. Part of what makes a conversation fluent is the links between its elements, which SOTA NMT models fail to capture. For instance, the latter utterance in the following exchange: *"They put something on the roof." "What?"* translates to Polish as *"Co takiego?" ("What something?").* The translation uses information unavailable in the utterance itself, i.e. the fact that *what* refers to the noun *something*. A sentence-level translation of *What?* would just be *Co?*, which is more universal, but also more ambiguous. Simply put, even when SentNMT pro-

[1] All examples throughout the report have been generated using Google Translate http://translate.google.com/, accessed 26 Nov 2020.

Proceedings of the 16th Conference of the European Chapter of the Associationfor Computational Linguistics: Student Research Workshop, pages 137–147
April 19 - 23, 2021. ©2021 Association for Computational Linguistics

duces a feasible translation, its context agnosticism may prevent it from producing a far better one.

There are growing appeals for developing NMT systems capable of incorporating additional information into hypothesis production: personalised NMT for extra-textual information (e.g. Sennrich et al., 2016; Elaraby et al., 2018; Vanmassenhove et al., 2018) and document-level NMT for intra-textual information (e.g. Bawden, 2019; Tiedemann and Scherrer, 2017; Zhang et al., 2018; Lopes et al., 2020). Evaluation methods predominant within both areas vary vastly from paper to paper, suggesting that for these applications a robust evaluation metric is not readily available. This view is further strengthened by the fact that Hassan et al. (2018), when assessing their MT for human parity, ignored document-level evaluation completely. Läubli et al. (2018) later disputed this choice, showing that professional annotators still overwhelmingly prefer human translation at the level of the document, and therefore human parity has not yet been achieved. This case study shows how much a robust and widely accepted document-level metric is needed.

Currently, researchers working on PersNMT and DocNMT conduct evaluation primarily by reporting the BLEU score for their systems. But they also commonly assert that the metric cannot reliably judge fine-grained translation improvements coming from context inclusion. As a way out, some of them report accuracy on specialised test suites (e.g. Kuang et al., 2018; Bawden, 2019; Voita et al., 2020) or manual evaluation. Although both have limited potential for generalisation, their attention to detail makes them superior tactics of evaluation for applications such as PersNMT and DocNMT.

In this work we utilise TV subtitles, a context-rich domain, in order to investigate whether MT of dialogue can be improved: directly, by **enhancing document coherence and cohesion** through incorporation of intra- and extra-textual information into translation, and indirectly, by **designing suitable evaluation methods for PersNMT and DocNMT**. Dialogue extracted from TV content is an attractive domain for two reasons: (1) there is an abundance of parallel dialogue corpora extracted purely from subtitles, and (2) the data is rich in or could potentially be annotated for a range of meta information such as the gender of the speaker.

In Section 2, we discuss relevant contextual phenomena. We then present the research on PersNMT and DocNMT, and the applicability of MT evaluation metrics to both. In Section 3 we delineate the research questions, the work conducted so far and our plans. Section 4 concludes the paper.

2 Background

2.1 Contextual phenomena

Two types of contextual phenomena relevant for MT of dialogue are explored: **cohesion** phenomena (related to information that can be found in the text) and **coherence** phenomena (related to the context of situation, which we consider to be external to the text). We emphasise that the phenomena explored below represent a subset of cohesion and coherence constituents, and that our interest in them arises from the difficulties they pose for MT of dialogue.

Cohesion phenomena Humans introduce cohesion into speech or written text in three ways: by choosing words related to those that were used before (*lexical cohesion*), by omitting parts of or whole phrases which can be unambiguously recovered by the addressee (*ellipsis and substitution*) and by referring to elements with pronouns or synonyms that the speaker judges recoverable from somewhere else in text (*reference*) (Halliday and Matthiessen, 2013). Cohesion phenomena effectively constitute links in text, whether within one utterance or across several. Figure 1 shows examples of how they can be violated by MT.

Cohesion-related tasks such as coreference or ellipsis resolution have attracted great interest in the recent years (e.g. Rønning et al., 2018; Jwalapuram et al., 2020). Previous research on cohesion within DocNMT has revealed that verb phrase ellipsis, coreference and reiteration (a type of lexical cohesion) may be particularly erroneous in MT (e.g. Tiedemann and Scherrer, 2017; Bawden et al., 2018; Voita et al., 2020).

Coherence phenomena Coherence is consistency of text with the context of situation (Halliday and Hasan, 1976). MT of dialogue may be erroneous due to models not having access to extra-textual information[2], e.g.: (a) speaker gender and number, (b) interlocutor gender and number, (c) social addressing, and (d) discourse situation. Different languages may render such phenomena differently, e.g. formality in German is expressed

[2]Note: the focus here is on *sentence-level translation utilising extra-textual context.*

EN	"It's just a social call." "A social call?"
PL$_{\text{MT}}$	"To tylko spotkanie towarzyskie." "Połączenie towarzyskie?" *("It's just a social gathering." "A social call?")*
PL$_{\text{ref}}$	"To tylko spotkanie towarzyskie." "Spotkanie towarzyskie?" *("It's just a social gathering." "A social gathering?")*
EN	I love it. We all do [=love it].
PL$_{\text{MT}}$	Kocham to. Wszyscy to robimy. *("We all do it.")*
PL$_{\text{ref}}$	Kocham to. Wszyscy to kochamy. *("We all love it.")*

Figure 1: Mistranslations of cohesion phenomena in translations. In the top example, *social call* is reiterated in source and reference, while MT opts for two different phrases, thereby decreasing lexical cohesion. The bottom example is verb phrase ellipsis, which does not exist in Polish and hence requires that the antecedent verb is repeated.

through the formal pronoun *Sie* (e.g. "Are you hungry?" becomes "*Bist du hungrig?*" when informal and "*Sind Sie hunrgig?*" when formal), while in Polish inflections of the pronoun *Pan/Pani/Państwo* ("*Mr/Mrs/Mr and Mrs*"), the formal equivalent of *ty/wy* ("*you*") are used. Then, as observed by Kranich (2014), some languages (such as English) prefer to express formality through politeness via word choices (e.g. *pleased* is a more formal *happy*)[3].

2.2 Personalised Neural Machine Translation

In PersNMT, the aim is to develop a system F capable of executing the following operation:

$$F(x_{SL}, e, TL) = x_{TL,e}$$

where x is the source sentence, p is the extra-textual information (e.g. speaker gender) and SL, TL are source and target language, respectively; $x_{TL,e}$ is then a contextual translation of x_{SL}.

This formulation is inspired by previous work within the area. Sennrich et al. (2016) control the formality of a sentence translated from English to German by using a side constraint. The model is trained on pairs of sentences (x_i, y_i), where y_i is either formal or informal, and a corresponding tag is prepended to the source sentence. At test time, the model relies on the tag to guide the formality of the translation hypothesis. A similar method has been used in Vanmassenhove et al. (2018) and in Elaraby et al. (2018) to address the problem of speaker gender morphological agreement. Moryossef et al. (2019) address the issue by modifying the source sentence during inference. They prepend the source with a minimal phrase implicitly containing all the relevant information; for example, for a female speaker and a plural audience, the augmented source yields "*She said to them: <src. sent.>*". Their method improves on multiple phenomena simultaneously (speaker gender and number, interlocutor gender and number) and requires little annotated data, but its performance relies entirely on the MT system's ability to utilise the added information. Furthermore, there are some side effects, e.g. the authors find the model's predictions to be often unintentionally influenced by the token *said*.

A similar method of tag-managed tuning has been used to train multilingual NMT systems (Johnson et al., 2017) and approximately control sequence length in NMT (Lakew et al., 2019). Outside MT, this method has been the driving force behind large pretrained controllable language models (Devlin et al., 2019; Keskar et al., 2019; Dathathri et al., 2019; Krause et al., 2020; Mai et al., 2020).

2.3 Document-level Neural Machine Translation (DocNMT)

Traditionally, NMT is a sentence-level (**Sent2Sent**) task, where models process each sentence of a document independently. Another way to do it would be to process the entire document at once (**Doc2Doc**), but it is much harder to train a reliable NMT model on document-long sequences. A compromise between the two is a **Doc2Sent** approach which produces the translation sentence by sentence but considers the document-level information as *context* when doing so (Sun et al., 2020).

Doc2Doc Tiedemann and Scherrer (2017) conduct the first Doc2Doc pilot study: they translate documents two sentences at once, each time discarding the first translated sentence and keeping the latter. They find that there is some benefit from doing so, albeit such benefit is difficult to measure. A larger setting was explored in (Junczys-Dowmunt, 2019): a 12-layer Transformer-Big (Vaswani et al., 2017) was trained to translate documents of up to 1000 subword units, with performance optimised by noisy back-translation, fine tuning and second-

[3]More examples can be found in the Appendix

pass post editing described in (Junczys-Dowmunt and Grundkiewicz, 2018). Finally, Sun et al. (2020) propose a fully Doc2Doc approach applicable to documents of arbitrary length. They split each document into $k \in 1, 2, 4, 8...$ parts and treat them as input data to the model, in what they call a **multi-relational** training, as opposed to **single relational** where only the whole document would be fed as input. Despite good results, the last two methods require enormous computational resources, and this limits their commercial application.

Doc2Sent When translating a sentence s_i a Doc2Sent model is granted access to document-level information $S \subseteq \{s_0...s_{i-1}, s_{i+1}...s_n\}$ and/or $T \subseteq \{t_0...t_{i-1}\}$ where n is the length of the document. The context information is either concatenated with the source sentence yielding a *uni-encoder* model (Tiedemann and Scherrer, 2017; Ma et al., 2020), or is supplied in an extra encoder yielding a *dual-encoder*[4] model (Zhang et al., 2018; Voita et al., 2020). In most approaches, the performance is optimised when shorter context (1-3 sentences) is used, though Kim et al. (2019) find that applying a simple rule-based *context filter* can stabilise performance for longer contexts. Ma et al. (2020) offer an improvement to uni-decoder which limits the sequence length in the top blocks of the Transformer encoder in the uni-encoder architecture, and Kang et al. (2020) introduce a reinforcement-learning-based *context scorer* which dynamically selects the context best suited for translating the critical sentence.

Jauregi Unanue et al. (2020) challenge the idea that DocNMT can implicitly learn document-level features, and instead propose that the models be *rewarded* when it preserves them. They focus on lexical cohesion and coherence and use respective metrics (Wong and Kit, 2012; Gong et al., 2015) to measure rewards. This method may be successful provided that suitable specialised evaluation metrics are proposed in the future. Nevertheless, more interest has been expressed in literature in achieving high performance w.r.t. such features as a by-product of an efficient architecture, as is the case with SOTA Sent2Sent architectures.

Other architectures DocRepair (Voita et al., 2019) is a monolingual post-editing model trained to repair cohesion in a document translated with SentNMT. Kuang et al. (2018) use two cache structures to influence the model's token predictions: a dynamic cache c_d of past token hypotheses with stopword removal and a topic cache c_t of most probable topic-related words. Finally, Lopes et al. (2020) compress the entire document into a vector and supply it as context during translation.

[4]Notation adopted from Ma et al. (2020).

2.4 Evaluation of Machine Translation

Many machine translation evaluation (MTE) metrics have been proposed over the years, much owing to the yearly WMT Metrics task (Mathur et al., 2020). They typically measure similarity between reference r, hypothesis h and source s, expressed in e.g. n-gram overlap (e.g. Papineni et al., 2002), cosine distance of embeddings (e.g. Zhang et al., 2020), translation edit rate (Snover et al., 2006) or trained on human judgements (Shimanaka et al., 2018), with the SOTA represented by COMET which combines the ideas of Zhang et al. and Shimanaka et al.: several distances between h, r and s are computed based on contextual embeddings from BERT.

Practically all of these metrics are developed to optimise performance at sentence level, an issue which until recently was not brought up often enough within the community. In the latest edition of the Metrics task at WMT (Mathur et al., 2020), a track for document-level evaluation was introduced. However, the organisers approached document-level evaluation as the average of human judgements on sentences in documents. This is not a reliable assessment, since the quality of a text is more than the sum or average of the quality of its sentences. This approach risks "averaging out" the severity of potential inter-sentential errors. Currently, DocNMT models are typically evaluated in terms of BLEU, showing modest improvements over a baseline (e.g. Voita et al., 2018, report 0.7 BLEU improvement). Several authors have argued that BLEU is not well suited to evaluating performance with respect to preserving cross-sentential discourse phenomena (Voita et al., 2020; Lopes et al., 2020). When applied to methods which improve only a certain aspect of translation, BLEU can indicate very little about the accuracy of these improvements. Furthermore, Kim et al. (2019) and Li et al. (2020) argue that even the reported BLEU gains in DocNMT models may not come from document-level quality improvements. Li et al. (2020) show that feeding the incorrect context can improve the metric by a similar amount.

To decide whether DocNMT yield any improvements, a more sophisticated evaluation method is needed. Following the observation that DocNMT improves on individual aspects of translation w.r.t. SentNMT, **test suites** grew in popularity among researchers (Bawden, 2019; Voita et al., 2020; Lopes et al., 2020). In particular, contrastive test suites (Müller et al., 2018) measure whether a model can repeatedly identify and correctly translate a certain phenomenon. They can be seen as robust collections of fine-grained multiple choice questions, yielding for each phenomenon an accuracy score indicative of performance. Producing these suites is time consuming and often requires expertise, but they are of extreme benefit to NMT. A sufficiently rich bed of test suites can evaluate the general robustness of a model, expressed as the average accuracy on these suites.

3 Addressing Research Questions

Within this PhD, we seek to answer three research questions (RQs):

RQ1 Can machine translation of dialogue be personalised by supplying it with extra-textual information?

RQ2 Is ellipsis problematic for MT, and can MT make use of marking of ellipsis and other cohesion devices to increase cohesion in translation of dialogue?

RQ3 How can automatic evaluation methods of MT be developed which confidently and reliably reward successful translations of contextual phenomena and, likewise, punish incorrect translations of the same phenomena?

3.1 Modelling Extra-Textual Information in Machine Translation

We hypothesise that supplying the MT model with extra-textual information might help it make better dialogue translation choices. Our hypothesis is motivated by two facts: (1) that human translators base their choices of individual utterances on the understanding of the discourse situation and ensure that each utterance preserves its original function and meaning, and (2) that many instances of utterances and phrases are impossible to interpret unambiguously in isolation from their context.

Tuning MT output with external information Previous works on supplying context via constraints or tags have been narrow in scope, predominantly employing tag controlling (see subsection 2.2). Following their success we plan to experiment with alternative neural model architectures which allow the incorporation of extra data into sequence-to-sequence transduction and assess whether they are fit for translation. If successful, we see many potential applications of such models in NMT, ranging from those explored in this thesis to limiting the length of the translation, fine-grained personalisation (e.g. on speaker characteristics) and more.

Per scene domain adaptation Neural machine translation models can be fine-tuned to a particular domain (e.g. medical transcripts) via domain adaptation (Cuong and Sima'an, 2017). Effective as it is, domain adaptation requires domain-specific data and that the model is trained on it (a time-consuming process). This technique is then inapplicable in scenarios where domains are fine-grained and the adaptation needs to be instantaneous. Per scene adaptation appears to be a promising solution to the problem of wrong lexical choices made by MT models when translating dialogue. The environment or scene in which dialogue occurs is often crucial to interpreting its meaning; a scene-unaware model may misinterpret the function of an utterance and produce an incorrect translation.

Within TV dialogue we define a scene as continuous action which sets boundaries for exchanges. Its characteristics can be expressed in natural language (e.g. extracts from plot synopsis), as tags (e.g. *school, student, sunny, exam*) or as individual categories (e.g. *battle*). Since scene context is document-level, this task can also be seen as a use case for combining PersNMT and DocNMT, and will be explored in this PhD.

3.2 Improving Cohesion for Machine Translation of Dialogue

Work within MT so far has only limitedly explored whether ellipsis poses a significant problem for translation (see Voita et al., 2020). We hypothesise that this is indeed the case: for some language pairs, the quality of machine-translated texts depend on the system's understanding of the ellipsis, when it is present in the source text. Since in dialogue ellipsis typically spans more than one utterance, it is poorly understood by SentNMT and the resulting MT quality is low (Figure 2).

To test our hypothesis, we will analyse ellipsis occurrences in dialogue data. We will use automatic methods to identify 1,000 occurrences of ellipsis in source text and mark spans of their occurrence

EN "I'm sorry, Dad, but you wouldn't understand." "Oh, sure, I would [understand], princess."
$\mathbf{PL_{MT}}$ "Przepraszam tato, ale nie zrozumiałbyś." "Och, oczywiście, księżniczko."
$\mathbf{PL_{ref}}$ "Przykro mi, tato, ale nie zrozumiałbyś." "Pewnie, że zrozumiałbym, księżniczko."

Figure 2: A wrongly translated exchange with ellipsis. In the source, the word *would* is a negation to *wouldn't* in the previous utterance. The MT system ignores *I would*: the backtranslation of PL_{MT} reads *"Oh, sure, princess."*

in the corresponding machine and reference translations. All cases will then be manually analysed from the following angles: (i) Is the ellipsis correctly translated? (ii) Is the resulting translation of ellipsis natural/unnatural? (iii) Does the reference translation make use of the elided content? (iv) If the model generates an acceptable translation, could the elided content nevertheless have been used to disambiguate it or make it more cohesive?

Next, we aim to build a DocNMT system which utilises marking of cohesion phenomena to make more cohesive translation choices[5] (Figure 3). We apply the insights from previous research, namely that the Transformer model may track cohesion phenomena when given enough context (Voita et al., 2018), that context preprocessing stabilises performance of contextual MT models (Kim et al., 2019), solutions to the problem of long inputs in DocNMT (e.g. Ma et al., 2020; Sun et al., 2020), and finally our own analysis of the problem.

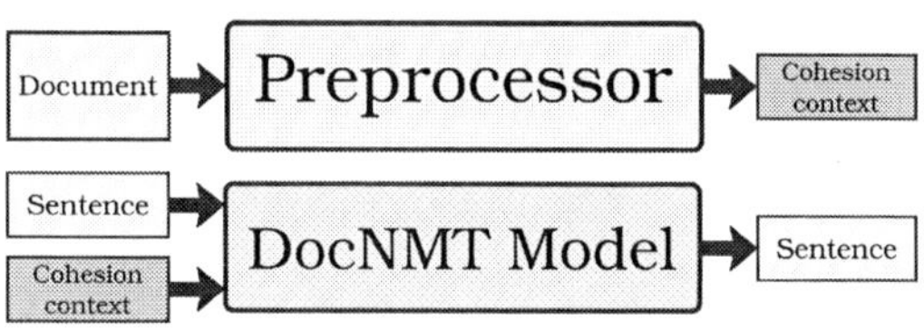

Figure 3: A draft of our DocNMT pipeline architecture. We preprocess the document to mark cohesion features. Then we use the output as the data for our model.

3.3 Applying Evaluation Metrics to Cohesion and Speaker Phenomena

Addressing RQ3 will involve testing the hypothesis that current common and SOTA automatic evaluation metrics fail to successfully reward translations which preserve contextual phenomena and, similarly, fail to punish those which do not.

We will develop a document-level test set of dialogue utterances in five languages, annotated for contextual phenomena. For each phenomenon, we will modify the reference translations to prepare several variations: one where all marked phenomena are translated correctly, another one where only 90% is translated correctly, then 80% etc. up to 0%. We will prepare a set of common and SOTA MT evaluation metrics and use them to produce scores for all variants, for all phenomena. If there exists a metric which gives a consistently lower score the more a phenomenon is violated, for all phenomena, then our hypothesis is incorrect and we will use that metric for evaluation in experiments. Otherwise, we will develop our own metric.

The aforementioned test set will also be converted to a contrastive test suite (Müller et al., 2018) and submitted as an evaluation method to WMT News Translation task. The data to be used here is a combination of the Serial Speakers dataset (Bost et al., 2020) and exports from OpenSubtitles (Lison and Tiedemann, 2016), yielding 5.6k utterances total, split into scenes and parallel in five languages.

We hope that this work will substantiate the flaws of sentence-level evaluation and prompt the community to work on context-inclusive methods.

4 Conclusions

This work is the proposal of a PhD addressing PersNMT and DocNMT in the dialogue domain. We have presented evidence that sentence-level MT models make cohesion- and coherence-related errors and offered several approaches via which we aim to tackle this problem. We plan to conduct extensive experiments to analyse the problem of ellipsis translation and of the use of sentence-level evaluation metrics to evaluate contextual phenomena. The outcome of this work will also include publicly available test suites, a document-level translation model, a personalised translation model and a context-aware evaluation metric.

Acknowledgements

This work was supported by the Centre for Doctoral Training in Speech and Language Technologies (SLT) and their Applications funded by UK Research and Innovation [grant number EP/S023062/1].

[5]Including elliptical structures in this step will depend on the result of the first experiment.

References

Rachel Bawden. 2019. *Going beyond the sentence : Contextual Machine Translation of Dialogue*. Ph.D. thesis, Université Paris-Saclay.

Rachel Bawden, Rico Sennrich, Alexandra Birch, and Barry Haddow. 2018. Evaluating discourse phenomena in neural machine translation. *NAACL HLT 2018 - 2018 Conference of the North American Chapter of the Association for Computational Linguistics: Human Language Technologies - Proceedings of the Conference*, 1:1304–1313.

Xavier Bost, Vincent Labatut, and Georges Linarès. 2020. Serial speakers: A dataset of TV series. *arXiv*.

Hoang Cuong and Khalil Sima'an. 2017. A survey of domain adaptation for statistical machine translation. *Machine Translation*, 31(4):187–224.

Sumanth Dathathri, Andrea Madotto, Janice Lan, Jane Hung, Eric Frank, Piero Molino, Jason Yosinski, and Rosanne Liu. 2019. Plug and Play Language Models: A Simple Approach to Controlled Text Generation. *arXiv*, pages 1–34.

Jacob Devlin, Ming-Wei Chang, Kenton Lee, and Kristina Toutanova. 2019. BERT: Pre-training of Deep Bidirectional Transformers for Language Understanding. In *Proceedings of the 2019 Conference of the North {A}merican Chapter of the Association for Computational Linguistics: Human Language Technologies, Volume 1 (Long and Short Papers)*, pages 4171–4186, Minneapolis, Minnesota. Association for Computational Linguistics.

Mostafa Elaraby, Ahmed Y. Tawfik, Mahmoud Khaled, Hany Hassan, and Aly Osama. 2018. Gender aware spoken language translation applied to English-Arabic. *2nd International Conference on Natural Language and Speech Processing, ICNLSP 2018*, pages 1–6.

Zhengxian Gong, Min Zhang, and Guodong Zhou. 2015. Document-Level Machine Translation Evaluation with Gist Consistency and Text Cohesion. In *Proceedings ofthe Second Workshop on Discourse in Machine Translation (DiscoMT)*, pages 33–40. Association for Computational Linguistics.

M A K Halliday and R Hasan. 1976. *Cohesion in English*. Longman, London.

M. A.K. Halliday and Christian M.I.M. Matthiessen. 2013. *Halliday's introduction to functional grammar: Fourth edition*. Routledge.

Hany Hassan, Anthony Aue, Chang Chen, Vishal Chowdhary, Jonathan Clark, Christian Federmann, Xuedong Huang, Marcin Junczys-Dowmunt, William Lewis, Mu Li, Shujie Liu, Tie-Yan Liu, Renqian Luo, Arul Menezes, Tao Qin, Frank Seide, Xu Tan, Fei Tian, Lijun Wu, Shuangzhi Wu, Yingce Xia, Dongdong Zhang, Zhirui Zhang, and Ming Zhou. 2018. Achieving Human Parity on Automatic Chinese to English News Translation. *arXiv*.

Inigo Jauregi Unanue, Nazanin Esmaili, Gholamreza Haffari, and Massimo Piccardi. 2020. Leveraging Discourse Rewards for Document-Level Neural Machine Translation. In *Proceedings of the 28th International Conference on Computational Linguistics*, pages 4467–4482, Barcelona, Spain (Online). International Committee on Computational Linguistics.

Melvin Johnson, Mike Schuster, Quoc V. Le, Maxim Krikun, Yonghui Wu, Zhifeng Chen, Nikhil Thorat, Fernanda Viégas, Martin Wattenberg, Greg Corrado, Macduff Hughes, and Jeffrey Dean. 2017. Google's Multilingual Neural Machine Translation System: Enabling Zero-Shot Translation. *Transactions of the Association for Computational Linguistics*, 5:339–351.

Marcin Junczys-Dowmunt. 2019. {M}icrosoft Translator at {WMT} 2019: Towards Large-Scale Document-Level Neural Machine Translation. In *Proceedings of the Fourth Conference on Machine Translation (Volume 2: Shared Task Papers, Day 1)*, pages 225–233, Florence, Italy. Association for Computational Linguistics.

Marcin Junczys-Dowmunt and Roman Grundkiewicz. 2018. MS-UEdin Submission to the WMT2018 APE Shared Task: Dual-Source Transformer for Automatic Post-Editing. In *Proceedings of the Third Conference on Machine Translation: Shared Task Papers*, pages 822–826, Belgium, Brussels. Association for Computational Linguistics.

Prathyusha Jwalapuram, Shafiq Joty, Irina Temnikova, and Preslav Nakov. 2020. Evaluating pronominal anaphora in machine translation: An evaluation measure and a test suite. *EMNLP-IJCNLP 2019 - 2019 Conference on Empirical Methods in Natural Language Processing and 9th International Joint Conference on Natural Language Processing, Proceedings of the Conference*, pages 2964–2975.

Xiaomian Kang, Yang Zhao, Jiajun Zhang, and Chengqing Zong. 2020. Dynamic Context Selection for Document-level Neural Machine Translation via Reinforcement Learning. In *Proceedings of the 2020 Conference on Empirical Methods in Natural Language Processing (EMNLP)*, pages 2242–2254, Online. Association for Computational Linguistics.

Nitish Shirish Keskar, Bryan McCann, Lav R. Varshney, Caiming Xiong, and Richard Socher. 2019. CTRL: A conditional transformer language model for controllable generation. *arXiv*, pages 1–18.

Yunsu Kim, Duc Thanh Tran, and Hermann Ney. 2019. When and Why is Document-level Context Useful in Neural Machine Translation? In *Proceedings of the Fourth Workshop on Discourse in Machine Translation (DiscoMT 2019)*, pages 24–34, Hong Kong, China. Association for Computational Linguistics.

Svenja Kranich. 2014. Translations as a Locus of Language Contact. In Juliane House, editor, *Translation: A Multidisciplinary Approach*, pages 96–115. Palgrave Macmillan UK, London.

Ben Krause, Akhilesh Deepak Gotmare, Bryan McCann, Nitish Shirish Keskar, Shafiq Joty, Richard Socher, and Nazneen Fatema Rajani. 2020. GeDi: Generative Discriminator Guided Sequence Generation. *arXiv*, pages 1–31.

Shaohui Kuang, Deyi Xiong, Weihua Luo, and Guodong Zhou. 2018. Modeling Coherence for Neural Machine Translation with Dynamic and Topic Caches. In *Proceedings of the 27th International Conference on Computational Linguistics*, pages 596–606, Santa Fe, New Mexico, USA. Association for Computational Linguistics.

Surafel Melaku Lakew, Mattia Di Gangi, and Marcello Federico. 2019. Controlling the Output Length of Neural Machine Translation. *arXiv*.

Guillaume Lample, Myle Ott, Alexis Conneau, Ludovic Denoyer, and Marc'Aurelio Ranzato. 2020. Phrase-based & neural unsupervised machine translation. *Proceedings of the 2018 Conference on Empirical Methods in Natural Language Processing, EMNLP 2018*, pages 5039–5049.

Samuel Läubli, Rico Sennrich, and Martin Volk. 2018. Has machine translation achieved human parity? A Case for Document-level Evaluation. *Proceedings of the 2018 Conference on Empirical Methods in Natural Language Processing, EMNLP 2018*, pages 4791–4796.

Bei Li, Hui Liu, Ziyang Wang, Yufan Jiang, Tong Xiao, Jingbo Zhu, Tongran Liu, and Changliang Li. 2020. Does Multi-Encoder Help? A Case Study on Context-Aware Neural Machine Translation. In *Proceedings of the 58th Annual Meeting of the Association for Computational Linguistics*, pages 3512–3518, Online. Association for Computational Linguistics.

Pierre Lison and Jörg Tiedemann. 2016. OpenSubtitles2016: Extracting Large Parallel Corpora from Movie and TV Subtitles. In *Proceedings of the Tenth International Conference on Language Resources and Evaluation (LREC'16)*, pages 923–929, Portorož, Slovenia. European Language Resources Association (ELRA).

António Lopes, M Amin Farajian, Rachel Bawden, Michael Zhang, and André F T Martins. 2020. Document-level Neural MT: A Systematic Comparison. In *Proceedings of the 22nd Annual Conference of the European Association for Machine Translation*, pages 225–234, Lisboa, Portugal. European Association for Machine Translation.

Shuming Ma, Dongdong Zhang, and Ming Zhou. 2020. A Simple and Effective Unified Encoder for Document-Level Machine Translation. In *Proceedings of the 58th Annual Meeting of the Association for Computational Linguistics*, pages 3505–3511, Online. Association for Computational Linguistics.

Florian Mai, Nikolaos Pappas, Ivan Montero, Noah A Smith, and James Henderson. 2020. Plug and Play Autoencoders for Conditional Text Generation. *arXiv*.

Nitika Mathur, Johnny Wei, Qingsong Ma, and Ondřej Bojar. 2020. Results of the WMT20 Metrics Shared Task. In *Proceedings of the Fifth Conference on Machine Translation*, pages 686–723, Online. Association for Computational Linguistics.

Amit Moryossef, Roee Aharoni, and Yoav Goldberg. 2019. Filling Gender & Number Gaps in Neural Machine Translation with Black-box Context Injection. In *Proceedings of the First Workshop on Gender Bias in Natural Language Processing*, pages 49–54, Florence, Italy. Association for Computational Linguistics.

Mathias Müller, Annette Rios, Elena Voita, and Rico Sennrich. 2018. A Large-Scale Test Set for the Evaluation of Context-Aware Pronoun Translation in Neural Machine Translation. In *Proceedings of the Third Conference on Machine Translation: Research Papers*, pages 61–72, Brussels, Belgium. Association for Computational Linguistics.

Kishore Papineni, Salim Roukos, Todd Ward, and Wei-Jing Zhu. 2002. Bleu: a Method for Automatic Evaluation of Machine Translation. In *Proceedings of the 40th Annual Meeting of the Association for Computational Linguistics*, pages 311–318, Philadelphia, Pennsylvania, USA. Association for Computational Linguistics.

Martin J. Pickering and Simon Garrod. 2004. Toward a mechanistic psychology of dialogue. *Behavioral and Brain Sciences*, 27(02).

Argentina Anna Rescigno, Johanna Monti, Andy Way, and Eva Vanmassenhove. 2020. A Case Study of Natural Gender Phenomena in Translation: A Comparison of Google Translate, Bing Microsoft Translator and DeepL for English to Italian, French and Spanish. In *Workshop on the Impact of Machine Translation (iMpacT 2020)*, pages 62–90, Virtual. Association for Machine Translation in the Americas.

Ola Rønning, Daniel Hardt, and Anders Søgaard. 2018. Sluice resolution without hand-crafted features over brittle syntax trees. *NAACL HLT 2018 - 2018 Conference of the North American Chapter of the Association for Computational Linguistics: Human Language Technologies - Proceedings of the Conference*, 2:236–241.

Rico Sennrich, Barry Haddow, and Alexandra Birch. 2016. Controlling politeness in neural machine translation via side constraints. *2016 Conference of the North American Chapter of the Association for Computational Linguistics: Human Language Technologies, NAACL HLT 2016 - Proceedings of the Conference*, pages 35–40.

Hiroki Shimanaka, Tomoyuki Kajiwara, and Mamoru Komachi. 2018. RUSE: Regressor Using Sentence Embeddings for Automatic Machine Translation Evaluation. In *Proceedings of the Third Conference on Machine Translation: Shared Task Papers*, pages 751–758, Belgium, Brussels. Association for Computational Linguistics.

Matthew Snover, Bonnie Dorr, Richard Schwartz, Linnea Micciulla, and John Makhoul. 2006. A study of translation edit rate with targeted human annotation. *AMTA 2006 - Proceedings of the 7th Conference of the Association for Machine Translation of the Americas: Visions for the Future of Machine Translation*, pages 223–231.

Gabriel Stanovsky, Noah A. Smith, and Luke Zettlemoyer. 2020. Evaluating gender bias in machine translation. *ACL 2019 - 57th Annual Meeting of the Association for Computational Linguistics, Proceedings of the Conference*, pages 1679–1684.

Zewei Sun, Mingxuan Wang, Hao Zhou, Chengqi Zhao, Shujian Huang, Jiajun Chen, and Lei Li. 2020. Capturing Longer Context for Document-level Neural Machine Translation: A Multi-resolutional Approach. *arXiv*.

Ilya Sutskever, Oriol Vinyals, and Quoc V. Le. 2014. Sequence to sequence learning with neural networks. *Advances in Neural Information Processing Systems*, 4(January):3104–3112.

Jörg Tiedemann and Yves Scherrer. 2017. Neural Machine Translation with Extended Context. In *Proceedings of the Third Workshop on Discourse in Machine Translation*, pages 82–92, Copenhagen, Denmark. Association for Computational Linguistics.

Eva Vanmassenhove, Christian Hardmeier, and Andy Way. 2018. Getting gender right in neural machine translation. *Proceedings of the 2018 Conference on Empirical Methods in Natural Language Processing, EMNLP 2018*, pages 3003–3008.

Ashish Vaswani, Noam Shazeer, Niki Parmar, Jakob Uszkoreit, Llion Jones, Aidan N. Gomez, Lukasz Kaiser, and Illia Polosukhin. 2017. Attention is all you need. *Advances in Neural Information Processing Systems*, pages 5999–6009.

Elena Voita, Rico Sennrich, and Ivan Titov. 2019. Context-Aware Monolingual Repair for Neural Machine Translation. In *Proceedings of the 2019 Conference on Empirical Methods in Natural Language Processing and the 9th International Joint Conference on Natural Language Processing (EMNLP-IJCNLP)*, pages 877–886, Hong Kong, China. Association for Computational Linguistics.

Elena Voita, Rico Sennrich, and Ivan Titov. 2020. When a good translation is wrong in context: Context-aware machine translation improves on deixis, ellipsis, and lexical cohesion. *ACL 2019 - 57th Annual Meeting of the Association for Computational Linguistics, Proceedings of the Conference*, pages 1198–1212.

Elena Voita, Pavel Serdyukov, Rico Sennrich, and Ivan Titov. 2018. Context-Aware Neural Machine Translation Learns Anaphora Resolution. In *Proceedings of the 56th Annual Meeting of the Association for Computational Linguistics (Volume 1: Long Papers)*, pages 1264–1274, Melbourne, Australia. Association for Computational Linguistics.

Billy T.M. Wong and Chunyu Kit. 2012. Extending machine translation evaluation metrics with lexical cohesion to document level. In *EMNLP-CoNLL 2012 - 2012 Joint Conference on Empirical Methods in Natural Language Processing and Computational Natural Language Learning, Proceedings of the Conference*, July, pages 1060–1068.

Jiacheng Zhang, Huanbo Luan, Maosong Sun, Fei Fei Zhai, Jingfang Xu, Min Zhang, and Yang Liu. 2018. Improving the transformer translation model with document-level context. *Proceedings of the 2018 Conference on Empirical Methods in Natural Language Processing, EMNLP 2018*, pages 533–542.

Tianyi Zhang, Varsha Kishore, Felix Wu, Kilian Q Weinberger, and Yoav Artzi. 2020. BERTScore: Evaluating Text Generation with BERT. In *8th International Conference on Learning Representations, ICLR 2020, Addis Ababa, Ethiopia, April 26-30, 2020*. OpenReview.net.

A Other examples

In this section we present an extended set of examples supporting our hypotheses stated in the main proposal. All examples in Figure 4, Figure 5 and Figure 6 show examples of mistranslated sentences where the error was related to a specific phenomenon: ellipsis in Figure 4, lexical cohesion in Figure 5 and reference in Figure 6. Figure 7, instead of highlighting translation errors, shows how a sentence in English can have several different translation candidates depending on the extra-textual context embedded in the situation (the corresponding translations are reference translations rather than MT-generated ones).

Context	What would they use it for?
Antecedent	[They would use it for]
EN	Grabbing the balls of a spy.
PL$_{MT}$	Łapie szpiega za jaja. *('He/she/they grab(s) the balls of a spy')*
PL$_{ref}$	Żeby łapać szpiega za jaja. *('For grabbing the balls of a spy')*
Context	A big, dumb, balding, North American ape with no chin.
Antecedent	[with]
EN	And a short temper.
PL$_{MT}$	I krótki temperament$_{nominative}$. *('And a short temper.')*
PL$_{ref}$	I z krótkim temperamentem$_{instrumental}$. *('And with a short temper.')*
Context	(...) with a record of zero wins and 48 defeats...
Antecedent	[a record of zero wins and 48]
EN	Oh, correction. Humiliating defeats, all of them by knockout–
PL$_{MT}$	Oh, korekta. Upokarzające porażki, wszystkie$_{nominative}$ przez nokautowanie... *('Oh, correction. Humiliating defeats, all of them by knockout...')*
PL$_{ref}$	Oh, korekta. Upokarzających porażek, wszystkich$_{genitive}$ przez nokautowanie... *('Oh, correction. Humiliating defeats, all of them by knockout...')*
Context	"I've only got two cupcakes for the three of you."
Antecedent	[two cupcakes]
EN	"Just take mine [=my cupcake]."
DE$_{MT}$	"Nimm einfach meine [=mine$_{fem}$]."
DE$_{ref}$	"Nimm einfach meinen [=mine$_{masc}$]."

Figure 4: Examples of translations where resolving ellipsis is crucial to generating a correct translation hypothesis. **Context** is the utterance containing the antecedent, and **Antecedent** is the content which is elided in the current utterance. In the first two examples from the top, the Polish translation requires including part of the antecedent in order to maintain cohesion. In the third example from the top, the antecedent decides the inflection of all the words relating to the word *defeats* which is repeated in the current utterance. Finally, the bottom example contains nominal ellipsis, and the model uses an incorrect inflection of *mein* since it fails to make the connection with the antecedent.

EN	"Sorry, Dad. I know you mean well." "Thanks for knowing I mean well."
PL$_{MT}$	"Przepraszam tato. Wiem, że chcesz dobrze." "Dzięki, że wiedziałeś, że chcę dobrze."
PL$_{ref}$	"Przepraszam tato. Wiem, że chcesz dobrze." "Dzięki, że wiesz, że chcę dobrze."
EN	"You're a dimwit." "Maybe so, but from now on... this dimwit is on easy street."
PL$_{MT}$	"Jesteś głupcem." *('You're a fool.')* "Może i tak, ale od teraz ... ten głupek *(dimwit)* jest na łatwej ulicy."
PL$_{ref}$	"Jesteś głupkiem."*('You're a dimwit.')* "Może i tak, ale od teraz ... ten głupek *(dimwit)* jest na łatwej ulicy."

Figure 5: Examples of mistranslated lexical cohesion. In the top example, although the MT model managed to translate most of the repeated phrase in the same way, it failed to maintain the verb *know* in the present tense. In the bottom example a different translation of *dimwit* is used in the two utterances. Note that it is okay for a model to give a different hypothesis to a word than the human translator would, as long as it agrees with the source *and* is cohesive with the rest of the text (i.e. all occurrences of the word are translated in the same way).

EN	The grabber. What would they use it for?
DE_{MT}	Der Grabber$_{masc}$. Wofür würden sie es$_{neut}$ verwenden?
DE_{ref}	Der Grabber$_{masc}$. Wofür würden sie ihn$_{masc}$ verwenden?
EN	Leave ideology to the armchair generals. It does me no good.
PL_{MT}	Ideologię$_{fem}$ zostawcie generałom foteli. Nic mi to$_{neut}$ nie da.
PL_{ref}	Ideologię$_{fem}$ zostawcie generałom foteli. Nic mi ona$_{fem}$ nie da.

Figure 6: Examples of mistranslated multi-sentence dialogue where reference is the violated phenomenon. In both examples, the gender of the referent is different in source and target languages, therefore the pronoun which refers to it is mistranslated.

EN	I never expected to be involved in every policy or decision, but I have been completely cut out of everything.
PL (fem)	Nigdy nie oczekiwałam wglądu w każdą decyzję, ale zostałam odcięta od wszystkiego.
PL (masc)	Nigdy nie oczekiwałem wglądu w każdą decyzję, ale zostałem odcięty od wszystkiego.
EN	And who have you called, by the way ?
PL (to masc)	Do kogo już dzwoniłeś?
PL (to fem)	Do kogo już dzwoniłaś?
PL (to Plural)	Do kogo już dzwoniliście?
PL (to Plural$_{fem}$)	Do kogo już dzwoniłyście?
EN	He was shot previous to your arrival?
PL (formal)	Został postrzelony przed pana przyjazdem?
PL (informal)	Został postrzelony przed Twoim przyjazdem?

Figure 7: Examples of situation phenomena that can occur in text: speaker gender agreement (top), addressee gender agreement (middle), formality (bottom).

Semantic-aware transformation of short texts using word embeddings: An application in the Food Computing domain

Andrea Morales-Garzón
University of Granada, Spain
andreamgmg@correo.ugr.es

Juan Gómez-Romero
University of Granada, Spain
jgomez@decsai.ugr.es

Maria J. Martin-Bautista
University of Granada, Spain
mbautis@decsai.ugr.es

Abstract

Most works in food computing focus on generating new recipes from scratch. However, there is a large number of new online recipes generated daily with a large number of users reviews, with recommendations to improve the recipe flavor and ideas to modify them. This fact encourages the use of these data for obtaining improved and customized versions. In this thesis, we propose an adaptation engine based on fine-tuning a word embedding model. We will capture, in an unsupervised way, the semantic meaning of the recipe ingredients. We will use their word embedding representations to align them to external databases, thus enriching their data. The adaptation engine will use this food data to modify a recipe into another fitting specific user preferences (e.g., decrease caloric intake or make a recipe). We plan to explore different types of recipe adaptations while preserving recipe essential features such as cuisine style and essence simultaneously. We will also modify the rest of the recipe to the new changes to be reproducible.

1 Introduction

Our dietary habits have a huge impact on health and, thus, in quality of life. In the last decades, the amount of nutritional data available has notably increased. This fact, together with the ubiquity of smartphones, has encouraged the use of machine learning techniques for automatizing some tedious and repetitive tasks as diet generation. In this context, the food computing concept refers to the use of food data to improve the quality of life as well as understanding human behavior (Min et al., 2019).

Recipes and their composition have been largely studied in food computing, especially in the food recommendation systems field (Teng et al., 2012). These systems mainly perform recipe-based nutrition assessment, looking for suitable combinations to user preferences. The use of predictive algorithms to understand relations between recipes has emerged in the last years (Sajadmanesh et al., 2017). Recently, authors have taken advantage of these tools to generate synthetic food data. Recipe generation is a current area of research, and the latest works in the area have put their interest in the creation of synthetic recipes. However, these works have focused on automatized text generation from scratch instead of taking direct advantage of the already existing recipes to generate new versions.

In this thesis, we will address the problem of partially-generation of recipes. Particularly, we will put our effort into recipe adaptation and recipe completion tasks. Online cooking communities and social media generate daily a huge amount of food data, mostly cooking recipes that users want to share with the world. In these communities, many users review the shared recipes, often giving feedback, customization, and suggestions for tasty versions of a given recipe. We plan to use this information to generate new recipe versions. Particularly, we will modify recipes to fulfill the user's requests. There are many reasons to modify a recipe, e.g., a diet restriction such as vegan or vegetarian diets, a lack of ingredients at home, to make the recipe tastier or cooking a kid-friendly version.

Also, many users follow restricted diets linked to nutritionist personalized assessment. A user would require a light version of a given recipe or including high-protein ingredients, among others. We propose to automatize the process of ingredient modification in a recipe and extend this idea with a recipe completion task. In both cases, we can consider several criteria simultaneously, such as those mentioned before. Thus, we tackle twofold challenges here; we have to preserve the semantic of the recipe and its essence while combining heterogeneous sources to incorporate nutrition and user knowledge during the adaptation.

Proceedings of the 16th Conference of the European Chapter of the Associationfor Computational Linguistics: Student Research Workshop, pages 148–154
April 19 - 23, 2021. ©2021 Association for Computational Linguistics

Here, a specific-domain language model can able us to tackle both purposes. We propose to use a fine-tuned word embedding model as the base of our contribution. We will use it to model the recipe ingredients to incorporate useful information from external sources (i.e., complete the ingredient data with nutrition information, user tips, and cuisine styles). Then, we will use the merged data in an adaptation function to find the most suitable foods to adapt a recipe to given restrictions. The semantic information combined with the external data will be the base of the adaptation engine. But adapting recipes do not only consist of dealing with ingredients. Likewise, we will use this model for a synthetic adaptation of title, recipe steps, and extra recipe data affected in the process.

2 Related work

Cooking recipes have been largely explored in food computing (Min et al., 2019). Last recipe-based works in food computing have surrounding agreed with the advantages of data mining techniques to understand how people cook. Regarding the use of natural language processing approaches to resolve food computing tasks, they have been mainly focused on the analysis of cuisines and ingredient relations (Min et al., 2019). From a wide perspective, these relations have been addressed by using the textual description of foods and flavor networks. The latter has been widely studied with statistical natural language processing methods (Takahashi et al., 2012; Chen, 2017; Chang et al., 2018). Our proposal is particularly related to the following topics.

Recipe generation and completion Creative cooking is the food computing area focused on the automatic generation of new recipes. Here, there is a distinction based on the approach. Synthetic recipes are created in two main ways. One is recipe completion, able to generate synthetic partial recipes from already existing ones. Completing recipes has also been studied in the frame of food recommendation systems. In (Cueto et al., 2019), the authors tackle the problem of completing partial recipes by using context-based recommendation. Recipe generation tasks have also considered the cuisine style for adapting recipes to other cultures (Kazama et al., 2018). In this case, they propose a neural network method to change ingredients for their equivalents in other cuisines. Regarding recipe generation, cooking recipes have been generated with natural text generation tasks (Aljbawi, 2020). Due to the repetitive results that are usually obtained with this approach, the authors in (Bosselut et al., 2018) proposed a synthetic recipe generation model that considered a reward to get more coherent and less repetitive texts.

Word embedding in food computing Word embedding models in food computing have been mainly focused on ingredient analysis. One of the more relevant works in this area is food2vec, where the author used a word embedding model trained with lists of ingredients to understand relations between ingredients and cuisines of the world (Altossar, 2015). Recipe2vec is another model trained in food data, in this case, for recipe retrieval purposes (BuzzFeed and Tasty, 2017). It has been mentioned the many advantages of embedding models referring to fusion heterogeneous food data for multiple purposes, where nutritional and social media textual data are integrated (Salvador et al., 2017) more specialized in resolving image recognition tasks rather than language processing. In (Chen et al., 2019), the authors used a word embedding model to detect ingredient relations to create pseudo-recipes. They used a model trained on a list of recipes to detect which ingredients appear together in recipes. They created a pseudo-recipe object based on this idea.

Transfer learning The state-of-the-art in NLP tasks is based in transfer learning models. It is very useful for specific-domains where data are limited since general-purpose models will perform poorly. This approach allows to train models with a bigger capacity but capturing the subtle essence of the problem addressed. The most well-known models using fine-tuning for specific tasks are BERT (Devlin et al., 2019) and GPT-2 (Budzianowski and Vulić, 2019) with excellent results. Transfer learning has been used in different specific areas, e.g., in biomedicine (Lee et al., 2019). To the best of our knowledge, transfer learning has not been proposed to extract semantic information from food item descriptions to combine heterogeneous sources.

Conditional text generation Controllable text generation is the area where sentences' attributes can be controlled by factors such as age, gender, or style (Prabhumoye et al., 2020). In this problem, we have a sequence output that is conditioned by the sequence input. Text generation language models have to assess the need for controlling specific parts of the task for resolving a specific problem (Keskar et al., 2019). In this line, recent approaches have put interest in style transfer techniques. Text style transfer has allowed adapting a synthetic text to different situations such as audiences, complexity, and other contextual circumstances (Li et al., 2020). Recent style transfer algorithms employ parallel data in supervised learning approaches and non-parallel data in seq2seq architectures for unsupervised approaches. Also, Variational Auto-Encoders have been applied for this aim by separating content and style in the latent space for better adjustment of the style (Fu et al., 2018).

3 Proposed methodology

We have divided our approach into two tasks explained in the following subsections.

3.1 Heterogeneous data-handling

The first problem that appears when modifying a recipe is obtaining enough food knowledge to be able to generate recipes that fulfill user preferences. One of the main challenges to address in food computing is the inherent difficulty in using food features from many different nutritional sources. Consequently, food items need previous processing to handle them jointly. According to this idea, we can use the item textual description to identify equivalent items between databases, allowing the joint use of these databases as a unique data collection (Morales-Garzón et al., 2020). Notice that ontology-based methods could perform well in this problem. But these models have problems when applied to ingredient-based tasks. They do not represent high detailed ingredients, and also have difficulty generalizing to online recipes. Furthermore, knowledge extraction has to be hand-crafted. To overcome this, we propose to model ingredient descriptions with a word embedding model. This unsupervised model can deal with arbitrary-sized text and capture the semantic of cooking.

Models Since the food domain is very-specific, general-purpose word embedding models will perform poorly. This issue can be solved by using pre-trained models and perform transfer learning. Deep models will be trained in large unlabeled text databases and, then, fine-tuned to the cooking domain. This approach will be able to capture automatically the semantic of cooking without human supervision. First, we will do a transfer learning task with a BERT language model (Devlin et al., 2019). Using BERT will able us to deal with one of the more compound facts when cooking: a same ingredient can be used in different forms and meals (e.g., a user could use flour for a cake, but also frying fish). In a sentence-based model, we will be able to represent the current context in which an ingredient is used. This fact will able us to find better food alternatives for each ingredient.

We plan to test the performance of our model replicating the process with GPT-2 (Budzianowski and Vulić, 2019). The main difference between BERT and GPT-2 is while BERT looks at the context of the word, GPT-2 only looks backward. In this thesis, we will explore both and discern the advantages of each one for the cooking domain.

Distance metrics We understand ingredient mapping as the search for an equivalent food in an external source. This similarity can be obtained by calculating the distance between ingredient descriptions. We consider an ingredient description as a short description text (e.g. "almonds toasted"). We plan to use food representations obtained with the embedding vectors to find food equivalences within databases. We plan to test the model performances with different metrics including word mover's distance as a baseline metric. We also plan to use a distance metric proposed in (Morales-Garzón et al., 2020), which has demonstrated to work remarkably well with food data descriptions.

Dataset We plan to use a pre-trained word embedding model trained on Wikipedia and Book Corpus datasets[1]. We will re-train the model in a food-based textual corpus. To do this, we will use a large recipe dataset available in archive.org[2]. The dataset contains more than 200,000 recipes with their preparation step texts. These texts contain meaningful information about the science of cooking such as ingredient combinations and cooking processes.

3.2 Adaptation engine

Deciding the most profitable version for a recipe is a very subjective process. Consequently, following human adaptation rules is difficult and very tedious. Our approach consists in using word embedding vectors to represent an existing cooking

[1] https://huggingface.co/models

[2] https://archive.org/details/recipes-en-201706

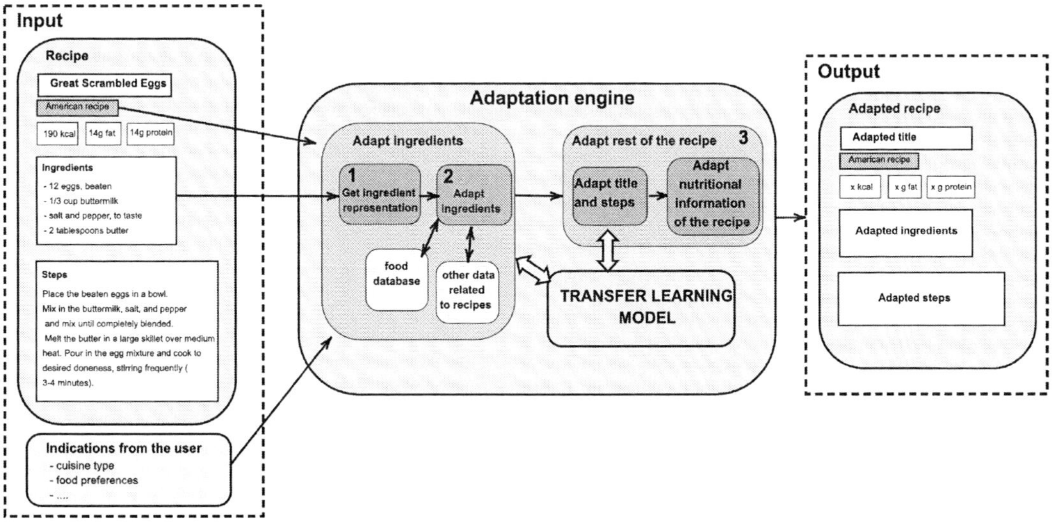

Figure 1: An overview of the procedure

recipe. For that, we will extract the ingredients from a recipe, and we will obtain their embedded representations with the transfer learning model. Once we have a representation of the ingredients, we proceed with adapting them to fit the user requirements. We will take advantage of the captured information in the model to adapt the ingredients (e.g., similarity relations between foods), with the aim of preserving the recipe essence. In this way, semantic relations between ingredients can influence the decision when changing an ingredient for other that fits in the recipe. Besides, not only changing the ingredients will result in a finished recipe. We will also generate automatic text from the ingredient list to make coherent cooking instructions. Thus, the process consists of three steps: (1) obtain a semantic representation of the ingredients, (2) adapt the recipe by changing the ingredients to other foods that fit, (3) modify the rest of the recipe accordingly, i.e., recipe preparation steps, nutrition information, and title if need. Since title and nutrition data can be easily obtained from the final ingredients, the challenge resides in altering the preparation text. Conditional generation and style transfer techniques will be used in this last step. At the end of this process, the user will have the full recipe with the list of ingredients and the cooking procedure, being able to reproduce it at home. See Figure 1 for a better understanding of this process.

Recipe modeling First, we will model a recipe with the transfer learning model. The ingredient information contained in an online recipe is short and may not be sufficient for making a quality adaptation. As introduced, we plan to combine the ingredients with food features such as cuisine style, nutrition information, packaging information, cooking tips, and potential ingredient relations. Unfortunately, this information has to be obtained from external heterogeneous sources. We will join this information in one object, merging the ingredient data with food knowledge from these external databases. Subsection 3.1 describes this procedure.

Ingredient adaptation One part of the recipe is properly adapting the ingredients. There are two main ways of adapting a recipe. In the first case, some ingredients of a recipe are replaced following a criterion, e.g., converting a given recipe into a vegan version, and, in the second case, it consists of suggestions to add new ingredients. In both cases, we can consider several criteria simultaneously. For example, the users would like to do a recipe but with fewer calories or more proteins.Here, we will design the proper adaptation function according to a multiobjective optimization problem with restrictions, e.g., maximizing the use of sweet ingredients while minimizing the calories. This has to be subjected to maintaining the coherence of the recipe.

Notice that only similarity-based functions will be suitable for maintaining the coherence of the recipe but they do not take into account other factors like calories. Thus, the ingredient adaptation task will consider the joint ingredient data obtained from the combination of the ingredient with external sources. Thus, we will be able to add adaptation knowledge to this step.

Feeding the adaptation procedure We can make use of user interactions with recipes to obtain information about how users react to some recipes. We will use online user interaction data with recipes to be considered in the adaptation function. We can exploit this data to measure which ingredient combinations are more appealing for the users. We will analyze this data to extract knowledge to feed the adaptation function.

Adaptation of the rest of the recipe Adapting a recipe does not just consist of changing the ingredients for another suitable option. We also need to adapt the preparation step to fit with the new ingredients. This part is compound because it needs to remain the coherence of the original recipe when possible. We plan to explore the use of word embedding approaches to partially-generate synthetic text using keywords. We will part from the original recipe, detecting those steps that must be modified. Notice that some recipe objects also contain nutrition tags for a serving. In this case, we will adapt this information using the ingredient data if allowed.

Dataset We plan to study recipes in specific cuisines. For that, we will use recipes extracted from Yummly. One of the tags stored in Yummly recipe data is the geographical origin of the recipe. There are several Yummly datasets online that we can use, with ingredients, preparation texts, and cuisine type[3]. Additionally, the Yummly website provide users' reviews, with their suggestions for altering the recipe, and recommendations of ingredients substitutions (and additions) to improve the taste of the dish.

Regarding nutritional food data, there are open-source nutrition dataset available for obtaining food data from the most common foods and dishes. One example is the USDA database, maintained by the Department of Agriculture in the United States (Gebhardt et al., 2008). There are also market product sources for access to typical food in specific zones of the world. Open Food Facts[4] is an open-source project with the aim of make worldwide food products accessible.

There are available resources about how users interact with recipes. The Food.com dataset[5] available in Kaggle provide this info for more than 200,000 recipes from the popular cooking site Food.com[6].

4 Evaluation

Validating recipe adaptations is a subjective procedure. Depending on the cultural factor, the type of meal, the flavors, and other intrinsic combinations, what could be an excellent recipe for a user, could result to be untasted for another different one. This variability makes it difficult to measure the adequacy of an adapted recipe. To tackle this variability, we plan to evaluate the proposed method with an online survey on both regular and expert users. For this, we will generate adapted recipes for different circumstances. Each recipe will receive a score, where the lowest value represents that the adapted recipe is disgusting and the highest is a very succulent recipe. Also, we plan to obtain adaptation suggestions in this step to use them as feedback for future improvement.

5 Strengths

With the arising of technology and, consequently, the large amount of recipes shared on the internet, food computing has played an undeniable role in recipe retrieval systems. These systems allow access to online recipes to speed up the recipe searching whenever a user wants to prepare a dish. We believe that the integration of our approach in the cited software could meet user needs when looking for cooking inspiration. Additionally, it is worth noting that a recipe-based word embedding model could be able to participate in multiple problems of food computing. One of its applications is using them for detecting recipe similarity to ensure variety in nutrition assessment systems.

We believe that food computing is not the only application of our approach. Personalized beauty treatment is another area in which our proposal could be useful. Commonly, there can be found on the internet many natural beauty care recipes consisting of a list of ingredients and instructions to create beauty remedies for different purposes. Among other many factors, this kind of treatment handles user expectations, allergies, and the cos-

[3]http://123.57.42.89/FoodComputing__Dataset.html

[4]https://es.openfoodfacts.org

[5]https://www.kaggle.com/shuyangli94/food-com-recipes-and-user-interactions

[6]https://www.food.com

metic composition of the treatment. A transfer learning model in this area could be applied to adapt these kinds of treatments to the user's needs.

6 Summary

Our proposal consists of using a transfer learning model in the food domain to adapt recipes to fulfill user needs. The challenge remains in using the model for two different tasks. First, we plan to use the model to complete ingredients information with data from external sources, such as nutritional data or cuisine traditions. Thus, we will employ this joined data for adapting a recipe to fulfill a need. Then, we will use the language model to adequate the rest of the recipe to be consistent with the adapted ingredients.

References

Bushra Aljbawi. 2020. Health-aware food planner: A personalized recipe generation approach based on gpt-2.

Jaan Altossar. 2015. Food2vec-augmented-cooking-machineintelligence. *Jaan Altossar's blog, last modified Dec*, 17.

Antoine Bosselut, Asli Celikyilmaz, Xiaodong He, Jianfeng Gao, Po-Sen Huang, and Yejin Choi. 2018. Discourse-aware neural rewards for coherent text generation. In *Proceedings of the 2018 Conference of the North American Chapter of the Association for Computational Linguistics: Human Language Technologies, Volume 1 (Long Papers)*, pages 173–184, New Orleans, Louisiana. Association for Computational Linguistics.

Paweł Budzianowski and Ivan Vulić. 2019. Hello, it's GPT-2 - how can I help you? towards the use of pretrained language models for task-oriented dialogue systems. In *Proceedings of the 3rd Workshop on Neural Generation and Translation*, pages 15–22, Hong Kong. Association for Computational Linguistics.

BuzzFeed and Tasty. 2017. Recipe2vec: How word2vec helped us discover related tasty recipes.

Minsuk Chang, Léonore V Guillain, Hyeungshik Jung, Vivian M Hare, Juho Kim, and Maneesh Agrawala. 2018. Recipescape: An interactive tool for analyzing cooking instructions at scale. In *Proceedings of the 2018 CHI Conference on Human Factors in Computing Systems*, page 451. ACM.

Meng Chen, Xiaoyi Jia, Elizabeth Gorbonos, Chnh T Hong, Xiaohui Yu, and Yang Liu. 2019. Eating healthier: Exploring nutrition information for healthier recipe recommendation. *Information Processing & Management*, page 102051.

Yuzhe Chen. 2017. *A statistical machine learning approach to generating graph structures from food recipes*. Ph.D. thesis, Brandeis University.

Paula Fermín Cueto, Meeke Roet, and Agnieszka Słowik. 2019. Completing partial recipes using item-based collaborative filtering to recommend ingredients. *arXiv preprint arXiv:1907.12380*.

Jacob Devlin, Ming-Wei Chang, Kenton Lee, and Kristina Toutanova. 2019. BERT: Pre-training of deep bidirectional transformers for language understanding. In *Proceedings of the 2019 Conference of the North American Chapter of the Association for Computational Linguistics: Human Language Technologies, Volume 1 (Long and Short Papers)*, pages 4171–4186, Minneapolis, Minnesota. Association for Computational Linguistics.

Zhenxin Fu, Xiaoye Tan, Nanyun Peng, Dongyan Zhao, and Rui Yan. 2018. Style transfer in text: Exploration and evaluation. In *Proceedings of the AAAI Conference on Artificial Intelligence*, volume 32.

Susan Gebhardt, L Lemar, D Haytowitz, P Pehrsson, M Nickle, B Showell, R Thomas, J Exler, and J Holden. 2008. Usda national nutrient database for standard reference, release 21. *United States Department of AgricultureAgricultural Research Service*.

Masahiro Kazama, Minami Sugimoto, Chizuru Hosokawa, Keisuke Matsushima, Lav R Varshney, and Yoshiki Ishikawa. 2018. A neural network system for transformation of regional cuisine style. *Frontiers in ICT*, 5:14.

Nitish Shirish Keskar, Bryan McCann, Lav R Varshney, Caiming Xiong, and Richard Socher. 2019. Ctrl: A conditional transformer language model for controllable generation. *arXiv preprint arXiv:1909.05858*.

Jinhyuk Lee, Wonjin Yoon, Sungdong Kim, Donghyeon Kim, Sunkyu Kim, Chan Ho So, and Jaewoo Kang. 2019. BioBERT: a pre-trained biomedical language representation model for biomedical text mining. *Bioinformatics*, 36(4):1234–1240.

Xiangyang Li, Guo Pu, Keyu Ming, Pu Li, Jie Wang, Yuxuan Wang, and Sujian Li. 2020. Review of text style transfer based on deep learning. *arXiv preprint arXiv:2005.02914*.

Weiqing Min, Shuqiang Jiang, Linhu Liu, Yong Rui, and Ramesh Jain. 2019. A survey on food computing. *ACM Computing Surveys (CSUR)*, 52(5):1–36.

Andrea Morales-Garzón, Juan Gómez-Romero, and María J Martin-Bautista. 2020. A word embedding model for mapping food composition databases using fuzzy logic. In *International Conference on Information Processing and Management of Uncertainty in Knowledge-Based Systems*, pages 635–647. Springer.

Shrimai Prabhumoye, Alan W Black, and Ruslan Salakhutdinov. 2020. Exploring controllable text generation techniques. *arXiv preprint arXiv:2005.01822*.

Sina Sajadmanesh, Sina Jafarzadeh, Seyed Ali Ossia, Hamid R Rabiee, Hamed Haddadi, Yelena Mejova, Mirco Musolesi, Emiliano De Cristofaro, and Gianluca Stringhini. 2017. Kissing cuisines: Exploring worldwide culinary habits on the web. In *Proceedings of the 26th international conference on world wide web companion*, pages 1013–1021.

Amaia Salvador, Nicholas Hynes, Yusuf Aytar, Javier Marin, Ferda Ofli, Ingmar Weber, and Antonio Torralba. 2017. Learning cross-modal embeddings for cooking recipes and food images. In *Proceedings of the IEEE conference on computer vision and pattern recognition*, pages 3020–3028.

Jun Takahashi, Tsuguya Ueda, Chika Nishikawa, Takayuki Ito, and Akihiko Nagai. 2012. Implementation of automatic nutrient calculation system for cooking recipes based on text analysis. *Lecture Notes in Computer Science (including subseries Lecture Notes in Artificial Intelligence and Lecture Notes in Bioinformatics)*, pages 789–794.

Chun-Yuen Teng, Yu-Ru Lin, and Lada A Adamic. 2012. Recipe recommendation using ingredient networks. In *Proceedings of the 4th Annual ACM Web Science Conference*, pages 298–307.

TMR: Evaluating NER Recall on Tough Mentions

Jingxuan Tu
Brandeis University
jxtu@brandeis.edu

Constantine Lignos
Brandeis University
lignos@brandeis.edu

Abstract

We propose the *Tough Mentions Recall* (TMR) metrics to supplement traditional named entity recognition (NER) evaluation by examining recall on specific subsets of "tough" mentions: *unseen mentions*, those whose tokens or token/type combination were not observed in training, and *type-confusable mentions*, token sequences with multiple entity types in the test data. We demonstrate the usefulness of these metrics by evaluating corpora of English, Spanish, and Dutch using five recent neural architectures. We identify subtle differences between the performance of BERT and Flair on two English NER corpora and identify a weak spot in the performance of current models in Spanish. We conclude that the TMR metrics enable differentiation between otherwise similar-scoring systems and identification of patterns in performance that would go unnoticed from overall precision, recall, and F1.

1 Introduction

For decades, the standard measures of performance for named entity recognition (NER) systems have been precision, recall, and F1 computed over entity mentions.[1] NER systems are primarily evaluated using exact match[2] F1 score, micro-averaged across mentions of all entity types. While per-entity-type scores available from the `conlleval` scorer (Tjong Kim Sang, 2002) are often reported, there are no widely-used diagnostic metrics that further analyze the performance of NER systems and allow for separation of systems close in F1.

This work proposes *Tough Mentions Recall* (TMR), a set of metrics that provide a fine-grained analysis of the mentions that are likely to be most challenging for a system: *unseen mentions*, ones that are present in the test data but not the training data, and *type-confusable mentions*, ones that appear with multiple types in the test set. We evaluate the performance of five recent popular neural systems on English, Spanish and Dutch data using these fine-grained metrics. We demonstrate that TMR metrics enable differentiation between otherwise similar-scoring systems, and the model that performs best overall might not be the best on the tough mentions. Our NER evaluation tool is publicly available via a GitHub repository.[3]

2 Related Work

Previous work in NER and sequence labeling has examined performance on out-of-vocabulary (OOV) tokens and rare or unseen entities. Ma and Hovy (2016) and Yang et al. (2018) evaluate system performance on mentions containing tokens not present in the pretrained embeddings or training data. Such analysis can be used broadly—Ma and Hovy perform similar analyses for part of speech tagging and NER—and can guide system design around the handling of those tokens.

Augenstein et al. (2017) present a thorough analysis of the generalization abilities of NER systems, quantifying the performance gap between seen and unseen mentions, among many other factors. Their work predates current neural NER models; the newest model they use in their evaluation is SENNA (Collobert et al., 2011). While prior work has considered evaluation on unseen mentions, it has focused on experimenting on English data, and the definition of "unseen" has focused on the tokens themselves being unseen (UNSEEN-TOKENS in our

[1] We use the term *mention* to refer to a specific annotated reference to a named entity—a span of tokens (*token sequence*) and an entity type. We reserve the term *entity* for the referent, e.g. the person being named. The traditional NER F1 measure is computed over mentions ("phrase" F1).

[2] While partial match metrics have been used (e.g. Chinchor and Sundheim, 1993; Chinchor, 1998; Doddington et al., 2004; Segura-Bedmar et al., 2013), exact matching is still most commonly used, and the only approach we explore.

[3] https://github.com/jxtu/EvalNER

Proceedings of the 16th Conference of the European Chapter of the Associationfor Computational Linguistics: Student Research Workshop, pages 155–163
April 19 - 23, 2021. ©2021 Association for Computational Linguistics

TRAINING SET	Newcastle$_{[LOC]}$ is a city in the UK$_{[LOC]}$.
TEST SET	John Brown$_{[PER]}$, the Newcastle$_{[ORG]}$ star from the UK$_{[LOC]}$, has...

	Newcastle [ORG]	John Brown$_{[PER]}$	UK$_{[LOC]}$
SEEN			✔
UNSEEN-TYPE	✔		
UNSEEN-TOKENS		✔	
UNSEEN-ANY	✔	✔	

Table 1: Example data and how mentions would be classified into unseen and type-confusable mention sets

work). We use the umbrella of "tough mentions" to cover a number of possible distinctions that can be made with regards to how unseen test set data is, and we experiment on multiple languages.

Mesbah et al. (2018) propose an iterative approach for long-tail entity extraction, focusing on entities of two specific types in the scientific domain. Derczynski et al. (2017) propose evaluation on a set of unique mentions, which emphasizes the ability of a system to recognize rarer entities. As entities and their types change quickly (Derczynski et al., 2015), recall on emerging entities is becoming a more critical measure in evaluating progress. Ribeiro et al. (2020) propose CHECKLIST, which can be applied to NER by using invariance tests; for example, replacing a mention with another one of the same entity type should not affect the output of the model. Fu et al. (2020) evaluate the generalization of NER models through breakdown tests, annotation errors and dataset bias. They examine the performance on subsets of entities based on the entity coverage rate between train and test set. They also release *ReCoNLL*, a revised version of CoNLL-2003 English with fewer annotation errors which we use in this work.

3 Unseen and Type-confusable Mentions

3.1 Unseen Mentions

Given annotated NER data divided into a fixed train/development/test split, we are interested in the relationship between the mentions of the training and test sets. We classify mentions into three mutually-exclusive sets described in Table 1: SEEN, UNSEEN-TYPE, and UNSEEN-TOKENS, and a superset UNSEEN-ANY that is the union of UNSEEN-TYPE and UNSEEN-TOKENS. **UK$_{[LOC]}$** appears in both the training and test set, so it is a SEEN mention. As there is no mention consisting of the token sequence *John Brown* annotated as any type in the test set, **John Brown$_{[PER]}$** is an UNSEEN-TOKENS mention.[4] While there is no mention with the tokens and type **Newcastle$_{[ORG]}$** in the training data, the token sequence *Newcastle* appears as a mention, albeit with a different type (LOC). **Newcastle$_{[ORG]}$** is an UNSEEN-TYPE mention as the same token sequence has appeared as a mention, but not with the type ORG.

3.2 Type-confusable Mentions

Token sequences that appear as mentions with multiple types in the test set form another natural set of challenging mentions. If **Boston$_{[LOC]}$**, the city, and **Boston$_{[ORG]}$**, referring to a sports team[5] are both in the test set, we consider all mentions of exactly the token sequence *Boston* to be *type-confusable mentions* (TCMs), members of TCM-ALL. We can further divide this set based on whether each mention is unseen. TCM-UNSEEN is the intersection of TCM-ALL and UNSEEN-TOKEN; TCM-SEEN is the rest of TCM-ALL.

Unlike Fu et al. (2020), who explore token sequences that occur with different types in the training data, we base our criteria for TCMs around type variation in the test data. Doing so places the focus on whether the model can correctly produce multiple types in the output, as opposed to how it reacted to multiple types in the input. Also, if type confusability were based on the training data, it would be impossible to have TCM-UNSEEN mentions, as the fact that they are type confusable in the training data means they have been seen at least twice in training and thus cannot be considered unseen. As our metrics compute subsets over the gold standard entities, it is natural to only measure recall and not precision on those subsets, as it is not clear exactly which false positives should be considered in computing precision.

3.3 Data Composition

We evaluate using the ReCoNLL English (Fu et al., 2020), OntoNotes 5.0 English (Weischedel et al., 2013, using data splits from Pradhan et al. 2013), CoNLL-2002 Dutch, and CoNLL-2002 Spanish (Tjong Kim Sang, 2002) datasets. We use ReCoNLL (Fu et al., 2020) in our analysis instead

[4]The matching criterion for the token sequence is case sensitive, requires an exact—not partial—match, and only considers mentions. **John Henry Brown$_{[PER]}$**, **john brown$_{[PER]}$**, or unannotated *John Brown* appearing in the training set would not make **John Brown$_{[PER]}$** a seen mention.

[5]For example: ***Boston$_{[ORG]}$* won the World Series in 2018.**

Set	LOC	ORG	PER	MISC	ALL
UNSEEN-ANY	17.9	45.9	**85.3**	35.5	47.6
UNSEEN-TOK.	17.5	41.6	**85.1**	35.1	46.1
UNSEEN-TYPE	0.4	**4.3**	0.2	0.4	1.5
TCM-ALL	7.1	**13.7**	0.4	1.0	6.3
TCM-SEEN	5.4	**9.5**	0.4	1.0	4.6
TCM-UNSEEN	1.7	**4.2**	0.0	0.0	1.7
All (Count)	1,668	1,661	1,617	702	5,648

Table 2: Percentage of all mentions in each subset, with total mentions in the final row (ReCoNLL English)

Set	LOC	ORG	PER	MISC	ALL
UNSEEN-ANY	24.4	30.8	**68.9**	60.9	39.6
UNSEEN-TOK.	22.4	29.2	**67.1**	58.8	37.8
UNSEEN-TYPE	2.0	1.6	1.8	**2.1**	1.8
TCM-ALL	**23.3**	7.5	1.1	4.7	10.7
TCM-SEEN	**22.6**	6.8	0.8	4.1	10.1
TCM-UNSEEN	**0.7**	**0.7**	0.3	0.6	0.6
All (Count)	1,084	1,400	735	340	3,559

Table 3: Percentage of all mentions in each subset, with total mentions in the final row (CoNLL-2002 Spanish)

of the CoNLL-2003 English data (Tjong Kim Sang and De Meulder, 2003) to improve accuracy as it contains a number of corrections.

Tables 2, 3, and 4 give the total mentions of each entity type and the percentage that fall under the proposed unseen and TCM subsets for the three CoNLL datasets.[6] Across the three languages, 39.6%–54.6% of mentions are unseen, with the highest rate coming from PER mentions. UNSEEN-TYPE contains under 2% of mentions in English and Spanish and almost no mentions in Dutch; it is rare for a token sequence to only appear in training with types that do not appear with it in the test data.

Similarly, TCMs appear in the English (10.7%) and Spanish (6.3%) data, but almost never in Dutch (0.2%). The differences across languages with regards to TCMs may reflect morphology or other patterns that prevent the same token sequence from appearing with multiple types, but they could also be caused by the topics included in the data. In English, the primary source of TCMs is the use of city names as sports organizations, creating LOC-ORG confusion.

[6]Tables for OntoNotes 5.0 English are provided in the appendix (Tables 16-17).

Set	LOC	ORG	PER	MISC	ALL
UNSEEN-ANY	36.8	52.2	**72.6**	51.2	54.6
UNSEEN-TOK.	36.8	52.1	**72.5**	50.9	54.4
UNSEEN-TYPE	0.0	0.1	0.1	**0.3**	0.2
TCM-ALL	0.1	0.0	0.2	**0.3**	0.2
TCM-SEEN	**0.1**	0.0	**0.1**	0.0	0.1
TCM-UNSEEN	0.0	0.0	0.1	**0.3**	0.1
All (Count)	774	882	1,098	1,187	3,941

Table 4: Percentage of all mentions in each subset, with total mentions in the final row (CoNLL-2002 Dutch)

4 Results

4.1 Models and Evaluation

We tested five recent mainstream NER neural architectures that either achieved the state-of-the-art performance previously or are widely used among the research community.[7] The models are CHAR-CNN+WORDLSTM+CRF[8](CHARCNN), CHARLSTM+WORDLSTM+CRF[8] (CHARLSTM), CASED BERT-BASE[9] (Devlin et al., 2019), BERT-CRF[10] (Souza et al., 2019), and FLAIR (Akbik et al., 2018).[11]

We trained all the models using the training set of each dataset. We fine-tuned English Cased BERT-Base, Dutch (Vries et al., 2019) and Spanish (Cañete et al., 2020) BERT models and used the model from epoch 4 after comparing development set performance for epochs 3, 4, and 5. We also fine-tuned BERT-CRF models using the training data, and used the model from the epoch where development set performance was the best within the maximum of 16 epochs.

All models were trained five times each on a single NVIDIA TITAN RTX GPU. The mean and standard deviation of scores over five training runs are reported for each model. It took approximately 2 hours to train each of FLAIR and NCRF++ on each of the CoNLL-2002/3 datasets, 12 hours to train FLAIR, and 4 hours to train NCRF++ on OntoNotes 5.0 English. It took less than an hour to fine-tune BERT or BERT-CRF models on each dataset. Hyperparameters for Spanish and Dutch models implemented using NCRF++ were taken from Lample et al. (2016). FLAIR does not provide hyperparameters for training CoNLL-02 Spanish, so we used

[7]We could not include a recent system by Baevski et al. (2019) because it was not made publicly available.

[8]Using the NCRF++ (Yang and Zhang, 2018) implementations: `https://github.com/jiesutd/NCRFpp`.

[9]NER implementation from `https://github.com/kamalkraj/BERT-NER`.

[10]A Cased BERT-Base Model with an additional CRF layer.

[11]`https://github.com/flairNLP/flair`

Model	Precision	Recall	F1
CharLSTM	91.92 (±0.29)	91.90 (±0.31)	91.91 (±0.28)
CharCNN	92.13 (±0.18)	91.93 (±0.18)	92.03 (±0.17)
Flair	**93.00 (±0.15)**	**93.66 (±0.08)**	**93.33 (±0.12)**
BERT	91.04 (±0.11)	92.36 (±0.13)	91.70 (±0.14)
BERT-CRF	91.13 (±0.15)	92.29 (±0.04)	91.70 (±0.08)

Table 5: Standard P/R/F1 (ReCoNLL-2003 English)

Model	Precision	Recall	F1
CharLSTM	87.12 (±0.42)	86.38 (±0.36)	86.90 (±0.40)
CharCNN	86.94 (±0.27)	86.28 (±0.33)	86.61 (±0.25)
Flair	**88.56 (±0.12)**	89.42 (±0.09)	**88.99 (±0.10)**
BERT	87.52 (±0.09)	**89.84 (±0.12)**	88.67 (±0.10)
BERT-CRF	87.29 (±0.33)	89.32 (±0.19)	88.29 (±0.26)

Table 6: Standard P/R/F1 (OntoNotes 5.0 English)

those for CoNLL-02 Dutch. We did not perform any other hyperparameter tuning.

4.2 Baseline Results

We first examine the performance of these systems under standard evaluation measures. Tables 5 and 6 give performance on ReCoNLL and OntoNotes 5.0 English datasets using standard P/R/F1. In English, Flair attains the best F1 in both datasets, although BERT attains higher recall for OntoNotes.[12]

BERT attains the highest F1 in Dutch (91.26) and Spanish (87.36); due to space limitations, tables are provided in the appendix (Tables 14-15). BERT-CRF performs similar or slightly worse than BERT in all languages, but generally attains lower standard deviation in multiple training runs, which suggests greater stability from using a CRF for structured predictions. The same observation also holds for Flair which also uses a CRF layer. We are not aware of prior work showing results from using BERT-CRF on English, Spanish, and Dutch. Souza et al. (2019) shows that the combination of Portuguese BERT Base and CRF does not show better performance than bare BERT Base, which agrees with our observations. F1 rankings are otherwise similar across languages. The performance of CharLSTM and CharCNN cannot be differentiated in English, but CharLSTM substantially outperforms CharCNN in Spanish (+2.53) and Dutch (+2.15).

[12]We are not aware of any open-source implementation capable of matching the F1 of 92.4 reported by Devlin et al. (2019). The gap between published and reproduced performance likely stems from the usage of the "maximal document context," while reimplementations process sentences independently, as is typical in NER. Performance of Flair is slightly worse than that reported in the original paper because we did not use the development set as additional training data.

Model	All	TCM-All	TCM-Seen	TCM-Unseen
CharLSTM	91.90	85.52 (±1.09)	87.36 (±0.70)	80.61 (±3.00)
CharCNN	91.93	85.58 (±1.08)	87.55 (±1.11)	80.36 (±3.37)
Flair	**93.66**	**88.47 (±0.51)**	**89.75 (±0.73)**	**87.76 (±1.86)**
BERT	92.36	88.28 (±0.74)	89.69 (±0.89)	85.46 (±1.74)
BERT-CRF	92.29	87.02 (±0.71)	89.43 (±0.76)	79.59 (±1.25)

Table 7: Recall over all mentions and each type-confusable mention subset (ReCoNLL-2003 English)

Model	All	U-Any	U-Tok.	U-Type
CharLSTM	91.90	86.94 (±0.58)	87.32 (±0.63)	75.29 (±2.54)
CharCNN	91.93	87.06 (±0.21)	87.48 (±0.18)	74.41 (±1.48)
Flair	**93.66**	**89.93 (±0.25)**	**90.31 (±0.19)**	78.53 (±2.94)
BERT	92.36	87.94 (±0.29)	88.02 (±0.31)	**85.29 (±2.04)**
BERT-CRF	92.29	87.55 (±0.14)	87.73 (±0.12)	82.12 (±1.53)

Table 8: Recall over all mentions and each unseen (U-) mention subset (ReCoNLL-2003 English)

4.3 TMR for English

We explore English first and in greatest depth because its test sets are much larger than those of the other languages we evaluate, and we have multiple well-studied test sets for it. Additionally, the CoNLL-2003 English test data is from a later time than the training set, reducing train/test similarity.

Revised CoNLL English. One of the advantages of evaluating using TMR metrics is that systems can be differentiated more easily. Table 7 gives recall for type-confusable mentions (TCMs) on ReCoNLL English. As expected, recall for TCMs is lower than overall recall, but more importantly, recall is less tightly-grouped over the TCM subsets (range of 8.17) than all mentions (1.76). This spread allows for better differentiation, even though there is a higher standard deviation for each score. For example, BERT-CRF generally performs very similarly to BERT, but scores 5.87 points lower for TCM-Unseen, possibly due to how the CRF handles lower-confidence predictions differently (Lignos and Kamyab, 2020). Flair has the highest all-mentions recall and the highest recall for TCMs, suggesting that when type-confusable mentions have been seen in the training data, it is able to effectively disambiguate types based on context.

Table 8 gives recall for unseen mentions. Although Flair attains higher overall recall, BERT attains higher recall on Unseen-Type, the set on which all models perform their worst. While there are few (85) mentions in this set, making assessment of statistical reliability challenging, this set allows us to identify an advantage for BERT in this specific subset: a BERT-based NER model is better able to produce a novel type for a token sequence

Model	ALL	TCM-ALL	TCM-SEEN
CHARLSTM	86.38	80.65 (±0.46)	82.24 (±0.46)
CHARCNN	86.28	79.80 (±0.41)	81.49 (±0.40)
FLAIR	89.42	**86.00 (±0.44)**	**87.39 (±0.51)**
BERT	**89.84**	84.72 (±0.18)	85.61 (±0.00)
BERT-CRF	89.32	85.46 (±0.40)	86.83 (±0.46)

Table 9: Recall over all mentions and each type-confusable mention subset (OntoNotes 5.0 English)

Model	ALL	U-ANY	U-TOKENS
CHARLSTM	86.38	72.71 (±0.80)	74.34 (±0.80)
CHARCNN	86.28	72.50 (±0.76)	74.10 (±0.75)
FLAIR	89.42	77.56 (±0.21)	79.05 (±0.16)
BERT	**89.84**	**79.97 (±0.11)**	**81.14 (±0.14)**
BERT-CRF	89.32	78.46 (±0.56)	79.63 (±0.61)

Table 10: Recall over all mentions and each unseen mention subset (OntoNotes 5.0 English)

only seen with other types in the training data.

OntoNotes 5.0 English. Examination of the OntoNotes English data shows that Flair outperforms BERT for type-confusable mentions, but BERT maintains its lead in overall recall when examining unseen mentions. Tables 9 and 10 give recall for type-confusable and unseen mentions.[13]

Summary. Table 11 gives a high-level comparison between BERT and Flair on English data. Using the TMR metrics, we find that the models that attain the highest overall recall may not perform the best on tough mentions. However, the results vary based on the entity ontology in use. In a head-to-head comparison between Flair and BERT on ReCoNLL English, despite Flair having the highest overall and TCM recall, BERT performs better than Flair on UNSEEN-TYPE, suggesting that BERT is better at predicting the type for a mention seen only with other types in the training data. In contrast, on OntoNotes 5.0 English, BERT attains the highest recall on UNSEEN mentions, but performs worse than Flair on TCMs. The larger and more precise OntoNotes ontology results in the unseen and type-confusable mentions being different than in the smaller CoNLL ontology. In general, Flair performs consistently better on TCMs while BERT performs better on UNSEEN mentions.

4.4 TMR for CoNLL-02 Spanish/Dutch

Tables 12 and 13 give recall for type-confusable and unseen mentions for CoNLL-2002 Spanish and Dutch.[14] The range of the overall recall for Spanish (11.80) and Dutch (17.13) among the five systems we evaluate is much larger than in English (1.76), likely due to systems being less optimized for those languages. In both Spanish and Dutch, BERT has the highest recall overall and in every subset.

While our proposed TMR metrics do not help differentiate models in Spanish and Dutch, they can provide estimates of performance on subsets of tough mentions from different languages and identify areas for improvement. For example, while the percentage of UNSEEN-TYPE mentions in Spanish (1.8) and ReCoNLL English (1.5) is similar, the performance for BERT for those mentions in Spanish is 34.04 points below that for ReCoNLL English. By using the TMR metrics, we have identified a gap that is not visible by just examining overall recall.

Compared with ReCoNLL English (6.3%) and Spanish (10.7%), there are far fewer type-confusable mentions in Dutch (0.2%). Given the sports-centric nature of the English and Spanish datasets, which creates many LOC/ORG confusable mentions, it is likely that their TCM rate is artificially high. However the near-zero rate in Dutch is a reminder that either linguistic or data collection properties may result in a high or negligible number of TCMs. OntoNotes English shows a similar rate (7.7%) to ReCoNLL English, but due to its richer ontology and larger set of types, these numbers are not directly comparable.

5 Conclusion

We have proposed Tough Mentions Recall (TMR), a set of evaluation metrics that provide a fine-grained analysis of different sets of formalized mentions that are most challenging for a NER system. By looking at recall on specific kinds of "tough" mentions—unseen and type-confusable ones—we are able to better differentiate between otherwise similar-performing systems, compare systems using dimensions beyond the overall score, and evaluate how systems are doing on the most difficult subparts of the NER task.

We summarize our findings as follows. For

[13]We do not display results for TCM-UNSEEN and UNSEEN-TYPE as they each represent less than 1% of the test mentions. BERT's recall for TCM-UNSEEN mentions is 19.51 points higher than any other system. However, as there are 41 mentions in that set, the difference is only 8 mentions.

[14]In Table 12, TCM-UNSEEN is not shown because it includes less than 1% of the test mentions (0.6%); in Table 13 UNSEEN-TYPE (0.2%) and TCM (0.2%) are not shown.

Dataset	Model	ALL	U-ANY	U-TOK.	U-TYPE	TCM-ALL	TCM-SEEN	TCM-UNSEEN
ReCoNLL-English	BERT				✔			
	FLAIR	✔	✔	✔		✔	✔	✔
Ontonotes 5.0	BERT	✔	✔	✔	N/A			N/A
	FLAIR				N/A	✔	✔	N/A

Table 11: Performance comparison between BERT and Flair on English data. A ✔ indicates higher recall under a metric. No comparisons are made for UNSEEN-TYPE and TCM-UNSEEN using OntoNotes due to data sparsity.

Model	ALL	U-ANY	U-TOK.	U-TYPE	TCM-ALL
CHARLSTM	79.76	70.56 (±0.93)	71.72 (±0.94)	46.25 (±3.86)	70.31 (±0.84)
CHARCNN	77.05	67.28 (±0.69)	68.13 (±0.51)	49.38 (±4.76)	68.48 (±0.68)
FLAIR	87.47	79.89 (±0.59)	81.65 (±0.50)	42.81 (±3.05)	77.02 (±1.23)
BERT	**88.85**	**83.04 (±0.58)**	**84.55 (±0.58)**	**51.25 (±3.39)**	**80.00 (±0.78)**
BERT-CRF	88.70	82.36 (±0.42)	83.93 (±0.40)	49.38 (±1.78)	79.74 (±0.63)

Table 12: Recall over all mentions and unseen and type-confusable mention subsets (CoNLL-2002 Spanish)

Model	ALL	U-ANY	U-TOKENS
CHARLSTM	77.35	66.32 (±0.23)	66.46 (±0.23)
CHARCNN	74.55	64.50 (±0.37)	64.61 (±0.32)
FLAIR	89.43	82.86 (±0.26)	83.00 (±0.26)
BERT	**91.68**	**86.65 (±0.17)**	**86.74 (±0.20)**
BERT-CRF	91.26	85.88 (±0.58)	85.94 (±0.58)

Table 13: Recall over all mentions and unseen mention subsets (CoNLL-2002 Dutch)

English, the TMR metrics provide greater differentiation across systems than overall recall and are able to identify differences in performance between BERT and Flair, the best-performing systems in our evaluation. Flair performs better on type-confusable mentions regardless of ontology, while performance on unseen mentions largely follows the overall recall, which is higher for Flair on ReCoNLL and for BERT on OntoNotes.

In Spanish and Dutch, the TMR metrics are not needed to differentiate systems overall, but they provide some insight into performance gaps between Spanish and English related to UNSEEN-TYPE mentions.

One challenge in applying these metrics is simply that there may be relatively few unseen mentions or TCMs, especially in the case of lower-resourced languages. While we are interested in finer-grained metrics for lower-resourced settings, data sparsity issues pose great challenges. As shown in Section 3.3, even in a higher-resourced setting, some subsets of tough mentions include less than 1% of the total mentions in the test set. We believe that lower-resourced NER settings can still benefit from our work by gaining information on pretraining or tuning models towards better performance on unseen and type-confusable mentions.

For new corpora, these metrics can be used to guide construction and corpus splitting to make test sets as difficult as possible, making them better benchmarks for progress. We hope that this form of scoring will see wide adoption and help provide a more nuanced view of NER performance.

Acknowledgments

Thanks to two anonymous EACL SRW mentors, three anonymous reviewers, and Chester Palen-Michel for providing feedback on this paper.

References

Alan Akbik, Duncan Blythe, and Roland Vollgraf. 2018. Contextual string embeddings for sequence labeling. In *Proceedings of the 27th International Conference on Computational Linguistics*, pages 1638–1649, Santa Fe, New Mexico, USA. Association for Computational Linguistics.

Isabelle Augenstein, Leon Derczynski, and Kalina Bontcheva. 2017. Generalisation in named entity recognition. *Comput. Speech Lang.*, 44(C):61–83.

Alexei Baevski, Sergey Edunov, Yinhan Liu, Luke Zettlemoyer, and Michael Auli. 2019. Cloze-driven pretraining of self-attention networks. In *Proceedings of the 2019 Conference on Empirical Methods in Natural Language Processing and the 9th International Joint Conference on Natural Language Processing (EMNLP-IJCNLP)*, pages 5360–5369, Hong Kong, China. Association for Computational Linguistics.

José Cañete, Gabriel Chaperon, Rodrigo Fuentes, and Jorge Pérez. 2020. Spanish pre-trained BERT model and evaluation data. In *Proceedings of the Practical ML for Developing Countries Workshop at ICLR 2020*.

Nancy Chinchor. 1998. Appendix b: MUC-7 test scores introduction. In *Seventh Message Understanding Conference (MUC-7): Proceedings of a Conference Held in Fairfax, Virginia, April 29 - May 1, 1998*.

Nancy Chinchor and Beth Sundheim. 1993. MUC-5 evaluation metrics. In *Fifth Message Understanding Conference (MUC-5): Proceedings of a Conference Held in Baltimore, Maryland, August 25-27, 1993*.

Ronan Collobert, Jason Weston, Léon Bottou, Michael Karlen, Koray Kavukcuoglu, and Pavel Kuksa. 2011. Natural language processing (almost) from scratch. *Journal of Machine Learning Research*, 12(Aug):2493–2537.

Leon Derczynski, Diana Maynard, Giuseppe Rizzo, Marieke van Erp, Genevieve Gorrell, Raphaël Troncy, Johann Petrak, and Kalina Bontcheva. 2015. Analysis of named entity recognition and linking for tweets. *Information Processing & Management*, 51(2):32–49.

Leon Derczynski, Eric Nichols, Marieke van Erp, and Nut Limsopatham. 2017. Results of the WNUT2017 shared task on novel and emerging entity recognition. In *Proceedings of the 3rd Workshop on Noisy User-generated Text*, pages 140–147, Copenhagen, Denmark. Association for Computational Linguistics.

Jacob Devlin, Ming-Wei Chang, Kenton Lee, and Kristina Toutanova. 2019. BERT: Pre-training of deep bidirectional transformers for language understanding. In *Proceedings of the 2019 Conference of the North American Chapter of the Association for Computational Linguistics: Human Language Technologies, Volume 1 (Long and Short Papers)*, pages 4171–4186, Minneapolis, Minnesota. Association for Computational Linguistics.

George Doddington, Alexis Mitchell, Mark Przybocki, Lance Ramshaw, Stephanie Strassel, and Ralph Weischedel. 2004. The automatic content extraction (ACE) program – tasks, data, and evaluation. In *Proceedings of the Fourth International Conference on Language Resources and Evaluation (LREC'04)*, Lisbon, Portugal. European Language Resources Association (ELRA).

Jinlan Fu, Pengfei Liu, and Qi Zhang. 2020. Rethinking generalization of neural models: A named entity recognition case study. *Proceedings of the AAAI Conference on Artificial Intelligence*, 34(05):7732–7739.

Guillaume Lample, Miguel Ballesteros, Sandeep Subramanian, Kazuya Kawakami, and Chris Dyer. 2016. Neural architectures for named entity recognition. In *Proceedings of the 2016 Conference of the North American Chapter of the Association for Computational Linguistics: Human Language Technologies*, pages 260–270, San Diego, California. Association for Computational Linguistics.

Constantine Lignos and Marjan Kamyab. 2020. If you build your own NER scorer, non-replicable results will come. In *Proceedings of the First Workshop on Insights from Negative Results in NLP*, pages 94–99, Online. Association for Computational Linguistics.

Xuezhe Ma and Eduard Hovy. 2016. End-to-end sequence labeling via bi-directional LSTM-CNNs-CRF. In *Proceedings of the 54th Annual Meeting of the Association for Computational Linguistics (Volume 1: Long Papers)*, pages 1064–1074, Berlin, Germany. Association for Computational Linguistics.

Sepideh Mesbah, Christoph Lofi, Manuel Valle Torre, Alessandro Bozzon, and Geert-Jan Houben. 2018. TSE-NER: An iterative approach for long-tail entity extraction in scientific publications. In *International Semantic Web Conference*, pages 127–143. Springer.

Sameer Pradhan, Alessandro Moschitti, Nianwen Xue, Hwee Tou Ng, Anders Björkelund, Olga Uryupina, Yuchen Zhang, and Zhi Zhong. 2013. Towards robust linguistic analysis using OntoNotes. In *Proceedings of the Seventeenth Conference on Computational Natural Language Learning*, pages 143–152, Sofia, Bulgaria. Association for Computational Linguistics.

Marco Tulio Ribeiro, Tongshuang Wu, Carlos Guestrin, and Sameer Singh. 2020. Beyond accuracy: Behavioral testing of NLP models with CheckList. In *Proceedings of the 58th Annual Meeting of the Association for Computational Linguistics*, pages 4902–4912, Online. Association for Computational Linguistics.

Isabel Segura-Bedmar, Paloma Martínez, and María Herrero-Zazo. 2013. SemEval-2013 task 9 : Extraction of drug-drug interactions from biomedical texts (DDIExtraction 2013). In *Second Joint Conference on Lexical and Computational Semantics (*SEM), Volume 2: Proceedings of the Seventh International Workshop on Semantic Evaluation (SemEval 2013)*, pages 341–350, Atlanta, Georgia, USA. Association for Computational Linguistics.

F. Souza, Rodrigo Nogueira, and R. Lotufo. 2019. Portuguese named entity recognition using BERT-CRF. *ArXiv*, abs/1909.10649.

Erik F. Tjong Kim Sang. 2002. Introduction to the CoNLL-2002 shared task: Language-independent named entity recognition. In *COLING-02: The 6th Conference on Natural Language Learning 2002 (CoNLL-2002)*.

Erik F. Tjong Kim Sang and Fien De Meulder. 2003. Introduction to the CoNLL-2003 shared task: Language-independent named entity recognition. In

Proceedings of the Seventh Conference on Natural Language Learning at HLT-NAACL 2003, pages 142–147.

Wietse de Vries, Andreas van Cranenburgh, Arianna Bisazza, Tommaso Caselli, Gertjan van Noord, and Malvina Nissim. 2019. BERTje: A Dutch BERT Model. *arXiv:1912.09582 [cs]*.

Ralph Weischedel, Martha Palmer, Mitchell Marcus, Eduard Hovy, Sameer Pradhan, Lance Ramshaw, Nianwen Xue, Ann Taylor, Jeff Kaufman, Michelle Franchini, et al. 2013. OntoNotes release 5.0 LDC2013T19.

Jie Yang, Shuailong Liang, and Yue Zhang. 2018. Design challenges and misconceptions in neural sequence labeling. In *Proceedings of the 27th International Conference on Computational Linguistics*, pages 3879–3889, Santa Fe, New Mexico, USA. Association for Computational Linguistics.

Jie Yang and Yue Zhang. 2018. NCRF++: An open-source neural sequence labeling toolkit. In *Proceedings of ACL 2018, System Demonstrations*, pages 74–79, Melbourne, Australia. Association for Computational Linguistics.

A Additional Tables

Please see the following pages for additional tables.

	Precision	Recall	F1
CHARCNN	76.74 (±0.36)	74.55 (±0.27)	75.63 (±0.26)
CHARLSTM	78.21 (±0.34)	77.35 (±0.21)	77.78 (±0.27)
FLAIR	90.11 (±0.15)	89.43 (±0.13)	89.77 (±0.14)
BERT	**91.26 (±0.23)**	**91.68 (±0.18)**	**91.47 (±0.18)**
BERT-CRF	90.75 (±0.47)	91.26 (±0.18)	91.00 (±0.32)

Table 14: Standard precision/recall/F1 for all types for each model trained on the CoNLL-2002 Dutch dataset

	Precision	Recall	F1
CHARCNN	77.75 (±0.22)	77.05 (±0.21)	77.40 (±0.20)
CHARLSTM	80.09 (±0.59)	79.76 (±0.63)	79.93 (±0.61)
FLAIR	86.96 (±0.23)	87.47 (±0.19)	87.21 (±0.20)
BERT	**87.36 (±0.52)**	**88.85 (±0.39)**	**88.10 (±0.45)**
BERT-CRF	87.25 (±0.38)	88.70 (±0.20)	87.97 (±0.29)

Table 15: Standard precision/recall/F1 for all types for each model trained on the CoNLL-2002 Spanish dataset

Mentions	ALL	GPE	PER	ORG	DATE	CARD	NORP	PERC	MONEY
UNSEEN-ANY	30.3	10.5	48.9	41.4	20.3	15.3	12.4	29.5	61.8
UNSEEN-TOKENS	29.4	9.9	48.0	40.8	19.7	14.9	12.0	29.5	60.2
UNSEEN-TYPE	0.9	0.6	0.9	0.6	0.6	0.4	0.4	0.0	1.6
TCM-ALL	7.7	11.5	1.7	4.9	3.2	15.4	18.5	0.0	5.1
TCM-SEEN	7.3	11.1	1.6	3.8	3.2	15.2	18.4	0.0	5.1
TCM-UNSEEN	0.4	0.4	0.1	1.1	0.1	0.2	0.1	0.0	0.0
Total (Count)	11,265	2,241	1,991	1,795	1,604	936	842	349	314

Table 16: Percentage of all mentions in each subset, with total mentions in the final row (OntoNotes 5.0 English). Due to space constraints, types are split across this table and the following one.

Mentions	TIME	ORD	LOC	WA	FAC	QUAN	PROD	EVENT	LAW	LANG
UNSEEN-ANY	41.5	3.6	39.1	**83.1**	80	73.3	52.6	47.6	75.0	22.7
UNSEEN-TOKENS	39.6	3.1	34.1	**78.9**	74.8	73.3	48.7	47.6	57.5	4.5
UNSEEN-TYPE	1.9	0.5	5.0	4.2	5.2	0.0	3.9	0.0	**17.5**	18.2
TCM-ALL	7.5	12.8	14	5.4	15.5	0.0	0.0	7.9	0.0	**54.5**
TCM-SEEN	7.5	12.8	14	2.4	14.8	0.0	0.0	7.9	0.0	**54.5**
TCM-UNSEEN	0.0	0.0	0.0	**3.0**	0.7	0.0	0.0	0.0	0.0	0.0
Total (Count)	212	195	179	166	135	105	76	63	40	22

Table 17: Percentage of all mentions in each subset, with total mentions in the final row (OntoNotes 5.0 English). Due to space constraints, types are split across this table and the preceding one.

The Effectiveness of Morphology-aware Segmentation in Low-Resource Neural Machine Translation

Jonne Sälevä
Brandeis University
jonnesaleva@brandeis.edu

Constantine Lignos
Brandeis University
lignos@brandeis.edu

Abstract

This paper evaluates the performance of several modern subword segmentation methods in a low-resource neural machine translation setting. We compare segmentations produced by applying BPE at the token or sentence level with morphologically-based segmentations from LMVR and MORSEL. We evaluate translation tasks between English and each of Nepali, Sinhala, and Kazakh, and predict that using morphologically-based segmentation methods would lead to better performance in this setting. However, comparing to BPE, we find that no consistent and reliable differences emerge between the segmentation methods. While morphologically-based methods outperform BPE in a few cases, what performs best tends to vary across tasks, and the performance of segmentation methods is often statistically indistinguishable.

1 Introduction

Despite the advances of neural machine translation (NMT), building effective translation systems for lower-resourced and morphologically rich languages remains a challenging process. The lack of large training data sets tends to lead to problems of vocabulary sparsity, a problem exacerbated by the combinatorial explosion of permissible surface forms commonly encountered when working with morphologically rich languages.

Current NMT systems typically operate at the level of *subwords*. Most commonly, these systems achieve vocabulary reduction by decomposing tokens into character sequences constructed by maximizing an information-theoretic compression criterion. The most widely used subword segmentation method is byte pair encoding, originally invented in the data compression literature by Gage (1994), and introduced to the MT community by Sennrich et al. (2016). Another approach to open vocabulary NMT has been to compose characters or character n-grams to form word representations (Ataman and Federico, 2018a; Ling et al., 2015).

As BPE has become mainstream, the question of whether segmenting words in a linguistically-informed fashion provides a benefit remains open. Intuitively, the translation task may be easier when using subwords that contain maximal linguistic signal, as opposed to heuristically derived units based on data compression. The greatest benefit may come in low-resource settings, where the training data is small and biases toward morphological structure may lead to more reusable units.

We seek to address this question by exploring the usefulness of linguistically-motivated subword segmentation methods in NMT, as measured against a BPE baseline. Specifically, we investigate the effectiveness of morphology-based segmentation algorithms of Ataman et al. (2017) and Lignos (2010) as alternatives to BPE at the word or sentence level and find that they do not lead to reliable improvements under our experimental conditions. We perform our evaluation using both BLEU (Papineni et al., 2002) and CHRF3 (Popović, 2015). In our low-resource NMT setting, all these methods provide comparable results.

The contribution of this work is that it provides insights into the performance of these segmentation methods using a thorough experimental paradigm in a highly replicable environment. We evaluate without the many possible confounds related to back-translation and other processes used in state-of-the-art NMT systems, focusing on the performance of a straightforward Transformer-based system. To analyze the performance differences between the various segmentation strategies, we utilize a Bayesian linear model as well as nonparametric hypothesis tests.

Proceedings of the 16th Conference of the European Chapter of the Associationfor Computational Linguistics: Student Research Workshop, pages 164–174
April 19 - 23, 2021. ©2021 Association for Computational Linguistics

Translation task	Split	Sentences	Tokens (EN)	Tokens (non-EN)
NE ↔ EN	Train	563,947	4,483,440	4,200,818
SI ↔ EN	Train	646,781	4,837,496	4,180,520
KK ↔ EN	Train (120k)	124,770	379,546	319,484
KK ↔ EN	Train (220k)	222,424	1,717,414	1,365,605
NE ↔ EN	Dev	2,559	46,267	37,576
SI ↔ EN	Dev	2,898	53,471	48,659
KK ↔ EN	Dev	2,066	45,975	37,258
NE ↔ EN	Test	2,835	51,455	43,802
SI ↔ EN	Test	2,766	50,973	46,318
KK → EN	Test	1,000	20,376	15,943
EN → KK	Test	998	24,074	19,141

Table 1: Number of sentences in raw corpora. The 120k and 220k training conditions for KK correspond to training KK↔EN models with/without an additional crawled corpus. The test sets for KK→EN and EN→KK are different from each other and mirror the released WMT19 data.

2 Related work

Attempts to create unsupervised, morphologically-aware segmentations have often been derived from the Morfessor family of morphological segmentation tools (Virpioja et al., 2013). In addition to extensions of Morfessor, such as *Cognate Morfessor* (Grönroos et al., 2018), Ataman et al. (2017) and Ataman and Federico (2018b) introduced the LMVR model, derived from Morfessor *FlatCat* (Grönroos et al., 2014), and applied it to NMT tasks on Arabic, Czech, German, Italian, Turkish and English, noting that LMVR outperforms a BPE baseline in CHRF3 and BLEU. Contrary to their results, however, Toral et al. (2019) find that using LMVR yielded mixed results: on a Kazakh-English translation task the authors observed marginal BLEU improvements over BPE, whereas for English-Kazakh, the authors reported LMVR to perform marginally worse than BPE in terms of CHRF3.

There have also been efforts to combine BPE with linguistically motivated approaches. For instance, Huck et al. (2017) propose to combine BPE with various linguistic heuristics such as prefix, suffix, and compound splitting. The authors work with English-German and German-English tasks, and observe performance improvements of approximately 0.5 BLEU compared to a BPE-only baseline. As another example, Weller-Di Marco and Fraser (2020) combine BPE with a full morphological analysis on the source and target sides of an English-German translation task, and report performance improvements exceeding 1 BLEU point over a BPE-only baseline.

Finally, even though Sennrich et al. (2016) originally only used the NMT training set to train their segmentation model, others have recently found benefit in adding monolingual data to the process. In particular, Scherrer et al. (2020) used both SentencePiece and Morfessor as segmentation models on an Upper Sorbian–German translation task and found a monotonic increase in BLEU when the segmentation model was trained with additional data, while at the same time keeping the NMT training data constant.

3 Experiments

To investigate the effect of subword segmentation algorithms on NMT performance, we train translation models using the Transformer architecture of Vaswani et al. (2017). We base our work on two recent datasets: FLoRes (Guzmán et al., 2019), and select languages from the WMT 2019 Shared Task on News Translation (Barrault et al., 2019). Corpus statistics for all corpora can be found in Table 1.

The FLoRes dataset consists of two language pairs, English-Nepali and English-Sinhala. To add another lower-resourced language, we use the Kazakh-English translation data from WMT19. In terms of morphological typology, both Nepali and Sinhala are agglutinative languages (Prasain, 2011; Priyanga et al., 2017), as is Kazakh (Kessikbayeva and Cicekli, 2014).

We conduct two sets of experiments on Kazakh to investigate how the amount of training data influences our results: first, we train only on

Segmentation	Sentence
Original	The nation slowly started being centralized and during
SentencePiece	_the _n ation _sl ow ly _start ed _being _cent ral ized _and _d ur ing
Subword-NMT	the n@@ ation s@@ low@@ ly star@@ ted being cen@@ tr@@ ali@@ z@@ ed and d@@ ur@@ ing
LMVR	the nation s +low +ly st +ar +ted be +ing c +ent +ral +ized and d +ur +ing
MORSEL	the nation s@@ low +ly start +ed being cen@@ tr@@ ali@@ z +ed and du@@ r +ing

Table 2: Examples of segmentation strategies and tokenization.

the WikiTitles and News Commentary corpora (`train120k`), followed by another set of experiments (`train220k`) where we include the web crawl corpus prepared by Bagdat Myrzakhmetov of Nazarbayev University. We also conducted experiments with Gujarati data from WMT19, but BLEU scores were too low to allow for meaningful analysis. For our models, we generally follow the architecture and hyperparameter choices of the FLoRes Transformer baseline, except for setting `clip_norm` to 0.1 and enabling FP16 training.

Despite the widespread use of auxiliary techniques such as back-translation we deliberately refrain from employing such techniques in this work. This is done to best isolate the effect of varying the subword segmentation algorithm, and to avoid the complexity of disentangling it from the effect of other factors. It should be noted, however, that such techniques were highly prevalent among of systems submitted to the KK↔EN WMT19 News Translation Shared Task: 64% used back-translation, 61% used ensembling, and 57% employed extensive corpus filtering (Barrault et al., 2019).

3.1 Subword segmentation algorithms

Below we describe our hyperparameter settings for the various subword segmentation algorithms. Sinhala and Nepali are tokenized using the Indic NLP tokenizer (Kunchukuttan, 2020), whereas for English and Kazakh we use the Moses tokenizer (Koehn et al., 2007). Example segmentations from actual data can be seen in Table 2.

The segmentation methods we evaluate learn their subword vocabularies from frequency distributions of tokenized text. The exception to this is SentencePiece, whose subword units are learned from sentences, including whitespace. In the case of English and Kazakh, these sentences are untokenized whereas for Nepali and Sinhala, preprocessing with the Indic NLP tokenizer is applied following the approach of Guzmán et al. (2019).

3.1.1 Subword-NMT and SentencePiece

As our baseline subword segmentation algorithm, we use the BPE implementation from Subword-NMT[1]. Throughout our experiments we use a joint vocabulary of the source and target and set the number of requested symbols to 5,000. For SentencePiece, we use the default BPE implementation[2] with a joint vocabulary size of 5,000 words. These choices are motivated by the general observation by Sennrich and Zhang (2019) that lowering BPE size improves translation quality in ultra-low resource conditions, and the specific value of 5,000 was previously used by Guzmán et al. (2019). The same small vocabulary size has been used elsewhere in the low-resource NMT literature, for instance by Roest et al. (2020) while training NMT systems for Inuktitut. We also conducted a hyperparameter sweep for 2,500, 5,000, 7,500 and 10,000 merge operations, but noticed no improvement over the choice of 5,000 motivated by prior work.

3.1.2 LMVR

For LMVR (Ataman et al., 2017), we utilize slightly modified versions of the sample scripts from the author's Github repository[3]. Our main modification is tuning the `corpusweight` hyperparameter in the Morfessor Baseline (Virpioja et al., 2013) model used to seed the LMVR model. Tuning is performed by maximizing the F1 score for segmenting the English side of the training data, using the English word lists from the Morpho Challenge 2010 shared task (Kurimo et al., 2010) as gold standard segmentations. After tuning the Morfessor Baseline model, we train a separate LMVR model for each language in a language pair using a vocabulary size parameter of 2,500 per language.

[1] https://github.com/rsennrich/subword-nmt

[2] https://github.com/google/sentencepiece

[3] https://github.com/d-ataman/lmvr

3.1.3 MORSEL

MORSEL (Lignos, 2010) provides linguistically-motivated unsupervised morphological analysis that has been shown to work effectively on small datasets (Chan and Lignos, 2010). While it provides derivations of morphologically complex forms via a combination of stems and affix rules, we modified it to provide a segmentation and then postprocessed its output to apply BPE to the stems to yield a limited-size vocabulary.

For example, on the English side of the NE-EN training data, MORSEL analyzes the word *algebraic* as resulting from the stem *algebra* being combined with the suffix rule *+ic*. A BPE model is trained on all of the stems in MORSEL's analysis, and when that is applied to the stem, it is segmented as `al@@ ge@@ br@@ a`. The stem and suffix are combined using a special plus character to denote suffixation, so the final segmentation is `al@@ ge@@ br@@ a +ic`. Tuning is performed as with LMVR, using the English word lists from the Morpho Challenge 2010 shared task (Kurimo et al., 2010) as a reference. We adjust the number of BPE units learned from the stems to keep the total per-language vocabulary below 2,500.

4 Results and analysis

Our experimental results can be seen in Table 3. All BLEU scores were computed using `sacrebleu`, and all CHRF3 scores using `nltk`. Each row consists of the mean and standard deviation computed across 5 random seeds for each configuration. We also plot the raw results in Figure 1. Table 4 gives counts for the number of times each segmentation approach was the top-performing one or statistically indistinguishable from it. Table 7 in the appendix gives p-values for all comparisons performed.

Overall, based on Tables 3 and 4, no segmentation method seems to emerge as the clear winner across translation tasks, although BPE applied at the token (Subword-NMT) or sentence (SentencePiece) level performs well consistently. Subword-NMT or SentencePiece perform best in 12 out of 16 cases (counting BLEU and CHRF3 for each translation task), while morphology-based methods rank best in 4 out of 16 cases. In particular, we note that morphology-based methods seem to achieve or tie the best BLEU performance for translation tasks involving SI, and best CHRF3 performance for

Segm. method	BLEU	CHRF3
EN-KK (train120k)		
LMVR	1.00 ± 0.12	**21.98** ± 0.41
MORSEL	0.94 ± 0.11	**21.24** ± 0.89
SentencePiece	1.04 ± 0.09	**21.48** ± 0.47
Subword-NMT	**1.32** ± 0.08	**22.12** ± 0.28
EN-KK (train220k)		
LMVR	1.82 ± 0.13	**22.74** ± 0.84
MORSEL	**2.06** ± 0.11	**22.88** ± 0.40
SentencePiece	**2.18** ± 0.08	**22.78** ± 0.43
Subword-NMT	1.94 ± 0.22	**22.62** ± 0.88
KK-EN (train120k)		
LMVR	1.70 ± 0.07	23.72 ± 0.44
MORSEL	**2.62** ± 0.08	**26.26** ± 0.36
SentencePiece	2.34 ± 0.21	24.64 ± 0.81
Subword-NMT	**3.14** ± 0.18	**25.92** ± 0.54
KK-EN (train220k)		
LMVR	9.42 ± 0.26	33.88 ± 0.76
MORSEL	**10.44** ± 0.48	**34.58** ± 0.88
SentencePiece	**10.02** ± 0.29	33.50 ± 0.54
Subword-NMT	**10.68** ± 0.34	**35.52** ± 0.41
EN-NE		
LMVR	4.32 ± 0.04	**31.00** ± 0.29
MORSEL	**4.38** ± 0.16	**31.28** ± 0.47
SentencePiece	**4.58** ± 0.15	**31.36** ± 0.35
Subword-NMT	**4.42** ± 0.16	30.96 ± 0.34
NE-EN		
LMVR	7.84 ± 0.11	**34.10** ± 0.16
MORSEL	5.30 ± 0.30	28.18 ± 0.97
SentencePiece	**8.42** ± 0.23	**34.40** ± 0.73
Subword-NMT	**8.46** ± 0.15	**34.18** ± 0.13
EN-SI		
LMVR	**1.44** ± 0.32	**28.22** ± 0.30
MORSEL	**1.12** ± 0.13	27.44 ± 0.34
SentencePiece	**1.08** ± 0.31	**27.56** ± 0.43
Subword-NMT	0.88 ± 0.13	26.78 ± 0.51
SI-EN		
LMVR	7.24 ± 0.22	32.16 ± 0.63
MORSEL	**7.78** ± 0.16	**34.32** ± 0.30
SentencePiece	**7.52** ± 0.08	**33.58** ± 0.43
Subword-NMT	**7.76** ± 0.25	**34.38** ± 0.38

Table 3: Mean and standard deviation of BLEU and CHRF3 across translation tasks and segmentation methods. Underlined values represent the highest mean scores. Bolded values are not significantly different ($p > 0.05$) than the highest score as determined by Dunn's test.

KK-EN with smaller training data (`train120k`) as well as EN-SI. However, when using LMVR, we fail to find the significant gains in BLEU compared to BPE reported by Ataman et al. (2017).

Comparing our results to Guzmán et al. (2019), we note that the scores are similar, although not directly comparable as we report lowercased BLEU

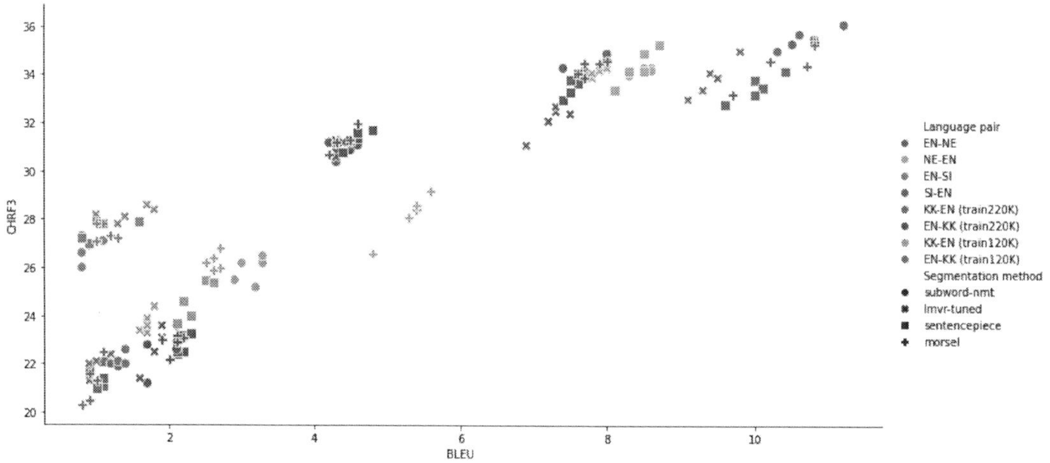

Figure 1: CHRF3 vs. BLEU with different translation tasks indicated by color and segmentation by marker shape.

Segmentation method	BLEU	CHRF3
Subword-NMT	6	6
SentencePiece	6	6
MORSEL	6	6
LMVR	1	5

Table 4: Number of times each segmentation method was or tied with the best-performing method under each metric, counted across all tasks.

Pairwise comparison	τ (BLEU)	τ (CHRF3)
SentencePiece - Subword-NMT	-0.05 $\pm$ 0.08	-0.07 $\pm$ 0.20
MORSEL - Subword-NMT	-0.12 $\pm$ 0.07	0.02 $\pm$ 0.18
LMVR - Subword-NMT	-0.26 $\pm$ 0.06	-0.19 $\pm$ 0.21

Table 5: Posterior means and standard deviations of $\tau_m - \tau_{Subword-NMT}$ (pairwise comparison with BPE) under the BLEU and CHRF3 models. Values are rounded to two decimal places.

scores.[4] They report EN-NE/NE-EN baseline BLEU scores of 4.3 and 7.6 using a single random seed, which are in line with our results in Table 3. For EN-SI/SI-EN, the authors report 1.2 and 7.2 BLEU, which likewise matches our findings. Even though our scores are low overall, they are as low as is to be expected using this approach, size of data, and languages. In order to compare our results to WMT19 participant systems, it is only meaningful to compare our system to baseline systems due to the widespread use of auxiliary training techniques, such as back-translation. For instance, Casas et al. (2019) report baseline NMT scores of 2.32 on KK-EN and 1.42 on EN-KK, which are in line with our MORSEL and SentencePiece results on KK-EN, and Subword-NMT results on EN-KK in the `train120k` condition.

4.1 Modeling BLEU and CHRF3

Based on Figure 1 and Tables 3 and 4, the BLEU and CHRF3 scores vary with both the translation task and segmentation method. Intuitively, the scores seem to cluster around a certain range for each translation task, and are perturbed slightly depending on the choice of segmentation method. To better disentangle the influence of these factors, we fit a Bayesian linear model to the experimental data, treating the final BLEU/CHRF3 score as a sum of a "translation task effect" η, a "segmentation method effect" τ, and a translation task-specific noise term ϵ.[5] The η and ϵ terms are estimated for each of the eight translation tasks (e.g. SI-EN and EN-SI are estimated separately), and τ is estimated for each of the four segmentation methods using results from all translation tasks.

To explicitly compare SentencePiece, LMVR and MORSEL to the Subword-NMT baseline, we also model the pairwise differences between each method's τ-term and that of Subword-NMT. The posterior inferences for these quantities can be seen in Table 5 and are plotted in the appendix. For BLEU, the differences for LMVR are several standard deviations below 0, suggesting that it performs worse than the Subword-NMT baseline

[4] We lowercased all data in preprocessing because MORSEL and Morfessor, which LMVR is derived from, are designed to operate on lowercase inputs.

[5] In the appendix, Section A gives details of our model, and Table 6 gives the point estimates of the posterior mean and standard deviation for η and τ.

when accounting for all translation tasks. Similarly, MORSEL is almost 2 standard deviations away from 0, though its posterior interval does cover 0. In both cases, the effect size is small, with a mean of -0.12 and -0.26 points of BLEU for MORSEL and LMVR, respectively. The reliability of this difference also disappears for LMVR under the CHRF3 model, where no segmentation method's posterior mean is several standard deviations away from 0.

We hypothesize that this greater discrimination among methods when using BLEU may originate from the differences between how BLEU and CHRF3 operate. Since CHRF3 is a character-level metric, it is less prone than BLEU to penalizing a given translation due to subword outputs that are *almost* correct. For instance, consider output of `do@@ gs` → `dogs` with `dog` as the reference; while CHRF3 awards credit for this as a partial match, BLEU treats it as entirely incorrect. This further underscores our observation that segmentation methods perform inconsistently across experimental conditions.

5 Conclusion and future work

Contrary to our hypothesis about the usefulness of morphology-aware segmentation, we see no consistent advantage, and possibly a small disadvantage, to using LMVR or MORSEL in this resource-constrained setting. By and large, our experiments and modeling show that no segmentation approach consistently achieves the best BLEU/CHRF3 across all translation tasks. BPE remains a good default segmentation strategy, but it is possible that LMVR, MORSEL, or similar systems may show larger performance advantages for languages with specific morphological structures.

Consequently, we believe further work is needed to better understand when morphology-aware methods are most effective and to develop methods that provide a consistent advantage over BPE. One such avenue of future work would be to broaden our analysis to more languages and include languages that are higher-resourced but morphologically rich and as well as ones that are lower-resourced but morphologically poor. Ortega et al. (2021), which we encountered during preparation of the final version of this paper, began to address these questions by comparing Morfessor with BPE and their own BPE variant on Finnish, Quechua and Spanish.

An alternative approach which we intend to pursue in future work is experimenting with supervised morphological segmenters or analyzers that can be efficiently developed even in lower-resourced settings. Incorporating such "gold standard" segmentations may make it clearer whether the unsupervised morphological segmenters are capturing linguistically-relevant structure.

Finally, there is the question of whether BPE can approximate a general representation for a language instead of converging on a corpus-specific set of subwords. To test this, one can add monolingual data and train the BPE segmentation on that larger data set. Ideally the new, "enriched" segmentations would depend less on the specific vocabulary of the training corpus. As noted above, Scherrer et al. (2020) observed this approach to be helpful in terms of BLEU. However, it remains unknown why the subwords derived from a larger corpus perform better, and whether better identification of morphological structure could be responsible.

We hope that this work and these ideas will catalyze further research, and that efficient methods for translating to and from lower-resourced languages can be developed as a result.

References

Duygu Ataman and Marcello Federico. 2018a. Compositional representation of morphologically-rich input for neural machine translation. In *Proceedings of the 56th Annual Meeting of the Association for Computational Linguistics (Volume 2: Short Papers)*, pages 305–311, Melbourne, Australia. Association for Computational Linguistics.

Duygu Ataman and Marcello Federico. 2018b. An evaluation of two vocabulary reduction methods for neural machine translation. In *Proceedings of the 13th Conference of the Association for Machine Translation in the Americas (Volume 1: Research Track)*, pages 97–110, Boston, MA. Association for Machine Translation in the Americas.

Duygu Ataman, Matteo Negri, Marco Turchi, and Marcello Federico. 2017. Linguistically motivated vocabulary reduction for neural machine translation from turkish to english. *The Prague Bulletin of Mathematical Linguistics*, 108(1):331–342.

Loïc Barrault, Ondřej Bojar, Marta R. Costa-jussà, Christian Federmann, Mark Fishel, Yvette Graham, Barry Haddow, Matthias Huck, Philipp Koehn, Shervin Malmasi, Christof Monz, Mathias Müller, Santanu Pal, Matt Post, and Marcos Zampieri. 2019. Findings of the 2019 conference on machine translation (WMT19). In *Proceedings of the Fourth Conference on Machine Translation (Volume 2: Shared*

Task Papers, Day 1), pages 1–61, Florence, Italy. Association for Computational Linguistics.

Noe Casas, José A. R. Fonollosa, Carlos Escolano, Christine Basta, and Marta R. Costa-jussà. 2019. The TALP-UPC machine translation systems for WMT19 news translation task: Pivoting techniques for low resource MT. In *Proceedings of the Fourth Conference on Machine Translation (Volume 2: Shared Task Papers, Day 1)*, pages 155–162, Florence, Italy. Association for Computational Linguistics.

Erwin Chan and Constantine Lignos. 2010. Investigating the relationship between linguistic representation and computation through an unsupervised model of human morphology learning. *Research on Language and Computation*, 8(2-3):209–238.

Philip Gage. 1994. A new algorithm for data compression. *C Users Journal*, 12(2):23–38.

Stig-Arne Grönroos, Sami Virpioja, and Mikko Kurimo. 2018. Cognate-aware morphological segmentation for multilingual neural translation. In *Proceedings of the Third Conference on Machine Translation: Shared Task Papers*, pages 386–393, Belgium, Brussels. Association for Computational Linguistics.

Stig-Arne Grönroos, Sami Virpioja, Peter Smit, and Mikko Kurimo. 2014. Morfessor FlatCat: An HMM-based method for unsupervised and semi-supervised learning of morphology. In *Proceedings of COLING 2014, the 25th International Conference on Computational Linguistics: Technical Papers*, pages 1177–1185, Dublin, Ireland. Dublin City University and Association for Computational Linguistics.

Francisco Guzmán, Peng-Jen Chen, Myle Ott, Juan Pino, Guillaume Lample, Philipp Koehn, Vishrav Chaudhary, and Marc'Aurelio Ranzato. 2019. The FLORES evaluation datasets for low-resource machine translation: Nepali–English and Sinhala–English. In *Proceedings of the 2019 Conference on Empirical Methods in Natural Language Processing and the 9th International Joint Conference on Natural Language Processing (EMNLP-IJCNLP)*, pages 6098–6111, Hong Kong, China. Association for Computational Linguistics.

Matthias Huck, Simon Riess, and Alexander Fraser. 2017. Target-side word segmentation strategies for neural machine translation. In *Proceedings of the Second Conference on Machine Translation*, pages 56–67, Copenhagen, Denmark. Association for Computational Linguistics.

Gulshat Kessikbayeva and Ilyas Cicekli. 2014. Rule based morphological analyzer of Kazakh language. In *Proceedings of the 2014 Joint Meeting of SIGMORPHON and SIGFSM*, pages 46–54, Baltimore, Maryland. Association for Computational Linguistics.

Philipp Koehn, Hieu Hoang, Alexandra Birch, Chris Callison-Burch, Marcello Federico, Nicola Bertoldi, Brooke Cowan, Wade Shen, Christine Moran, Richard Zens, Chris Dyer, Ondřej Bojar, Alexandra Constantin, and Evan Herbst. 2007. Moses: Open source toolkit for statistical machine translation. In *Proceedings of the 45th Annual Meeting of the Association for Computational Linguistics Companion Volume Proceedings of the Demo and Poster Sessions*, pages 177–180, Prague, Czech Republic. Association for Computational Linguistics.

Anoop Kunchukuttan. 2020. The IndicNLP Library. https://github.com/anoopkunchukuttan/indic_nlp_library/blob/master/docs/indicnlp.pdf.

Mikko Kurimo, Sami Virpioja, Ville T Turunen, et al. 2010. Proceedings of the Morpho Challenge 2010 workshop. In *Morpho Challenge Workshop 2010*. Aalto University School of Science and Technology.

Constantine Lignos. 2010. Learning from unseen data. In *Proceedings of the Morpho Challenge 2010 Workshop*, pages 35–38.

Wang Ling, Isabel Trancoso, Chris Dyer, and Alan W Black. 2015. Character-based neural machine translation. *ArXiV*.

John E. Ortega, Richard Castro Mamani, and Kyunghyun Cho. 2021. Neural machine translation with a polysynthetic low resource language. *Machine Translation*.

Kishore Papineni, Salim Roukos, Todd Ward, and Wei-Jing Zhu. 2002. Bleu: a method for automatic evaluation of machine translation. In *Proceedings of the 40th Annual Meeting of the Association for Computational Linguistics*, pages 311–318, Philadelphia, Pennsylvania, USA. Association for Computational Linguistics.

Maja Popović. 2015. chrF: character n-gram F-score for automatic MT evaluation. In *Proceedings of the Tenth Workshop on Statistical Machine Translation*, pages 392–395, Lisbon, Portugal. Association for Computational Linguistics.

Balaram Prasain. 2011. *Computational analysis of Nepali morphology: A model for natural language processing*. Ph.D. thesis, Faculty of Humanities and Social Sciences of Tribhuvan University.

Rajith Priyanga, Surangika Ranatunga, and Gihan Dias. 2017. Sinhala word joiner. In *Proceedings of the 14th International Conference on Natural Language Processing (ICON-2017)*, pages 220–226, Kolkata, India. NLP Association of India.

Christian Roest, JK Spenader, and A Toral Ruiz. 2020. Morphological segmentation of polysynthetic languages for neural machine translation: The case of inuktitut. mastersthesis, University of Groeningen.

Yves Scherrer, Stig-Arne Grönroos, and Sami Virpioja. 2020. The University of Helsinki and aalto university submissions to the WMT 2020 news and low-resource translation tasks. In *Proceedings of the Fifth Conference on Machine Translation*, pages 1129–1138, Online. Association for Computational Linguistics.

Rico Sennrich, Barry Haddow, and Alexandra Birch. 2016. Neural machine translation of rare words with subword units. In *Proceedings of the 54th Annual Meeting of the Association for Computational Linguistics (Volume 1: Long Papers)*, pages 1715–1725, Berlin, Germany. Association for Computational Linguistics.

Rico Sennrich and Biao Zhang. 2019. Revisiting low-resource neural machine translation: A case study. In *Proceedings of the 57th Annual Meeting of the Association for Computational Linguistics*, pages 211–221, Florence, Italy. Association for Computational Linguistics.

Antonio Toral, Lukas Edman, Galiya Yeshmagambetova, and Jennifer Spenader. 2019. Neural machine translation for English–Kazakh with morphological segmentation and synthetic data. In *Proceedings of the Fourth Conference on Machine Translation (Volume 2: Shared Task Papers, Day 1)*, pages 386–392, Florence, Italy. Association for Computational Linguistics.

Ashish Vaswani, Noam Shazeer, Niki Parmar, Jakob Uszkoreit, Llion Jones, Aidan N Gomez, Łukasz Kaiser, and Illia Polosukhin. 2017. Attention is all you need. In *Advances in neural information processing systems*, pages 5998–6008.

Sami Virpioja, Peter Smit, Stig-Arne Grönroos, Mikko Kurimo, et al. 2013. Morfessor 2.0: Python implementation and extensions for Morfessor baseline. *Technical Report.*

Marion Weller-Di Marco and Alexander Fraser. 2020. Modeling word formation in English–German neural machine translation. In *Proceedings of the 58th Annual Meeting of the Association for Computational Linguistics*, pages 4227–4232, Online. Association for Computational Linguistics.

A Bayesian Linear Model Details

Mathematically, our model can be expressed as:

$$\phi_{lm} = \eta_l + \tau_m + \epsilon_l \tag{1}$$

where $\phi_{lm} \in \{\text{BLEU, CHRF3}\}$, η_l and τ_m represent the "translation task effect" and "segmentation method effect," and ϵ_l is a translation task-specific variance term.

To initialize our Bayesian linear model from Equation 1, we set the following priors. For the BLEU model, $\eta_l \sim \mathcal{N}(4, 3)$ and $\tau_m \sim \mathcal{N}(0, 1)$.

Segmentation method effect	τ (BLEU)	τ (CHRF3)
LMVR	-0.09 ± 0.47	0.41 ± 0.50
MORSEL	0.05 ± 0.47	0.63 ± 0.50
SentencePiece	0.12 ± 0.47	0.53 ± 0.50
Subword-NMT	0.17 ± 0.47	0.60 ± 0.50
Pairwise comparison	τ (BLEU)	τ (CHRF3)
SentencePiece - Subword-NMT	-0.05 ± 0.08	-0.07 ± 0.20
LMVR - Subword-NMT	-0.26 ± 0.06	-0.19 ± 0.21
MORSEL - Subword-NMT	-0.12 ± 0.07	0.02 ± 0.18
Translation task effect	η (BLEU)	η (CHRF3)
EN-KK (train120k)	1.01 ± 0.47	21.16 ± 0.52
EN-KK (train220k)	1.94 ± 0.47	22.21 ± 0.51
EN-NE	4.36 ± 0.47	30.60 ± 0.50
EN-SI	1.07 ± 0.47	26.95 ± 0.52
KK-EN (train120k)	2.39 ± 0.48	24.58 ± 0.56
KK-EN (train220k)	10.07 ± 0.48	33.81 ± 0.54
NE-EN	7.41 ± 0.56	32.02 ± 0.82
SI-EN	7.51 ± 0.47	33.05 ± 0.54

Table 6: Posterior means and standard deviations for τ and η under the BLEU and CHRF3 models.

For the CHRF3 model, $\eta_l \sim \mathcal{N}(15, 7)$ and $\tau_m \sim \mathcal{N}(0, 1)$. The priors are the same regardless of translation task or segmentation method. For our noise terms, we use a $\epsilon_l \sim \text{HalfCauchy}(5)$ prior in all models. Our rationale for these priors is that η_l should place most of its probability mass within the observed range of BLEU/CHRF3, whereas τ_m should, *a priori*, take on positive and negative values with equal probability, reflecting a lack of prior information. All models are fit using PyMC3, and MCMC posterior inference performed using the No-U-Turn Sampler.

All posterior means for η are close to the average BLEU/CHRF3 scores per translation task observed in Table 3, and fall between 1.01 and 10.07 for the BLEU model, and 21.16 and 33.81 for the CHRF3 model. In contrast, the posterior means for τ are universally small: -0.09, 0.05, 0.12, and 0.17 for LMVR, MORSEL, SentencePiece and Subword-NMT, respectively, with a posterior standard deviation of 0.47. The τ-terms under the CHRF3 model exhibit a similar pattern: 0.41, 0.63, 0.53, 0.60, with a posterior standard deviation of 0.50. Compared to the posterior standard deviation, as well as translation task effects η, the τ-terms are practically 0. This, in conjunction with our analysis using Dunn's test, suggests that there is not a segmentation method that consistently works best across translation tasks.

Figures 2 and 3 show posterior predictive distributions for the BLEU and CHRF3 models. Figure 4 shows the posterior distribution of pairwise differences between each of the other segmentation methods and Subword-NMT.

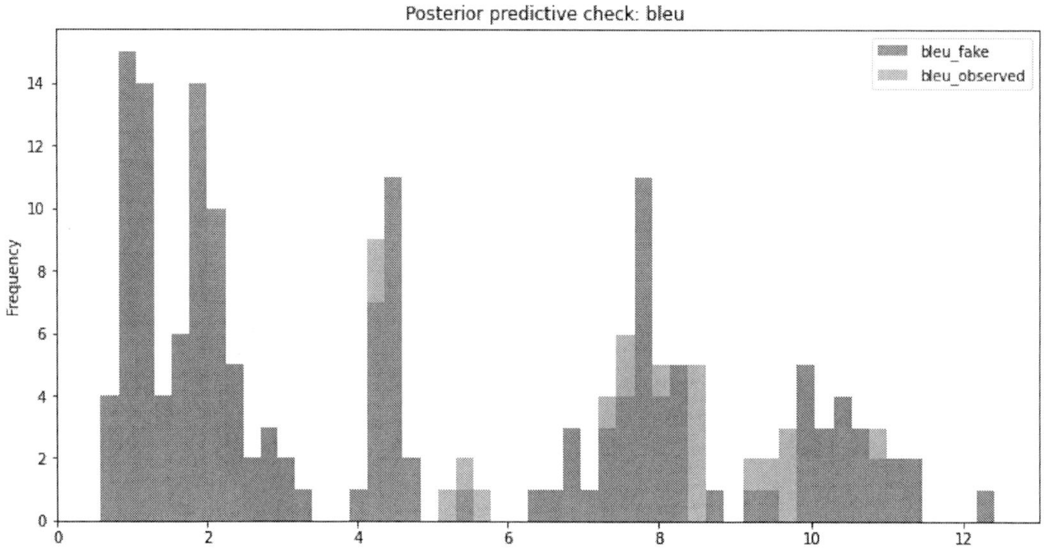

Figure 2: Posterior predictive distribution of BLEU under the Bayesian linear model.

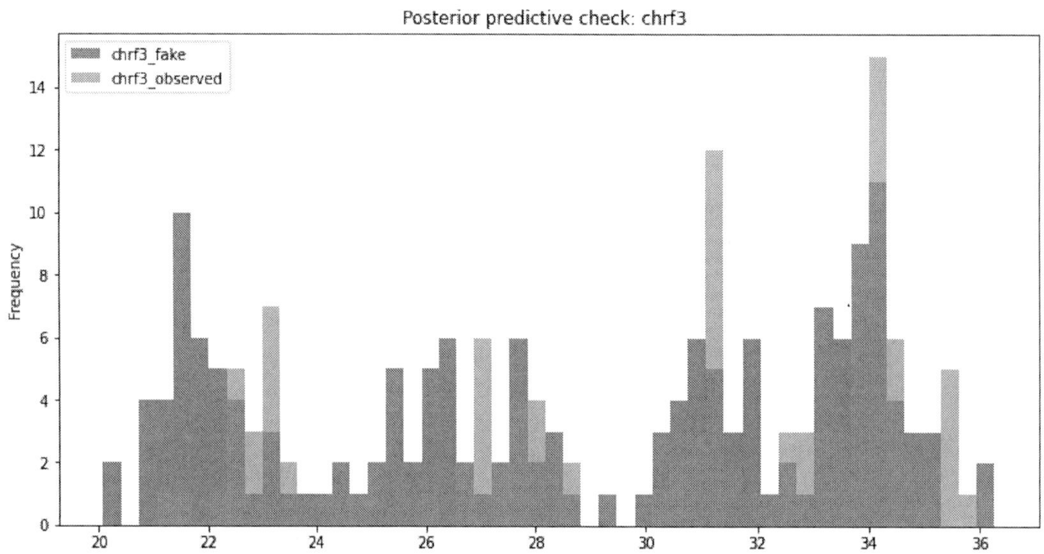

Figure 3: Posterior predictive distribution of CHRF3 under the Bayesian linear model.

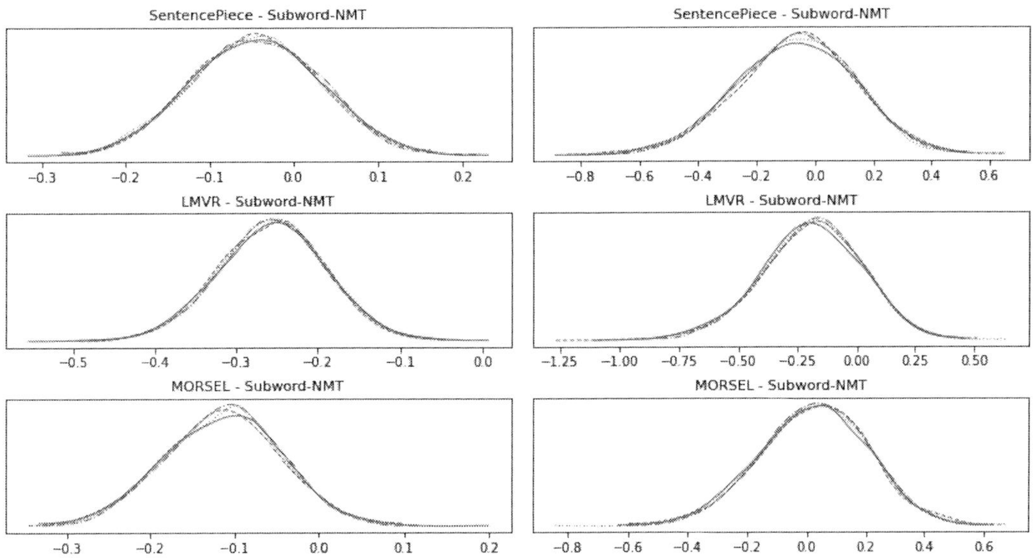

Figure 4: Posterior distribution of pairwise differences $\tau_m - \tau_{\text{Subword-NMT}}$ in the BLEU model (left) and CHRF3 model (right). Note: $m \in \{\text{SentencePiece, LMVR, MORSEL}\}$

Language pair	Segmentation method	p-value (BLEU)	p-value (CHRF3)
EN-NE	LMVR	**0.014**	0.071
EN-NE	MORSEL	0.057	0.466
EN-NE	SentencePiece	1.000	1.000
EN-NE	Subword-NMT	0.137	**0.046**
NE-EN	LMVR	**0.036**	0.405
NE-EN	MORSEL	**0.001**	**0.002**
NE-EN	SentencePiece	0.872	1.000
NE-EN	Subword-NMT	1.000	0.767
EN-SI	LMVR	1.000	1.000
EN-SI	MORSEL	0.246	**0.036**
EN-SI	SentencePiece	0.071	0.091
EN-SI	Subword-NMT	**0.003**	**0.000**
SI-EN	LMVR	**0.002**	**0.001**
SI-EN	MORSEL	1.000	0.851
SI-EN	SentencePiece	0.080	0.057
SI-EN	Subword-NMT	0.850	1.000
KK-EN (train220k)	LMVR	**0.001**	**0.009**
KK-EN (train220k)	MORSEL	0.592	0.149
KK-EN (train220k)	SentencePiece	0.069	**0.002**
KK-EN (train220k)	Subword-NMT	1.000	1.000
EN-KK (train220k)	LMVR	**0.002**	0.788
EN-KK (train220k)	MORSEL	0.216	0.768
EN-KK (train220k)	SentencePiece	1.000	1.000
EN-KK (train220k)	Subword-NMT	**0.037**	0.893
KK-EN (train120k)	LMVR	**0.000**	**0.001**
KK-EN (train120k)	MORSEL	0.140	1.000
KK-EN (train120k)	SentencePiece	**0.011**	**0.026**
KK-EN (train120k)	Subword-NMT	1.000	0.611
EN-KK (train120k)	LMVR	**0.008**	0.872
EN-KK (train120k)	MORSEL	**0.001**	0.068
EN-KK (train120k)	SentencePiece	**0.032**	0.096
EN-KK (train120k)	Subword-NMT	1.000	1.000

Table 7: Dunn's test p-values for BLEU and CHRF3. Boldface indicates statistical significance at the $\alpha = 0.05$ level.

Making Use of Latent Space in Language GANs for Generating Diverse Text without Pre-training

Takeshi Kojima, Yusuke Iwasawa, Yutaka Matsuo
Department of Technology Management for Innovation
The University of Tokyo
7-3-1 Hongo, Bunkyo-ku, Tokyo 113-8656, Japan
t.kojima,iwasawa,matsuo@weblab.t.u-tokyo.ac.jp

Abstract

Generating diverse texts is an important factor for unsupervised text generation. One approach is to produce the diversity of texts conditioned by the sampled latent code. Although several generative adversarial networks (GANs) have been proposed thus far, these models still suffer from mode-collapsing if the models are not pre-trained. In this paper, we propose a GAN model that aims to improve the approach to generating diverse texts conditioned by the latent space. The generator of our model uses Gumbel-Softmax distribution for the word sampling process. To ensure that the text is generated conditioned upon the sampled latent code, reconstruction loss is introduced in our objective function. The discriminator of our model iteratively inspects incomplete partial texts and learns to distinguish whether they are real or fake by using the standard GAN objective function. Experimental results using the COCO Image Captions dataset show that, although our model is not pre-trained, the performance of our model is quite competitive with the existing baseline models, which requires pre-training.

1 Introduction

Generative adversarial networks (GANs) (Goodfellow et al., 2014) have recently received significant attention in the field of unsupervised text generation, which aims to generate realistic texts by unsupervised learning approach.

For language GANs, the diversity of the generated texts is an important evaluation metric. There are mainly two approaches to produce the diversity of texts by the generative models. One approach, which includes SeqGAN (Yu et al., 2017) and LeakGAN (Guo et al., 2018), is to generate the diverse texts by sampling words during the text-generation process. The generators of these models set the initial state as zero and randomly sample every word depending on the word distribution, and thus we cannot control the generated text depending on any conditions. The other approach, which includes TextGAN (Zhang et al., 2017) and FM-GAN (Chen et al., 2018), produces the diversity of texts depending on the randomly sampled latent code from the prior distribution. These models set the latent code information at the initial state or the input of every time step for the generator.

In this paper, we propose a GAN model that aims to improve the approach to generating diverse texts from the latent space. As for TextGAN and FM-GAN, the generator almost decisively selects each word using soft-argmax approximation to generate a sentence depending on the latent space information. To avoid mode-collapsing, instead of using standard GAN objective function, the discriminator of each model respectively measures the Maximum Mean Discrepancy (MMD) or the Feature Mover's Distance (FMD) between the true text representations and fake ones. These models succeed in generating diverse texts if the generators are pre-trained by a Variational Autoencoder. However, it is verified that these methods still fall into mode-collapsing if the generator is not pre-trained (Section 4.3.1). One of the possible reasons for the mode-collapsing is the deterministic word sampling process through a soft-argmax approximation from the beginning of the training. Deterministic word sampling process hinders the generator from exploring a variety of text generation, which may lead the generator to fall into sub-optimal point. The second possible reason is that the discriminator tries to discriminate the completed sentences. Generating a good-completed sentence from the beginning of the training is too difficult for the generator because the possible number of combinations of words increases exponentially if the number of words sampled becomes large. Therefore, there is a possibility that, without pre-training, the

Proceedings of the 16th Conference of the European Chapter of the Associationfor Computational Linguistics: Student Research Workshop, pages 175–182
April 19 - 23, 2021. ©2021 Association for Computational Linguistics

discriminator does not serve useful signals to the generator if the discriminator looks at only completed sentences. Based on these assumptions, our model adopts the following approach: The generator randomly samples words depending on the word probability distribution using the Gumbel-Softmax distribution (Jang et al., 2016). To ensure that the texts generated are conditioned upon the latent code, a reconstructor is introduced, which is fed the generated sentence and outputs the reconstructed latent code. The generator and the reconstructor cooperatively minimize the reconstruction loss. The discriminator of our model iteratively inspects incomplete partial texts and learns to distinguish whether they are real or fake using the standard GAN objective.

We trained our model using the COCO Image Captions dataset (Lin et al., 2014) for the experiment. The results show that although our model is not pre-trained, its performance is quite competitive with the existing baseline models. We also found that, by controlling the weight of the reconstruction loss coefficient, our model can obtain a higher diversity of generated texts even when texts are generated by greedy decoding.

2 Related Work

The language GANs, in which the generator and discriminator optimize their objective functions in an adversarial manner to generate realistic texts, have two main perspectives.

As the first perspective, a reinforcement learning approach is used for optimizing the generator. SeqGAN (Yu et al., 2017), LeakGAN (Guo et al., 2018), MaskGAN (Fedus et al., 2018), RankGAN (Lin et al., 2017), RL-GAN (Caccia et al., 2019), and ScratchGAN (de Masson d'Autume et al., 2019) are typical models. These models are non-differentiable from the discriminator to the generator. Therefore, the generator cannot be optimized using a standard GAN approach. Instead, the output of the discriminator is regarded as a reward for the sampling of words, and the expected rewards are maximized to optimize the generator. This reinforcement approach generally produces the diversity of texts during the word sampling process.

As the second perspective, the model is end-to-end differentiable from the discriminator to the generator. TextGAN (Zhang et al., 2017), RelGAN (Nie et al., 2018), and FM-GAN (Chen et al., 2018) are typical models. The sampling of words is approximated using a soft-argmax approximation or the Gumbel-Softmax distribution, which is used to create approximated one-hot vectors by lowering the temperature of the softmax function. Some models of this approach produce the diversity of texts by sampling latent code from the prior distribution. Note that GSGAN (Kusner and Hernández-Lobato, 2016) is also an end-to-end differentiable model for discretized data, but does not verify the effectiveness in the case of text generation.

Model	Generate text Conditioned by Latent space	Require Pretraining
SeqGAN, LeakGAN, etc	No	Yes (MLE)
ScratchGAN, COT, MLE	No	No
TextGAN, FM-GAN	Yes	Yes (VAE)
Ours[GAN], VAE-Based	Yes	No

Table 1: Summary of previous studies, where (·) indicates a pretraining approach. MLE, Maximum Likelihood Estimator; VAE, Variational Autoencoder.

Other text generation approaches beyond those described above also exist, such as a VAE-based model (Bowman et al., 2016; Bao et al., 2019) and COT(Lu et al., 2019) among others (Gagnon-Marchand et al. (2019), Li et al. (2019)).

To the best of our knowledge, our approach is the first GAN model that does not require variational Autoencoder pre-training and is able to generate texts conditioned by the latent code[1]. Previous studies are summarized in Table 1.

3 Model

Figure 1 shows a schematic illustration of the proposed method. We describe the details in the following paragraphs.

Our goal is to generate sentences conditioned by the latent space in a GAN framework. When training language GANs, if the discriminator only looks at the complete sentences, the generator obtains no learning signals early in the training be-

[1]For FM-GAN, no description regarding the necessity of pre-training is provided in this paper. However, their released code refers to the pre-training procedure and is available at `https://github.com/vijini/FM-GAN`. We also verified that a model without VAE pre-training cannot achieve the expected performance (Figure 3).

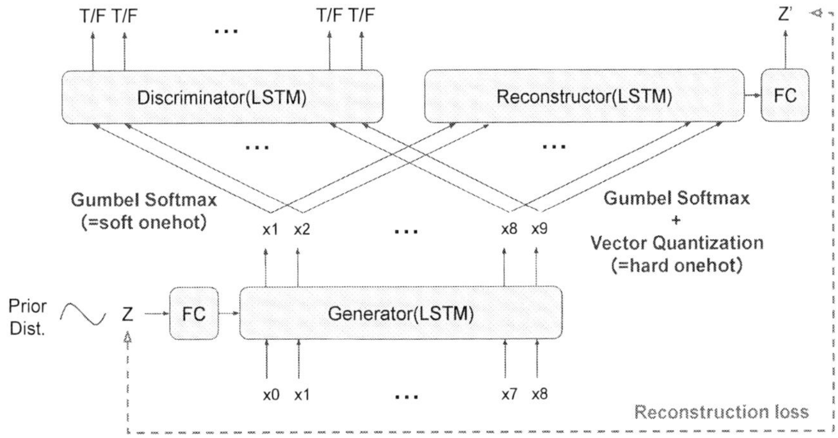

Figure 1: Overview of our model. The latent code z sampled from the prior distribution is fed into the fully connected layer and set as the initial state of the generator. The generator iteratively generates soft one-hot vectors of words using the Gumbel-Softmax distribution. The discriminator is fed the soft one-hot vectors and outputs the dense reward iteratively for the GAN loss. The reconstructor is fed the vector-quantized hard one-hot vectors and outputs the reconstructed latent code for the reconstruction loss. This network is end-to-end differentiable from the discriminator/reconstructor to the generator.

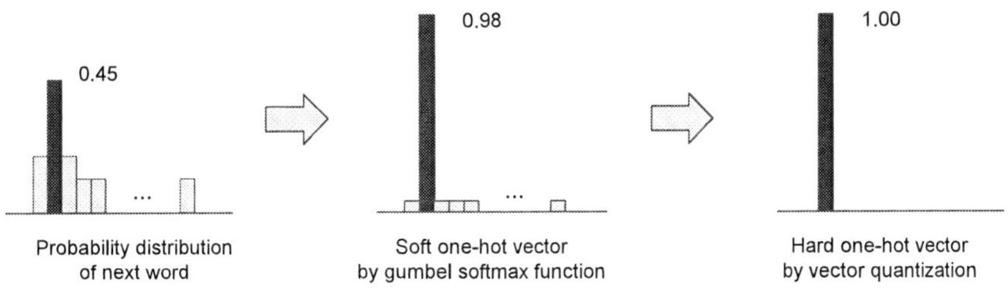

Figure 2: Example of vector quantization of words from soft one-hot vector to hard one-hot vector. This approach can back-propagate the loss from the reconstructor to the generator using only the sampled word parameters. Implementation details: hard one-hot = onehot(Argmax(soft one-hot)) - StopGradient[soft one-hot] + soft one-hot

cause the complete sentences generated are easily determined to be fake by the discriminator(de Masson d'Autume et al., 2019). To address this problem, following the idea of Fedus et al. (2018), Semeniuta et al. (2018), and de Masson d'Autume et al. (2019), our discriminator D_ϕ iteratively inspects incomplete partial texts and learns to distinguish whether they are real or fake. Therefore, the generator can obtain more informative signals from the recurrent discriminator during the iterative word sampling process. By using this recurrent discriminator, it is expected that our model does not require pre-training, as reported in ScratchGAN (de Masson d'Autume et al., 2019). The objective function of the discriminator D_ϕ is the same as that in ScratchGAN, except that the generator p_θ generates a sequence of tokens $\{x_1, ..., x_T\}$ depending on the sampled latent code z from the prior distribution $p(z)$.

$$\max_{\phi} \sum_{t=1}^{T} \mathbb{E}_{p^*(x_t|x_{<t})}[logD_\phi(x_t|x_{<t})] \quad (1)$$

$$+\sum_{t=1}^{T} \mathbb{E}_{p(z)p_\theta(x_t|z,x_{<t})}[log(1 - D_\phi(x_t|x_{<t}))],$$

where $x_{<t} := \{x_1, .., x_{t-1}\}$ denotes a sequence of words before timestep t, and p^* is the real data distribution.

In a practical sense, the typical word sampling process makes the differentiability from the discriminator to the generator impossible because sampling a word from a word probability distribution is equivalent to creating a non-differentiable one-hot vector. As a workaround, we use the Gumbel-Softmax distribution (Jang et al., 2016), which enables our model to sample words from p_θ by creating an approximated one-hot vector while making the differentiability from the discriminator to the generator possible. Here, we call this one-hot vector a "soft one-hot vector." The Gumbel-Softmax distribution used to create the soft one-hot vector $\tilde{x}$ is set as follows:

$$\begin{aligned} \tilde{x} &= softmax((log(p_\theta) + g)/\tau_1) \\ \text{where } p_\theta &= softmax(o/\tau_2) \end{aligned} \tag{2}$$

Here, g is a randomly sampled value from the Gumbel distribution $Gumbel(0, 1)$, o is the output from the generator. Note that τ_1 is the Gumbel-Softmax temperature, and τ_2 is the word probability distribution temperature.

To ensure that the texts generated are conditioned by the sampled latent code, our model introduces a reconstructor R_ψ, which is fed the generated text and outputs a reconstructed latent code to minimize the reconstruction loss between the latent code and the reconstructed code. The generator p_θ and reconstructor R_ψ are optimized simultaneously. Therefore, the objective function of the reconstructor is added to that of the generator multiplied by a coefficient λ.

$$\min_{\theta,\psi} \sum_{t=1}^{T} \mathbb{E}_{p(z)p_\theta(x_t|z,x_{<t})}[log(1 - D_\phi(x_t|x_{<t}))]$$

$$+\lambda \mathbb{E}_{p(z)p_\theta(x_1..,x_t)}\left[\frac{1}{N_z}||R_\psi(x_1,..,x_t)-z||_2^2\right] \tag{3}$$

where N_z denotes the dimension size of the latent code z. It should be noted that the joint distribution $p_\theta(x_1...x_t)$ is decomposed into the iterative conditional distribution $p_\theta(x_1...x_t) = p_\theta(x_1)p_\theta(x_2|x_1)...p_\theta(x_t|x_{<t})$ such that conditional sampling can be executed using the Gumbel-Softmax distribution described above.

We found several heuristic approaches for stabilizing the training. As the first, vector quantization (Van Den Oord et al., 2017) is applied to the soft one-hot vector to create a "hard one-hot vector" for the reconstructor input. Vector quantization can back-propagate the loss from the reconstructor to the generator using only the sampled word parameters. By using this approach, reconstruction loss training is stabilized. Figure 2 illustrates an example of the vector quantization process. As the second technique, if a blank token is chosen at any time step by the Gumebel softmax of the generator, the rest of the sentence is automatically padded with blank tokens. The pseudocode is given in Appendix C.

4 Experiment

First, we describe the data setting and evaluation metrics for the experiment. Second, we describe the experimental results to better evaluate the performance of our model.

4.1 Data Setting

We experimentally evaluated the quality and diversity of our generated models using a real sentence dataset, i.e., COCO Image Captions (Lin et al., 2014). We used the same sampled data as in Zhu et al. (2018), which consist of 10,000 training texts and 10,000 evaluation texts[2]. The maximum sentence length was 37 tokens, the average length of the sentence was 11.3 tokens, and the vocabulary size was 6577. For the experiment, the end of the text was padded with blank tokens.

4.2 Evaluation Metrics

The quality and diversity of the generated text were measured using the Negative BLEU score and the Self-BLEU score (Zhu et al., 2018), respectively. In tuition, the BLEU score measures the quality of the generated sentences through a comparison with real sentences from the viewpoint of how much the N-gram words overlap. The negative BLEU score is defined as the -1 $*$ BLEU score. The Self-BLEU scores measure the diversity of every generated sentence by comparing with the other generated sentences by inspecting how much the N-gram words overlap. Therefore, a lower value indicates a better performance for both metrics. We draw the temperature curve(Caccia et al., 2019) for each model, in which the texts are generated by gradually changing the temperature of the softmax function, and plotting the quality and diversity score for every temperature point on a two-dimensional quality-diversity canvas. Therefore, the closer the curve is to the origin, the better the performance of the model. We plot the results for temperatures at intervals of 0.0 to 1.0 with 0.1 increments. Note that at a temperature of 0.0, the model generates the text using a greedy approach, which can be interpreted as temperature $\tau \to 0$. In principle, as the temperature decreases, the quality of the generated texts increases, but the diversity decreases. Thus, the greedy decoding case is the upper leftmost point on each temperature curve. We generate 10,000 texts from the trained model at every temperature

[2]The dataset is available at `https://github.com/geek-ai/Texygen/tree/master/data`

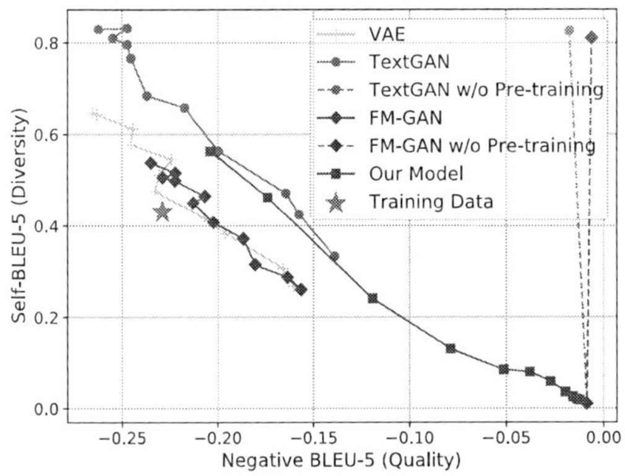

Figure 3: Performance comparison of our model with baseline models. The lower value indicates the better performance for diversity and quality metrics.

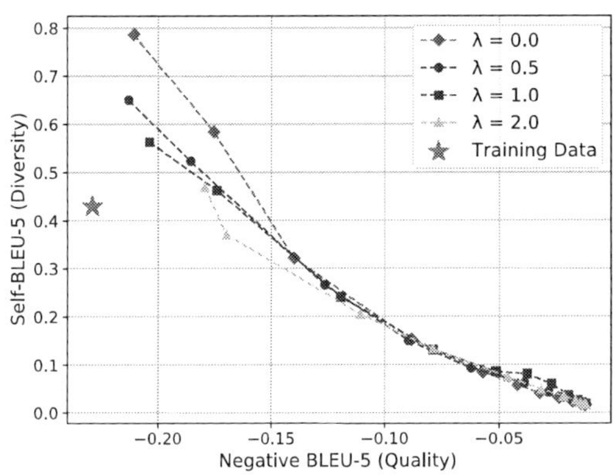

Figure 4: Effect of changing reconstruction loss coefficient λ.

for evaluation. The generated sample texts can be found at Table 2. Note that in the Gumbel-Softmax distribution, the changing target of the temperature is τ_2, and not τ_1 in equation (2).

4.3 Results

4.3.1 Comparison with Baseline Models

We compared the performance of our model with the baseline models: VAE, FM-GAN, and TextGAN. VAE used the CNN-LSTM autoencoder architecture as in Gan et al. (2017). FM-GAN and TextGAN require VAE pre-training. Our model settings and hyperparameter details can be found in Appendix A and B. Figure 3 illustrates the temperature curves for each model to compare the performance from the viewpoint of quality and diversity. This result indicates that the overall performance of our model is slightly inferior to that of the baseline models, but is quite competitive despite our model not being pre-trained. We also evaluated FM-GAN and TextGAN without pre-training case. Both of them achieved far worse performance than the pre-trained case. This result indicates that these models without pre-training fall into mode-collapsing.

4.3.2 Effect of Changing Value of λ

We observe the effect of changing the value of the reconstruction coefficient λ in equation (3) on the performance of our model. Figure 4 shows the temperature curves for different coefficients. The result indicates that, as the value of λ increases, the performance of our models improves. However, if the value of λ is too high such as $\lambda = 2.0$, the quality of the generated sentence significantly worsens. We also found that for the greedy decoding case, which is the upper-left point of each curve, as λ increases, the diversity of the generated sentences increases and the quality-diversity distribution becomes closer to that of the training data. Greedy decoding is the most extreme case for verifying if the generated sentences are conditioned by the latent space. Therefore, it can be assumed that the reconstruction loss has the ability to make the generated text more dependent on the latent space information.

5 Conclusion and Discussion

This paper proposed a GAN model that aims to improve the approach to generating diverse texts conditioned by a latent space. In a quantitative experiment using the COCO Image Captions dataset, it was shown that although our model is not pre-trained, its performance is quite competitive with the existing baseline models, which require pre-training. Future work will include further improvements to the performance of our model, and application of our model to other tasks that need to transform the data between domains through a latent space, such as improving the quality and diversity of machine translation or multi-modal learning related to text generation.

References

Yu Bao, Hao Zhou, Shujian Huang, Lei Li, Lili Mou, Olga Vechtomova, Xin-yu Dai, and Jiajun Chen. 2019. Generating sentences from disentangled syntactic and semantic spaces. In *Proceedings of the 57th Annual Meeting of the Association for Computational Linguistics*.

Samuel R. Bowman, Luke Vilnis, Oriol Vinyals, Andrew Dai, Rafal Jozefowicz, and Samy Bengio.

Real Data	a bicycle replica with a clock as the front wheel. a black honda motorcycle parked in front of a garage. a room with blue walls and a white sink and door. a car that seems to be parked illegally behind a legally parked car a large passenger airplane flying through the air. there is a gol plane taking off in a partly cloudy sky. blue and white color scheme in a small bathroom. this is a blue and white bathroom with a wall sink and a lifesaver on the wall. a blue boat themed bathroom with a life preserver on the wall
VAE	a bathroom sink with only the tub in the bathroom a large boy and a plane sitting on the landing . a clock tower with pots and windows a car at an open door leading to a bunch of foot . office space force force jet on display during day . an image of benches on a street and chairs being terminal . a large airplane flying in the open of a kitchen . a couple of an airplane flying through the clear blue oven . an airplane with some chairs on a table by the counter .
FM-GAN	a man wearing two sheep on a blue umbrella a group of birds standing around a table in a forest . a bathroom with a vanity , sink , and white and shower . a building with a clock on a clock tower a large white plane sits on a sidewalk in the kitchen . a row of cars are parked outside the street at an intersection . a woman looks plays in the kitchen an orange and woman walking around a park bench . a man standing in the kitchen at a tv .
TextGAN	a person with a football standing in front of a house an old airplane flying through a blue sky above a house . a man sitting on a bed with a dog and fries inside a car . a group of people riding bicycles down a city street . two motorcycles lined up with green seats in snow . a man wearing glasses wearing glasses and black bookbag riding a horse down a street . a bathroom with a toilet , shower , and toilet , trash can on the wall a cat drinking the back of a white toilet paper a man and motorcycle riders are riding on the road
Our Model	a small bird sit on a white bathroom with a mirror seat . two chefs counter standing in front of a toilet . a modern black and white checkered oven underneath area . looking off from you doors from doors . a white kitchen with chrome space at cabinets . a racing plane in a sky by land on a track . there is a yellow bathroom stands next to a toilet under a mirror . a kitchen with wooden appliances in flight a bathroom that has a mirror and a wall and basket . an image of men are crossing from the car .

Table 2: Randomly selected samples of COCO Image Captions from real data, VAE, FM-GAN, TextGAN, and our model. Text generations are based on greedy decoding for all models.

2016. Generating sentences from a continuous space. In *Proceedings of The 20th SIGNLL Conference on Computational Natural Language Learning*.

Massimo Caccia, Lucas Caccia, William Fedus, Hugo Larochelle, Joelle Pineau, and Laurent Charlin. 2019. Language gans falling short. In *International Conference on Learning Representations*.

Liqun Chen, Shuyang Dai, Chenyang Tao, Haichao Zhang, Zhe Gan, Dinghan Shen, Yizhe Zhang, Guoyin Wang, Ruiyi Zhang, and Lawrence Carin. 2018. Adversarial text generation via feature-mover's distance. In *Advances in Neural Information Processing Systems*, pages 4666–4677.

William Fedus, Ian Goodfellow, and Andrew M Dai. 2018. Maskgan: Better text generation via filling in the _. In *International Conference on Learning Representations*.

Jules Gagnon-Marchand, Hamed Sadeghi, Md Akmal Haidar, and Mehdi Rezagholizadeh. 2019. Salsa-text: self attentive latent space based adversarial text generation. In *Canadian Conference on Artificial Intelligence*, pages 119–131. Springer.

Zhe Gan, Yunchen Pu, Ricardo Henao, Chunyuan Li, Xiaodong He, and Lawrence Carin. 2017. Learning generic sentence representations using convolutional neural networks. In *Proceedings of the 2017 Conference on Empirical Methods in Natural Language Processing*, pages 2390–2400.

Ian Goodfellow, Jean Pouget-Abadie, Mehdi Mirza, Bing Xu, David Warde-Farley, Sherjil Ozair, Aaron Courville, and Yoshua Bengio. 2014. Generative adversarial nets. In *Advances in neural information processing systems*, pages 2672–2680.

Jiaxian Guo, Sidi Lu, Han Cai, Weinan Zhang, Yong Yu, and Jun Wang. 2018. Long text generation via adversarial training with leaked information. In *AAAI*.

Sepp Hochreiter and Jürgen Schmidhuber. 1997. Long short-term memory. *Neural Computation*, 9(8):1735–1780.

Eric Jang, Shixiang Gu, and Ben Poole. 2016. Categorical reparameterization with gumbel-softmax. *arXiv preprint arXiv:1611.01144*.

Diederik P. Kingma and Jimmy Ba. 2015. Adam: A method for stochastic optimization. In *3rd International Conference on Learning Representations, ICLR*.

Matt J Kusner and José Miguel Hernández-Lobato. 2016. Gans for sequences of discrete elements with the gumbel-softmax distribution. *arXiv preprint arXiv:1611.04051*.

Zhongliang Li, Tian Xia, Xingyu Lou, Kaihe Xu, Shaojun Wang, and Jing Xiao. 2019. Adversarial discrete sequence generation without explicit neuralnetworks as discriminators. In *The 22nd International Conference on Artificial Intelligence and Statistics*, pages 3089–3098.

Kevin Lin, Dianqi Li, Xiaodong He, Zhengyou Zhang, and Ming-Ting Sun. 2017. Adversarial ranking for language generation. In *Advances in Neural Information Processing Systems*, pages 3155–3165.

Tsung-Yi Lin, Michael Maire, Serge Belongie, James Hays, Pietro Perona, Deva Ramanan, Piotr Dollár, and C Lawrence Zitnick. 2014. Microsoft coco: Common objects in context. In *European conference on computer vision*, pages 740–755. Springer.

Sidi Lu, Lantao Yu, Siyuan Feng, Yaoming Zhu, and Weinan Zhang. 2019. Cot: Cooperative training for generative modeling of discrete data. In *International Conference on Machine Learning*, pages 4164–4172.

Cyprien de Masson d'Autume, Shakir Mohamed, Mihaela Rosca, and Jack Rae. 2019. Training language gans from scratch. In *Advances in Neural Information Processing Systems*, pages 4300–4311.

Weili Nie, Nina Narodytska, and Ankit Patel. 2018. Relgan: Relational generative adversarial networks for text generation. In *International conference on learning representations*.

Stanislau Semeniuta, Aliaksei Severyn, and Sylvain Gelly. 2018. On accurate evaluation of gans for language generation. *arXiv preprint arXiv:1806.04936*.

Aaron Van Den Oord, Oriol Vinyals, et al. 2017. Neural discrete representation learning. In *Advances in Neural Information Processing Systems*, pages 6306–6315.

Lantao Yu, Weinan Zhang, Jun Wang, and Yong Yu. 2017. Seqgan: Sequence generative adversarial nets with policy gradient. In *Thirty-first AAAI conference on artificial intelligence*.

Yizhe Zhang, Zhe Gan, K. Fan, Z. Chen, Ricardo Henao, Dinghan Shen, and L. Carin. 2017. Adversarial feature matching for text generation. In *ICML*.

Yaoming Zhu, Sidi Lu, Lei Zheng, Jiaxian Guo, Weinan Zhang, Jun Wang, and Yong Yu. 2018. Texygen: A benchmarking platform for text generation models. *SIGIR*.

A Model Settings

- For the generator, reconstructor, and discriminator, we used long short-term memory (LSTM) (Hochreiter and Schmidhuber, 1997).
- Two different fully connected layers are set to linearly transform z into the initial states C_0 and H_0 respectively for the LSTM network of the generator.
- Positional information of 8-dimensions in size (de Masson d'Autume et al., 2019) is concatenated with the word embeddings in each network.
- A dropout is applied to the word embeddings before the word embeddings are fed into each LSTM network of the discriminator.
- All trainable parameters are optimized using Adam (Kingma and Ba, 2015). A weight decay is applied to all trainable parameters of the discriminator using an L2 penalty.
- The prior distribution of Latent space is defined as Gaussian distribution $G(0, 1)$.

B Hyperparameters of Our Model for COCO Image Captions Experiment

- LSTM feature size of the discriminator: 64
- LSTM feature size of the generator: 128
- LSTM feature size of the reconstructor: 128
- Dimension size of latent code z: 8
- Learning rate for Adam: 0.0002
- β_1 for Adam: 0.5
- β_2 for Adam: 0.999
- Minibatch size: 256
- Dropout rate for word embedding: 0.1
- τ_1 in Equation (2): 0.1
- τ_2 in Equation (2): 0.1
- λ in Equation (3): 1.0
- Weight decay rate: 0.0001
- Iteration size: 50000

C Training Algorithm of Our Model

Algorithm 1

GS:=GumbelSoftmax,
VQ:=VectorQuantization,
SG:=StopGradient

Require: initial generator parameter θ, discriminator parameter ϕ, reconstructor parameter ψ.

while θ, ϕ, ψ has not converged **do**
  Sample $x \sim p^*(x)$, $z \sim p(z)$
  for $t = 1, ..., T$ **do**
    if $Argmax(\tilde{x}_{t-1}) = BlankID$ **then**
      $\tilde{x}_t \leftarrow Onehot(BlankID)$
    else
      $\tilde{x}_t \leftarrow GS(P_\theta(\tilde{x}_t|z, \ddot{x}_{<t}))$
    end if
    $\dot{x}_t \leftarrow VQ(\tilde{x}_t)$
    $\ddot{x}_t \leftarrow SG(\dot{x}_t)$
  end for
  $D_t \leftarrow -\frac{1}{T}\sum_{t=1}^{T} logD_\phi(x_t|x_{<t})$
  $D_f \leftarrow -\frac{1}{T}\sum_{t=1}^{T} log(1 - D_\phi(\tilde{x}_t|\tilde{x}_{<t}))$
  $\mathcal{L} \leftarrow D_t + D_f$
  $\phi \leftarrow Adam(\nabla_\phi \mathcal{L}, \phi)$

  Sample $z \sim p(z)$
  for $t = 1, ..., T$ **do**
    if $Argmax(\tilde{x}_{t-1}) = BlankID$ **then**
      $\tilde{x}_t \leftarrow Onehot(BlankID)$
    else
      $\tilde{x}_t \leftarrow GS(P_\theta(\tilde{x}_t|z, \ddot{x}_{<t}))$
    end if
    $\dot{x}_t \leftarrow VQ(\tilde{x}_t)$
    $\ddot{x}_t \leftarrow SG(\dot{x}_t)$
  end for
  $D_f \leftarrow \frac{1}{T}\sum_{t=1}^{T} log(1 - D_\phi(\tilde{x}_t|\tilde{x}_{<t}))$
  $\mathcal{L} \leftarrow D_f + \lambda R_\psi(\dot{x}_1, ..., \dot{x}_T)$
  $\theta \leftarrow Adam(\nabla_\theta \mathcal{L}, \theta)$
  $\psi \leftarrow Adam(\nabla_\psi \mathcal{L}, \psi)$
end while

Beyond the English Web: Zero-Shot Cross-Lingual and Lightweight Monolingual Classification of Registers

Liina Repo[*†] **Valtteri Skantsi**[*°†] **Samuel Rönnqvist**[*] **Saara Hellström**[*]
Miika Oinonen[*] **Anna Salmela**[*] **Douglas Biber**[‡] **Jesse Egbert**[‡]
Sampo Pyysalo[*] **Veronika Laippala**[*]

[*]University of Turku [°]University of Oulu [‡]Northern Arizona University

[*]{tlkrep,valtteri.skantsi,saanro,sherik,mhtoin,annsaln,sampo.pyysalo,mavela}@utu.fi
[°]{valtteri.skantsi}@oulu.fi [‡]{douglas.biber,jesse.egbert}@nau.edu

Abstract

We explore cross-lingual transfer of register classification for web documents. Registers, that is, text varieties such as blogs or news are one of the primary predictors of linguistic variation and thus affect the automatic processing of language. We introduce two new register-annotated corpora, FreCORE and SweCORE, for French and Swedish. We demonstrate that deep pre-trained language models perform strongly in these languages and outperform previous state-of-the-art in English and Finnish. Specifically, we show 1) that zero-shot cross-lingual transfer from the large English CORE corpus can match or surpass previously published monolingual models, and 2) that lightweight monolingual classification requiring very little training data can reach or surpass our zero-shot performance. We further analyse classification results finding that certain registers continue to pose challenges in particular for cross-lingual transfer.

1 Introduction

Text genre or *register* (Biber, 1988), such as discussion forum, news article or poem, is one of the most important predictors of linguistic variation (Biber, 2012). Thus, register affects crucially also the automatic processing of language (Mahajan et al., 2015; Webber, 2009; Van der Wees et al., 2018). Yet, despite its importance, register information is not available in web-crawled datasets that are widely used e.g. for pre-training language models in modern NLP. This is a challenge, as better structured language resources would also enable more detailed understanding and more sophisticated use of this data.

While web register identification would allow better realization of the potential offered by web-crawled datasets, most previous web register identification studies have been limited by skewed datasets, low performance, and near-exclusive focus on English. For example, Asheghi et al. (2014) and Pritsos and Stamatatos (2018) reported comparatively strong results, but their evaluations were based on datasets representing only a subset of the registers found online. With the CORE corpus, Egbert et al. (2015) were the first to present a dataset featuring the full extent of registers found on the open, searchable English web. While Biber and Egbert (2016b) demonstrated the possibility of automatic register classification using Stepwise Discriminant Analysis, improvements in modeling and more efficient methods remained necessary in order to reach practical levels of performance.

A challenge in modeling web registers is that web documents drawn from the unrestricted web do not always fit discrete classes but could rather be described in a continuous space (Biber and Egbert, 2018; Sharoff, 2018). Not all documents have clear characteristics of one single register, or even any register at all. This has shown also in relatively low inter-annotator agreement for web register annotation (Crowston et al., 2010).

Very recently, however, the advances brought to NLP by neural networks have shown that registers can be identified also in a corpus featuring the full range of online language variation (Laippala et al., 2020a). Laippala et al. (2019) extended the possibilities of web register identification beyond English by presenting an online register corpus on Finnish (FinCORE) and demonstrating that web registers can be modeled also in a cross-lingual setting.

In this paper, we substantially extend on this early work on cross-lingual web register identification through the following contributions: 1) we

[†]The marked authors contributed equally to this paper.

Proceedings of the 16th Conference of the European Chapter of the Associationfor Computational Linguistics: Student Research Workshop, pages 183–191
April 19 - 23, 2021. ©2021 Association for Computational Linguistics

General register category	English	Finnish	French	Swedish
NA Narrative	36.46 %	34.95 %	22.33 %	28.32 %
IN Informational description	19.24 %	17.03 %	20.74 %	27.68 %
OP Opinion	16.23 %	15.23 %	6.33 %	6.60 %
ID Interactive discussion	6.77 %	6.29 %	8.03 %	3.57 %
HI How-to/Instructions	3.08 %	6.47 %	3.08 %	2.80 %
IP Informational persuasion	2.75 %	20.04 %	24.15 %	16.82 %
LY Lyrical	1.32 %	0.00 %	0.33 %	0.14 %
SP Spoken	1.21 %	0.00 %	0.83 %	0.14 %
Empty	1.20 %	0.00 %	0.00 %	0.00 %
Hybrids	11.74 %	0.00 %	14.19 %	13.93 %
Total	**48452**	**2226**	**1818**	**2182**

Table 1: Proportional register distribution and total number of documents in CORE, FinCORE, FreCORE and SweCORE. Hybrids include all documents annotated with several register labels, and Empty refers to documents not assigned any label.

introduce manually annotated web register datasets for two new languages, French and Swedish, 2) we demonstrate competitive performance for cross-lingual transfer of a register classification model from English to other languages in a zero-shot setting, and 3) we analyze zero-shot vs. monolingual training for register classification and remaining challenges in both. In particular, using Transformer-based pre-trained language models, we show that a zero-shot cross-lingual approach outperforms monolingual results achieved by a previously proposed state-of-the-art method for all the three language pairs (En-Fr, En-Sv, and En-Fi), and that strong monolingual performance can be achieved with limited training data.

2 Data

We use four register-annotated corpora representing the unrestricted open web: the English CORE and Finnish FinCORE, which have been introduced in previous work (Egbert et al., 2015; Laippala et al., 2019), and two new corpora, FreCORE for French and SweCORE for Swedish. These novel datasets are released under open licences together with this paper.[1] With these new resources, the possibilities for web register identification expand substantially.

FreCORE and SweCORE are random samples of the 2017 CoNLL datasets (Ginter et al., 2017) originally drawn from Common Crawl. Both datasets were deduplicated using Onion (Pomikálek, 2011) with 0.7 threshold and n-gram length of 5. All material not belonging to the body of text, such as boilerplate, was removed. Titles, however, were preserved. The cleaning and pre-processing steps follow the procedure suggested in Laippala et al. (2020b). The register annotation of the datasets was conducted individually by two trained annotators with a linguistics background. Uncertain cases were discussed and resolved together with an annotation supervisor. The inter-annotator agreement, counted prior to the discussions, was 78% F1-score for FreCORE and 84% for SweCORE. This can be considered as a lower bound.

All datasets are similarly annotated across languages, and they all apply the same hierarchical register class taxonomy originally introduced for CORE. It includes eight main registers (e.g., Narrative) and approximately 30 sub-registers (e.g., News report within Narrative). The main and sub-register categories are illustrated in the appendix. When a document shares characteristics of several registers, it can be assigned several labels both at the main and sub-register level. These documents are called *hybrids*. As our focus in this paper is on general register categories, we initially pre-process all four corpora to remove the more specific sub-register labels.

The general register categories and their distributions as well as the average document length and standard deviation for all classes are presented in Table 1 and Table 2, respectively. The register class Empty consists of texts whose register the annotators could not agree on. Due to the very small number of each type of hybrid label combination in the data, in Tables 1 and 2, the class Hybrids includes all documents that have more than one label. Table 1 reveals that the register distributions in the four languages are broadly similar, featuring Narrative, Informational description, and

[1] Available at `https://github.com/TurkuNLP/Multilingual-register-corpora`

Register	English		Finnish		French		Swedish	
	mean	std.	mean	std.	mean	std.	mean	std.
NA	1081	2490	649	2170	623	2284	602	2461
IP	1066	3370	301	391	325	493	426	2225
IN	1353	3373	989	4755	1446	9688	323	626
OP	1595	4021	739	1188	857	1835	1055	1825
HI	1007	1402	277	285	623	1130	437	508
ID	1079	4042	2017	8907	970	1579	577	885
LY	468	1114	-	-	387	314	263	225
SP	2047	3335	-	-	999	939	525	178
Empty	13345	3215	-	-	-	-	-	-
Hybrids	1290	3141	-	-	1170	3296	859	1207
All	1083	2747	713	3295	703	3900	482	1446

Table 2: Average length (number of words) and standard deviation of Finnish, French, Swedish and English documents.

hybrids among the four most frequent categories. The top four also include Informational persuasion in FinCORE, FreCORE, and SweCORE, while in CORE this label is relatively infrequent. Additionally, Opinion is notably more frequent in CORE and FinCORE than in FreCORE and SweCORE. These differences may reflect differences in data compilation. Table 2 shows that, on average, English documents are longer than documents in other languages, whereas Swedish documents tend to be shortest. Overall the number of words in a document in most of the classes show large variation, with the longest documents containing tens of thousands of words.

3 Experimental setup

The architectures and models we are using are presented below.[2] We perform multi-label document classification, where each document can have zero, one, or several register labels. The experiments are divided into 1) a monolingual setup with training and evaluation on Finnish, French, Swedish, and English (as reference), and 2) a zero-shot cross-lingual setup with training on English and evaluation on the other languages.

BERT, Bidirectional Encoder Representations from Transformers (Devlin et al., 2019) is a state-of-the-art deep bidirectional language model pre-trained on large unlabelled corpora. BERT's architecture is a multi-layer Transformer encoder that is based on the original Transformer architecture introduced by Vaswani et al. (2017). We use cased BERT models (TensorFlow versions) through the Huggingface Transformers library (Wolf et al., 2020) with the following language-specific models: the original English BERT, Finnish FinBERT (Virtanen et al., 2019), French FlauBERT (Le et al., 2020) and Swedish KB-BERT (Malmsten et al., 2020). Additionally, we use Multilingual BERT (mBERT) (Devlin et al., 2019), which was pre-trained on monolingual Wikipedia corpora from 104 languages with a shared multilingual vocabulary.

XLM-RoBERTa (XLM-R, Conneau et al. (2020)) is a multilingual language model that follows the Cross-lingual Language Modeling (XLM) approach (Conneau and Lample, 2019) and is based on the RoBERTa model (Liu et al., 2019), which shares the architecture of BERT. The authors argue that XLM and mBERT are undertuned and that the improved and prolonged training procedure of RoBERTa in combination with more data – on average two orders of magnitude more for low-resource languages – is key to improving cross-lingual performance. XLM-R is trained on 2.5TB of filtered Common Crawl (Wenzek et al., 2020) data comprising of monolingual texts in 100 languages. It is claimed to be the first multilingual model to outperform monolingual models, as well as Multilingual BERT in a number of experiments (Conneau et al., 2020; Libovický et al., 2020; Tanase et al., 2020).

We also apply a **CNN** (Convolutional Neural Network) based architecture following Kim (2014), as our baseline model. We modify the cross-lingual CNN used by Laippala et al. (2019) to a multi-label setting. We use the multilingual word vectors introduced by Conneau et al. (2018). The CNN employs a convolution layer with ReLU activation,

[2]The code is available at: `https://github.com/TurkuNLP/Multilingual-register-corpora`

Model	Monolingual					Cross-lingual				
	Train-	Dev		Test		Train-	Dev		Test	
	Test	F1 (%)	Std.	F1 (%)	Std.	Test	F1 (%)	Std.	F1 (%)	Std.
CNN	Fi	59.04	(0.67)	58.04	(1.02)	En-Fi	40.53	(1.11)	41.56	(0.20)
mBERT	Fi	65.91	(0.85)	64.83	(1.16)	En-Fi	51.02	(2.92)	50.21	(0.74)
XLM-R large	Fi	76.25	(0.45)	**73.18**	(1.35)	En-Fi	**61.60**	(2.01)	**61.35**	(1.26)
FinBERT	Fi	**76.28**	(1.23)	72.98	(0.74)					
CNN	Fr	59.78	(1.10)	58.14	(1.10)	En-Fr	46.44	(0.51)	46.78	(1.80)
mBERT	Fr	70.74	(1.67)	68.66	(0.63)	En-Fr	56.73	(1.54)	55.04	(0.66)
XLM-R large	Fr	**77.38**	(0.51)	**76.92**	(0.24)	En-Fr	**65.66**	(0.52)	**64.27**	(1.58)
FlauBERT large	Fr	73.93	(0.93)	72.56	(1.40)					
CNN	Sv	69.43	(0.56)	67.89	(1.01)	En-Sv	43.74	(0.82)	43.78	(1.00)
mBERT	Sv	76.91	(0.45)	76.43	(0.46)	En-Sv	62.37	(0.82)	62.53	(0.78)
XLM-R large	Sv	**82.61**	(0.37)	**83.04**	(0.62)	En-Sv	**70.49**	(0.58)	**69.22**	(1.66)
KB-BERT	Sv	80.15	(0.50)	80.75	(0.09)					
CNN	En	64.56	(0.78)	64.03	(0.30)					
mBERT	En	72.80	(0.21)	73.06	(0.09)					
XLM-R large	En	**75.80**	(0.12)	**75.68**	(0.05)					
BERT large	En	74.01	(0.42)	74.07	(0.28)					

Table 3: Monolingual and zero-shot cross-lingual classification results (N=3). Best results for each experiment shown in bold.

a max-pooling layer and sigmoid activation.

The French and Swedish data were divided into training, development and test sets using stratified sampling with a 50/20/30 split. For BERT-based models we used large model size when available to maximize model performance. We used the maximum sequence length of 512 tokens (with truncation at the end) and batch size of 7, and performed a grid search on learning rate ($8e^{-6}$–$6e^{-5}$) and number of training epochs (3–7). For the CNN, we performed a grid search on the kernel size (1–2), learning rate ($1e^{-4}$–$1e^{-2}$), and prediction threshold (0.4, 0.5, 0.6).

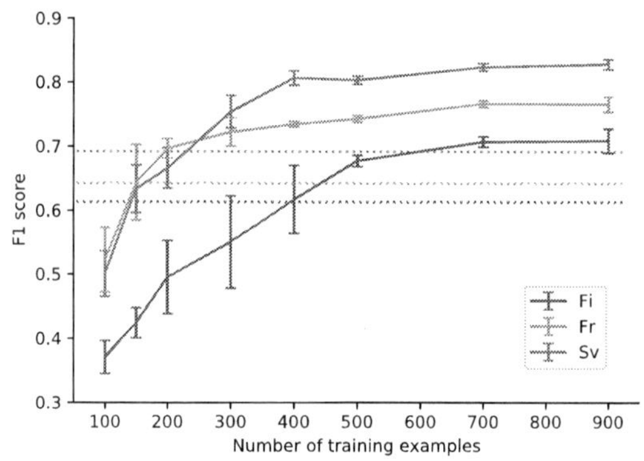

Figure 1: Monolingual performance when training with varying number of examples (solid lines) in relation to zero-shot cross-lingual performance when training on full English set (dotted lines). Error bars represent standard deviations (N=6).

4 Results

In Table 3, we present the primary results on English, Finnish, French and Swedish monolingual classification with the models described in Section 3, as well as cross-lingual results with English as the source language and Finnish, French and Swedish as target languages. We report the mean and standard deviation of F1 over three repetitions.

In monolingual settings, XLM-R large performs competitively compared to monolingual models and clearly outperforms both mBERT and the CNN baseline. The lead of XLM-R over monolingual models is substantial in all cases except for the FinBERT model, where the two perform within one standard deviation of each other. Our results support the claimed competitiveness of XLM-R large with monolingual models, mentioned in Section 3.

English, Finnish and French BERT models achieve similar monolingual test results (73–74% F1-score), while the Swedish KB-BERT achieves the highest F1-score (81%). The Finnish classification task is seemingly easier due to smaller number of classes, nevertheless, other factors may cause the difficulty of the task to differ between languages. For instance, the measured human inter-annotator agreements at 78% (Fr) and 84% (Sv) F1-score (see Section 2) represent a theoretical upper bound for the classification task and reflect the tendency of

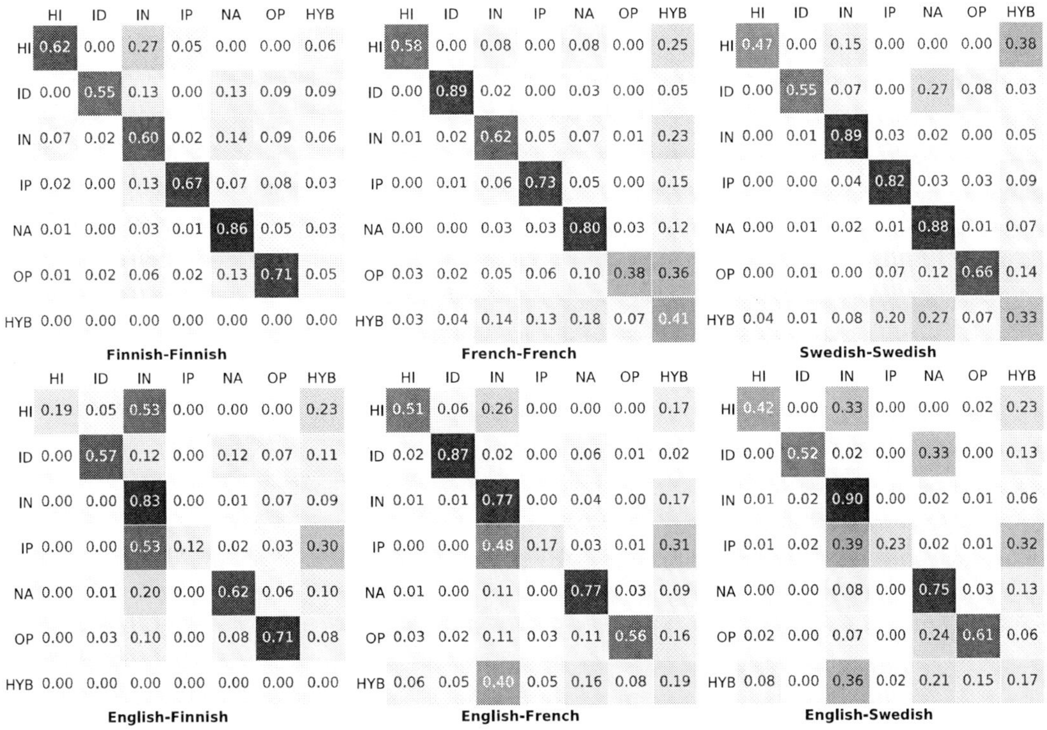

Figure 2: Confusion matrices presenting class label observations (rows) vs. class label predictions (columns) in monolingual (upper row) and cross-lingual (lower row) settings. The numbers and coloring represent the proportions of predictions per row. HYB is a combination of all hybrid cases with multiple labels.

Swedish being easier to classify; the level of agreement has not been reported for Finnish. Although not strictly comparable, our results clearly outperform the previous state-of-the-art results achieved with the CNN (Laippala et al., 2019) in terms of F1, which in turn outperforms Biber and Egbert (2016b), who used the same corpus but in multiclass setting.

Furthermore, Table 3 shows very strong zero-shot cross-lingual results with XLM-R large, with F1-scores in the 61–69% range. This represents a remarkably consistent relative decrease of 16.2–16.6% (11.8–13.8% absolute) from the monolingual scores of XLM-R. Its lead over mBERT increases from 6.6–8.4% absolute F1 to 7.8–11.4% in the cross-lingual settings, whereas its lead over the CNN goes from 15.1–18.8% to 17.5–25.4%. Most interestingly, the zero-shot XLM-R even beats the monolingually trained CNN baselines by a significant margin for Finnish and French, while its lead remains within a standard deviation for Swedish.

In Figure 1, we illustrate the effect of training monolingual XLM-R large models with varying train set sizes and compare the performance against the reported zero-shot performance. The optimal monolingual hyperparameter settings for each language are used, while training the model instances on 100–900 examples each. We see that zero-shot cross-lingual performance is surpassed already with about 150 training instances for French, 225 for Swedish and 400 for Finnish, while performance seems to converge around 500.

Previous studies have shown repeatedly that registers vary considerably in terms of how well they are linguistically defined and thus how well they can be automatically identified (Biber and Egbert, 2018, 2016a; Laippala et al., 2020a). For instance, while texts in the IN (Informational description) and NA (Narrative) classes, such as Encyclopedia articles and Sports reports, have very distinctive characteristics and can be identified with a very high reliability, others, such as Information blogs in the IN class or Advice in the OP (Opinion) class receive much lower scores.

Figure 2 presents confusion matrices on the predictions in monolingual and cross-lingual settings, using the best-performing model.[3] For the sake of simplicity, the multi-label predictions have been

[3]See appendix for class-specific F1 results.

collapsed into multi-class by including all hybrids under one label HYB in Figure 2. In the monolingual settings, we can see that particularly hybrids present a challenge. This is expected, as they feature characteristics of several registers. Additionally, while IP (Informational persuasion) and NA are predicted with high performance in all three languages, the other classes display more variation. For instance, ID (interactive discussion) reaches an F1-score of 90% (see appendix) in French monolingual setting, whereas in Swedish and Finnish it is frequently misclassified, most likely because of the small number of examples in the training data.

The hybrids are also frequently misclassified in cross-lingual settings. Interestingly, register classes also feature clear differences in the extent to which the cross-lingual transfer affects the identification performance. The register class IN tends to be predicted strongly in all zero-shot language pairs. This is probably due to the IN class including documents with strong cross-lingual signals. For instance, IN includes Encyclopedia articles (see appendix), such as Wikipedia texts, that tend to be very similar across languages.

While most of the non-hybrid classes experience a small drop in performance, the identification rate for IP and HI (How-to/Instructions) drops dramatically in cross-lingual settings in all language pairs. The decrease of IP can be linked to its smaller proportion in the English data (see Section 2), but the drops experienced by IP and HI can also reflect the variation displayed by registers across languages. Biber (2014) showed that registers, such as spoken texts, display functional similarities across languages, which obviously is needed for high-quality transfer in register identification. However, analyzing the English CORE registers, Laippala et al. (2020a) noted that some registers, such as many blogs, depend highly on lexical characteristics reflecting the discussion topics. These topics, however, may vary extensively between languages. This, again, may complicate the transfer learning for these classes.

5 Discussion and conclusions

Despite the many opportunities that reliable recognition of text register would introduce for the analysis and use of web documents and many efforts to address this task over the years, only limited progress has been made toward unrestricted web document register classification. Previous work has also focused almost exclusively on English.

In this study, we have introduced manual register annotation compatible with that of the large English CORE corpus for two languages previously lacking such a resource, namely French and Swedish. We also demonstrated that state-of-the-art multilingual neural language models can support zero-shot transfer of register annotations from English to a Germanic, Romance and Finnic language at levels of performance broadly comparable or better to previously published monolingual results on CORE.

Moreover, we demonstrated that small amounts of monolingual training data are needed to reach or surpass this level of performance, which attests that reliable register identification in a new language is readily attainable using current pre-trained language models. We further compared and analysed the results for monolingual and cross-lingual register classifiers, finding that certain registers as well as hybrid texts combining several register characteristics continue to pose challenges in particular for cross-lingual transfer. In future work, we will build on these results to extend multi- and cross-lingual modeling in order to create massive multilingual register-annotated web corpora.

Acknowledgments

We thank for the financial support of the Emil Aaltonen Foundation and Academy of Finland. We also wish to acknowledge CSC – IT Center for Science, Finland, for computational resources.

References

Rezapour Noushin Asheghi, Katja Markert, and Serge Sharoff. 2014. Semi-supervised graph-based genre classification for web pages. In *Proceedings of TextGraphs-9*, pages 39–47. Association for Computational Linguistics.

Douglas Biber. 1988. *Variation across speech and writing*. Cambridge University Press.

Douglas Biber. 2012. Register as a predictor of linguistic variation. *Corpus linguistics and linguistic theory*, 8(1):9–37.

Douglas Biber. 2014. Using multi-dimensional analysis to explore cross-linguistic universals of register variation. *Languages in contrast*, 14(1):7–34.

Douglas Biber and Jesse Egbert. 2016a. Register variation on the searchable web: A multi-dimensional analysis. *Journal of English Linguistics*, 44(2):95–137.

Douglas Biber and Jesse Egbert. 2016b. Using grammatical features for automatic register identification in an unrestricted corpus of documents from the open web. *Journal of Research Design and Statistics in Linguistics and Communication Science*, 2:3–36.

Douglas Biber and Jesse Egbert. 2018. *Register variation online*. Cambridge University Press.

Alexis Conneau, Kartikay Khandelwal, Naman Goyal, Vishrav Chaudhary, Guillaume Wenzek, Francisco Guzmán, Edouard Grave, Myle Ott, Luke Zettlemoyer, and Veselin Stoyanov. 2020. Unsupervised cross-lingual representation learning at scale. arXiv preprint arXiv:1911.02116.

Alexis Conneau and Guillaume Lample. 2019. Cross-lingual language model pretraining. In *Advances in Neural Information Processing Systems*, pages 7059–7069. Curran Associates, Inc.

Alexis Conneau, Guillaume Lample, Marc'Aurelio Ranzato, Ludovic Denoyer, and Hervé Jégou. 2018. Word translation without parallel data. *CoRR*, abs/1710.04087.

Kevin Crowston, Barbara Kwaśnik, and Joseph Rubleske. 2010. Problems in the use-centered development of a taxonomy of web genres. In *Genres on the Web*, pages 69–84. Springer.

Jacob Devlin, Ming-Wei Chang, Kenton Lee, and Kristina Toutanova. 2019. BERT: Pre-training of deep bidirectional transformers for language understanding. In *Proceedings of the 2019 Conference of the North American Chapter of the Association for Computational Linguistics: Human Language Technologies, Volume 1 (Long and Short Papers)*, pages 4171–4186. Association for Computational Linguistics.

Jesse Egbert, Douglas Biber, and Mark Davies. 2015. Developing a bottom-up, user-based method of web register classification. *Journal of the Association for Information Science and Technology*, 66:1817–1831.

Filip Ginter, Jan Hajič, Juhani Luotolahti, Milan Straka, and Daniel Zeman. 2017. CoNLL 2017 shared task - Automatically annotated raw texts and word embeddings. LINDAT/CLARIN digital library at the Institute of Formal and Applied Linguistics, Charles University.

Yoon Kim. 2014. Convolutional neural networks for sentence classification. In *Proceedings of the 2014 Conference on Empirical Methods in Natural Language Processing (EMNLP)*, pages 1746–1751. Association for Computational Linguistics.

Veronika Laippala, Jesse Egbert, Douglas Biber, and Aki-Juhani Kyröläinen. 2020a. Exploring the role of lexis and grammar for the stable identification of register in an unrestricted corpus of web documents. *Language resources and evaluation*.

Veronika Laippala, Roosa Kyllönen, Jesse Egbert, Douglas Biber, and Sampo Pyysalo. 2019. Toward multilingual identification of online registers. In *Proceedings of the 22nd Nordic Conference on Computational Linguistics*, pages 292–297. Linköping University Electronic Press.

Veronika Laippala, Samuel Rönnqvist, Saara Hellström, Juhani Luotolahti, Liina Repo, Anna Salmela, Valtteri Skantsi, and Sampo Pyysalo. 2020b. From web crawl to clean register-annotated corpora. In *Proceedings of the 12th Web as Corpus Workshop*, pages 14–22. European Language Resources Association.

Hang Le, Loïc Vial, Jibril Frej, Vincent Segonne, Maximin Coavoux, Benjamin Lecouteux, Alexandre Allauzen, Benoît Crabbé, Laurent Besacier, and Didier Schwab. 2020. FlauBERT: Unsupervised language model pre-training for French. In *Proceedings of the 12th Language Resources and Evaluation Conference*, pages 2479–2490. European Language Resources Association.

Jindřich Libovický, Rudolf Rosa, and Alexander Fraser. 2020. On the language neutrality of pre-trained multilingual representations. arXiv preprint arXiv:2004.05160.

Yinhan Liu, Myle Ott, Naman Goyal, Jingfei Du, Mandar Joshi, Danqi Chen, Omer Levy, Mike Lewis, Luke Zettlemoyer, and Veselin Stoyanov. 2019. RoBERTa: A robustly optimized BERT pretraining approach. arXiv preprint arXiv:1907.11692.

Anuj Mahajan, Sharmistha Jat, and Shourya Roy. 2015. Feature selection for short text classification using wavelet packet transform. In *Proceedings of the Nineteenth Conference on Computational Natural Language Learning*, pages 321–326. Association for Computational Linguistics.

Martin Malmsten, Love Börjeson, and Chris Haffenden. 2020. Playing with words at the national library of Sweden – making a Swedish BERT. arXiv preprint arXiv:2007.01658.

Jan Pomikálek. 2011. *Removing boilerplate and duplicate content from web corpora*. Ph.D. thesis, Masaryk university, Faculty of informatics.

Dimitrios Pritsos and Efstathios Stamatatos. 2018. Open set evaluation of web genre identification. *Language Resources and Evaluation*, 52(4):949–968.

Serge Sharoff. 2018. Functional text dimensions for the annotation of web corpora. *Corpora*, 1(13):65–95.

Mircea-Adrian Tanase, Dumitru-Clementin Cercel, and Costin-Gabriel Chiru. 2020. UPB at SemEval-2020 task 12: Multilingual offensive language detection on social media by fine-tuning a variety of BERT-based models. arXiv preprint arXiv:2010.13609.

Ashish Vaswani, Noam Shazeer, Niki Parmar, Jakob Uszkoreit, Llion Jones, Aidan N Gomez, Łukasz Kaiser, and Illia Polosukhin. 2017. Attention is all you need. In *Advances in neural information processing systems*, pages 5998–6008. Curran Associates, Inc.

Antti Virtanen, Jenna Kanerva, Rami Ilo, Jouni Luoma, Juhani Luotolahti, Tapio Salakoski, Filip Ginter, and Sampo Pyysalo. 2019. Multilingual is not enough: BERT for Finnish. arXiv preprint arXiv:1912.07076.

Bonnie Webber. 2009. Genre distinctions for discourse in the Penn TreeBank. In *Proceedings of the Joint Conference of the 47th Annual Meeting of the ACL and the 4th International Joint Conference on Natural Language Processing of the AFNLP*, pages 674–682. Association for Computational Linguistics.

Marlies Van der Wees, Arianna Bisazza, and Christof Monz. 2018. Evaluation of machine translation performance across multiple genres and languages. In *Proceedings of the Eleventh International Conference on Language Resources and Evaluation (LREC 2018)*. European Language Resources Association (ELRA).

Guillaume Wenzek, Marie-Anne Lachaux, Alexis Conneau, Vishrav Chaudhary, Francisco Guzmán, Armand Joulin, and Edouard Grave. 2020. Ccnet: Extracting high quality monolingual datasets from web crawl data. In *Proceedings of the 12th Conference on Language Resources and Evaluation (LREC 2020)*, pages 4003–4012. European Language Resources Association.

Thomas Wolf, Julien Chaumond, Lysandre Debut, Victor Sanh, Clement Delangue, Anthony Moi, Pierric Cistac, Morgan Funtowicz, Joe Davison, Sam Shleifer, et al. 2020. Transformers: State-of-the-art natural language processing. In *Proceedings of the 2020 Conference on Empirical Methods in Natural Language Processing: System Demonstrations*, pages 38–45. Association for Computational Linguistics.

A Appendix

Tables 4 and 5 present the detailed results for the zero-shot cross-lingual and monolingual register classification experiments, respectively. Table 6 presents the register taxonomy with the main registers and their sub-registers.

	En-Fi		En-Fr		En-Sv	
	F1	**Std.**	**F1**	**Std.**	**F1**	**Std.**
HI	48.43 %	1.98 %	55.12 %	5.65 %	62.91 %	0.60 %
ID	69.79 %	6.06 %	87.48 %	2.05 %	52.05 %	3.07 %
IN	44.43 %	0.32 %	58.68 %	0.17 %	68.81 %	0.20 %
IP	52.79 %	5.72 %	53,57 %	2.53 %	51.45 %	1.88 %
LY	0.00 %	0.00 %	66.67 %	0.00 %	95.24 %	6.73 %
NA	77.85 %	0.80 %	75.18 %	0.32 %	78.36 %	0.70 %
OP	70.32 %	1.59 %	59.26 %	1.51 %	60.57 %	0.32 %
SP	0.00 %	0.00 %	79.08 %	7.53 %	0.00 %	0.00 %

Table 4: Class-wise F1-scores and standard deviations on cross-lingual experiments

	Fi-Fi		Fr-Fr		Sv-Sv	
	F1	**Std.**	**F1**	**Std.**	**F1**	**Std.**
HI	64.02 %	1.94 %	58.81 %	0.59 %	70.70 %	4.56 %
ID	66.18 %	3.54 %	90.37 %	1.58 %	60.48 %	3.21 %
IN	58.68 %	1.59 %	74.00 %	0.40 %	87.79 %	0.29 %
IP	75.74 %	2.34 %	80.02 %	1.04 %	81.75 %	1.10 %
LY	–	–	66.67 %	0.00 %	0.00 %	0.00 %
NA	82.38 %	0.98 %	77.02 %	1.16 %	86.66 %	0.69 %
OP	67.10 %	2.05 %	66.23 %	3.08 %	75.37 %	1.66 %
SP	–	–	65.28 %	1.96 %	0.00 %	0.00 %

Table 5: Class-wise F1-scores and standard deviations on monolingual experiments

Narrative
News report / news blog, sports report, personal blog, historical article, fiction, travel blog, community blog, online article
Informational description
Description of a thing, encyclopedia article, research article, description of a person, information blog, FAQ, course material, legal terms / condition, report, job description
Opinion
Review, opinion blog, religious blogs/sermon, advice
Interactive discussion
Discussion forum, question-answer forum
How-to/Instructions
How-to/instruction, recipe
Informational Persuasion
Description with intent to sell, news+opinion blog / editorial
Lyrical
Songs, poem
Spoken
Interview, formal speech, TV transcript

Table 6: All register classes. Main registers are shown in bold.

Explaining and Improving BERT Performance on Lexical Semantic Change Detection

Severin Laicher, Sinan Kurtyigit, Dominik Schlechtweg, Jonas Kuhn and Sabine Schulte im Walde
Institute for Natural Language Processing, University of Stuttgart
{laichesn,kurtyisn,schlecdk,jonas,schulte}@ims.uni-stuttgart.de

Abstract

Type- and token-based embedding architectures are still competing in lexical semantic change detection. The recent success of type-based models in SemEval-2020 Task 1 has raised the question why the success of token-based models on a variety of other NLP tasks does not translate to our field. We investigate the influence of a range of variables on clusterings of BERT vectors and show that its low performance is largely due to orthographic information on the target word, which is encoded even in the higher layers of BERT representations. By reducing the influence of orthography we considerably improve BERT's performance.

1 Introduction

Lexical Semantic Change (LSC) Detection has drawn increasing attention in the past years (Kutuzov et al., 2018; Tahmasebi et al., 2018; Hengchen et al., 2021). Recently, SemEval-2020 Task 1 and the Italian follow-up task DIACR-Ita provided a multi-lingual evaluation framework to compare the variety of proposed model architectures (Schlechtweg et al., 2020; Basile et al., 2020). Both tasks demonstrated that type-based embeddings outperform token-based embeddings. This is surprising given that contextualised token-based approaches have achieved significant improvements over the static type-based approaches in several NLP tasks over the past years (Peters et al., 2018; Devlin et al., 2019).

In this study, we relate model results on LSC detection to results on the word sense disambiguation data set underlying SemEval-2020 Task 1. This allows us to test the performance of different methods more rigorously, and to thoroughly analyze results of clustering-based methods. We investigate the influence of a range of variables on clusterings of BERT vectors and show that its low performance is largely due to orthographic information on the target word which is encoded even in the higher layers of BERT representations. By reducing the influence of orthography on the target word while keeping the rest of the input in its natural form we considerably improve BERT's performance.

2 Related work

Traditional approaches for LSC detection are type-based (Dubossarsky et al., 2019; Schlechtweg et al., 2019). This means that not every word occurrence is considered individually (token-based); instead, a general vector representation that summarizes every occurrence of a word (including polysemous words) is created. The results of SemEval-2020 Task 1 and DIACR-Ita (Basile et al., 2020; Schlechtweg et al., 2020) demonstrated that overall type-based approaches (Asgari et al., 2020; Kaiser et al., 2020; Pražák et al., 2020) achieved better results than token-based approaches (Beck, 2020; Kutuzov and Giulianelli, 2020; Laicher et al., 2020). This is surprising, however, for two main reasons: (i) contextualized token-based approaches have significantly outperformed static type-based approaches in several NLP tasks over the past years (Ethayarajh, 2019). (ii) SemEval-2020 Task 1 and DIACR-Ita both include a subtask on binary change detection that requires to discover small sets of contextualized usages with the same sense. Type-based embeddings do not infer usage-based (or token-based) representations and are therefore not expected to be able to find such sets (Schlechtweg et al., 2020). Yet, they show better performance on binary change detection than clusterings of token-based embeddings (Kutuzov and Giulianelli, 2020).

3 Data and evaluation

We utilize the annotated English, German and Swedish datasets (ENG, GER, SWE) underlying

Proceedings of the 16th Conference of the European Chapter of the Associationfor Computational Linguistics: Student Research Workshop, pages 192–202
April 19 - 23, 2021. ©2021 Association for Computational Linguistics

SemEval-2020 Task 1 (Schlechtweg et al., 2020). Each dataset contains a list of target words and a set of usages per target word from two time periods, t_1 and t_2 (Schlechtweg et al., submitted). For each target word, a Word Usage Graph (WUG) was annotated, where nodes represent word usages, and weights on edges represent the (median) semantic relatedness judgment of a pair of usages, as exemplified in (1) and (2) for the target word *plane*.

(1) Von Hassel replied that he had such faith in the **plane** that he had no hesitation about allowing his only son to become a Starfighter pilot.

(2) This point, where the rays pass through the perspective **plane**, is called the seat of their representation.

The final WUGs were clustered with a variation of correlation clustering (Bansal et al., 2004) (see Figure 1 in Appendix A, left) and split into two subgraphs representing nodes from t_1 and t_2 respectively (middle and right). Clusters are interpreted as senses, and changes in clusters over time are interpreted as lexical semantic change. Schlechtweg et al. then infer a binary change value $B(w)$ for Subtask 1 and a graded change value $G(w)$ for Subtask 2 from the two resulting time-specific clusterings for each target word w.

The evaluation of the shared task participants only relied on the change values derived from the annotation, while the annotated usages were not released. We gained access to the data set, which enables us to relate performances in change detection to the underlying data.[1] We can also analyze the inferred clusterings with respect to bias factors, and compare their influence on inferred vs. gold clusterings. A further advantage of having access to the underlying data is that it reflects more accurately the annotated change scores. In SemEval-2020 Task 1 the annotated usages were mixed with additional usages to create the training corpora for the shared task, possibly introducing noise on the derived change scores.

4 Models and Measures

BERT Bidirectional Encoder Representations from Transformers (BERT, Devlin et al., 2019) is a transformer-based neural language model designed to find contextualised representations for text by analysing left and right contexts. The base version processes text in 12 different layers. In each layer, a contextualized token vector representation is created for every word. A layer, or a combination of multiple layers (we use the average), serves as a representation for a token. For every target word, we feed the usages from the SemEval data set into BERT and use the respective pre-trained cased base model to create token embeddings.[2]

Clustering LSC can be detected by clustering the token vectors from t_1 and t_2 into sets of usages with similar meanings, and then comparing these clusters over time (cf. Schütze, 1998; Navigli, 2009). This section introduces the clustering algorithms and clustering performance measures that we used. **Agglomerative Clustering** (AGL) is a hierarchical clustering algorithm starting with each element in an individual cluster. It then repeatedly merges those two clusters whose merging maximizes a predefined criterion. We use Ward's method, where clusters with the lowest loss of information are merged (Ward Jr, 1963). Following Giulianelli et al. (2020) and Martinc et al. (2020a), we estimate the number of clusters k with the **Silhouette Method** (Rousseeuw, 1987): we perform a cluster analysis for each $2 \leq k \leq 10$ and calculate the silhouette index for each k. The number of clusters with the largest index is used for the final clustering. The **Jensen-Shannon Distance** (JSD) measures the difference between two probability distributions (Lin, 1991; Donoso and Sanchez, 2017). We convert two time specific clusterings into probability distribution P and Q and measure their distance $JSD(P, Q)$ to obtain graded change values (Giulianelli et al., 2020; Kutuzov and Giulianelli, 2020). If P and Q are very similar, the JSD returns a value close to 0. If the distributions are very different, the JSD returns a value close to 1. **Spearman's Rank-Order Correlation Coefficient** ρ measures the strength and the direction of the relationship between two variables (Bolboaca and Jäntschi, 2006) by correlating the rank order of two variables. Its values range from -1 to 1, where 1 denotes a perfect positive relationship between the two variables, and -1 a perfect negative relationship. 0 means that the two variables are not related.

[1] We had no access to the Latin annotated data. For the ENG clustering experiments we use the full annotated resource containing three additional graphs (Schlechtweg et al., submitted).

[2] We first clean the GER usages by replacing historical with modern characters.

Cluster bias We perform a detailed analysis on what the inferred clusters actually reflect. We test hypotheses on *word form*, *sentence position*, *number of proper names* and *corpus*. The influence strength of each of these variables on the clusters is measured by the **Adjusted Rand Index** (ARI) (Hubert and Arabie, 1985) between the inferred cluster labels for each test sentence and a labeling for each test sentence derived from the respective variable. For the variable *word form*, we assign the same label to each use where the target word has the same orthographic form (same string). If ARI = 1, then the inferred clusters contain only sentences where the target word has the same form. For *sentence position* each sentence receives label 0, if the target word is one of the first three words of the sentence, 2, if the target word is one of the last three words, else 1.[3] For *proper names* a sentence receives label 0, if no proper names are in the sentence, 1, if one proper name occurs, else 2.[4] The hypothesis that proper names may influence the clustering was suggested in Martinc et al. (2020b). For *corpora*, a sentence is labeled 0, if it occurs in the first target corpus, else 1.

Average measures Given two sets of token vectors V_1 and V_2 from t_1 and t_2, **Average Pairwise Distance** (APD) is calculated by randomly picking n vectors from both sets, calculating their pairwise cosine distances $d(x, y)$ where $x \in V_1$ and $y \in V_2$ and averaging over these. (Schlechtweg et al., 2018; Giulianelli et al., 2020). We determine n as the minimum size of V_1 and V_2. **APD-OLD/NEW** measure the average of pairwise distances within V_1 and V_2, respectively. They are calculated as the average distance of max. $10,000$ randomly sampled unique combinations of vectors from either V_1 or V_2. **COS** is calculated as the cosine distance of the respective mean vectors for V_1 and V_2 (Kutuzov and Giulianelli, 2020).

5 Results

5.1 Clustering

Because of the high computational load, we apply the clustering only to the ENG and the GER part of the SemEval data set. For this, we use BERT to create token vectors and cluster them with AGL, as described above. We then perform a detailed analysis of what the clusters reflect.[5]

We report a subset of the clustering experiment results in Table 1, the complete results are provided in Appendix B. Table 1 shows JSD performance on graded change (ρ), clustering performance (ARI) as well as the ARI scores for the influence factors introduced above, across BERT layers. For each influence factor we add two baselines: (i) The random baseline measures the ARI score of the influence factor using random cluster labels, and (ii) the actual baseline measures the ARI score between the true cluster labels and the influence factor. In other words, (i) and (ii) respectively answer the question of how strong the influence factor is by chance, and how strong it is according to the human annotation. The values of the two baselines are crucial: If an influence factor has an ARI score greater than both baselines, the clustering reflects the influence factor more than expected. If additionally the influence factor has an ARI score greater than the actual performance ARI score, the clustering reflects the partitioning according to the influence factor more than the clustering derived from human annotations.

Word form bias As explained above, the word form influence measures how strongly the inferred clusterings represent the orthographic forms of the target word. Table 1 shows that for both GER and ENG the form bias of the raw token vectors (column 'Token') is extremely high and always yields the highest influence score for each layer combination of BERT. Additionally, the influence of the word form is significantly higher when using lower layers of BERT. This fits well with the observations of Jawahar et al. (2019) that the lower layers of BERT capture surface features, the middle layers capture syntactic features and the higher layers capture semantic features of the text. With the first layer of BERT the sentences are almost exclusively (.9) clustered according to the form of the target word (e.g. plural/singular division). Even in the higher layers word form influence is considerable in both languages (layer 12: $\approx .4$). This strongly overlays the semantic information encoded in the vectors, as we can see in the low ρ and ARI scores, which are negatively correlated with word form

[3] We assume that especially the beginning and ending of a sentence have a strong influence.

[4] The influence of proper names is only measured for ENG, since no POS-tagged data was readily available for GER.

[5] We also run most of our experiments with k-means (Forgy, 1965). Both algorithms performed similarly with a slight advantage for AGL. We therefore only report the results achieved using AGL.

	Layer	Token	Lemma	TokLem
ρ	1	-.141	-.033	.100
	12	.205	.154	.168
	9-12	.325	**.345**	.293
ARI	1	.022	.041	.045
	12	.116	.111	.158
	9-12	.150	.159	**.163**
Form	1	**.907**	.014	.014
	12	**.389**	**.018**	**.077**
	9-12	**.334**	**.018**	**.051**
Position	1	.001	**.026**	**.024**
	12	**.012**	**.012**	**.015**
	9-12	.002	**.007**	**.003**
Corpora	1	**.019**	**.021**	**.033**
	12	**.078**	**.056**	**.082**
	9-12	**.056**	**.044**	**.063**
Names	1	-.007	.010	.010
	12	**.025**	**.027**	**.033**
	9-12	.019	**.022**	**.026**

	Layer	Token	Lemma	TokLem
ρ	1	-.265	-.062	-.170
	12	.123	.427	**.624**
	9-12	.122	.420	.533
ARI	1	.033	.002	.003
	12	.119	.159	**.161**
	9-12	.155	.142	.154
Form	1	**.706**	.024	.004
	12	**.439**	**.056**	**.150**
	9-12	**.420**	**.047**	**.094**
Position	1	.005	**.023**	**.027**
	12	-.002	.005	-.002
	9-12	**.009**	**.018**	**.012**
Corpora	1	.074	.003	.005
	12	**.110**	**.095**	**.096**
	9-12	**.107**	.068	**.089**
Names	1	-	-	-
	12	-	-	-
	9-12	-	-	-

Table 1: Overview of English clustering scores (left) and German clustering scores (right). Bold font indicates best scores for ρ and ARI (top) or scores above all corresponding baselines for influence variables (bottom).

influence.[6]

The word form bias seems to be lower in GER than in ENG (layer 1: .7 vs. .9). However, this is misleading, as our approach to measure word form influence does not capture cases where vectors cluster according to subword forms as in the case of *Ackergerät*. Its word forms differ as to whether they are written with an 'h' or not, as in *Ackergerät* vs. *Ackergeräth*. As a manual inspection shows this is strongly reflected in the inferred clustering. However, these forms then further subdivide into inflected forms such as *Ackergeräthe* and *Ackergeräthes*, which is reflected in our influence variable. For these cases, our approach tends to underestimate the influence of the variable.

In order to reduce the influence of word form we experiment with two pre-processing approaches: (i) We feed BERT with lemmatised sentences (Lemma) instead of raw ones. (ii) We only replace the target word in every sentence with its lemma (TokLem). TokLem is motivated by the fact that BERT is trained on raw text. Thus, we assume that BERT is more familiar with non-lemmatised sentences and therefore expect it to work better on raw text. In order to continue working with non-lemmatised sentences we only remove the target word form bias by exchanging the target word with its lemma.

As we can see in Table 1, lemmatisation strongly reduces the influence of word form, as expected.[7] Accordingly, ρ and ARI improve. However, it also leads to deterioration in some cases. Also, TokLem reduces the influence of word form and in most cases yields the overall maximum performance. The ARI scores for both languages are similar ($\approx$ .160) while the ρ performance varies very strongly between languages, achieving a very high score for GER (.624).

Replacing the target word by its lemma form seems to shift the word form influence in the different layers: Especially for GER, layers 1 and 1+12 show the highest influences (.706 and .687) with Token (see also Appendix B). In combination with TokLem, both layers are influenced the least (.004 and .046). For ENG we see the same effect for layer 1.

Other bias factors We can see in Table 1 that most influences are above-baseline. As explained above, the word form bias heavily decreases using higher layers of BERT. For all other influences the bias increases when using high layers of BERT.

[6]Note that it is very difficult to reach high ARI scores because ARI incorporates chance.

[7]In some cases it is however above the baselines, indicating that word form is correlated with other sentence features.

This may be because decreasing the word form influence reveals the existence of further –less strong but still relevant– influences. The same is observable with the Lemma and TokLem results, since there the form influence is decreased or even eliminated. While for ENG the influence scores mostly increase using Lemma and TokLem, for GER only the position influence increases, while corpora influence decreases. This is probably because the corpora influence is to some extent related to word form, which often reflects time-specific orthography as in *Ackergeräth* vs. *Ackergerät*, where the spelling with the "h" mostly occurs in the old corpus.

Influence of position and proper names seems to be less important but the respective scores are still most of the times higher than the baselines. So overall the reflection of the two corpora seems to be the most influential factor apart from word form. Often the corpus bias is almost as high as the actual ARI score.

5.2 Average Measures

For the average measures we perform experiments for all three languages (ENG, GER, SWE).

Layers Because we observe a strong variation of influence scores with layers, as seen in Section (5.1), we test different layer combinations for the average measures. The following are considered: 1, 12, 1+12, 1+2+3+4 (1-4), 9+10+11+12 (9-12). As shown in Table 2, the choice of the layers strongly affects the performance. We see that for APD the higher layer combinations 12 and 9-12 perform best across all three languages, while the latter is slightly better (.571, .407 and .554). Interestingly, these two are the only layer combinations that do not include layer 1. All three layer combinations that include layer 1 are significantly worse in comparison. While COS performs best with layer combination 1-4 for ENG (.390), for GER and SWE we see a similar trend as with APD. Again, the higher layer combinations perform better than the other three, which all include layer 1. For GER layer combination 12 (.472) performs best, while 9-12 yields the highest result for SWE (.183). Our results are mostly in line with the findings of Kutuzov and Giulianelli (2020) that APD works best on ENG and SWE, while COS yields the best scores for GER.

Pre-processing As with the clustering, we try to improve the performance of the average measures by using the two above-described pre-processing approaches. We perform experiments only for three layer combinations in order to reduce the complexity: (i) 12 and (ii) 9-12 perform best and are therefore obvious choices. (iii) From the remaining combinations 1+12 shows the most stable performance across measures and languages. Table 3 shows the performance of the pre-processings (Lemma, TokLem) over these three combinations. We can see that both APD and COS perform slightly worse for ENG when paired with a pre-processing (exception to this is 1+12 Lemma). In contrast, GER profits heavily: While APD with layer combinations 12 and 9-12 performs slightly worse with Lemma, and slightly better with TokLem, we observe an enormous performance boost for layer combination 1+12 (.643 Lemma and .731 TokLem). We achieve a similar boost for all three layer combinations with COS as a measure. We reach a top performance of .755 for layer 12 with TokLem. SWE does not benefit from Lemma. We observe large performance decreases, with the exception of combination 1+12 (APD). The APD performance of layers 12 and 9-12 is slightly worse with TokLem. However, layers 1+12, which performed poorly without pre-processing, reaches peak performance of .602 with TokLem. All COS performances increase with TokLem, but are still well below the APD counterparts. The general picture is that GER and SWE profit strongly from TokLem.

Layer	APD			COS		
	ENG	GER	SWE	ENG	GER	SWE
1	.297	.205	.228	.246	.246	.089
12	.566	.359	.529	.339	**.472**	.134
1+12	.455	.316	.280	.365	.373	.077
1-4	.431	.227	.355	**.390**	.297	.079
9-12	**.571**	**.407**	**.554**	.365	.446	**.183**

Table 2: Token performance for different layer combinations across languages.

Word form bias In order to better understand the effects of layer combinations and pre-processing, we compute correlations between word form and model predictions. To lessen the complexity, only layer combination 1+12 (which performed worst overall and includes layer 1), layer combination 9-12 (which performed best overall) in combination with Token and the superior TokLem are considered. The results are presented in Table 4. We observe similar findings for all three languages. The correlation between word form and APD pre-

		Layer	Token	Lemma	TokLem
ENG	APD	12	**.566**	.483	.494
		1+12	.455	**.483**	.455
		9-12	**.571**	.493	.547
	COS	12	**.339**	.251	.331
		1+12	**.365**	.239	.193
		9-12	**.365**	.286	.353
GER	APD	12	.359	.303	**.456**
		1+12	.316	.643	**.731**
		9-12	.407	.305	**.516**
	COS	12	.472	.693	**.755**
		1+12	.373	.698	**.729**
		9-12	.446	.689	**.726**
SWE	APD	12	**.529**	.214	.505
		1+12	.280	.368	**.602**
		9-12	**.554**	.218	.531
	COS	12	.134	-.019	**.285**
		1+12	.077	.012	**.082**
		9-12	.183	-.002	**.284**

Table 3: Performance of pre-processing variants for three layer combinations.

		Layer	Token	TokLem
ENG	APD	1+12	.613	-.026
		9-12	.068	.090
	COS	1+12	.246	-.062
		9-12	.020	.004
GER	APD	1+12	.554	.271
		9-12	.292	.105
	COS	1+12	.387	-.017
		9-12	.205	-.008
SWE	APD	1+12	.730	.176
		9-12	.237	.048
	COS	1+12	.429	-.031
		9-12	.277	-.035

Table 4: Correlations of word form and predicted change scores.

dictions is strong (.613, .554 and .730) for layers 1+12 without pre-processing. The correlation is much weaker with layers 9-12 (.068, .292 and .237) or TokLem (−.026, .105 and .176). This is in line with the performance development that also increases using layers 9-12 or TokLem. Both approaches (different layers, pre-processing) result in a considerable performance increase as described previously. Using layer combination 9-12 with TokLem further decreases the correlation (with the exception of ENG). However, the performance is better when only one of these approaches is used. The correlation between word form and COS model predictions is weaker overall (.246, .387 and .429). We see a similar correlation development as for APD, however this time the performance of ENG does not profit from the lowered bias (see Table 3). Both GER and SWE see a performance increase when the word form bias is lowered by either using layers 9-12 or TokLem.

Polysemy bias The SemEval data sets are strongly biased by polysemy, i.e., a perfect model measuring the true synchronic target word polysemy in either t_1 or t_2 could reach above .7 performance (Schlechtweg et al., 2020). We use APD-OLD and APD-NEW (see Section 4) to see whether we can exploit this fact to create a purely synchronic polysemy model with high performance. We achieve moderate performances for ENG and GER (.274/.332 and .321/.450 respectively) and a good performance for SWE (.550/.562). While the performance for ENG and GER is clearly below the high-scores, the performance is high for a measure that lacks any kind of diachronic information. And in the case of SWE, the performance of both APD-OLD and APD-NEW is just barely below the high-scores (cf. Table 3). Note that regular APD (in contrast to COS) is, in theory, affected by polysemy (Schlechtweg et al., 2018). It is thus possible that APD's high performance stems at least partly from this polysemy bias. This is supported by comparing the SWE results of APD and COS in Table 3: COS is weakly influenced by polysemy and performs poorly, while APD has higher performance, but only slightly above the purely synchronic measures APD-OLD/NEW.

6 Conclusion

BERT token representations are influenced by various factors, but most strongly by target word form. Even in higher layers this influence persists. By removing the form bias we were able to considerably improve the performance across languages. Although we reach comparably high performance with clustering for graded change detection in German, average measures still perform better than cluster-based approaches. The reasons for this are still unclear and should be addressed in future research. Furthermore, we used BERT without fine-tuning. It would be interesting to see how fine-tuning interacts with influence variables and whether it further improves performance.

References

Ehsaneddin Asgari, Christoph Ringlstetter, and Hinrich Schütze. 2020. EmbLexChange at SemEval-2020 Task 1: Unsupervised Embedding-based Detection of Lexical Semantic Changes. In *Proceedings of the 14th International Workshop on Semantic Evaluation*, Barcelona, Spain. Association for Computational Linguistics.

Nikhil Bansal, Avrim Blum, and Shuchi Chawla. 2004. Correlation clustering. *Machine Learning*, 56(1-3):89–113.

Pierpaolo Basile, Annalina Caputo, Tommaso Caselli, Pierluigi Cassotti, and Rossella Varvara. 2020. Overview of the EVALITA 2020 Diachronic Lexical Semantics (DIACR-Ita) Task. In *Proceedings of the 7th evaluation campaign of Natural Language Processing and Speech tools for Italian (EVALITA 2020)*, Online. CEUR.org.

Christin Beck. 2020. DiaSense at SemEval-2020 Task 1: Modeling sense change via pre-trained BERT embeddings. In *Proceedings of the 14th International Workshop on Semantic Evaluation*, Barcelona, Spain. Association for Computational Linguistics.

Sorana-Daniela Bolboaca and Lorentz Jäntschi. 2006. Pearson versus spearman, kendall's tau correlation analysis on structure-activity relationships of biologic active compounds. *Leonardo Journal of Sciences*, 5(9):179–200.

Jacob Devlin, Ming-Wei Chang, Kenton Lee, and Kristina Toutanova. 2019. BERT: Pre-training of deep bidirectional transformers for language understanding. In *Proceedings of the 2019 Conference of the North American Chapter of the Association for Computational Linguistics: Human Language Technologies, Volume 1 (Long and Short Papers)*, pages 4171–4186, Minneapolis, Minnesota. Association for Computational Linguistics.

Gonzalo Donoso and David Sanchez. 2017. Dialectometric analysis of language variation in twitter. In *Proceedings of the Fourth Workshop on NLP for Similar Languages, Varieties and Dialects*, pages 16–25, Valencia, Spain.

Haim Dubossarsky, Simon Hengchen, Nina Tahmasebi, and Dominik Schlechtweg. 2019. Time-Out: Temporal Referencing for Robust Modeling of Lexical Semantic Change. In *Proceedings of the 57th Annual Meeting of the Association for Computational Linguistics*, pages 457–470, Florence, Italy. Association for Computational Linguistics.

Kawin Ethayarajh. 2019. How contextual are contextualized word representations? comparing the geometry of BERT, ELMo, and GPT-2 embeddings. In *Proceedings of the 2019 Conference on Empirical Methods in Natural Language Processing and the 9th International Joint Conference on Natural Language Processing (EMNLP-IJCNLP)*, pages 55–65, Hong Kong, China. Association for Computational Linguistics.

Edward W. Forgy. 1965. Cluster analysis of multivariate data: Efficiency vs. interpretability of classifications. *Biometrics*, 21:768–780.

Mario Giulianelli, Marco Del Tredici, and Raquel Fernández. 2020. Analysing lexical semantic change with contextualised word representations. In *Proceedings of the 58th Annual Meeting of the Association for Computational Linguistics*, pages 3960–3973, Online. Association for Computational Linguistics.

Simon Hengchen, Nina Tahmasebi, Dominik Schlechtweg, and Haim Dubossarsky. 2021. Challenges for computational lexical semantic change. In Nina Tahmasebi, Lars Borin, Adam Jatowt, Yang Xu, and Simon Hengchen, editors, *Computational Approaches to Semantic Change*, volume Language Variation, chapter 11. Language Science Press, Berlin.

Lawrence Hubert and Phipps Arabie. 1985. Comparing partitions. *Journal of Classification*, 2:193–218.

Ganesh Jawahar, Benoît Sagot, and Djamé Seddah. 2019. What does BERT learn about the structure of language? In *Proceedings of the 57th Annual Meeting of the Association for Computational Linguistics*, pages 3651–3657, Florence, Italy. Association for Computational Linguistics.

Jens Kaiser, Dominik Schlechtweg, and Sabine Schulte im Walde. 2020. OP-IMS @ DIACR-Ita: Back to the Roots: SGNS+OP+CD still rocks Semantic Change Detection. In *Proceedings of the 7th evaluation campaign of Natural Language Processing and Speech tools for Italian (EVALITA 2020)*, Online. CEUR.org. Winning Submission!

Andrey Kutuzov and Mario Giulianelli. 2020. UiO-UvA at SemEval-2020 Task 1: Contextualised Embeddings for Lexical Semantic Change Detection. In *Proceedings of the 14th International Workshop on Semantic Evaluation*, Barcelona, Spain. Association for Computational Linguistics.

Andrey Kutuzov, Lilja Øvrelid, Terrence Szymanski, and Erik Velldal. 2018. Diachronic word embeddings and semantic shifts: a survey. In *Proceedings of the 27th International Conference on Computational Linguistics*, pages 1384–1397, Santa Fe, New Mexico, USA. Association for Computational Linguistics.

Severin Laicher, Gioia Baldissin, Enrique Castaneda, Dominik Schlechtweg, and Sabine Schulte im Walde. 2020. CL-IMS @ DIACR-Ita: Volente o Nolente: BERT does not outperform SGNS on Semantic Change Detection. In *Proceedings of the 7th evaluation campaign of Natural Language Processing and Speech tools for Italian (EVALITA 2020)*, Online. CEUR.org.

Jianhua Lin. 1991. Divergence measures based on the shannon entropy. *IEEE Transactions on Information Theory*, 37:145–151.

Matej Martinc, Syrielle Montariol, Elaine Zosa, and Lidia Pivovarova. 2020a. Capturing evolution in word usage: Just add more clusters? In *Companion Proceedings of the Web Conference 2020*, WWW '20, pages 343—-349, New York, NY, USA. Association for Computing Machinery.

Matej Martinc, Syrielle Montariol, Elaine Zosa, and Lidia Pivovarova. 2020b. Discovery Team at SemEval-2020 Task 1: Context-sensitive Embeddings not Always Better Than Static for Semantic Change Detection. In *Proceedings of the 14th International Workshop on Semantic Evaluation*, Barcelona, Spain. Association for Computational Linguistics.

Roberto Navigli. 2009. Word sense disambiguation: a survey. *ACM Computing Surveys*, 41(2):1–69.

Matthew Peters, Mark Neumann, Mohit Iyyer, Matt Gardner, Christopher Clark, Kenton Lee, and Luke Zettlemoyer. 2018. Deep contextualized word representations. In *Proceedings of the 2018 Conference of the North American Chapter of the Association for Computational Linguistics: Human Language Technologies*, pages 2227–2237, New Orleans, LA, USA.

Ondřej Pražák, Pavel Přibákň, Stephen Taylor, and Jakub Sido. 2020. UWB at SemEval-2020 Task 1: Lexical Semantic Change Detection. In *Proceedings of the 14th International Workshop on Semantic Evaluation*, Barcelona, Spain. Association for Computational Linguistics.

Peter J Rousseeuw. 1987. Silhouettes: A graphical aid to the interpretation and validation of cluster analysis. *Journal of computational and applied mathematics*, 20:53–65.

Dominik Schlechtweg, Anna Hätty, Marco del Tredici, and Sabine Schulte im Walde. 2019. A Wind of Change: Detecting and Evaluating Lexical Semantic Change across Times and Domains. In *Proceedings of the 57th Annual Meeting of the Association for Computational Linguistics*, pages 732–746, Florence, Italy. Association for Computational Linguistics.

Dominik Schlechtweg, Barbara McGillivray, Simon Hengchen, Haim Dubossarsky, and Nina Tahmasebi. 2020. SemEval-2020 task 1: Unsupervised Lexical Semantic Change Detection. In *Proceedings of the 14th International Workshop on Semantic Evaluation*, Barcelona, Spain. Association for Computational Linguistics.

Dominik Schlechtweg, Sabine Schulte im Walde, and Stefanie Eckmann. 2018. Diachronic Usage Relatedness (DURel): A framework for the annotation of lexical semantic change. In *Proceedings of the 2018 Conference of the North American Chapter of the Association for Computational Linguistics: Human Language Technologies*, pages 169–174, New Orleans, Louisiana.

Dominik Schlechtweg, Nina Tahmasebi, Simon Hengchen, Haim Dubossarsky, and Barbara McGillivray. submitted. DWUG: A large Resource of Diachronic Word Usage Graphs in Four Languages.

Hinrich Schütze. 1998. Automatic word sense discrimination. *Computational Linguistics*, 24(1):97–123.

Nina Tahmasebi, Lars Borin, and Adam Jatowt. 2018. Survey of Computational Approaches to Diachronic Conceptual Change. *arXiv e-prints*.

Joe H Ward Jr. 1963. Hierarchical grouping to optimize an objective function. *Journal of the American Statistical Association*, 58(301):236–244.

A Word Usage Graphs

Please find an example of a Word Usage Graph (WUG) for the German word *Eintagsfliege* in Figure 1 (Schlechtweg et al., 2020, submitted).

B Extended clustering performances and influences

Please find the full results of our cluster experiments in Tables 5 and 6.

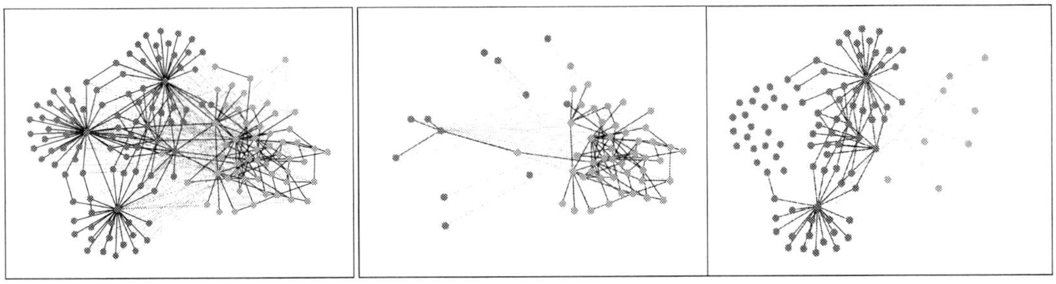

full t_1 t_2

Figure 1: Word Usage Graph of German *Eintagsfliege*. Nodes represent uses of the target word. Edge weights represent the median of relatedness judgments between uses (**black**/gray lines for **high**/low edge weights). Colors indicate clusters (senses) inferred from the full graph. $D_1 = (12, 45, 0, 1)$, $D_2 = (85, 6, 1, 1)$, $B(w) = 0$ and $G(w) = 0.66$.

		Layer	Token	Lemma	TokLem
Performance	ρ	1	-.141	-.033	.100
		12	.205	.154	.168
		1+12	-.316	.130	.081
		6+7	.075	-.103	.017
		9-12	.325	**.345**	.293
	ARI	1	.022	.041	.045
		12	.116	.111	.158
		1+12	.022	.141	.149
		6+7	.119	.111	.145
		9-12	.150	.159	**.163**

		Layer	Token	Lemma	TokLem
Performance	ρ	1	-.265	-.062	-.170
		12	.123	.427	**.624**
		1+12	-.252	.235	.401
		6+7	.002	.464	.320
		9-12	.122	.420	.533
	ARI	1	.033	.002	.003
		12	.119	.159	**.161**
		1+12	.037	.064	.080
		6+7	.101	.158	.152
		9-12	.155	.142	.154

Table 5: English clustering performance (left) and German clustering performance (right).

		Layer	Token	Lemma	TokLem
Form	Influence	1	.907	.014	.014
		12	.389	.018	.077
		1+12	.881	.020	.057
		6+7	.572	.013	.028
		9-12	.334	.018	.051
	Random	1	.002	.002	.002
		12	-.001	.001	-.001
		1+12	-.002	-.001	-.001
		6+7	.001	.002	.001
		9-12	-.001	-.001	-.002
	Baseline	1	.017	.017	.017
		12	.017	.017	.017
		1+12	.017	.017	.017
		6+7	.017	.017	.017
		9-12	.017	.017	.017
Position	Influence	1	.001	.026	.024
		12	.012	.012	.015
		1+12	-.001	.019	.007
		6+7	-.002	.018	-.003
		9-12	.002	.007	.003
	Random	1	.001	.003	.001
		12	.001	-.001	-.001
		1+12	-.001	-.001	-.001
		6+7	.001	-.001	-.001
		9-12	.001	.001	-.001
	Baseline	1	-.002	-.002	-.002
		12	-.002	-.002	-.002
		1+12	-.002	-.002	-.002
		6+7	-.002	-.002	-.002
		9-12	-.002	-.002	-.002
Corpora	Influence	1	.019	.021	.033
		12	.078	.056	.082
		1+12	.027	.050	.074
		6+7	.034	.035	.050
		9-12	.056	.044	.063
	Random	1	.001	-.001	.003
		12	.001	.001	.001
		1+12	-.001	.001	.001
		6+7	.001	.001	.002
		9-12	.002	.001	.002
	Baseline	1	.018	.018	.018
		12	.018	.018	.018
		1+12	.018	.018	.018
		6+7	.018	.018	.018
		9-12	.018	.018	.018
Names	Influence	1	-.007	.010	.010
		12	.025	.027	.033
		1+12	.018	.022	.027
		6+7	.012	.016	.027
		9-12	.019	.022	.026
	Random	1	-.001	-.002	-.002
		12	-.001	.001	.001
		1+12	-.001	.001	-.001
		6+7	-.001	.001	.001
		9-12	-.001	-.001	.001
	Baseline	1	.019	.019	.019
		12	.019	.019	.019
		1+12	.019	.019	.019
		6+7	.019	.019	.019
		9-12	.019	.019	.019

		Layer	Token	Lemma	TokLem
Form	Influence	1	.706	.024	.004
		12	.439	.056	.150
		1+12	.687	.039	.046
		6+7	.503	.050	.050
		9-12	.420	.047	.094
	Random	1	-.001	-.002	.020
		12	-.001	.001	.021
		1+12	-.001	-.001	.020
		6+7	.002	.001	.019
		9-12	.001	-.001	.021
	Baseline	1	.036	.036	.036
		12	.036	.036	.036
		1+12	.036	.036	.036
		6+7	.036	.036	.036
		9-12	.036	.036	.036
Position	Influence	1	.005	.023	.027
		12	-.002	.005	-.002
		1+12	.002	.021	.013
		6+7	.010	.020	.018
		9-12	.009	.018	.012
	Random	1	.001	.001	.001
		12	.001	-.001	.001
		1+12	-.001	-.001	.002
		6+7	-.001	.001	.001
		9-12	-.001	.001	.001
	Baseline	1	.005	.005	.005
		12	.005	.005	.005
		1+12	.005	.005	.005
		6+7	.005	.005	.005
		9-12	.005	.005	.005
Corpora	Influence	1	.074	.003	.005
		12	.110	.095	.096
		1+12	.077	.024	.052
		6+7	.101	.058	.075
		9-12	.107	.068	.089
	Random	1	-.001	-.001	.001
		12	.001	-.001	.001
		1+12	-.001	.001	.002
		6+7	-.001	.001	-.001
		9-12	-.001	.001	-.001
	Baseline	1	.083	.083	.083
		12	.083	.083	.083
		1+12	.083	.083	.083
		6+7	.083	.083	.083
		9-12	.083	.083	.083
Names	Influence	1	-	-	-
		12	-	-	-
		1+12	-	-	-
		6+7	-	-	-
		9-12	-	-	-
	Random	1	-	-	-
		12	-	-	-
		1+12	-	-	-
		6+7	-	-	-
		9-12	-	-	-
	Baseline	1	-	-	-
		12	-	-	-
		1+12	-	-	-
		6+7	-	-	-
		9-12	-	-	-

Table 6: English clustering influences (left) and German clustering influences (right).

Why Find the Right *One*?

Payal Khullar
Language Technologies Research Centre
International Institute of Information Technology Hyderabad
Gachibowli, Hyderabad, India.
payal.khullar@research.iiit.ac.in

Abstract

The present paper investigates the impact of the anaphoric one words in English on the Neural Machine Translation (NMT) process using English-Hindi as source and target language pair. As expected, the experimental results show that the state-of-the-art Google English-Hindi NMT system achieves significantly poorly on sentences containing anaphoric *ones* as compared to the sentences containing regular, non-anaphoric *ones*. But, more importantly, we note that amongst the anaphoric words, the noun class is clearly much harder for NMT than the determinatives. This reaffirms the linguistic disparity of the two phenomenon in recent theoretical syntactic literature, despite the obvious surface similarities.

1 Introduction

English has three distinct lexemes spelled as one– the regular third person indefinite pronoun, such as in (1); the indefinite cardinal numeral (determinative), such as in (2); and regular common count noun, such as in (3).

1. One must obey the laws of the state at all times.
2. Could you pass me one one glass of water here.
3. It is important that we take care of our loved ones.

A visible difference in their orthographic base form is not observable. However, these can be totally differentiated on the basis of their morphological, syntactic, and semantic functions in the language. Note that the examples presented in (1), (2) and (3) are non-anaphoric one words. Coming to the anaphoric class of *one*– we have two subtypes. The first one belongs to the determinative category, as seen in (4); and the second one is a noun, as in (5).

4. I bought three red glasses, but she bought only one.
5. After looking at all the glasses, I decided to buy this small one.

As expected, the determinative anaphoric ones behave like a determiner, and the one-anaphora behave like nouns in a sentence. Note that the plural form of the determinative one in example (4) is *some*, but that of one-anaphora in (5) is *ones*. They are also different with respect to the kind of antecedents they take. The constituent whose repetition the determinative anaphora avoids is the whole NP, *a glass*. But in case of one-anaphora, it is the noun head optionally with one or more of its modifiers *red glass*, but never the whole NP (Payne et al., 2013).

Like other cohesive devices like pronouns and ellipsis, anaphoric ones make language less redundant and more engaging (Menzel, 2017; Mitkov, 1999; Halliday and Hasan, 1976). Resolving the information encoded in such structures is not hard for humans as they can easily disambiguate meanings from linguistic or extralinguistic context, cognitive commonsense extension as well as logical reasoning (Chen, 2016). However, all of this is not that straightforward for a machine. In fact, anaphoric ones can potentially present a special challenge for Machine Translation (MT) since the meaning of the word does not come from its most frequent usage as a cardinal number, but instead relies on its context, thereby becoming unavailable overtly at the surface syntax for text processing.

2 Previous Work

The determinative anaphoric ones have been discussed majorly as an instance of noun ellipsis, nominal ellipsis or noun phrase ellipsis (NPE) in linguistics (Halliday and Hasan, 1976; Dalrymple et al., 1991b; Lobeck, 1995; Lappin, 1996; Hobbs and Kehler, 1997; Hardt, 1999; Johnson,

Proceedings of the 16th Conference of the European Chapter of the Associationfor Computational Linguistics: Student Research Workshop, pages 203–208
April 19 - 23, 2021. ©2021 Association for Computational Linguistics

2001; Wijnen et al., 2003; Merchant, 2004; Frazier, 2008; Chung et al., 2010; Merchant, 2010; Goksun et al., 2010; Gunther, 2011; Rouveret, 2012; Lindenbergh et al., 2015; van Craenenbroeck and Merchant, 2013; Park, 2017; Hyams et al., 2017; Kim et al., 2019). One-anaphora, on the other hand, has been referred to as noun anaphora, one-insertion, one-substitution and pronominalization (Menzel, 2017, 2014; Kayne, 2015; Hankamer and Sag, 2015; Payne et al., 2013; Corver and van Koppen, 2011; Gunther, 2011; Culicover and Jackendoff, 2005; Akhtar et al., 2004; Cowper, 1992; Luperfoy, 1991; Dalrymple et al., 1991a; Dahl, 1985; Radford, 1981; Baker, 1978; Halliday and Hasan, 1976; Bresnan, 1971).

To the best of our knowledge, the earliest computational approach to one-anaphora comes from Gardiner (2003), who presents several linguistically-motivated heuristics to distinguish one-anaphora from other non-anaphoric uses of one in English, and later from Ng (2005) that uses Gardiner's heuristics as features to train a simple Machine Learning (ML) model. Another seminal work on the anaphoric *one* comes from Recasens et al. (2016) where it has been treated as one of the several sense anaphoric relations in English. The authors create sAnaNotes corpus where they annotate one third of the OntoNotes corpus for sense Anaphora. They use a Support Vector Machine (SVM) classifier - LIBLINEAR implementation (Fan et al., 2008) along with 31 lexical and syntactic features, to distinguish between the anaphoric and the non-anaphoric class. Trained and tested on one-third of the OntoNotes dataset annotated as the SAnaNotes corpus, their system achieves 61.80% F1 score on the detection of all anaphoric relations, including one-anaphora. The detection and resolution of the determinative one anaphor, on the other hand, has been carried out as a part of computational research on noun ellipsis (Khullar et al., 2020b, 2019).

Recent research shows that discourse devices such as pronominal anaphora, ellipsis, deixis and lexical cohesion create inconsistencies in MT output (Voita et al., 2019; Mitkov, 2004). Unlike these discourse devices, however, the exact role of anaphoric ones in NLP tasks such as MT has not been studied. In the present paper, we conduct a data-driven study to study this extent and nature of this impact, using English and Hindi as source and target language pairs.

Point	Fluency	Adequacy
4	Flawless	Perfect/Ideal
3	Few errors	Mostly correct
2	Many errors	Somewhat correct
1	Unacceptable	Unrelated to source

Table 1: 4-Point Numeric scale for judging the fluency and adequacy of the translations.

3 Experiment

3.1 Curating Test sets

We prepare three test sets– the first containing sentences with determinative anaphoric ones; the second containing one-anaphora; and the third containing regular non-anaphoric one words. For the first test set, we randomly choose 750 sentences from the NoEl corpus (Khullar et al., 2020b), the curated dataset prepared by (Khullar et al., 2019) and the sAnaNotes corpus (Recasens et al., 2016); for the second, we take 750 sentences from (Khullar et al., 2020a) and (Recasens et al., 2016); and for the third, pick 750 sentences each from Cornel movie dialogs dataset (Danescu-Niculescu-Mizil and Lee, 2011) and The British National Corpus (2001), manually checked to contain non-anaphoric ones. We also undertake translation of these 2,250 sentences to assist automatic evaluation. The translation is carried manually by a professional translator, who is bilingual in English and Hindi. We get up to three translations for each sentence, which are then verified by a native Hindi speaker.

3.2 Obtaining Translations

To get the English sentences translated into Hindi, we use Google NMT (GNMT). The system comprises a deep LSTM network with 8 encoder and 8 decoder layers with attention and residual connections (Wu et al., 2016). It serves us well for our experiment as its performance is at par with the current state-of-the-art NMT systems and is also freely available for translations between English and Hindi. This system is run on the three test sets and the translations are saved for analysis.

3.3 Evaluation

In automatic evaluation, we get a BLEU (Bilingual Evaluation Understudy Score) (Papineni et al., 2002) score of 39.72 for the sentences in the first test set, 38.21 in the second and 41.46 in the third. We also try manual evaluation, where four evaluators rate the translations of all sentences from the three test sets for their *fluency*) or syntactic correctness and (*adequacy* or translation accuracy. The evaluation of all the metrics is done on a 4-point Likert scale, see Table 1 for reference. The assigned scores by different raters are totalled and averaged for all the given sentences. We use the Fleiss's Kappa coefficient (Fleiss, 1971) to calculate the inter-annotator agreement between multiple evaluators. We get a score of 0.83 for fluency and 0.77 for adequacy that confirms reliability of the evaluation.

4 Results and Discussion

As can be seen, BLEU is the lower for the sentences containing anaphoric ones as compared to non-anaphoric ones. However, this may not be indicative of a trend as the test set is small and the difference observed is not that huge. Coming to manual evaluation, a total of 389 sentences from the first set, 601 from the second test set and 202 sentences from the third set get a rating of either 1 or 2 in the adequacy evaluation perspective. See Table 2. This shows that a majority of the sentences containing anaphoric one words are either poorly translated or have major translation quality errors, although they are grammatically still acceptable.

English (source text)	*The name is the same as the original one.*
Translation (Hindi)	नाम मूल एक के समान है
Transliteration	naam mool ek ke samaan hai
Gloss	नाम/name मूल/original एक/CRD(1) के/ ADP समान/equal है/AUX
Meaning	The name is the same as original number one.

Figure 1: Translation of an English sentence containing one-anaphora to Hindi. The one-anaphora gets translated as non-anaphoric cardinal numeral one in the target language.

About 90% of the sentences containing the non-anaphoric instances of *one* are translated rather well by the system. Most of the errors observed are due to the incorrect translation of named entities and incorrect subject-verb agreement for gender marking. We do not encounter any errors that are caused due to incorrect translation of the word one in the target language.

English (source text)	*Because you have a hypothesis, an Important one.*
Translation (Hindi)	क्योंकि आप एक परिकल्पना है, एक महत्वपूर्ण है
Transliteration	Kyunkii aap ek parikalpanaa hai, ek mahatvapoorna hai
Gloss	kyunkii/because aap/you ek/one parikalpanaa/hypothesis hai/AUX ek/ one mahatvapoorna/important hai/ AUX
Meaning	Because you are a hypothesis, an Important one.

Figure 2: Translation of an English sentence containing determinative anaphoric *one* to Hindi. The one-anaphora gets translated incorrectly as a pronoun in the target language.

In comparison to the sentences contaning the non-anaphoric one words, the sentences containing anaphoric one words are translated much poorly. Within the latter, we note that the highest number of wrong translations are for the sentences with one-anaphora. The errors observed in such incorrect translations can be categorized into three types. In the first type, the anaphoric one words are translated into non-anaphoric *one* expressions, specifically as the cardinal numeral, in the target language. For example in Figure 1, the one-anaphora in the English sentence, which means *name* as seen from preceding context, gets translated as cardinal numeral one in the target language. Out of 750 sentences, a total of 232 sentences exhibit this error. One possible reason for this error could be the most common occurrence of the word *one* in English as a cardinal number (Gardiner, 2003). Hence, in case of ambiguity, the word *one* is more likely to be treated as a cardinal number by the MT system. The second type of errors are where the anaphoric one gets translated as a pronoun in the target language. Such errors occur very few times–only 25 from all sentences in our test set. See Figure 2 for one such example. Finally, in the third type of errors, the one-anaphora gets completely disregarded by the translation system and the translated sentence shows no equivalent lexeme to the anaphor. Note that these errors result into poor translation adequacy, but a majority of the translated sentence are more or less grammatically acceptable as per the rules of the target language, as seen in Figure 1 and Figure 2. They can, however, also become

Test set	Evaluation Perspective	1	2	3	4
Determinative Anaphora	Fluency	102	159	**291**	198
(750)	Adequacy	188	**210**	199	153
One-anaphora	Fluency	94	188	**354**	114
(750)	Adequacy	**309**	292	85	66
Non-anaphoric ones	Fluency	59	98	263	**330**
(750)	Adequacy	94	101	**304**	251
&					

Table 2: Evaluation scores of the sentences in the test sets containing determinative anaphoric *ones*, one-anaphora and non-anaphoric one words. There are 750 sentences in each test set. The highest values in each row are highlighted.

totally absurd in meaning in some cases, as can be seen in Figure 2.

As compared to one-anaphora, the severity of wrong translations for determinative anaphoric *ones* is slightly less. Hindi is morphologically richer as compared to English. We observe that the error in the translations come from copying of wrong agreement morphology on the verb in the absence of the noun whose repetition the determinative anaphoric *one* avoids. See Figure 3 for one such example. This also implies that although such sentences get a lower rating for fluency, they rate higher for translation adequacy.

From a long time in traditional syntactic literature, right from Baker (1978), one-anaphora and determinative anaphoric one words have been clubbed together, with frequent interchangeable uses of them in discussions and analysis. It is only recently (Payne et al., 2013) that the morphological, syntactic and semantic differences between the two anaphoric forms have been extensively discussed. Note that although recent work by Kayne (2015) aims to render all instances of the word *one* a homogeneous internal structure, comprising a classifier merged with an indefintive article through a variety of examples, he too identifies subtypes within this class and points out how they behave differently than one another. Our simple experiment highlights the differences between these two forms, restating their linguistic analysis and advocating for a disparate treatment for them in future Computational Linguistics and NLP research.

Finally, in the sentences that are correctly translated, we observe that a majority of the one-anaphora and the determinative anaphoric ones get translated exactly into their antecedent. This means that the anaphoric expression *per se* is lost in the target language. For instance, the corresponding expression for one-anaphora in Hindi is *vaala* (singular, masculine). We see only 69 out of 750 translated sentences actually containing this lexeme. It is not surprising that 66 out of such sentences are rated 4 in the evaluation.

It is debatable, however, to claim that a translation that contains an anaphoric expression similar to the source is of better quality as compared to the translation that only copies the antecedent and replaces the anaphor with it. While both achieves nearly the same meaning and are grammatically acceptable, in our experiment, the former type were rated higher. It could be, then, argued that the latter added redundant information which might not be desirable in most cases.

English (source text)	*She bought two baskets from the store, so we only took one.*
Translation (Hindi)	उसने स्टोर से दो बास्केट खरीदी, इसलिए हमने केवल एक ही लिया।
Transliteration	usne store se do basket khariidii, isliye hamne keval ek hii liyaa
Gloss	us/she ne/ERG store se/ADP do/ CRD(2) basket khariidii/bought.**Fem**, isliye/so ham/we ne/ERG keval/only ek/ CRD(1) hii/PRT liyaa/took.**Mas**
Meaning	*She bought two baskets from the store, so we only took one.*
Notes	Wrong gender agreement on the verb.

Figure 3: Translation of an English sentence containing determinative anaphoric one to Hindi. Although the translation is fine, the wrong agreement morphology on the verb makes it grammatically incorrect.

5 Conclusion

In the present paper, we performed a simple experiment to investigate the impact of anaphoric and non-anaphoric one words on Neural Machine Translation process using English and Hindi as source and target language pair. Evaluation by manual methods revealed that anaphoric instances of the word one are much harder to translate as compared to the non-anaphoric one words. We also conclude that within the anaphoric class, one-anaphora are harder to translate than determinative anaphors, which reaffirms the linguistic disparity between the two phenomenon as shown in recent syntactic research. The long term goal of such a study is to improve the quality of translation of discourse structures such as anaphoric ones.

References

Nameera Akhtar, Maureen Callanan, Geoffrey K Pullum, and Barbara C Scholz. 2004. Learning antecedents for anaphoric one. *Cognition*, 4:141â145.

Carl Lee Baker. 1978. Introduction to generative transformational syntax. *Englewood Cliffs, NJ:: Prentice-Hal.*

Joan Bresnan. 1971. A note on the notion âidentity of sense anaphoraâ. *Linguistic Inquiry*, 2:589â597.

Wei Chen. 2016. The motivation of ellipsis. *Theory and Practice in Language Studies*, 6(11):2134–2139.

Sandra Chung, William Ladusaw, and James McCloskey. 2010. Sluicing (:) between structure and inference. *In Representing language: Essays in honor of Judith Aissen.*

The British National Corpus. 2001. *Oxford University Computing Services on behalf of the BNC Consortium*, (2).

Norbert Corver and Marjo van Koppen. 2011. Np-ellipsis with adjectival remnants: a micro-comparative perspective. *Natural Language & Linguistic Theory*, 29(2):371–421.

Elizabeth A. Cowper. 1992. A concise introduction to syntactic theory. *Chicago, IL: University of Chicago Press.*

Jeroen van Craenenbroeck and Jason Merchant. 2013. Ellipsis phenomena. In *The Cambridge Handbook of Generative Syntax*, pages 701–745.

Peter W Culicover and Ray Jackendoff. 2005. Simpler syntax. *Oxford, England: Oxford University Press.*

Deborah Anna Dahl. 1985. The structure and function of one-anaphora in english. *Ph.D. thesis, University of Minnesota.*

Mary Dalrymple, Stuart M. Shieber, and Fernando C.N. 1991a. Ellipsis and higher order unification. *Linguistics and Philosophy*, 14:399â452.

Mary Dalrymple, Stuart M. Shieber, and Fernando C. N. Pereira. 1991b. Ellipsis and higher-order unification. *Linguistics and Philosophy*, 14(4):399–452.

Cristian Danescu-Niculescu-Mizil and Lillian Lee. 2011. Chameleons in imagined conversations: A new approach to understanding coordination of linguistic style in dialogs. In *Proceedings of the Workshop on Cognitive Modeling and Computational Linguistics, ACL 2011.*

Rong-En Fan, Kai-Wei Chang, Cho-Jui Hsieh, Xiang-Rui Wang, and Chih-Jen Lin. 2008. Liblinear: A library for large linear classification. volume 9, page 1871â1874.

Joseph Fleiss. 1971. Measuring nominal scale agreement among many raters. *Psychological Bulletin*, 76.

Lyn Frazier. 2008. Processing ellipsis: A processing solution to the undergeneration problem? In *Proceedings of the 26th West Coast Conference on Formal Linguistics.*

Mary Gardiner. 2003. *Identifying and resolving one-anaphora.* Department of Computing, Division of ICS, Macquarie University.

Tilbe Goksun, Tom W. Roeper, Kathy Hirsh-Pasek, and Roberta Michnick Golinkoff. 2010. From noun-phrase ellipsis to verbphrase ellipsis: The acquisition path from context to abstract reconstruction.

Christine Gunther. 2011. Noun ellipsis in english: adjectival modifiers and the role of context. *The structure of the noun phrase in English: synchronic and diachronic explorations*, 15(2):279–301.

Michael Alexander Kirkwood Halliday and Ruqaiya Hasan. 1976. Cohesion in english. *Longman London*, page 76.

Jorge Hankamer and Ivan Sag. 2015. Deep and surface anaphora. *Linguistic Inquiry*, 7:391–428.

Daniel Hardt. 1999. Dynamic interpretation of verb phrase ellipsis. *Linguistics and Philosophy*, 22(2):187–221.

Jerry R. Hobbs and Andrew Kehler. 1997. A theory of parallelism and the case of vp ellipsis. In *Proceedings of the 35th Annual Meeting of the Association for Computational Linguistics and Eighth Conference of the European Chapter of the Association for Computational Linguistics*, ACL '98/EACL '98, pages 394–401, Stroudsburg, PA, USA. Association for Computational Linguistics.

Nina Hyams, Victoria Mateu, and Lauren Winans. 2017. Ellipsis meets wh-movement: sluicing in early grammar.

Kyle Johnson. 2001. What vp ellipsis can do, and what it canât, but not why. pages 439–479. In The Handbook of Contemporary Syntactic Theory, Mark Baltin and Chris Collins (eds.). Blackwell Publishers.

Richard S Kayne. 2015. English one and ones as complex determiners. *New York University*.

Payal Khullar, Allen Anthony, and Manish Shrivastava. 2019. Using syntax to resolve npe in english. In *Proceedings of Recent Advances in Natural Language Processing*, pages 535–541.

Payal Khullar, Arghya Bhattacharya, and Manish Shrivastava. 2020a. Finding the right one and resolving it. In *Asian chapter of Association of Computational Linguistics*.

Payal Khullar, Kushal Majmundar, and Manish Shrivastava. 2020b. Noel: An annotated corpus for noun ellipsis in english. In *Language Resources Evaluation Conference*.

Nayoun Kim, Laurel Brehm, and Masaya Yoshida. 2019. The online processing of noun phrase ellipsis and mechanisms of antecedent retrieval. *Language, Cognition and Neuroscience*, 34(2):190–213.

Shalom Lappin. 1996. The interpretatin of ellipsis. In *The Handbook of Contemporary Semantic Theory*, pages 145–176. Blackwell Publishers.

Charlotte Lindenbergh, Angeliek van Hout, and Bart Hollebrandse. 2015. Extending ellipsis research: The acquisition of sluicing in dutch. *BUCLD 39 Online Proceedings Supplement*, 39.

Anne Lobeck. 1995. *Functional Heads, Licensing, and Identification*. Oxford University Press.

Susann Luperfoy. 1991. Discourse pegs: A computational analysis of context-dependent referring expressions. *Ph.D. thesis, University of Texas at Austin*.

Katrin Menzel. 2014. A corpus linguistic study of ellipsis as a cohesive device1. *Proceedings of Corpus Linguistics*.

Katrin Menzel. 2017. *Understanding English-German contrasts: a corpus-based comparative analysis of ellipses as cohesive devices*. Ph.D. thesis, Universitat des Saar- Â¨ landes, Saarbrucken.

Jason Merchant. 2004. Fragments and ellipsis. *Linguistics and Philosophy*, 27(6):661–738.

Jason Merchant. 2010. *Three Kinds of Ellipsis: Syntactic, Semantic, Pragmatic?*

R. Mitkov. 2004. Introduction: Special issue on anaphora resolution in machine translation and multilingual nlp. *Machine Translation*, 14:159–161.

Ruslan Mitkov. 1999. *Anaphora Resolution*. Oxford University Press.

Hwee Tou Ng, Yu Zhou, Rober Dale, and Mary Gardiner. 2005. A machine learning approach to identification and resolution of one-anaphora. pages 1105–1110.

Kishore Papineni, S. Roukos, T. Ward, and Wei-Jing Zhu. 2002. Bleu: a method for automatic evaluation of machine translation. In *ACL*.

Dongwoo Park. 2017. *When does ellipsis occur, and what is elided?* PhD dissertation, University of Maryland.

John Payne, Geoffrey K. Pullum, Barbara C. Scholz, and Eva Berlage. 2013. Anaphoric one and its implications. *Language*, 4:794â829.

Andrew Radford. 1981. Transformational syntax: A studentâs guide to chomskyâs extended standard theory. *Cambridge, UK: Cambridge University Press.*

Marta Recasens, Zhichao Hu, and Olivia Rhinehart. 2016. Sense anaphoric pronouns: Am i one? page 1â6.

Alain Rouveret. 2012. Vp ellipsis, phases and the syntax of morphology. *Natural Language & Linguistic Theory*, 30(3):897â963.

Elena Voita, Rico Sennrich, and Ivan Titov. 2019. When a good translation is wrong in context: Context-aware machine translation improves on deixis, ellipsis, and lexical cohesion.

Frank Wijnen, Tom W. Roeper, and Hiske van der Meulen. 2003. Discourse binding: Does it begin with nominal ellipsis?

Yonghui Wu, Mike Schuster, Zhifeng Chen, Quoc V. Le, Mohammad Norouzi, Wolfgang Macherey, Maxim Krikun, Yuan Cao, Qin Gao, Klaus Macherey, Jeff Klingner, Apurva Shah, Melvin Johnson, Xiaobing Liu, Åukasz Kaiser, Stephan Gouws, Yoshikiyo Kato, Taku Kudo, Hideto Kazawa, Keith Stevens, George Kurian, Nishant Patil, Wei Wang, Cliff Young, Jason Smith, Jason Riesa, Alex Rudnick, Oriol Vinyals, Greg Corrado, Macduff Hughes, and Jeffrey Dean. 2016. Google's neural machine translation system: Bridging the gap between human and machine translation. *CoRR*, abs/1609.08144.

Association for Computational Linguistics
209 N. Eighth Street
Stroudsburg, Pennsylvania 18360

ISBN 978-1-7138-2915-7

CURRAN ASSOCIATES INC.
proceedings.com